GEORGE STREET, OUR STREET

A Poor Family's Richest Years in Chicago

by

Melvin E. Giles

Oakdale Press

CHICAGO

Published by Oakdale Press, P. O. Box 621, Lombard, IL 60148.

Manufactured in the United States of America

Library of Congress Catalog Number: 96-72438

ISBN 0-9656364-0-2

First Edition, March 1997

For my daughters and my nieces and nephews.

Dedicated to the memory of my mother, Mildred, who not only gave me life, but a lifetime of love and encouragement, and to the memory of my brothers who taught me to love life – namely Harvey, from whom I learned to accept responsibility, and Curtis, from whom I learned the meaning of courage.

There are several very good people for whose encouragement and assistance I wish to offer my thanks: To Joe Beary, for his friendship and for persuading me to continue writing; to Felicia Reed, for her timely encouragement, very necessary criticism and valued editorial suggestions; to Jean L. Baker, fellow author, for blazing the publishing trail; finally to John Nelson of DRM, for his valuable aid in producing this book.

Most of all, I wish to thank my wife, Marge, for being my unswerving advocate.

Where Did Everyone Go?

Picnics on the Fourth, at the same old grove,
Beckoned our family to gather once more,
For cook-outs, contests, and games to be played,
Till darkness sent us home, with muscles sore.

Then time stepped in, as it always will,
Forcing its changes in the choosing of sides,
Some who shared life would drift apart,
While others would scatter far and wide.

Sadder changes altered our family's number,
Wrought by passing years and the Grim Reaper,
Old folks in their time, yet others before,
Caused our sense of loss to be much deeper.

Fiery rockets burst with cannon's roar,
Releasing showers of color for all to see,
Reminding me of Fourths of bygone years,
But who's left to watch? Only me.

From: *"Reflections"*
       Copyright 1981
       Melvin E. Giles

Chapter 1

The Edge of Manhood

Strains of Sibelius' magnificent "Finlandia" waxed and waned on the undulating breeze of a balmy, late June evening. Lane Tech High School's orchestra was playing superbly, as the long awaited commencement exercises of June, 1952 were well under way, outdoors. The weather bureau's prediction of a chance of showers was beginning to look like "no chance" and the 600 graduating seniors of the all-boys school were relieved. At the Senior Rally their principal had decreed, "If the ceremony begins outdoors, we'll complete it outdoors!" to the cheers of the same 600 seniors. If it had been raining when the ceremonies began, only forty percent of the attending relatives and guests who filled all of the seats in the football stadium would have been admitted to their indoor Auditorium.

Of all those candidates for graduation, sitting in formations of a block "L" and "T" on the football field, one of the happiest was a seventeen-year-old named Gene Ryan. Even as he sat through the interminable speeches that had been customary and expected at these occasions, he was overjoyed because he had survived four arduous years at this school. Gratified also, that at least his mom, Kathleen, was in the crowd and he knew that she was pleased with him. How much more joyful the occasion would have been, if only his two older brothers, Bob and Dave, the remaining members of his immediate family could have been there.

As the speakers droned on, his youthful, active mind sought diversion, busying itself intermittently, with concerns about the future that young men of their day had, then with nostalgic memories of times and events gone by.

In addition to the usual anxieties of continuing their education or going into a trade or directly to other work, a major concern to Gene and to most of the graduating seniors was the bitter war in Korea. Graduation Day had fallen on the eve of the second anniversary of its outbreak, half a world away. Many of Gene's classmates had older brothers or friends from their neighborhoods, who had shipped out to Korea and had been wounded, suffered frostbite, or had returned in government-issued caskets.

Many of his classmates had offered that they too, wondered if each of them might one day face every warrior's moment of truth: whether to stand their ground in the face of the enemy or to bolt and run. In recalling Shakespeare's words describing how a coward dies a thousand times, while a valiant man dies only once, Gene and his friends hoped that if it came to pass, that they could summon the courage required to stand their ground as men.

The war was the reason his brothers couldn't be there that evening. Enlisting in February of the year before, Bob in the Air Force and Dave in the Army, they fortunately, had been assigned to posts in Germany. The odds had been great against duty in Europe, since seven of the eight companies in Dave's training battalion had been assigned to duty in Korea, while his was sent to Germany. Although Gene's brothers were unable to attend, they had both written, offering him their congratulations and telling him they were proud of him, for he was the first to finish all four years of high-school.

Accomplishing one of the toughest tasks he'd ever undertaken, Gene also felt some pride in himself. Lane Tech was Chicago's elite high school, having a stringent academic program, while emphasizing physical fitness. For Gene, his schooling at Lane had also been tough psychologically, having experienced more than the ordinary amount of hazing and social exclusion by many of his classmates during his first two years of high school.

A stripling adolescent weighing in at a puny 100 pounds and standing just five feet tall when he arrived here four years ago, Gene realized quickly that high school wasn't going to be easy for him. At thirteen years of age, he was a year younger than most of his 1,266 fellow freshmen, and with a speech impediment; two conditions which made starting over and making friends with all of those strangers difficult. During his grade school years, hospital stays and childhood illnesses had caused long absences from classes, but he had been able to keep up with his studies and skipped two grades, graduating in seven years.

Back in his sophomore year, Gene had considered quitting school, like his brother Dave had. In quitting school however, he would have been required to attend a continuation school, one day a week until he was seventeen, but he would graduate from Lane at that same age, if he stuck it out. Besides, he had never been a quitter before and certainly didn't want to become one.

After deciding to stay in school, Gene's academic life improved. In his junior and senior years Gene grew taller and heavier, coming to be accepted by fellow students. Stan Janowicz, once one of his steadiest antagonists, had in fact become a good friend. Being of average height, Stan was very muscular and athletic. He had needled Gene for their first two years, until Gene had endured just enough and stood up to him and said, "Let's you and me meet outside after school!"

When Stan stopped laughing, he put his hand on Gene's shoulder, saying, "Either you're crazy, or you've got guts! All of this time, I figured you for being chicken. Guess I was wrong. Friends?" After shaking Gene's hand, Stan in the following two years had often come to Gene for academic help, developing a mutual trust with him, and becoming his good friend.

One driving force, for which Gene had his brother Dave to thank, originated with Dave's prediction that Gene would never graduate from Lane. Just before Gene was to enter Lane, Dave told him, "You won't make it because a runt like you can't take the mockery and derision that you're gonna get in that place." In saying that, Dave was ready to duck the punch he thought his brother might throw, for Dave remembered when just a couple of years earlier he last called Gene, "Runt." Gene had gotten angry enough to sucker-punch young Davey in the stomach, and half-Nelson him to the ground where he didn't let him up until Dave promised to stop calling him "Runt."

Dave had imparted an added incentive for Gene, when he

promised, "If, through some miracle you can take it all and make it through four years at Lane and are able to graduate, I will give you a hundred dollars in cash. In fact, I'll also give you a gold ring mounted with a diamond and a ruby."

Gene questioned him with, "When is this treasure to be placed in my hands?"

Dave replied, "On the day you graduate from Lane."

Graduation Day had arrived but not any overseas package wrapped in brown paper or even a money order. Gene thought aloud, "Where's the ring Dave? And the money you promised me?" He wondered if it had been just a ploy used by Dave, to make him angry and determined enough to stay his course at Lane. If so, it had worked, for the Runt was graduating. He hadn't given up! In time, Gene would write off the ring and money which were never to come, remembering the only physical limitation his brother Dave ever had: A short memory when it came to paying off bets.

Life must be like a roller-coaster, Gene thought and if so, the first seventeen years of his life had been like the long first hill of the "Bobs." He was feeling the same exhilaration from surviving it all, that one experienced after coming down and around the first hill and tight turn of the legendary Riverview amusement park roller-coaster.

Surviving was what Gene Ryan had learned to do best. All of the trials he and his family endured during those early years, had conditioned him to resist giving in to any misfortune. Many times in his young life, he had been down, but never out, beginning with his birth.

Kathleen Ryan's wish for a Christmas baby had faded with the passing of that long-ago Christmas, but two days later, her son Gene was born at home. Hearing out-of-sight voices murmuring, she wondered why neither her sisters nor the doctor had brought her newborn baby to her so she could see him. Demanding to see her baby, he was brought to her and she was shown only a side view of his good side. Later, old Doc Anderson quietly came to her bedside and informed Kathleen, "Your baby has been born with a cleft lip and palate and he is unable to swallow. I don't hold out much hope of him living past sundown."

4

Kathleen, though crushed, didn't abandon hope but prayed for his life, instead. Her prayers and the continuous massaging of his throat by her sister, Etta, and a caring neighbor, Mrs. Bergt, finally caused him to begin swallowing and he survived.

In the late hours of many nights at a Texas hospital, when Gene was barely two years old and suffering from acute double pneumonia, Kathleen again prayed for her son's life. Little Gene, barely able to breathe was given last rites, while the doctors had held out scant hope for his survival but his mother's prayers were answered again when he recovered.

Learning what he needed to do in order to survive, he had won on his own the numerous fights forced upon him as a youngster, fights that even his mom had never known about. Every trial he had ever faced was overcome through some inner strength and help from above. He had learned to regard giving up as no option at all. Now he was ready to face the world as a young man.

As the speakers droned on, Gene's retrospective memory ride took him further into the past. Back to those long-ago early days he remembered with his immediate family, through the long years of living with his grandparents and many hospital stays. But his greatest memory of all had always been the reunion with his mother and brothers at the house on George Street, where they renewed the bond of familial love that had sustained them through years of separation; a bond that they would always share.

Chapter 2

All Hers To Give

Gene, the youngest and smallest of Kathleen's three sons, was still too young at the time to remember the trip from Texas in late March of 1937. Kathleen had told him of the long, tiring train ride, one which culminated in a slow-paced roll past the run-down ugliness that for many years had been Chicago's back yard. She also told him how their weary little family huddled in the back seat of a cab, peering through its vapor-fogged windows while stuck in traffic outside the train station's sooty facade. They shivered from the cold, their flour-sack trousers and light cotton jackets worn in Texas too flimsy for a dismal, damp and cold day in Chicago. Leaden clouds hung low in the sky, threatening to unload an early-spring snow, yet had only managed a cold drizzle to slicken down the Loop's cobblestone streets.

As their cab stood idling in the rain, a shower of shouted curses began pelting it, vented by angry men whose epithets were getting louder and closer. Crash!! The cab's side window exploded from a brick thrown in rage at the stalled taxicab. Spewing shards of glass everywhere, the projectile narrowly missed the Runt's older brother Davey, caromed off the back of the front seat and fell to the floor. Miraculously, no one in the cab had been injured but being helpless observers inside a "scab cab" embroiled in the violence of a nationwide taxi drivers' strike was a frightening introduction to the "City of Big Shoulders."

They had just arrived "safely" in the big city, but were confused, scared, and somewhat lost. For a few moments, Kathleen had even mulled over the notion that maybe they ought to return to the train station and catch the next train bound for the friendly

Red River Valley. Hearing the story of their unwelcome reception retold over ensuing years the Runt would, as a young man, recall the tale whenever he got into a taxicab.

Like thousands of farmers forced off their land by the Dust Bowl's erosion into poverty, Kathleen had been forced by circumstances to leave Texas. Dust Bowl refugees had either gone out West to work as pickers in California or up North to industrial cities like Chicago or Detroit. Wanting more for her sons than a dirt poor farm, Kathleen had decided to go northward with them, hoping to find work and a better place to raise them. Plus, her youngest son needed corrective surgery and she had heard that hospitals in the North had better facilities. Kathleen also had another, even more compelling reason for leaving her beloved Texas. She had finally left Hank Ryan, her husband of ten years, a farmer whom she married at eighteen for love, a family, and with the hopes of a good life. In those days that meant simply having a place to live, clothing, and food on the table.

Even though Hank was ten years her senior when they were married, it had been a good life for a few years. Hank Ryan, although an impassive man and stingy husband, was a good father. When each of their sons were just babies, he showed unusual patience as he took turns holding and carrying them when they cried most of the night from colic. Tougher and meaner than his wiry 140 pounds on a five-foot-seven frame might lead one to believe, Hank's presence commanded respect from most other men in town. He could work all day, every day, in the fields and when Saturday night came around, he burned the rosin off his bow, playing fiddle all night at the town dance. Like many men of his generation and circumstance, Hank's needs and wants were simple.

Renting their land and house from its owner, Hank and Kathleen were tenant farmers, owning only their livestock and tools, while trying to earn a living from the slow-yielding, begrudging earth. Working in the wilting Texas heat and humidity, Kathleen had picked the bolls of cotton from innumerable rows of cotton plants along with her husband, hauling along up to a hundred pounds of cotton in a sack, even late into her pregnancies. It was the lot of a cotton farmer's wife to do the cooking, cleaning, childbearing, and when possible, help her man in the fields. Rural folks didn't expect much from life and seemed to get less.

Each year, whether it had been good or bad, an agreed percentage of the proceeds from the sale of their harvested crop was given over to the landlord as payment for the use of his land. Cotton was King in the northeastern corner of Texas, the primary crop on most farms in that area, but too many cotton farms had produced a surplus of cotton, which brought down its market price.

In response to the cotton market being down, the Federal government supported cotton prices by paying cash subsidies to farm landlords who were supposed to pass the subsidies on to any tenants or sharecroppers working their land, but most of them didn't. Farmers protested the unfairness of their landlords who shared in the profits from the land yet refused to pass on much-needed price support payments. Also working against cotton farmers, in combination with low prices was the reduction in crop yield each year as the soil became poorer and dustier. For Hank and Kathleen, their time as tenant farmers appeared to be running out.

As their cotton crops gradually grew more spindly in the eroding soil, Hank found a way to subsidize their meager farm income that was definitely not encouraged, let alone supported by the Federal government. Setting up a still in the woods on their back acreage, Hank and his brother John began distilling the best illegal whiskey in the county. The quality of his product was confirmed by Kathleen's father, Grandpaw Kelly, who would in years to come, colorfully describe how his son-in-law, Hank, used to sneak in through the back door of the courthouse over at the county seat, delivering his moonshine to some of the judges.

Unfortunately, it wasn't long before Hank and John took to drinking too freely of their own distilled product, and Hank began staying out late and sometimes he didn't come home at all. In time, it seemed that drinking with his rowdy friends had taken on more appeal for Hank than spending time with his wife and family. When he did come home less often, the hours were passed in useless, heated arguments, verbal abuse of his thin, rundown wife, and neglect of their three undernourished sons.

After several years of such behavior, it became evident that Hank had no intention of changing his ways, and a bone-weary Kathleen decided that she wanted more out of life for herself than an abusive marriage but even more for her sons. She wanted them to have a better chance in life and the opportunity to get a good education. Gnawing away at her was also the need to have her youngest son's cleft lip and palate repaired and hospitals up North were said to have some good plastic surgeons who might be able to help him. Up until then, Hank had usually shrugged off Kathleen's suggestions for surgical repair of their youngest boy's defect. Then one day he finished by saying, "In time maybe we'll get it fixed. Maybe he'll grow out of it." It was a response that was totally unacceptable and deemed to be ignorant by their son's mother who defiantly shouted, "No, he won't!"

Still considered attractive by many who those who knew her, Kathleen was a slender brown-eyed woman about five feet four, with auburn hair. She came to believe that the time had come for her to make a new life for her sons and herself, away from their father. In 1937, despite many believing the Great Depression to be over, the national unemployment rate was hovering around twenty percent of the population. The Depression wasn't over for them.

Not wanting to stay in the badly-hit Southwest, nor go out to California where there were reports of many unlucky, out-of-work Okies being turned back at the California state line, Kathleen leaned toward going northward. Writing to family members who had moved up North to Chicago the year before, she asked about conditions there. Despite receiving negative news that unemployment was high and half the country was on strike, Kathleen wrote back and borrowed the train fare from her folks. Just before Easter, with the dimmest of chances and brightest of hopes, Kathleen bundled up her three sons and boarded a northbound train to Chicago.

The sons she so deeply loved were Bobby, who at eight years of age was truly his father's son, handsome with dark eyes and dark hair, with a sharp mind and a strong, wiry build. The two younger boys, Davey and the Runt, at four and two years of age, were also on the thin side but possessed sandy hair and dark eyes. Unlike Bobby, they favored Kathleen's side of the family, who were mostly fair-haired.

Settling on Chicago's North Side, Kathleen found a place for them to live with reasonable rent. It was on the second floor of a run-down gray clapboard two-flat on Fullerton Avenue just west of Southport Avenue. By moving in just up the street from her parents, who had only moved North before Christmas of the year before, Kathleen felt less alone in the strangeness of the big, noisy city. Not alone but darned near broke, she desperately checked the sparse want ads for any job that she could find.

Like most rural young women of her time, Kathleen was adept at sewing, a talent which soon landed her a night-shift job as a seamstress, sewing dress clothes at a clothing factory just up Fullerton Avenue, a block or so from where she lived. Not unusual, except that the clothes she and her co-workers made would never be worn on the street, since the attire was purchased only by funeral directors, to be the final dress attire that recently deceased would wear to their graves.

While Kathleen worked, Bobby undertook the job of taking care of his two younger brothers and putting them to bed each night. His younger brothers obeyed him faithfully as their mom had instructed them. They also obeyed because each of the boys seemed to grasp that Kathleen had chosen a difficult road and they tried very hard to be well-behaved for her. Often, they would go to their grandmaw's for lunch, where they encountered the Kellys' revolving door lunchroom. Two of their aunts and both uncles were still living at home and working a couple of blocks away. Each of the four came home quickly for lunch at slightly different times. It made for frequent but short, animated conversation between the young boys and their loving extended family.

By working very hard, Kathleen was able to improve their lives somewhat during the next year as Kathleen's small paycheck allowed her and her sons to eat regularly, regaining their health. From early on, Kathleen impressed on her sons the philosophy of savoring what little they had and not dwelling on those things which they did not have. They were happy that one thing they would always have was each other and the love they felt for each other. It was unfortunate for them that the single year they enjoyed together was all they were allowed to have, for their short-lived happiness in their new home, came to an unexpected end one day.

Answering the abrupt, loud pounding on their door, Kathleen found herself face-to-face with a juvenile welfare officer. Stern-faced and uncompromising, he stated, "Our office received a report that you have been abandoning your three children by leaving them unsupervised during the day."

Kathleen replied, "They're not unsupervised! Mah oldest boy is with 'em all the time, watchin' 'em with a sharp eye and he's real responsible for a boy nine years old."

"He's too young, ma'am. We just can't allow you to leave your children unsupervised. And if you can't find someone to take care of them, we will. We can make them wards of the county and take care of them ourselves! You'd better make other arrangements and soon. I'll be back in ten days. Good day to you!"

As he turned to leave Kathleen closed the door abruptly behind him. She heard his heavy footsteps clomp down the creaking hall stairs, followed by the slam of the downstairs door. Like a mother tiger whose cubs were threatened, Kathleen angrily shouted to unhearing county ears, "Y'all will take them away from me over mah dead body!"

Frantically, Kathleen began a desperate attempt to find someone to care for her sons during the evenings because she would never allow the county to take her sons away from her. In the post-Depression era, few, if any, day care facilities were available. Kathleen couldn't have afforded one anyway. Reluctantly, she went to her mother, Grandmaw Kelly, in search of assistance, asking her if she could watch her grandsons while Kathleen worked. It was unfortunate for everyone that the aftermath of the Great Depression had left her parents very sympathetic but financially and logistically unable to take in and feed three growing boys all week, in addition to their four grown children still at home. As another alternative however, Grandmaw Kelly offered, "Ah'd be willin' to take in one of the boys who could stay with us all the time, if'n that's alright with y'all."

"Ah'll keep it in mind," Kathleen replied. "Though Ah'd much rather keep 'em all together."

After exhausting all other possibilities, a despondent, guilt-ridden Kathleen was forced into making the most heart-rending decision that she would ever make: she would have to split her little family apart for at least a few years. Kathleen tearfully decided to move to a smaller apartment where she would live alone, take her youngest boy to live with her parents, and arrange to board her two older boys in an orphan home.

The Runt would always remember the hint of cigar smoke in the warm, wood-paneled office of a North Side orphanage. Within the large, dimly-lit, quiet room, a green-shaded banker's lamp warmly illuminated the somber area around the bespectacled, soft-spoken man's desk. In front of that desk, the four Ryans sat as the superintendent of the orphanage, a kindly old gentleman, listened to Kathleen's plight. Hearing her out, the superintendent approved Kathleen's arrangement of room and board on a monthly basis for the two older boys, Bobby and Davey, at the orphanage which, from that day forward, would always be referred to as "the Home." Kathleen's last-ditch, hopeful request to keep all of her sons together was denied when only the two older boys were accepted, for the superintendent told her, "Your youngest son is too young and frail for us to take him in on a room and board basis. Besides, we have no facilities or procedures for the post-operative care he will require after his corrective surgeries."

Thus, the Runt was destined to be the one child that his grandparents had offered to take care of for a while; a while that would last until he was nearly ten years old.

The few days which Kathleen had been given to comply with the county's directive, all too quickly passed, coming to an end one chilly, rainy night. On their last night together, Kathleen spent the remaining, fleeting hours with her sons, sharing with each of them the sad task of packing their few belongings. Along with the small cardboard box of clothes and personal items that each son would carry away, they would also be taking a part of Kathleen's heart with them. All too soon, the hours having flown, it was their bedtime and the young mother reluctantly tucked her boys into bed for what would be the last time. Holding back the flood of overwhelming grief building up within her chest, she bid each them "Goodnight and sweet dreams," as their young eyelids grew heavy in the dim light.

Sweet dreams were not to be Kathleen's that night or any other night for a very long time. During that night anguish and worry conspired to rob her of the sleep she so desperately needed, as she tossed and turned throughout the night. To thwart her anguish she prayed for the strength that might somehow, someway, allow her to carry out the tortuous, heart-breaking tasks she was to face in the coming day soon to dawn.

Raindrops drummed against the drafty window's panes, driven by a blustery wind strong enough to sway the huge trees across the street. Awakening to the rattle of a wind-blown, loose, window-sash, the Runt stirred fitfully. It was a miserable beginning to a day which, in itself was to hold no joy for any of them. Donning his shirt and trousers, he thought of the wonderful times that his mom, his brothers, and he had relished together, while living in this rundown house that had been transformed into a cozy home by their mother's caring love. Gone would be the fun-filled trips by streetcar, then walking to nearby Fullerton beach, the hours of carefree play in Chicago's parks, and occasional Sunday picnics.

Slowly Bobby and Davey began carrying their boxes of belongings down the stairway as Kathleen experienced difficulty in swallowing, for her heart was in her throat as she followed the two older boys, while holding her youngest son's hand. Burning tears welled in her eyes and made it difficult to see the steps while she may have been holding her youngest son's hand for guidance as well. Reaching the hall at the bottom of the stairs, they fumbled with the loose doorknob, opened the door and shuffled out onto the old porch. As the boys turned to look back at their home once more, the Runt would long remember the weathered door which seemed to be one big, glass panel, and the gray paint peeling off the door and the clapboard siding of the house. He also wouldn't forget the porch-shaking rattle of the loose-latched door as it noisily, ominously closed for the last time behind them.

Kathleen had fervently prayed in the darkness of the night before, asking her Creator for the strength and courage to face this day and for a glimmer of understanding on the part of her sons. Finding the strength she had sought, Kathleen was able to hold back her own bitter tears at the dreaded moment of separation at the Home. Just over three, the Runt didn't understand why his brothers had to go away. Five-year-old Davey tried but didn't really comprehend why he had to live away from his mother. Only her big boy, Bobby, really understood, yet shed no tears. At nine, he remembered what his father, in earlier times had drummed into him: "Big boys don't cry," the age-old macho teaching which has caused so many men to be buried before their time.

As Kathleen and the Runt sadly waved goodbye to Bobby and Davey the two boys were ushered away down the hallway by one of the staff. Turning the corner at the end of the hallway Davey leaned back for one last glimpse and a final wave goodbye. Then, as he disappeared, Kathleen began to sob. Although Bobby had held back his tears, the warm, brown eyes which Kathleen had passed on to and shared with her sons, would never be sadder than they had seemed to be on a blustery, rainy day in late spring.

Leaving her two older sons and a large part of her heart at the Home, Kathleen and her still-tearful youngest son walked to the bus stop. After they boarded the bus, she explained to him that they were going to Grandmaw and Grandpaw's just up the street from the apartment, where he would be able to stay every day and night, for a little while. She pointed out that, "You liked going there for lunch. Wouldn't y'all like to live there for a while?"

"Maybe for a little while," he grudgingly agreed.

Promising him, "Ah'll see you soon and we'll visit Bobby and Davey then," she hoped to comfort him.

In saying that it wouldn't be long before they got together and visited Bobby and Davey at the Home, she made him feel a little better. On the darkest, most tragic day of her life, all of Kathleen's efforts had been focused on doing what had to be done. She tried as hard as she could, to ease the traumatic sorrow of her sons, while at the same time, masking the pain of her own heartbreak.

Greeted warmly by his grandparents, the Runt felt more than

welcome. His grandparents' presence would ease the pain of his mother's departure, at least for a little while. Then as they resumed their normal evening routine, his ears listened for the doorbell's ring, hopefully anticipating his mother's return, not yielding easily to the thought of her leaving him there. Later, after bedtime, he lay alone on the couch, a cold, strange bed, missing his brother Davey who always slept next to him. As the last light went out, a blanket of darkness fell over him, and he began to miss his mother and brothers terribly.

For the first time, his mother hadn't been there to tuck him in or give him a goodnight kiss and hug. For the next six years, with the exception of an occasional overnight stay at one of his aunts, he would know the emptiness of no one tucking him in or kissing him goodnight. Despite trying very hard, he just couldn't be a big boy, like his brother Bobby had been. Sadness too overwhelming for a three-year-old boy caused him to cry into his pillow until he fell asleep. It would only be the first of many nights that he was to cry himself to sleep.

An hour earlier, his brokenhearted mother had arrived home, rain-soaked and chilled to the bone. Kathleen had subjugated her own anguish until she returned to the stark loneliness of her now-empty apartment. Missing were the childish voices and tittering laughter of her now-absent sons. Cocking her head, she listened intently, as if she may have heard the echo of young boys' voices, but the stony, empty silence of solitude only stifled all other sounds within the apartment's walls. Half-aloud, half-whispered, the young mother lamented having been blessed with three sons who had been hers alone for just one year, but now were only hers to give to other homes. "Why did things have to be this way?" she cried out in despair.

She felt a constriction within her, as if the imagined bands of tape that had been wrapped tightly across her chest all day now seemed to tighten even more and her breathing became difficult. The headache that plagued her throughout the day was intensifying to the point where it seemed that her head would burst. Then finally, it began. First, the slight paralysis in her throat, followed by the burning of her eyes until the first tears welled. Then,

The effect of the picture's composition was a diamond-shaped circle formed by a family with very little to their names, except love and each other.

hopelessly, Kathleen gave in to her despair and wept, then prayed, and continued to weep until she had no tears left to cry.

It was long after midnight when she awoke and sadly realized that it hadn't all been just a bad dream, but an unending, terrible nightmare in which she was yet entangled. Her hands tied by Fate and circumstance, she longed for consolation. Just to be able to talk to someone, but no one was there to listen to her plaintive tale or help her to unburden herself of the traumatic memories of the day just ended. Pulling her weary body up, she sat in her bed and gazed through reddened, irritated eyes at the wall above her bed. There hung the large sixteen-inch-high, colored picture in an old-fashioned oval frame of their little family, taken on Easter Sunday, the year before.

In the picture, she was sitting on the first step of their peeled-paint porch. Two steps up Bobby was standing behind her, while Davey and the Runt were standing one step up on opposite sides of her. Bobby's hands were reaching out to the shoulders of his brothers, while her hands were reaching out to hold the hands of her two younger sons. The effect of the picture's composition was a diamond-shaped circle formed by a family with very little to their names, except love and each other.

Slowly, resolutely, Kathleen got out of bed, took the treasured picture down from its hook, shuffled over to the kitchen table and slumped into a hard, wooden chair. Prying the stubborn retaining tacks loose with only her fingernails, she removed the picture from its frame, turned it over and while looking at the back of the picture, prepared to open her heart to her sons, writing a heartfelt note to them. In her exhausted state of mind she tried to think of the right words to say, to tell of her pain and how much she loved them and how she hoped that someday, God would bring them back together again. Unable to compose her thoughts, she simply began writing what she felt and of her hopes and prayers, saying:

I only hope that I can live long enough to see you boys grown, married, and happy, something I haven't been very often in my life. All I ask and pray for is that we'll always be as close as we are in this picture. No one or anything will ever come between us. I love you

three boys with all my heart and I always will. May
God help us through the years to come.

Love,

Your mother

Placing the picture back in its frame, she re-hung it, and went
back to bed where she finally drifted off to sleep. She had, in an
unusual manner, been able to tell her sons how she felt and in
doing so, had relieved some of the painful helplessness she felt.
For many years to come, Kathleen's prayer and her fondest hope
would be one and the same, that somehow, God would help her to
take care of her sons and see them grow to manhood.

Within the next week, Kathleen sold off her furniture and
arranged to move out of the large, empty apartment which had
become a vale of tears. It was soon to be the end of the last day
in the place which had once been such a happy home for them. A
woman living alone didn't need five rooms and getting a lower
rent would help her to pay for Bobby and Davey's room and board
at the Home. Soon she would walk over to the furnished one-room
flat where she had already taken her belongings. Kathleen,
haunted by memories all week, began to be haunted once again by
young, friendly ghosts and a thousand now-bittersweet memories.

Steeling herself against impending heartache, Kathleen slowly
closed the upstairs door on those grasping, reaching memories,
and painfully descended the stairs. Each of her footsteps on the
creaky, old treads evoked a squeak or crack, echoing off the bare
walls of the empty stairway. Hollow, faceless voices haunted her,
seeming to call her from behind as she made her way slowly down
the stairway. Reaching the foyer downstairs, the guilt-ridden,
heartbroken young mother closed the old, rattling outside door one
last time, then walked along the rain-washed, gray sidewalk, a
gray which matched the sky. On toward the corner she went with
tear-filled eyes straining to focus straight ahead. She dared not
look back.

Chapter 3

The Early Years at Grandmaw's

From that first lonely night, Kathleen's youngest boy counted the long days and nights since he last saw his mother not knowing that by counting them, he only made them seem to pass even more slowly. Then two weeks after he last saw her, the day came, as Kathleen had promised, when they were able to visit Davey and Bobby. The Home allowed visiting on every other Sunday and each of the four of them would come to live for those long-awaited Sundays.

The anticipation of seeing his mother and brothers caused the Runt to waken long before Kathleen arrived. After stopping by to pick up her youngest son at her parents' home, Kathleen and he walked across the street to the streetcar stop at Southport and Fullerton where they would then wait. Throughout the four seasons, whether in muggy heat, driving rain, or freezing cold, they waited patiently for the tram in order to visit Bobby and Davey. Pitching and rolling noisily along its bright ribbons of steel, the streetcar became just another part of the excitement.

A block from the Home stood a grocery store where the Runt and his mother always stopped for fresh fruit or candy. Opening the door, his sense of smell was greeted by the tantalizing odors of fresh fruits and vegetables. Fruit and candy snacks were always taken along on their excursions to the park or the playground and since they were rare treats for the boys, none of the snacks ever went to waste.

On some lucky occasions Kathleen's brother, Chick, drove them to the Home where he would also visit with them, filling the role of a male family figure by spending time with them and playing ball or other games. Other times, their Aunt Etta or Aunt Maybelle might come along instead. Being away so much from their family, it was always a case of "the more visitors, the merrier the time" for the boys.

Being together during those hours was treasured by each of them, as they learned that one of the greatest pleasures in life was simply to be with those you loved. But precious hours passed too quickly by, for soon the tolling of five o'clock beckoned Bobby and Davey back to their dormitories. Since they were billeted by age groups and being four years apart, they hadn't been allowed to stay together in the same dormitory, which only increased their feeling of separation. In leaving Davey behind, the Runt felt as though part of him was being left behind too, for they had been the closest two brothers of all. Leaving his brothers would never get easier for the Runt and it was always followed closely by having to bid his beloved mother goodbye for two weeks. Fourteen days between visits with his immediate family often seemed like an eternity to the little boy.

On visiting Sundays, their recreational activities were usually dictated by the season and the weather. They passed the time by staying in the family day room and auditorium in the winter or on rainy days but dashing outside to play on the grounds in the spring and fall. During the summertime, they often trekked over to the local park and its swimming pool where they all could play ball and swim. There they had learned to love the water, getting a head start toward becoming good swimmers.

When visiting hours were over, the return trip didn't seem as lonely during summer days of sunshine and warm breezes as Kathleen and her youngest walked past green lawns and trees back toward the Addison Street bus stop. Winter's bleakness however, caused their return trip to be much less pleasant because of its shorter days, which found the Runt and his mother trudging those two long blocks through the bone-chilling cold, the snow, and the darkness. But those late Sunday afternoon return trips during the starkness of winter were brightened part of the way. Passing the block-long, power-generating station, the bright, golden light from the sodium-vapor street lamps would light up an entire block, and in projecting their glow upward, seemed to penetrate and warm up the cold, dark, wintry sky. Those bright lights illuminated the night and would always illuminate his memory.

Visiting at the Home would go on for four of the six years that the Runt was to be away from them, from 1938 through 1942. He would come to feel very alone on those Sunday afternoons in the neighborhood, when no other kids were out playing and seven more days were to pass before he could see his family again. Often he wondered where other people went on Sundays, for the streets and alleys appeared to be deserted with a quiet that was overwhelming. He wasn't alone in that regard, for his mother and brothers all came to feel the loneliness of those in-between Sundays, when they weren't able to visit. Years later, after they would be reunited, Sunday afternoons would serve as a quiet reminder of all these years apart.

Even though the little boy spent every other one of his Sundays gaining familial experiences with his more permissive, immediate family, the other Sundays and every week day would be spent in the different, more restrictive environment of his grandmaw's home. For the better part of six years, his childhood would be exposed to two different avenues of socialization and in a sense, he would live one little boy's life, but within two separate, family environments.

While the Runt missed his immediate family so terribly at first, he eventually realized there was little that he could do about it. As the long weeks passed, he gradually adjusted to staying with his grandparents, although the term "adjusted" may be an understatement. While his soft-spoken mother, Kathleen, had been a loving, easygoing mother to her sons, it would become apparent in the years to come, that she hadn't inherited her gentle nature from Grandmaw Kelly, who was less tolerant of mistakes.

As a young woman, Grandmaw Kelly had been a lovely blue-eyed blonde of fair complexion. In addition, Grandmaw was Irish to the bone, possessed a fiery temper and believed in confrontation rather than accommodation. The many passing years had done little to take the edge off her temperament and from most people's perspective, she appeared to have matured into a strict matriarch who angered quickly and forgave slowly.

However, through day-to-day contact, her grandson would learn in time, that by maintaining a tough facade, she'd been able to conceal a tenderhearted side of her which was evident to him on limited occasions. For example, if she were to find a stray animal, her guard dropped instantly, for small creatures held the key to unlocking her compassion. Years later, he would come to realize that it may have been a protective ruse she used: preventing others from exploiting her tender side, by keeping it hidden within her.

Kitchens were the early family entertainment centers at that time, the place where many old family tales and secrets were passed along during the many daytime hours that Grandmaw Kelly and her grandson shared in the kitchen. Delegated small tasks such as the sorting of dry beans, or breaking off carrot-tops, he would listen with rapt attention while she crocheted, cooked, or mended, and related, sometimes repeated, those colorful, warm stories of the days when her children, the Runt's mother, aunts and uncles, were growing up. As her grandson watched her preparing supper, he asked, "Grandmaw, was cooking supper for such a big family a hard job?"

"It wasn't so hard to cook for all them mouths," she responded, then continued, "less'n we got some unwelcome visitors," which led her into one of her favorite stories, the one about the Pruitts, a freeloading family they knew while living in Kansas.

Every Sunday back then, just about the time dinner, which is what Southerners call the midday meal, was put on the table, Mr. and Mrs. Pruitt and their brood of ravenous brats from a few miles down the road would stop by for a neighborly Sunday visit. Naturally they expected to be, and always were, invited to stay and share dinner with the Kelly family. Until one scorching Sunday when temperatures on the Great Plains were raised by hellfire winds, and accompanied by the arrival of the Pruitt family, which finally got Grandmaw Kelly's Irish up.

The Kellys were gathering for their Sunday dinner when one of the Kelly boys came running breathlessly in through the back door. Regaining his breath, he put his family on red alert when he blurted out, "The Pruitts just turned into our road down by the creek!" Patience exhausted, Grandmaw Kelly suddenly emulated

General Pershing, giving everyone orders to hurry and stash all the food up on the pantry shelf and put the dishes in the sink.

Tantalizing aromas of tasty, southern-fried chicken, potatoes slathered in gravy, and steamed corn had telegraphed the Kelly menu to the Pruitts who were now debarking from their horse and buggy. Anticipating a luscious Sunday dinner, the smiling Pruitts tapped ever so lightly on the weathered screen door, offering only a, "How are y'all?"

Grandmaw Kelly cheerfully returned their greeting and in asking them to come in, she apologized, saying, "Ah'm pow'rful sorry Ah cain't invite y'all to sit down to dinner but we'uns done finished what little we had. But y'all are sure welcome to stay and sit a spell."

A furtive glance at the sink full of dishes needing to be washed and dried must have jogged Missus Pruitt's memory for she replied, "No, no. We'uns hadn't planned to stay but jest a few minutes. Jest stopped to see how things were with y'all. Ah jest suddenly remembered that we'uns have to take the buckboard o'er to the Brown's and borrow a coupla bales of hay which we ran short on. We'uns will be leaving right now."

And leave they did, yet strangely enough, they never came back to mooch another Sunday dinner again.

Grandmaw Kelly often told her grandson how she used to be able to run like a deer and bragged that "No matter how big mah children had growed, when they tried to escape a whippin' by runnin' away from me, Ah could always ketch 'em!"

Until one day he asked, "You could catch all of 'em?"

His grandmaw then admitted some fallibility when she corrected herself, saying "All but one, yore Aunt Etta." She continued, "Dang her hide, she ran like she had wings on her feet 'cause Ah never could ketch her!"

While he personally had never tested her speed, even with a running start, the Runt could vouch for his grandmaw having faster hands than Sugar Ray. If he was caught misbehaving, and knowing what was coming, there was still no way the little guy could avoid her swift hand of justice. His grandmaw was no dummy either, for she used a belt in order to keep from hurting her hands while spanking kids.

Like the Invisible Man, the Runt's grandmaw seemed to move unseen, when it suited her. Many times after she spied him playing, engrossed any activity of which she might not approve, his brightest day's sunlight could suddenly be eclipsed by her dark, shadowy form. Looking up, the Runt would see his grandmaw, who had materialized out of nowhere, poised to dispense her swift, certain, and painful justice.

Professing Christian principles, Grandmaw Kelly often told her grandson biblical stories about God and His Son who died on a cross, His admonition to love one's neighbor, and the wonders of Heaven. This confused the little boy who wondered just how strong her belief was and how true her stories of God were, when in contradiction she often spoke ill of other races and creeds.

Grandpaw Kelly however, had been cut from quite a different bolt of cloth, in that he was more down to earth and fun-loving. He had probably been quite a rake when he was young, handsome, and of course, single. Of average height, he possessed broad shoulders and exceptional upper-body strength, a vestige of the days he spent laying track. Friendly brown eyes, black hair, and a quick, sincere smile were his trademark. One glance at a picture of him in his youth, tanned from working every day in the sun, and one could see why Grandmaw Kelly had been swept off her feet by him. Though not a farmer, Grandpaw worked with his hands, and always traveled to where the work was, hence the Kellys had lived in quite a few places, contributing to their accumulation of stories.

While at times the Runt's grandmaw displayed her prejudices, his grandpaw was tolerant of all races, nationalities, and religions, causing frequent, minor disagreements between them. He was a good man who just didn't get to church as often as he would've liked. One of the old man's favorite recollections was the time when their neighbor in Arkansas came to their aid when their old house burned to the ground. Although the neighbor didn't believe in God, he had more charity in his heart than many church-goers of Grandpaw Kelly's acquaintance and had opened his home to them and their children, to stay as long as was necessary. Grandpaw Kelly especially liked to make reference to that neighbor whenever his dear spouse displayed a bit too much Christian zeal, and he would zing her by saying, "The most Christian man Ah ever met was an atheist!"

Although the Runt loved his grandmaw, it was somehow just a little easier to love the good-natured old man with shoulders that seemed as wide as a doorway, who never tired of retelling his colorful stories of bygone days in the South. Born in 1879, Grandpaw Kelly claimed to be a cousin to the notorious James Boys and while working as an iceman, had delivered ice to Cole Younger of the Younger Brothers. He boldly professed to having risen to great heights in his young life, but chiefly due to a brief fling at painting smokestacks. He owed his broad, muscular shoulders to the hard work during his years as a gandy dancer on track-laying gangs, pounding down countless spikes for growing railroads. It seemed to be that Grandpaw Kelly had done a lot of living in his life! Was all of it true? The Runt had never thought to ask, because he never doubted his hero.

When he was young, Grandpaw Kelly had been a good dancer and a hard worker. Those abilities contributed to the zest for living everyone knew him to possess. One dark night, along a lonely Louisiana road, it nearly came to an end. After working all week near Shreveport, he was hitchhiking the 90 miles to his home and family in Texarkana, Texas. Hearing a motor vehicle far down the road behind him he turned in the darkness to face the bright light from the oncoming vehicle. Seeing only one headlight coming toward him, he assumed that it belonged to a motorcycle and turned his back to it, doubting that he would be getting a lift. Closer and closer the noisy vehicle came, when in the same moment he turned and saw it was a car with its right headlight out, he was struck down and the pain of impact blacked out his consciousness.

Coming to, he was acutely aware of severe pain in his leg, vaguely aware of a very dim light, and smelled the pungent odor of strong chemicals. He felt cold, for the air was cool enough to cause the sheet draped over his face to feel damp and cold. Slowly he was able to uncover his face, then he struggled to raise his head and look about the room, only to spy several gurneys with sheet-covered bodies upon them. Oh God, he was in a morgue! Coming in shortly after, a very astonished attendant saw that he was alive and ran to get the doctor. Young Grandpaw Kelly had been presumed to be dead at the accident site, transported to the hospital in Shreveport and taken to its morgue.

After his traumatic "resurrection," the doctors treated his badly-injured leg, and released him return to Texarkana, to his home and family. This tragedy of errors continued on after he complained of severe pain to the staff at the Texarkana hospital who sent him home after only superficial examination and treatment of his injured right leg. A day or two later, the leg became extremely painful and he returned to the hospital in Texarkana where the medical staff saw that it had become infected and gangrene had set in, whereupon they sent him back to the better facilities at Shreveport.

Unable to save his leg, a surgeon at the Shreveport hospital amputated Grandpaw Kelly's right leg at mid-thigh, under a local anesthetic. On that fateful night along a Louisiana road, in one fleeting, horrible moment, a hit and run driver had destroyed Grandpaw Kelly's right leg. In doing so, he had robbed him of the opportunity to enjoy so many activities which had been a large part of his life.

Often in the late afternoon, the little boy waited down at the corner outside the bar and grill for the old man to come home from his job as an inspector at Belmont Radio, just to walk the last block with him. As he waited, his hungry, young stomach rumbled as he smelled the delightful scent of food wafting on the current of warm air expelled by the bar and grill's exhaust fan.

His eyes brightened as the old man slowly came into view. Walking wasn't easy for Grandpaw Kelly, wearing a heavy, wooden, artificial leg. To walk on it, he had to swing his hip to move the artificial leg alongside and forward, which made walking a laborious effort; hazardous in winter, and torturous in the hot summer. Some days he would leave the artificial leg off and walk with crutches for a while. His grandson never heard him complain about the pain that he must have experienced but on bad days, the pain was clearly visible in his grandpaw's face.

At home in the evening, after supper and before the dawn of television, the kitchen was the family gathering place. In those days, families spent long winter evenings around the kitchen's large, round table, keeping the parlor neat as a pin, in case company dropped by. Winter's cold nights also forced economic reasons onto the Kellys for gathering in the kitchen.

Standing like a sentinel on guard in the area between the dining-room and the parlor, was a nickel-plated, four-foot-high coalstove, but to conserve coal, it was nearly always held to a small fire, with just enough heat to keep walls from cracking, but not enough heat to warm those two rooms sufficiently for humans to sit in. The front of the stove contained a grillwork of small mica-paned windows through which the fiery, orange-red coals could be seen. Often, on cold winter nights, the Runt fell asleep in the warmth of his divan bed while watching the flickering orange light dancing on the ceiling and walls.

Within their small, dimly-lit kitchen, warmed by the large, black, wood-burning stove, all family members were part of a captive audience for Grandpaw Kelly, the official storyteller who reigned supreme. Visual effects weren't necessary, for the old man's vivid descriptions and colorful detail allowed a listener's imagination to conjure up any necessary images. On those rare occasions when the old man's voice wearied, the huge, maple-finished, superheterodyne radio, standing on the floor under the kitchen window, served as the family's backup entertainment. Over the coming years, many long, wintry evenings would pass to the sound of early Country and Western music that was widely derogated as "Hillbilly Music" by Northerners, World War II news broadcasts of the Allies' progress, and other long-silent radio programs of the Early Forties.

The years 1938 and 1939 were busy times within Grandmaw and Grandpaw Kelly's household. As mentioned before, the Runt's uncle Chick and aunts still lived at the Kelly home and those of working age worked close enough that they came home for lunch. Uncle Chick worked at a machine shop with Les Collins, a young guy who lived in the apartment downstairs. Les, who was short, fair, and handsome, was awful cute and real nice, to hear Chick's sister Maybelle tell it. She cared enough about him to marry Les later that same year. Aunt Etta and Aunt Maybelle and their married brother, Uncle Clay, all worked over at Belmont Radio, just a little ways east on Fullerton. Being so close, they also came home for lunch.

The Runt experienced few dull moments from about half-past eleven until one o'clock, since everyone came in for lunch at different times causing it to seem like a revolving-door lunch counter that kept Grandmaw Kelly busy serving lunch till after one o'clock. The youngest member of the family sat in wide-eyed wonder, watching and listening to his mother's sisters, brothers, and sister-in-law exchanging news, gossip, ideas, and jibes. They were a group of very close, young people whose love of life and each other was shown each day in the way they dealt with each other. He gained the knowledge that their family and its members were of paramount importance to each of them.

Even the newlyweds, Uncle Clay and his wife Anita, back from their honeymoon in Lubbock, Texas, made it over to Grandmaw's for lunch nearly everyday, and one day the young boy asked them how they had met. Uncle Clay's brown cow's-eyes twinkled when he realized he had a willing listener.

Explaining, Uncle Clay told how he had moved to Chicago along with his sisters, Etta and Maybelle, a couple of years earlier. While walking along Fullerton Avenue one day a sign in the front window of one of the local taverns caught his eye. Advertising for a Western string music artist, the sign advised that applicants should bring their own instruments. At work the next day, Clay mentioned the sign to a friend of his who frequented that particular tavern and learned that his buddy already had a part-time gig there. Feeling that he was a qualified guitar player and that he had an "in," Uncle Clay hurried home after work, grabbed his guitar and strutted confidently into the tavern, not knowing that this would be the where and when of meeting the love of his life.

Sitting at a table waiting hopefully for an audition, enjoying a soft-drink and a cigarette was a young woman. Since she sat with her back to Clay, all he could see was that she was dressed in a white blouse, a fringed, black, cowgirl skirt, a black Western hat and boots. As he approached her, she removed her fiddle from its case and began tuning it up. Turning slightly now, Clay was in front of her and he was stupefied by the prettiest gal he had ever seen, possessing wavy blonde hair and crystal clear, blue eyes that seemed to read his mind.

Like a hungry bear drawn to honey in a tree, Clay approached the young lady's table, and asked her, "Do you mind if Ah jest sit down here and talk with y'all?"

"Go right ahead, Ah don't own the table and chairs in this place," she answered.

"Thanks, Ah do appreciate yore kindness," responded Clay, thinking that she had spunk; he liked that in a woman.

His extroverted, gregarious personality could charm the birds out of the trees, while her southern drawl was music to his Dixie-born ears. As they talked, he learned that her name was Anita Travis, from a town near Effingham, in Southern Illinois. "So why are y'all here?" he asked.

"To apply for the Western string artist's job."

"Oh, Oh."

"What's wrong?"

"Me too."

Separately they each auditioned for the musician's job but for reasons of nervousness or lack of experience, neither one was hired for the job. As she made ready to leave, spellbound Clay, not wanting this charming, southern girl to get away, just blurted out, "Would y'all like to drop by mah home for a while and meet mah family? The same ones Ah was jest telling you about?" Disbelieving he had actually said that, Clay was utterly flabbergasted by her reply.

"Sure, Ah'd like to meet yore sisters and others in yore family. It's a long way back home and Ah don't know a soul in this big city."

Upon bringing her home, Uncle Clay's family took to her immediately, treating her like one of their own, especially Aunt Etta who felt that she had already gained another sister. It had been love at first sight for both of them and they were married a year later in 1938, and their little boy, Bucky, would be born another year later.

Still too young to be away from home and soon to graduate from Thomas School, was the Runt's youngest aunt, who was nine years older than he. Although her given name was Elizabeth, the family called her Betty. Later, in life, the Runt would, after six years of living in the same house with her, call her "Hopeless." In those years Betty would eventually come to be more like an older sister, the sister he never had and many times was grateful that he hadn't. Betty had often been instructed by Grandmaw Kelly to keep a watchful eye on her little nephew and she did. Well, most of the time. Needless to say, watching her oldest sister's pain-in-the-neck, know-it-all kid probably wouldn't have ranked high on Betty's list of things she liked most to do.

In her early teens, Betty was enduring the onslaught of puberty. It wasn't the best of times to be saddled with the unwanted responsibility of her nephew's welfare. If a teenaged boy stopped to talk with Betty, the Runt might just have to shift for himself. If Betty heard one of the young, two-legged, neighborhood wolves howling and tried to get out of the house to talk to him, Grandmaw Kelly asked her to take her little nephew for a walk, knowing it would cramp Betty's style. The Runt always scored lot of points with Betty for that. He went more places being dragged along by Betty, than places he wanted to go. One pleasant, summer evening found him being cooled in the breezes generated by speeding cars zooming past him, as he stood fear-frozen in the middle of Fullerton Avenue, where she had left him in a huff! Regretting her hasty actions a few moments later, she thought it might be best for her to go back and drag him away before a carelessly-driven car did.

Contributing to the young boy's survival, was the attention and nurturing he received from all of his aunts. "Do you want to come home with us tonight?" was an invitation to adventure for him. His Aunt Etta and Aunt Maybelle occasionally asked him to come along whenever one of them took in a movie or if sometimes Aunt Maybelle's husband Les had to work nights over at the machine shop.

Walking unsteadily out of the Hollywood theatre one chilly midnight, the cold night air blurred the little boy's eyes rousing him from the drowsiness brought on by a movie too dull for a five-year-old. Walking along with Aunt Maybelle, home alone since his uncle Les had been rotated to the night shift that week, they reached the six-corner intersection of Fullerton, Clybourn, and Ashland, where the large, flickering, rainbow-colored, neon ball atop the gas station across the street had dazzled him to alertness.

Wide-awake now and warm in his green snowsuit, he was suddenly talking Maybelle's ear off, playing his own version of Twenty Questions, with queries such as, "I've never been to Riverview, is it bright like this?"

"Yes, but it's much bigger and brighter."

"What's a gas station for?"

"For people to buy gas for their cars."

"How do they get all those colors on that ball?"

"They're different colored lights."

"How do they turn it on and off?"

"It's automatic."

"Is somebody inside it turning the colors on and off?"

"No, that's automatic too."

Not until after his aunt had tucked him into bed, did her nephew finally switch off. Maybelle couldn't help but wonder if her sister's youngest son might not have been just as happy if she had skipped taking him to see a movie and taken him over to watch the gas station's neon ball instead.

Occasionally, yet by sheer coincidence, Betty took him to places that a five-year-old such as he, might enjoy being. Places and events such as a movie at the Hollywood theatre within walking distance on Fullerton near Greenview, the Christopher House, or the annual church carnival at Saint Josaphat's on Southport. There, during his very first exciting Ferris Wheel ride, he experienced exhilaration which he hadn't known before, enjoying the wheel, while riding in the same open car together with Betty, who showed him that high rides were nothing to fear.

Betty often invited her girlfriends over to play on the front porch, and sometimes their games would include Betty's "cute little nephew," a phrase which when uttered, gave Betty a tendency to gag. Having little choice, the nephew in question didn't object much, since most of the time the other girls were more pleasant toward him than Betty. The Runt's objections were quickly voiced however, when the girls began to play house and he had to play the part of the baby, or if they tried dressing him up as a girl. That was the last straw! He'd struggle loose and race down the gangway and into the house to tell his grandmaw, who, at least once every other year, went outside and told Betty to play nicely. Yeah, sure she will. Stick around, Grandmaw, you don't know her like he does!

One memory of Betty that the Runt would always carry with him was that very sad moment in her young life which occurred during the funeral they held for Tony. Tony was her sweet, gray tabby cat, an affectionate ball of fur who had contracted a feline virus and died. It was customary among the neighborhood kids to have some sort of ceremony to send their pets off to that great "Pet Home In The Sky," and so a funeral was arranged in the Kelly's backyard by Betty and Grandmaw Kelly.

A damp chill hung in the air and the unrelenting rain made that sad occasion even gloomier. Several of the neighborhood kids came to Grandmaw Kelly's house and as the cold rain continued to fall, they stood sadly around while Grandmaw Kelly, who loved animals with all her heart, buried Betty's furry friend under the back porch stairs. She had picked that particular spot because it would be sheltered from the elements in the years to come. Dampened to the bone, feeling chilly and sad, the Runt turned and there stood a heartbroken Betty standing in the rain, holding a brightly colored paper umbrella, its colors running, as she sobbed for her deceased little friend. Her sadness touched him and he too began to cry, not only for Tony but for Betty too. He wished in his young heart and child's mind, that he could have been a doctor who could have saved Tony, or a scientist who might have been able to bring Tony back to life for Betty.

Still troubled later while getting ready for bed, he asked his grandmaw, "Do cats go to Heaven when they die, Grandmaw?"

"Ah've always sorta believed that cats had their own Heaven to go to."

Gaining some comfort from her belief, the little boy retired to the dining room, climbed into his bed on the couch, said a prayer for their departed, furry friend, dozed off and began to dream. Instead of sweet dreamland, he found himself stumbling along in a gradually descending, narrow tunnel, in which the Runt could hardly see for the all-encompassing darkness. A slippery path in the damp soil offered little footing and the close, dank air that smelled of a cellar during a rainy spell made it hard to breathe. Despite wanting to turn around and run back out into the fresh air, something told him to keep going. Fearfully going on, he saw a dim light reflected on the wall, coming from around the bend and in rounding that bend, he found himself in a small, white-walled hospital ward.

Somehow, he was aware that it was a cat hospital and in looking around, found their newly-departed Tony recovering in bed, with only his white-capped head visible above the white sheet, pulled up to his chin. Seeing the boy, Tony greeted him by name. Seeing the look of intense surprise in the young boy's face, Tony spoke to him saying, "That's right! I can talk. All of us can talk here, in Cat Heaven. Please don't worry about me. We've got good doctors here and all of my pain is gone. Some of the many other cats tell me this is a wonderful place, so I'll be fine here."

Saying, "Goodbye, Tony," the Runt awakened suddenly from a child's wishful dream, yet for a long time believed that cats truly did have their own Heaven.

One of the little friends who came for Tony's sendoff was Fritzie Schumacher, a six-year-old girl from next door. Fritzie's mother and the Runt's grandmother thought it would be nice if the two children, being close in age could play together. Indeed it was. After several weeks they became good friends who played together often in the yard, and joined in games like "Hide and Seek" and "Red Rover" with other kids out in front on the sidewalk. A year older than he, slender Fritzie had big brown eyes, shiny, dark brown hair that ended in ringlets, and she laughed a lot. Because he blushed easily, his Aunts Etta, Maybelle, and Betty teased him about his "little girlfriend," when the two of them just happened to be two little kids who enjoyed playing together and were good friends. Their sweet, young friendship would be short-lived, for the Runt's grandparents would soon move away, taking him with them.

Rent receipts had piled up for much too long and the Kelly's decided that it was time for them to buy a home of their own. In the spring of 1940, they settled on one within their means, a tan and brown, frame cottage on Lakewood just north of Diversey. Before he knew it, moving-day was upon them and his uncle Chick's red stake-truck parked alongside the house, where the alley met the street, was proof of that. Requiring several trips using the truck, they moved from the two-flat on Southport at Fullerton over to Lakewood, less than a mile away.

As the last truckload stood ready to go, the Runt sat in the back seat of his uncle Clay's car talking with Aunt Anita, who sat in the front seat holding her little son, Bucky, in her arms. At the curb they waited for Uncle Clay to return to the car, when Fritzie slowly, sheepishly, came up to the side window of the shiny, navy-blue Chevy to tell the Runt goodbye, then stepped back onto the sidewalk. Soon his Uncle Clay got back in the car and started it up. As they slowly pulled away the little boy waved through the back window to Fritzie, who kept waving as her image grew smaller and smaller, until finally, she disappeared from view. Aunt Anita, consoled her teary-eyed nephew by saying, "Don't be sad, you'll get to see her again." Poor Aunt Anita had no way of knowing that what she had said was untrue. In watching his Southport Avenue home and little Fritzie fade quickly into the distance, the young boy couldn't have known then that he was seeing his little friend go out of his life forever, for he would not be fortunate enough for their paths to ever cross again.

Chapter 4

Right Side Of The Tracks

His grandparents' home on Lakewood consisted of two tan, clapboard buildings on a city-sized lot abutting an alley. The buildings, connected by a wooden sidewalk, comprised a six-room, three-bedroom cottage referred to as "the big house," on the front portion of the lot and a two-room, one-bedroom house referred to as "the little house," on the back of the lot. Between them, along the fence, was a large coal shed, a structure the Runt would visit many times during his years there. Neither house had a central heating plant, requiring the use of coal-fired stoves, nor did either house have indoor toilet facilities. Lacking basements, the little house had been built on a slab while the big house had only a sand-floored cellar.

Eager to explore his new environment the Runt was everywhere during the first few days checking out closets and hideaways at least twice. But only once did the Runt venture to descend into the cellar, for in his child's mind it was a damp, dark, subterranean world of the unknown. His eagerness had often overruled a cautious approach but the Spring Equinox of 1940 taught him a valuable lesson in not moving to quick judgments.

Sitting down to breakfast one morning about three weeks after moving in, the Runt turned from his breakfast of corn meal mush and looked out the window to see the boughs of trees swaying in the wind. "I'm tired of this cold weather," he whined.

His grandmaw replied with, "Then y'all will be pleased to know that today's the first day of Spring."

He answered, "I didn't know that! I'm sure glad to hear that Spring has finally come 'cause Winter's too cold!"

As he ate, the little boy chewed and swallowed faster, simply because he was in a hurry to go outside and play. At only five years of age, he believed that since it was the first day of Spring, the weather outside was spring-like. While his grandmaw busied herself with needlework in the dining room, he opened the door and hurried outside, clad in only his shirt and trousers. As the door slammed shut behind him a frigid, late-winter blast of wind caught him square in the face chilling every part of his body, and driving him quickly back into the house.

"Grandmaw, if Spring is here, why is it still so cold outside?" he shouted through chattering teeth to his grandmaw still crocheting in the dining room.

She explained, better late than never, "Well silly, it gets warm over a couple a' months, not all at once."

In April, Uncle Chick set about the task of fabricating indoor toilet facilities on the enclosed back porch, the only space that had been available. In addition, hot water had to be heated in a large, oval pan called a boiler, upon the gas range or the wood stove, since no water heater had been installed yet. While Chick did a great job of building the facilities, the fact remained, that the porch was unheated and during winter presented certain challenges to one's comfort level. One's sleepiness in the morning vanished in a split-second, when they sat down on an ice-cold toilet seat! Emerging from a warm bath into near-frigid room temperatures could be described as invigorating, at the very least! Also, one needed to always remember to leave water faucets dripping in order to prevent freezing and bursting of water pipes.

Zoned as a residential neighborhood, this portion of Lakewood Avenue was unique due to the two sets of railroad tracks belonging to the Milwaukee Railroad which ran down the middle of the unpaved street. A house facing a street with a railroad's switch line running down its middle may not seem like a great location to adults but to a young boy's way of thinking, it made a fantastic playground during the warmer months.

Unfortunately, the spur switch which allowed shifting of the tracks to allow coal cars to be shunted off from the train to the nearby coal yards was located between the tracks right in front of

A house facing a street with a railroad's switch line running down its middle may not seem like a great location to adults, but to the Runt's way of thinking it made a fantastic playground.

his grandparents house! The switch stood as a test of strength to the boys in the neighborhood; if a kid couldn't throw the switch, he was considered a weakling. As long as the Runt lived there, he was never able to throw that heavy switch. Each day its massive black handle would taunt him to give it a try and each day he would fail, never being able to force the switch past its apex. The bigger boys had no problem throwing the switch but some of them were mischievous in that they wouldn't put the switch back the way it should be. A brakeman then had to dismount from a halted train and throw the switch to its proper position before the train could continue on.

As the earth-shaking switch trains slowly passed, sometimes a grizzled engineer turned toward him and waved back to him, as he stood in awe, memorizing each railroad's initials on refrigerator cars, boxcars, and gondolas. Proud railroads that had forged a steel trail in helping to build our country had become instantly identified by their initials such AT&SF, B&O, C&O, GN, and PRR. He learned to distinguish whether the cars were empty or full by how much they swayed and the degree of sink he detected in the rails as the heavy cars rolled past. Slowly but surely, the little boy was becoming a railroad man in his heart, often day-dreaming of someday running one of those mighty diesel giants along some high-speed track.

A special treat was enjoyed, on delivery days when the train crew went about the task of shunting off interspersed coal cars into the coal yard or refrigerator cars down a little farther into the George Street meat-packer's spur. The engine shuttled forward pulling its load of cars until it was in position. Then it backed up until a brakeman disconnected one or more cars, which then rolled smoothly onto the spur into the coal yard. Then the engine backed up toward the packing company where the process was repeated with refrigerator cars. It was like watching a steel-rail ballet. The experienced engineers were soft-touch artists, knowing just how much push to give the freed cars so that they rolled all the way into the coal yard or packing company spur with a minimal impact on colliding with standing cars already there.

Only once did the Runt see a young engineer's miscue, when

a coal-car juggernaut slowly rolled to a silent stop a hundred feet from the coal yard. It was a mistake that was easily remedied however, when the novice engineer revved up the diesels, slowly made contact with the stray car, then accelerated and hit the air brakes just enough to send the straggling gondola into the coal yard.

Most of the time, when there were no trains running, a single railroad track became a high-wire in the imagination of the World's Greatest High-Wire Walker, while the ties themselves made a challenging triple jump course. Along those tracks, the Runt also learned the fundamental physics of extreme pressure and its generation of heat. When the pressure of locomotive wheels was applied to small pieces of sandstone, the stones were pulverized in a flash. Various sizes of nails placed on the rails before a train passed, were flattened under the extreme pressure of the huge, steel, flanged wheels. The Runt's first lesson in extreme pressure and high temperatures came instantly, when he excitedly picked up a flattened nail immediately after a train passed, receiving a burn which smarted for several hours.

Nature detests a void and although the Kelly's had loved their long-departed cat, Tony, the time had come to bring another pet into the house. Other cats would be fortunate enough to find their way into Grandmaw Kelly's home and heart in the coming years. Hearing a persistent meow at the door one cool morning, she opened the door to find a half-grown, gray tabby cat which was promptly taken in and named Tiger. Later, there would be Blackie, who arrived as a beautiful kitten having a black coat with white splotches and eventually grew into a huge male cat possessing a propensity for fighting and carousing at night. Tiger had accepted Blackie as a kitten and they always got along despite their both being intact males. Of course, none of Grandmaw Kelly's cats, dogs, or birds ever fought, because they knew she didn't want them to. She possessed a rare, yet marvelous gift of being able to talk to the animals and they appeared to understand everything she told them.

Tiger, on several occasions, had rescued the Runt from a fate worse than death, for the young boy hated green peppers. He disdained the small green pepper chunks in his lunch salad but felt compelled by Grandmaw's stern glare to stay at the table until he finished them. A chunk of green pepper concealed in his lowered hand always brought Tiger under the Runt's side of the table and when Grandmaw wasn't looking, another piece of green pepper disappeared! Tiger never complained.

Blackie, for half of his long life, would bear the mutilated ear he suffered while he was out one night, coming home battered and bloody but presumed to be victorious. No other cat ever seen around their Lincoln-Diversey neighborhood, could have held its own against an oversized cat like Blackie for very long.

With the passing of couple of years, the Runt became aware of a few advantages in having a "big sister" around. Getting out of the house more often was the primary perk. If he forced himself to be nice, she wouldn't mind having him around. Staying up late occasionally was another perk, since his grandparents didn't think to send him off to bed while Betty was still up, under the impression that the time wasn't that late. Another advantage of staying close to Betty was listening to great "pop" songs on the radio in the afternoon when she got home from school and the "Hit Parade" once a week. Sometimes after a boring day, it was like a shot of adrenaline when Betty got home from school and talked about stuff that she did. Grandmaw Kelly didn't want him playing with the radio during the day but Betty could turn it on and let it blast! The Runt thought that his grandmaw had always liked her better, anyway.

Thanks to Betty, he had listened to everything from "Swing" orchestras such as Glenn Miller's, with its unique arrangements, to pop ballads by singers who possessed really great voices, such as Frank Sinatra, Perry Como, Helen O'Connell and Jo Stafford. Betty's influence aided the Runt in gaining a long-lasting perspective and appreciation of many types of music from a generation earlier than his own.

Musical influence of another stripe was exerted upon him by his grandparents who listened to the radio nearly every evening. Having spent most of their lives in the rural South and Southwest, the older Kellys preferred to listen to music that had sprung from that region. On week nights, they always tuned in to WJJD, owned then by Plough, Incorporated, and which broadcasted at 1160 kilowatts. WJJD's broadcasts in those days may have been tied to sundown and the need for farmers to rise early, since its signoff time early in the evening varied with the length of the day. In that bygone era, WJJD broadcasted a nightly program called "The Suppertime Frolic," which was hosted during its long nighttime reign by radio personality Randy Blake. Randy's play list was limited to Country and Western performers of the Forties, including singers like Eddy Arnold, Ernest Tubb, Bob Wills and the Texas Playboys, and lesser known performers such as Grandpaw Jones, T. Texas Tyler and the married team of Lulubelle and Scotty.

On Saturday nights, the big attraction was a live broadcast by radio station WLS, "The Prairie Farmer Station," which came from downtown Chicago's Eighth Street Theatre. With stars like Patsy Montana and Gene Autry, the evening-long "National Barn Dance" was country music's central attraction at that time and Chicago was its focal point.

Hearing this same genre of music every night, the Runt was to develop a lifelong appreciation for Country and Western music, which endured in spite of many derogatory comments from his young friends and classmates who always referred to it as "Hillbilly Music." They weren't interested in the explanation he offered which he had often heard, that Country music was written about events in everyday life while Western music told stories about places. It would be people like the Runt, his relatives, and many others like them, who kept the love for country music alive in the North, decades before it would be "cool" to appreciate "Country Music."

Radio could be a very entertaining medium, especially in its treatment of drama, since radio only set the stage and plot for its audience, allowing their minds to weave the details. One unforgettable Sunday evening mystery program stood out above all others. Known as "Lights Out," it gave the Runt fearful shivers he wouldn't soon forget. After ceremoniously following the deep-voiced announcer's eerie instructions to turn off the lights, the evening's suspenseful tale slowly, meticulously unfolded, while the family all huddled together in pitch-black darkness. Shivers crept up his spine as he sat staring into the darkness of the kitchen as it reached out to engulf him, listening to a terrifying story. The hideous eye, staring at him in the dark, was simply the glowing, green light of the radio dial, the only illumination in the room.

Rapt within this realm of horror, the Runt listened to the broadcast's ghastly moans and screams with one ear, while his other ear hearkened to every creak and groan emanating from the nether regions of the old house. His mind couldn't shut out the answer he got one rainy afternoon, when he asked his resident uncle what it was like, down in their cellar, and his uncle Chick flippantly answered that the devil was probably down there. Small wonder that the Runt's scary memories of childhood lingered the longest.

Getting back to Betty, if the Runt were pressed for an honest opinion, he'd admit that she was an extroverted person who could be fun to tag along with. Often she unknowingly aided in passing some of his lonely hours, when he listened to her singing from another room, some of the popular songs of the day. She possessed a pleasant singing voice that the Runt enjoyed listening to but before he would let her know, he would rather have been forced to eat boiled potatoes.

At times when Betty wasn't around, it didn't mean that he was alone, since his Uncle Chick and Aunt Maybelle also made his stay on Lakewood a pleasant one. Chick still lived at home while the Runt's married aunt, Maybelle, who would treat him with genuine compassion throughout the coming years, moved into the little house on the rear of the lot with her husband, Les Collins, and their baby son, Roy.

Chick, only in his mid-twenties, with steel grey eyes, chestnut hair and an engaging smile was seldom home evenings because he worked nights during the week or on weekends went out with his fiancee, Helen Page. As a rule, during weekdays, Chick rose sometime around mid-morning and would usually kid around with his nephew. Frequently, they played on the patience of Grandmaw Kelly, probably driving her blood pressure through the roof goofing around at the kitchen table, imitating various barnyard animals while she was cooking.

In what had become a daily ritual, the Runt saw his uncle off to work before Grandpaw Kelly came home. With his young nephew trailing along, Chick would stroll out in front of the house in time to catch the switch train coming through the middle of Lakewood about that same time of day. Calling out "So long," Chick would then run alongside one of the freight cars, grab a rung of its ladder, climb up, and ride the half-mile down the tracks to his job at a machine shop along the tracks near Fullerton.

Having seen his uncle off to work, the Runt continued walking the half-block along the tracks to Diversey where he waited for his grandpaw to walk home from the streetcar stop at Southport and Diversey. Waiting was always a pleasure, since just up Diversey was the huge bakery that baked Wonder Bread, whose sweet, tantalizing fresh-baked-bread aroma was nearly overpowering.

On one stifling, sunny afternoon, as he stood waiting for Grandpaw at Diversey, the Runt's love for furry animals betrayed him when a little white dog came trotting past and he reached down to pet the dog. In an instant, the dog turned and bit the Runt on his index finger. Feeling the pain of rejection by a furry creature more than the pain of his wound, the Runt ran home to his grandmaw's house. There he was quickly attended to by Betty and Grandmaw Kelly, who disinfected the bite, then wrapped it in a bandage. It was one of the times when his Lord must have been watching over him, for the little stray dog had continued on its way and the possibility of rabies had never been mentioned.

One day, the Runt didn't get to walk to the corner and wait. Instead, his old grandpaw came home early, lacking his usual happy-go-lucky air. Approaching retirement age, he had been laid-off from his job inspecting radio components. "Laid-off" was a new phrase the Runt learned that afternoon. It was a term whose original meaning implied the temporarily idling of part of a company's work force, subject to recall when business picked up. It had, by then, as now, become an employer's euphemism for discharging workers that they just didn't want on their payroll anymore. Losing his job was devastating to Grandpaw Kelly and it would be the old man's last regular employment, although for years afterward, he would sell newspapers at local newsstands, where everyone came to know him as "Pop."

Often the Runt carried lunch and a jar of coffee that Grandmaw Kelly made, up to the newsstand at Southport and Diversey for his grandpaw. Lingering for a while with his idol, he helped the old man by running the fifteen feet to the cars at the curb with the newspaper. During evenings in the kitchen, he had overheard his grandparents talking and was hurt more than once by hearing of the impatience of drivers who drove off, in too much of a hurry to wait for his crippled grandpaw to limp that distance to their cars.

In those days when all breaking news came through the newspapers and radio, there were enough readers, coverage and circulation to support all of Chicago's five major daily newspapers, which were the Times, News, Sun, American, and Tribune. Soon, the old man was lucky enough to get the corner of Lincoln, Racine, and Diversey, a good corner, a block away from home, where he earned a living in spite of daily newspapers selling for 3 cents each, while all Sunday newspapers were a dime. The newsstand was also right on the corner only three feet away from the curb. When his grandpaw worked mornings, the little boy would sometimes come up to help him and that's where he got to know Big Mike.

A ruddy-faced, big-boned Irishman who stood six-feet four, yet seemed ten feet tall, Big Mike Clancy was the traffic cop at the six-cornered intersection and he had his hands full, that he did. In all kinds of weather, Big Mike was there, directing traffic in conjunction with the signals, or whenever he wanted to override the signals. Often he'd step out into the curb lane of traffic, put up his big mitt and give a blast on his whistle that could have shut down the nearest factory. There is no way any driver could have not heard the shrill piping of Big Mike's whistle. The Runt did wonder though, if high-pitched noises could shatter glass, why none of the windows at the corner had been blasted into shards by Big Mike's whistle.

After getting the attention of everyone within three blocks,

Big Mike would then personally escort an elderly lady across the street or carry some shaggy neighborhood dog across to safety. The Runt would later see just how red Big Mike could look, when the raw winds of February would blow icy-cold in his craggy face, yet the huge, friendly cop always, always had a smile for everyone passing by. Since Grandpaw Kelly, like all newsstand vendors during winter, kept a fire going in a 55 gallon barrel right next to the newsstand, many times Big Mike would surely be found, passin' the early morning with the old man, and keepin' a bit warmer in the process.

Out-of-town company came to stay during the late summer of 1940, when Grandmaw Kelly's sister's boy, Earl Kirk, had hitch-hiked over five-hundred miles from his family's home in Springfield, Missouri. Earl, who could do no wrong in his aunt's eyes, stayed for a few weeks while scouting for a decent job but was unsuccessful in finding one. It was unfortunate, because during his stay with the Kellys, the Runt got to know Earl as a very likable, smart young man who was always kind toward others.

Earl, a tall, pleasant but boyish-looking, blond kid who had just turned twenty, treated everyone with the politeness of a young southern gentleman. Having a love of outdoor fun and good times in common, Earl and Chick had hit it off well and spent a couple of Saturdays together fishing and hunting. Since he was the oldest of several children, his family needed his help back on the farm. Had he been able to find a job up north, he could have helped them financially. Planning to go home, Earl was troubled by the weather almanac's prediction of an early Fall, and decided to return to Springfield over Labor Day weekend, so as not to miss the Ozarks' beautiful golden scenery. He was also leery of staying too long up in the North, because late Fall and early Winter's freezing rain offered very hazardous driving weather in the Ozarks.

While they had no way of knowing it at the time, those who had met and liked young Earl, had seen him for the last time. In less than three years World War II would snuff out his young life.

Chapter 5

The Peaceful Years

It had been nearly three years now since Kathleen had been forced into splitting up her family. Enough time for some of her pain to subside and time during which she established another home, lost her Texas drawl, and filled her empty hours with her work, where she gained a few trusted friends.

Lately her best friend, Gloria Wills, had begun to annoy her with repeated encouragement to meet a really great guy that Gloria thought Kathleen should get to know. The really great guy happened to be a friend and co-worker of Gloria's fiance, Richard Denton, and his name was Don Averill. Weary of Gloria's insistence that Don might be "Mister Right," Kathleen voiced her concerns that Don might be "Mister Wrong Again." Reassured by Gloria that this wouldn't be the case, Kathleen finally agreed to meet him and the meeting was quickly and easily arranged since Don, too, worked at the same company.

In addition to being tall and well-built, Don's curly, sandy hair framed a tanned face, which only emphasized his clear blue eyes. While Kathleen's first impressions noted that Don had a pleasant personality, she only met with him for lunch at work for several weeks until she was finally convinced that he was truly as nice as everyone said he was.

Eventually she decided to go out with Don and after a couple of months, to her complete surprise he asked, "When do you think I can meet your sons? Because I'd sure like to see them and get to know them."

"I think it might be just a little soon and I can't really answer that just yet Don, but I'm glad that you'd like to meet them," Kathleen replied.

Don's answer came two weeks later as Kathleen brought a broad smile to Don's always cheerful face when she mentioned, "Sunday is visiting day at the Home. If you wouldn't mind it might be a good idea if you could take me over to my folks' place to pick up my youngest son and then go along with us to the orphanage."

In the weeks and months that followed, visiting Sundays became playful, even more enjoyable, carefree times when Don went along with them. Having the gift of empathy with youngsters, Don could play their games with them, yet was still able to elicit their respect. He was also able to take them many places that they hadn't seen before, knowing just the kinds of places that young boys would enjoy being and the activities that would appeal to them.

These were the most special times in the Runt's heart, when Kathleen, Don, Gloria, and Richard would take the boys on fun-filled, exciting picnics to the forest preserves, to fish and wade near the dams on hot summer days. Fostering a sense of family, these occasions were the closest things to family outings that any of the boys could ever remember in their young lives.

By mid-1941, Kathleen and Don had become engaged, planning to marry in the summer of '42. Idolizing Don, the boys couldn't have been happier and he had shown that he truly cared about them. Don was an ideal prospect for a stepdad, being smart, kind, athletic, and loved by all of the boys who hoped that in the next year they might all be able to get back together in a happy home.

While visiting days became even more enjoyable, the Runt, who still resided with his grandparents, had begun to really enjoy the other days because his Aunt Maybelle and Uncle Les included him on many of their day trips. Living in the little house on the back of the lot, they would stop by and take their nephew with them whenever they took their infant son, Roy, to the park or to the movies. Sometimes they might just bring home ice cream for which the words, "Dixie Cup" became synonymous to the Runt. Maybelle often treated her nephew like another son, even buying identical Christmas gifts for him and little Roy over several Christmases.

He'd always remember a lovely picnic day during late Spring of 1941, that he spent playing on the lawn with his aunt, uncle, and cousin, in Lincoln Park. Listening to a portable radio that didn't plug in anywhere was a strangely different experience for him. It seemed that whenever his aunts or uncles were around, a radio was usually playing. After leaving the park they stopped to visit the Elks Memorial, but he overheard that because he was a minor they weren't allowed to tour the inside of the memorial. He felt badly that they had been denied the chance to walk through its exhibits which they had wanted to see, because he was with them.

Often Maybelle and Les took him to the movies at the East Theatre just a few doors east of Reimer's drug store. Located at the six-corners intersection of Racine, Diversey, and Lincoln, the bright pink letters of Reimer's neon sign proclaimed it to have been established in 1894. A special treat was enjoyed when they stopped there on the way home from the movies for nothing matched the sweet flavor of a malted milk shake from Reimer's fountain. A perfect touch was the small package of cookies that accompanied such a dairy delight.

Those boyhood memories would stay with him a lifetime. But so would other, less pleasant memories such as the one that stemmed from the time his Aunt Maybelle and Uncle Les had taken him with them to see a matinee showing of "The Mummy's Hand." The Runt spent half of the movie looking away from the screen, too scared to look at the wrapped, ragged monster but had seen enough to remember the mummy's face, his reaching hand, and how he dragged his foot. Arriving home the tired, yet contented little boy forgot about the scary movie that he had seen earlier and drifted off to sleep.

In that night's darkest hour, while sleeping fitfully on the divan in the dining room, the Runt awakened from a bad dream and stared past the surrounding darkness into the living room. The bright glare from the street light in front of the house beamed through clear windows, projecting the lace curtain's pattern onto the walls, while the light's eerie, yellow glow framed the archway. Then he saw it. Something slowly edged out from behind the archway, eclipsing the light. It was a shape that he had seen earlier that evening in the movie: the distinct, round head of the Mummy!

48

Not yet panic-stricken the scared young boy strained his eyes, staring to be sure of what was really there but saw only the archway. There! It edged out from the archway again. Panic grabbed him by the throat! He jumped from the divan and hit the light switch, while keeping his wide-open young eyes on that archway. The lights revealed nothing but the painted archway and nothing alarming, except his grandmaw's shouts to turn off the light and get back to bed! Lying there in the dark, the alert, young boy fought hard to stay awake and keep his watch on the archway but Morpheus finally overcame him, wrestling him back to sleep.

Other scary memories were caused by night vision trickery which often led the Runt to experience a fright that many other kids probably encountered at least once during their childhood. The "Bedroom Ghost" was an apparition spawned by a child's well-established habit of hanging clothing up on the back of their bedroom door. To wake up in the dark and see a light-colored object in the room, a child might stare and envision a ghost moving in front of their bedroom door. Staring harder, the child might see the object seem to wave its arms. If the child flicked on a light, the cowardly "ghost" vanished into the light-colored garment, hanging on the door.

Many children of the Runt's era also believed in a generally accepted truth. Well, accepted by those kids who believed that they were safe from harm, if they hid under the covers of their bed. A companion belief was that things which go bump in the night somehow lost their power when confronted by protective bed covers. The Runt deemed this to be so after one strange nightmare, during which he fought off a flock of sparrows. Waking up in the totally dark room, he imagined that the sparrows had exited the nightmare with him and were clamoring to get him! He outwitted them by ducking his head under the covers with the rest of his body, thwarting their efforts to peck his eyes out. He felt that the feathered little demons hadn't been able to get through the covers. Safe in his sanctuary, his heavy, weary eyelids closed in sleep shortly afterward.

Wonderful events also occurred in those days and counted among them was the wedding of his uncle Chick and his new aunt,

Helen, who were married in June of 1941, in a simple ceremony. The Runt had idolized his uncle Chick and always accepted Helen as pretty and nice. The family had arranged a wedding reception for close friends and family only, at the Kellys' home.

His uncle's wedding was important in the Runt's mind primarily because it was a long-anticipated, happy occasion in the Kelly family. It also meant that at last, the young lad could stop sleeping on the old, cold leather divan in the dining room, move into Chick's old bedroom, and sleep in a real bed again. Also helping to make the occasion unforgettable would be the hangover the Runt was to suffer, throughout the long hours of the next day.

When liquid refreshments were ordered for the reception, the event's planners had neglected to order soft drinks for those who might have preferred them and for a distinctly small minority who shouldn't have been drinking beer in the first place. A frost-covered keg of beer had been provided for the guests' refreshment and the Runt, a thirsty boy of six, had very often heard the term, "any port in a storm."

Although he believed that he shouldn't do it, the Runt repeatedly tapped the keg for a small glass of beer but disdained its bitter taste and after a few sips would pour it out and get another. It seemed that beer didn't taste as bitter when it was cold, right out of the keg. Only his uncle Chick had seen him when he came over to draw several glasses for guests but Chick just grinned, shook his head and walked away. No one else knew what the little sot had been doing until after everyone had left, whereupon he got sick. It was then that Grandmaw Kelly became acutely aware of what her grandson had done all evening.

His nausea and the late hour were the only things that kept the Runt from yet another close encounter with his grandmaw's belt. Aside from her angry tirade, during which she pointedly told him that she was glad he was sick, that he deserved to be sick, Grandmaw Kelly didn't talk to him all day Sunday. Needless to say, the malaise which afflicted him the next day was a much more powerful deterrent to drinking than any of her scolding. It caused her grandson to lose any and all interest in beer-drinking for many years afterwards.

A few months later, September's dry breezes carried a hint of coolness together with the long-awaited sound of school bells anticipated by the Runt. That golden post-Labor Day Tuesday morning found him patiently waiting for his aunt Helen to drop by and whisk him off to school for his first day. Backlogged work at Kathleen's plant had forced his mom to miss enrolling her youngest son in school and she had asked Chick's new bride, Helen, to get him registered. While he missed his mom's company, the Runt didn't mind too much, because he liked his new aunt, who was always very nice to him, had a soft voice and was an attractive pretty lady.

Having already learned his alphabet and other academic necessities through his grandpaw's tutoring, everyone thought he was ready for school. The placement advisor, after listening to Helen explain that her nephew had been schooled by his grandfather, agreed that the boy, who was already six years old, should begin his schooling in Mrs. Ellen Kosterman's first grade class instead of kindergarten. Being the last student assigned to her he took a seat at the desk given him by Mrs. Kosterman and surveyed this strange, new place.

As his eyes traversed the room he saw that several rollers had been installed above the blackboards, still clean from a washing over the summer, in the front of the room. In time he learned that those rollers contained rolled-up maps of his own country and far-off places in the world. Four other blackboards along the hall side of the room were actually sliding doors which opened vertically and concealed a coat-closet as long as the room and it was about four feet wide. What a great hiding-place it would make! The desks were one-piece desk and seat combinations, bolted to the wooden floor. In counting the number of desks in the room, he tallied forty-eight, in six rows of eight desks each, with little more than half of the desks occupied. In the corner of the room, on the wall near the door was an old Seth Thomas pendulum clock, made of reddish-brown wood, with hands that slowly moved, as he kept watching them. Eventually, he would find that almost all of the rooms were laid out in the same manner, except that some of the clocks didn't work and the desks in the higher grades were bigger.

Taking to school like a duck to water, he would learn quickly, excelling in his schoolwork throughout his first three semesters, all with Mrs. Kosterman, who took a special interest in him. Brunette, with a dark complexion, she wore thick glasses which made her eyes seem as though they were looking into his mind, and perhaps they could. Seeming to be a very intelligent woman, Mrs. Kosterman also possessed a warm personality, and had a manner of conveying ways to study faster and find answers easier.

If schoolwork could ever be considered a pleasure it certainly seemed to be so in her class, where she encouraged him to learn as much as he could and not wait for others to "catch up." When his assignments were done, she encouraged him to study something else while he was waiting. Mrs. Kosterman's teaching methods would be the benchmark against which he would measure succeeding teachers during his elementary school education.

In those days it seemed that the majority of Agassiz School's teachers were older, unmarried women of Irish descent. While thoroughly dedicated to the education of youngsters from all walks of life, each of them had probably been grossly underpaid for the task that they had undertaken. Fortunately for their students, the teachers somehow succeeded in educating their young charges. Multiplication tables were taught using visual aids and by repetition until a student learned them by rote. Often in spelling and reading, catch phrases were associated with rules to remember, or clues were embedded, such as pronouncing "separate" as "sePARate" and pronouncing "boundary" as "bounDAIRY," so that students would not only learn but remember what they had learned. In short, those wonderful teachers drummed their subject into each and every student until that little internal light went on and the steel-trap portion of each student's mind locked the knowledge away in its long-term memory.

One day, Mrs. Kosterman set up a special field trip for the Runt and two other students at Northwestern University where they could participate in a special teachers' workshop for advanced students. Afterwards, Mrs. Kosterman took them all to lunch and encouraged them to have dessert. The Runt wasn't accustomed to dessert and it was also the first time the Runt had ever heard of

New York Cherry ice cream but he tried it and it would always be his favorite ice cream flavor. Was it to be his favorite because of its flavor or because it reminded him of a very unusual day with a very special teacher? Who knows?

While his grandpaw had diligently prepared him for the academic portion of his education, the old man hadn't thought to warn the unsuspecting boy about the darker, more painful side of school days to be encountered in his school career. A "different" child quickly learns how cruelly undiplomatic other children can be, when the afflicted child is abruptly made to realize that he is different. The Runt hadn't realized the degree of his speech defect until it was coldly brought to his attention by some of his classmates, whose straight, unglossed candor eventually degraded into taunts. At first, he tried explaining to them why he was different but his attempt to gain their understanding only gained him more mockery.

After the failure of this tactic he tried turning the other cheek in order to keep his antagonists from knowing how much their deliberate insults had stung. Only emboldened by his deference, which was interpreted as weakness, the taunts gave way to shoves, then punches. Only when enough blows landed upon him to anger him, would the Runt retaliate. Rage-induced adrenaline brought his arms up and into a flurry of swift punches, while the rage insulated him against any pain from blows. He learned what he believed was necessary, very quickly, in order to survive in a school of hard knocks.

In time, the repeated pattern of abuse and response caused the young boy's anger threshold to diminish until mere taunts themselves were met with anger. Learning the routine, he adapted to becoming angry quickly and to land the first blow, in order to avoid the unnecessary pain of being pummeled first. Later in life he would have to work very hard to subdue the urge to anger quickly.

An unfortunate fact of life then, as it is now, is that it doesn't take long for a minority of insensitive children to put an easygoing, congenial, little boy onto the road to becoming another angry, defensive, young man. The only benefit the Runt had derived from such a pattern of behavior was that it strengthened his determination to prevail against the adversities that he would encounter in life.

In the interim, his mother had been busy in her search for someone who could make her son's life a little easier, a search that was soon to bear fruit. Never far from the forefront of Kathleen's mind was another of her major reasons for bringing her sons to Chicago and she had been inquiring at different hospitals about their treatment programs for children with birth defects. Having heard about the Childrens Memorial Hospital from friends, Kathleen was given hope that she might qualify to receive medical help for her youngest son.

With this hope to guide her, Kathleen and her youngest son rode the Lincoln Avenue streetcar down to the six corners of Lincoln, Halsted and Fullerton. From there they walked on a bright, autumn morning, past the Aetna State Bank and down Fullerton Parkway to the Thomas D. Jones Memorial Clinic. The young boy was amazed by the number of red-brick buildings they passed that were associated with the hospital.

At the first check-in station located under a bright, turquoise-globed light, Kathleen and her boy were told to take a seat. They learned quickly that several different waiting periods would be necessary in order to see a doctor. Bureaucratic inefficiency was not the reason why they waited so often and for so long. Rather, it was the large number of hopeful patients from other needy families, in search of a level of medical treatment unavailable to them elsewhere, who also waited in hope and weren't disappointed.

Ever-observant, the waiting young boy's eyes took in everything he saw. A large clearly-numbered clock dominated the wall of each crowded yet neat, clinic waiting room, the legend under its numbers indicating that the time shown on its face was "Naval Observatory Time." The patients and their parents who represented all races and creeds, brought their own reading material, for they knew they were going to wait quite a while.

Some of the waiting rooms held wondrous sights for children of all ages. These were the brightly-lit scenes recessed within the walls behind glass and composed of hand-carved miniature figures; animals, homes, barns, and landscapes which were amazing to study. Ubiquitous, enchanting, miniature scenes which aided in the passing of many clinic waiting hours for the Runt and his contemporaries. It was unfortunate that the little boy didn't remember the names of the craftsmen whose hands had created the multitude of brightly colored fantasy scenes. They were far too many in number to have been created by one person or one family.

While waiting all of those hours during the many visits, the Runt had seen that other boys and girls had been born with the same condition as he. One day, the chief of plastic surgery had great news for Kathleen when he told her that they could close her son's open palate; in effect, creating a palate where none had existed. Although school had already begun early that month, Kathleen agreed that the surgery should be scheduled soon.

Admitted on a Wednesday and getting his bearings on Thursday, the Runt's operation had been scheduled for early Friday afternoon. Having no food and little water all day Friday, he felt hungry and lonely. In late afternoon, his loneliness and anxiety quickly dissipated when his mom and grandmaw came into the room. No two people would ever be more welcome than they were at that moment. They talked with him, cheering him up and when the orderly rolled the gurney in, the little boy willingly hopped on it for the ride to the Operating Room. Pushed to a stop and long wait in the hall outside of the O. R., fear crept up on him as he studied the hall and the small room open to his left where large cylindrical tanks of different gases were stored.

His fears were allayed by the sweet voice of a dark-haired scrub nurse dressed in a green cotton uniform, who asked him if he felt nervous and then told him that he was just going to take a nap and when he woke up, his life would be much better. Shortly afterwards, he was wheeled into the brilliant white O. R. and transferred to the operating table. Looking up, he saw the glass of the large, circular ceiling light which hadn't yet been turned on and in its glass lens he watched the reflections of the doctors and nurses moving around him. "Hi son," piped the kindly male voice behind a cotton mask, as the huge ceiling light came on brightly. "I want you to count slowly to one hundred when I tell you to start," the voice said.

Then a cool, wet cloth was laid over his eyes and something that felt like a vegetable strainer was placed over his nose and mouth as the voice implored him to begin counting. He began to count slowly but it was difficult to breathe, for the ether was so pungent and sickly sweet. As he counted "four," then "five," a drum began to beat loudly, then he realized it was his own heart beating. "Six." He heard a very high-pitched squeal and saw a pinpoint of light off in the pitch-black distance. "Seven." The single light was now a triangle of three lights; the squeal was getting louder, the lights starting to revolve in a circle. "Eight." The lights spun dizzily in a circle as they got closer. "Nine." Soon the drum beat louder and faster, the squealing in his ears reached a crescendo, and the lights were upon him! The thunderous locomotive bearing down on him suddenly veered off to his right, just missing him, as the deafening drumbeat and piercing squeal suddenly went silent and a cloak of blackness fell over him.

"Sonny? Are you awake, honey?" The sweetness of his mother's voice penetrated the blackness but his eyes were not opening. Finally the dim light of the hospital room was in his eyes and he saw his loving mother's face. He was back! He had gone from that scary tunnel to an empty black place but now he was back in his room and his mom was there with him. Her presence was all that mattered, not the pain within his nose and mouth nor the fire burning in his throat. The rest of the evening and night would be lost traversing the labyrinth of coming in and out of the blessed anesthetic haze dulling the pain. He was asleep when his mother finally left for home later that evening.

For the next four weeks this room would be his home. Whether sunny days or stormy, he would spend hours looking to the outside world through the barred windows, across the lawn, and out over the cityscape. His panoramic view was exceptional and he enjoyed counting the church steeples. He remembered that religious training for Bobby, Davey, and all of the children at the Home was addressed by the Home who bussed all of the children weekly, to St. Paul's, a North Side Evangelical and Reformed church located across the street from Childrens Memorial Hospital. So on Sunday, he would ask for and receive permission to stand at a window on the Orchard Street side and look down at Saint Paul church's front entrance, watching for his brothers to arrive from the Home for services so he might call out to them. He never got to see them.

Outside, life was still going on and he wanted to get back to the fresh air and sunshine visible just outside of his barred hospital window. It wasn't that he was treated badly, he simply missed his family and school friends. From the first night of his post-op recovery, the nurses had treated him like a little prince and he would always remember several of their names. His favorite of all was known to him only as Miss Dean, whom he came to adore as one would adore a fairy godmother. She was the lovely brunette who first made his acquaintance during the early morning hours that followed his long post-surgery night. She brought him a cool drink of water when it seemed that the back of his throat was on fire and she stayed, carefully giving him water one spoonful at a time.

Days would pass before he would get accustomed to the stitches across the roof of his mouth that felt like a latticework of wire. His tongue became irritated from the constant grating against them. Eating, needless to say was extremely slow and difficult and how he yearned for the fourteen days to pass, when the tormenting stitches would be removed.

On one of those first days, he lay in his bed reading one of the many books he would finish during his stay. A noise at the door interrupted the silence in his room, then a voice, "You must have a lot of friends at your school. Where do you want me to put all of these letters?" Looking up, he saw one of his favorite nurses carrying a cardboard box filled with envelopes of all sizes. Springing up and turning to the side of his bed, he asked the nurse to move the tray over and put them on it.

His heart jumped with joy as he began opening them and saw that these were notes and cards from his classmates. Many of the letters even contained coins. For the remainder of that day, he forgot the discomfort of stitches and the quiet pain of loneliness. He had been remembered by his teacher and little classmates and their letters reminded him that he wasn't really alone after all.

Monday of the third week began with a cheerful greeting from the head nurse who came in to say, "I came in to make sure that you didn't sleep all day, because today the doctor is going to remove your stitches! Do you think you're up to it?" That was the news he had been waiting for! In late morning she eased the boy into a wheel chair and piloted him up the hall to one of the treatment rooms where one of the surgeons slowly removed fifteen stitches from his palate. They then allowed him to return to his room with the admonition that he would have to stay about two more weeks and that at mealtimes he should chew slowly and carefully during that time, just so he wouldn't damage any healing tissue. Paying very keen attention, the little boy felt absolutely great and couldn't wait to eat lunch without those awful stitches in the way.

It momentarily escaped him, that his mouth was now more normal than it had ever been. Weeks later, on a return visit, the plastic surgeon would show him the before and after pictures documenting the profound change between when he had no palate tissue and the very lucky boy who was given a palate, constructed by the chief of plastic surgery at Childrens Memorial. In remembering that his grandmaw had told him of Jesus who had been able to work miracles, the little boy thanked his Lord that night, for the blessed miracle which he had allowed this gifted, unselfish surgeon and his associates to perform on him.

On the next Monday the big day had come! A month after his surgery, he was going home! In the hours before he was to be discharged, several of the wonderful nurses who had tended to him stopped in to tell him goodbye, and he felt sad leaving them but wanted to go home very badly. Even the kindly, bespectacled, chief of plastic surgery and his able assistant, whose gifted hands had worked their miracle on his palate, stopped by to see him one last time. They said goodbye to their young patient and cautioned Kathleen that her son's resistance would be low and she should try to keep him from catching a cold.

As Kathleen and her son left the hospital, early afternoon thunderstorms lashed the city and the driving sheets of cold, penetrating rain combined with late October temperatures to chill them to the bone. Walking through puddles to the streetcar stop and waiting under an umbrella that had been of little use had caused Kathleen to voice her concern that her boy might come down with a cold. Arriving at Grandmaw Kelly's home, a hubbub of activity began in order to get him dry and warmed up.

Having shucked his wet clothes and bundled up in a warm blanket, the chilled, weakened ex-patient sat by the warmth of their wood-burning kitchen stove, absorbing its welcome heat. Warming up at last, the little boy dozed off, safe and reassured in the cozy comfort of his grandmaw's home. He awoke the next day feeling weak and too queasy to eat breakfast. Around noon, his grandmaw cooked up some hot chicken noodle soup and he ate a small bowl, then a large bowl. It couldn't have just been soup, it had to be a magic elixir because he felt much better right away. A woman of many talents and moods, his grandmaw also had it within her to be a kind, southern version of Florence Nightingale when the situation required it. The Runt was going to be okay, she would see to that.

Chapter 6

Who's Pearl Harbor?

"I don't remember it being such a long walk to school," muttered a weakened Runt as he trudged toward Agassiz School. Despite his being mentally prepared and eager to return to school, he plodded along on leaden legs. Four weeks of bed rest and inactivity had weakened his already frail body but the desire to see his classmates and resume his studies overrode the fatigue he felt. Further east on Wolfram he walked and as he approached Seminary Avenue, he saw the corner of the playground's six-foot high, light-green iron-spike fence. Coming across Wolfram from his house was his friend, blond-haired, amiable Ronald Dane, who smiled and asked the Runt how he was and told him that he and lots of his other friends had missed him while he was gone.

Sitting down at his old desk, the young boy noticed a new student, whom he, for some strange reason, would for a while consider to be an interloper, having moved into his classroom while he was gone. Mrs. Kosterman introduced him to his new classmate, little Marjorie Cribbens, who had moved into the neighborhood in October. Given the desk next to the Runt, she opened a two word dialog, saying, "Hello," and receiving only a curt "Hello" in response. It took time for him to get used to someone new coming into his class although she was sort of cute and nice. Slender and blue-eyed, with full cheeks that reminded him of a chipmunk, he kinda liked her.

After he returned to classes, the Runt found that the surgical correction now enabled him to do things that were impossible for him before. Now he could suck up fluids through a drinking straw properly, he could whistle, and he could almost blow up a balloon and he was grateful to the surgical staff of Childrens Memorial who had made these improvements possible. How wonderful it must be, he thought, to be a plastic surgeon like his benefactor and have the ability to perform miracles like these for children who desperately needed his help. Once more he gave consideration to becoming a doctor someday.

His improved speech would reduce the number of times that kids made fun of him but he still retained a partial cleft palate which would cause him to always have some speech deficiency, resulting in teasing by others. It was an adjustment that he would have to make, over time. It was fortunate for him that religion had been instilled in him by his grandmaw. The cushioning effect of a religious belief was needed sometimes, when taunting by the other boys got under the little boy's skin.

From friendly classmates, the Runt learned about the services and Sunday School classes at the God's Love Mission on Lincoln Avenue that had been founded many years before by Rev. T. M. Hofhurst. Arriving home, he picked the best time he could to broach the subject, then anxiously asked his grandmaw if he could go to Sunday School at the mission next Sunday. Surprisingly, she seemed to warm to the idea, saying that he should go and maybe he would find Jesus. Conversely, it would be while he attended the little mission on one of many Sundays, that Jesus would quietly find him.

Saint Alphonsus' Sunday bells roused him from sleep as they always had, but this Sunday he had to hurry. Finishing his breakfast quickly, he hurried out the door, ran through the alley over to Lincoln Avenue, and up Lincoln to the mission. Taking a seat in the front row of chairs, always the last to be occupied, he looked around, trying to read the placards and inscribed wall panels. Soon, when he learned to read better, he would commit their scriptures to memory, especially the white poster board on the side wall, painted in red and blue lettering, which contained the words of John 3:16:

"For God so loved the world he gave his only begotten Son that whosoever believeth in Him shall not perish but have everlasting life."

The boy would always carry those words with him in his mind and heart, for they so simply and succinctly told, not of a harsh, cruel God, but of a forgiving God's love for the world. On the wall behind the lectern were painted three large tablets, the scriptures on two would in time, escape his memory, but inscribed on the middle tablet were the words "I am the Way, the Truth, and the Life," words that had been attributed to Jesus. The hymns that were sung that Sunday and many other Sundays, were the same hymns the Runt had heard at home and in a few of the movies that he had seen. Though later in life he would attend other churches, many of those old hymns sung at the mission would always remain in his memory and close to his heart, most notably the hymn, "Are You Washed in the Blood of the Lamb?"

"Sonny, please come with me," a lady whispered in his ear at the end of the service. Following her, he learned that the lady was Mrs. Hofhurst, wife of the founder. She ushered him over to one of several small Sunday School classes on the left side of the large hall. Each class was enclosed and separated from the others by what looked like oversized sheets suspended from encircling wire. Opening the white curtain, Mrs. Hofhurst introduced him to his Sunday School teacher, Sister Esther.

In the following months he would come to know Sister Esther as the most patient, wonderful person he had ever met in his young life, next to his mom and aunt Maybelle. Flaxen-haired with blue eyes, she was old, maybe twenty-two, but she had gained a new admirer. Under her angelic spell he would attend her class for the entire school year, never missing a Sunday. Through her patience with their questions and her dedicated, vivid story-telling of the life and gospel of Jesus in weeks to come, the Runt and his classmates would come to know and believe in Jesus as their Lord.

Sundays began for him as they always had at his grandmaw's home on Lakewood. Upon rising, he often felt a kinship with Victor Hugo's hunchback, Quasimodo, in that they were both sensitive to the pealing of bells. Four blocks away, over on Wellington and Southport stood the magnificent stone edifice of Saint Alphonsus Catholic Church. Reaching out over that half-mile, the incessant pealing of the bells roused him briskly from his Sunday morning slumber. Where he formerly had risen slowly, the young boy now had an objective: get to Sunday School for Sister Esther's class.

On Sundays when he visited with his family, he chattered incessantly to Kathleen on the swaying streetcar, telling her what he had learned that morning, giving Kathleen a feeling of well-being, and perhaps a sore ear, knowing that her youngest boy's religious instruction would be in capable hands during their separation. Attending Sunday School classes at the mission also gave the lonely boy something to look forward to on those non-visiting Sundays, helping the days and weeks pass more quickly, into early winter.

Curled up all snug and warm under the covers on a chilly late November morning, he suddenly realized that his grandmaw had failed to waken him at the usual time. After a few minutes of frantic scurrying, he raced out the back door, ten minutes late. It was nearly nine o'clock, class starting time, when he approached the corner of Lincoln, Diversey, and Racine.

"Hey lad! You're runnin' a bit late this morning," boomed Big Mike as he spied the anxious youngster in a hurry.

"I woke up late this morning, Mike."

"Wait a minute, lad," Mike shouted, then striding to the curb, he turned his head to the left and looked up Lincoln Avenue. Then he raised his hand and motioned toward a maroon Ford waiting at the curb, signaling its occupants to pull up. As it loomed closer, the boy saw the legend "POLICE 53" on its side door. Oh no! Were they going to haul him in just for being a few minutes late?

As the squad car eased to a stop at the curb, Big Mike sauntered over and asked of the two detectives inside, "Would you be takin' this lad over to Agassiz School?"

The cop nearest the curb gave the kid a stern look, then grinned and asked, "You sure you don't want us to run him down to the station?" Opening the back door, they motioned for the Runt to get in and as the light changed, they drove off with a wave from Big Mike.

As a scared Runt answered their polite questions, he looked around the squad car and glancing sideways saw something that took his breath away! Stuck in between the seat and the armrest was a deadly-looking shotgun! In all his young life he had always respected the police but seeing that shotgun subtly reinforced his belief in the benefits of staying on the right side of the law.

In two minutes, the detectives pulled up in front of the school where they dropped him off and he waved goodbye. While he appreciated their lift, he thought of how awful it would have been if he had been a criminal and they had taken him down to the station, instead. It was a nice feeling: having nothing to hide, and having things go well.

Although this squad car would be repainted a light gray the next year and it would be replaced by squadrols numbered "253" in years to come, the Runt and all of the kids in the 37th precinct would simply refer to this same Sheffield detective squad and/or their police car as "53." Most of the neighborhood kids would come to know and respect the law through routine stops by the police to talk to the kids, as part of regular patrols of the area.

Yes, it was nice when things went well but on the following Sunday the Runt learned that life was full of unexpected twists and turns which can change one's plans.

It was early in December of 1941, on a calm Sunday afternoon as the Runt was taking some soup sent by his grandmaw back to his aunt Maybelle and uncle Les in their home on the back of the lot. The usual music on the radio had been interrupted by an announcement to which they were listening as he knocked and went in.

Worry clouded her face as Maybelle asked him, "Was Grandmaw listening to the radio up at the big house?"

"No," he answered hesitantly, "she wasn't. Why?"

"Hurry back up there and tell Grandmaw to turn on the radio! Pearl Harbor was attacked!"

Hearing the urgency in her voice, he ran back up to the house, hurried in and relayed the message, "Grandmaw, Aunt Maybelle wants you to turn on the radio. And Grandmaw, who's Pearl Harbor?"

"What made y'all ask that? Pearl Harbor's a place, not a woman."

"Because Aunt Maybelle said, 'Pearl Harbor was attacked.'"

His grandmaw went pale. Hurrying over to the radio she turned it on and after an eternity of waiting for it to warm up she heard a newscaster repeating that the Japanese had bombed the U. S. Navy's port at Pearl Harbor and it could mean war.

Just when it seemed to Kathleen and her sons, that their ever-brightening world might soon include a father figure, sudden, hellish events on that small island in the Pacific dashed their hopes. Those same destructive bombs that tore apart the Arizona and its sister ships in Battleship Row, had also ripped the Ryans' dream apart.

Within weeks the whirlwind of war whisked Don away, as it would so many other good men, who went off to serve their country. Millions of families all over the world, found that they would have to put their dreams aside for the duration, or give them up altogether, as World War II cut its bloody swath of carnage and destruction through most of the next four turbulent years.

In the chaotic months of 1942 that followed the war's outbreak, like so many other brave men were doing, the Runt's uncles went to their local recruiting office. It was early Summer before his uncle Chick became an active member of the Army. To Chick's younger brother Clay's regret, military service was not to be for him although it may have been a blessing for his wife Anita, and their three-year-old son, Buck. Clay's childhood bout with polio, a crippler of many kids in that era, had left him with a limp, causing him to be classified as 4F, physically unsuitable. Although he was prevented from serving his country like his brother Chick, it didn't keep him from feeling war's pain. Clay would later watch, with tears in his eyes, as his older brother went off into a shooting war, not knowing if he would ever see him again.

During late January of that chaotic time, the Runt had been given a double-promotion by Mrs. Kosterman as a reward for achievement but it meant having to adjust to new classmates a half-year older than he. It wouldn't be a big deal however, since he had heard that this was a time for all sorts of adjustments by everyone and he thought he had a small adjustment to make.

Lucky for him he still had his familiar reference point of Sunday School classes. Yet, as the summer season approached, all too soon, the Runt's spellbinding Sunday School classes would be at an end. On the last Sunday of June, Sister Esther cheerfully bade her pupils goodbye for the Summer, sweetly asking them to be sure to come back to her class in the Fall. She then mentioned that she was sorry but she wouldn't be attending the annual mission picnic that next Sunday, since she was going to make the long trip home where she planned to spend the Summer.

Except for getting a ride to the picnic from one of the other Sunday School teachers, the Runt had attended the picnic by himself. Freed from his grandmaw's watchful eyes, the Runt was everywhere, partaking of everything. Refreshments, food, and games blurred his entire day in the sun, except for a short while when he got in on the tug-of-war. Needless to say, by the time he arrived at his grandmaw's home that evening, he had burned himself out, falling asleep across the bed while taking off his socks.

Weeks later, movies of the picnic were shown on a Sunday evening at the mission and he was accompanied by his grandparents. None of them had any idea that the Runt would be a featured player in the movies. Most of his activities that afternoon had been recorded for posterity, including the tug-of-war during which he helped pull on one side, then ran around to the other side and pulled with the opposing group, repeating his actions several times. He hadn't remembered doing that so many times and was mortified when all of the people burst into laughter. They were having a good time with it while he felt like crawling under his chair.

The rest of the Summer seemed to be a series of appointments at the clinic until the Runt had been scheduled for another operation, this time to be done before school started. While his cleft lip had been corrected in Texas, when he was just several weeks old, the doctors at Childrens Memorial Hospital felt that they should attempt to improve on the closure by operating once more. Again, he went through all the procedures, from admitting through post-op. The best part of this stay in the hospital was that some of the nurses had remembered him from his previous stay. He adored them all because they were so friendly and kind to him.

Only staying in the hospital for a week after this surgery, he was discharged with the stitches still in his upper lip which raised a lot of eyebrows among his neighborhood playmates. He couldn't wait for those ugly stitches to be removed, since they were a source of stares and in a few cases, ridicule. One of the first things he did was write his uncle Chick and let him know that he was supposed to be better looking because of the operation. It was important to him to tell his uncle so he would know. Chick kidded him in writing back, "Sure pal, those doctors at the hospital might have told you that you're gonna be better looking but you'll never be better looking than me!"

Two weeks after the operation, the stitches were removed but unlike his palate operation, he didn't seem to notice much improvement, although he hadn't had to miss any school classes this time around.

The year following the outbreak of the war had been a hectic time of military men moving from one assignment to another, coming home for a leave, then being shipped out. Needing stability in his life during this time, Gene benefited from the consistent relationship between his mother and Don. All during 1942, while Don was half a world away, across the Pacific, he and Kathleen sustained each other's morale by writing faithfully; his letters always asking about the boys and hers answering with the latest news about them and the situation on the homefront. Indelible images remained in the Runt's mind, retained from the last time he saw Don, who had worn his uniform. Among those images were the castles on Don's Army brass, which Don had said indicated that he was in the Corps of Engineers and that engineers built bridges and moved hills out of the Army's way. Whenever they wrote to Don, the Runt always questioned his stepfather-to-be as to what he had built lately.

During the Summer of that year the Grim Reaper came again for one of the Ryan boys, only to be denied once more. Every year the Home sent all of its young residents to summer camps, and the boys went by truck to Three Oaks, Michigan, where they enjoyed two weeks of the great outdoors. The great outdoors meant outdoor activities and outdoor plumbing, the latter having made it necessary to build a new latrine. Among the group of older boys assigned the task of digging the excavation for the latrine was big brother Bobby.

While digging about six or seven feet down, a trickling of sand quickly became a sudden cave-in, causing tons of sandy, loose, Michigan soil to tumble back into the ditch, most of it burying Bobby. In a flurry of activity, every counselor and boy in camp raced to the dig and took turns shoveling furiously. Davey heard about the mishap from a friend who breathlessly came running up to shout, "Your brother's buried alive!"

Davey ran his legs off to join the diggers who still hadn't found Bobby. After several minutes more, one of the boys gave a solid object a whack with the flat of his shovel-blade and complained that he hit a rock. A wise and cautious counselor shouted, "Hold it! Don't hit it again! Let's see what you've found!"

Scooping dirt away from the object by hand, they found that the "rock" was really Bobby's head! Hurriedly the counselors scooped away an opening for him to breathe and were able to hear him. Bobby was still alive! Within minutes they pulled him out of the suffocating sand and although he was groggy from lack of oxygen and sported a huge bump on his head, he was okay.

Only after the boys came home from camp did Kathleen or their youngest brother learn about it. Previously, Bobby had sprained his wrist and later had an operation for appendicitis, while Davey had broken his wrist, but this had been the closest call either of them had while at the Home. The event was recorded for posterity and the family album two days after the incident, when Bobby climbed back down into the yawning excavation, and stood, hands on hips, smiling upward for the picture which Davey took from the edge of the ditch!

God also must have been watching over their kid brother and his friend, when one day in late Summer, the Runt was playing in the alley with young Frankie Manning, a neighbor kid and current classmate. Finding a chunk of dry-ice which had fallen off a passing truck, the Runt ran and took a discarded, empty, aspirin bottle out of the garbage can. Taking some water from his grand-maw's garden hose, he and Frankie filled the aspirin bottle with water and dropped in a chip of the dry-ice.

Watching the bottle's benign bubbles busily rising to the surface was intriguing but posed no problem for them. Not until they proceeded to screw on the bottle's metal cover. Since each of them wanted to keep it, they playfully kept taking it away from each other. In the moment that Frankie had yanked the bottle toward him out of the Runt's fingers, the bottle, over-pressurized with carbon dioxide gas, exploded.

Frankie, who was a pretty tough kid, screamed in pain as the bottle burst in front of his face and chest. The Runt's finger suddenly felt like fire and he saw the blood poring from a deep cut in his finger. Both of them ran to their respective homes for First Aid. In a stroke of good fortune, Betty happened to be home with Grandmaw and she had a First Aid kit which she had put together for a high-school course.

Treating his cut quickly and thoroughly, Betty didn't know that her nephew was getting off light. Moments later, a knocking at the back door turned out to be Frankie's sixteen-year-old sister, Violet, wanting to know if they had any hydrogen peroxide. Violet said that Frankie had cuts on his face and chest but miraculously, had escaped injury to his eyes. Frankie's smooth face would always carry a couple of tiny scars as a reminder of his and the Runt's foolishness. More than once afterwards, the two boys recounted how lucky they had been and how easily they could have lost their sight.

There comes a time in every little boy's young life when he is smitten by the charms of an older woman. That time came for the Runt during the days of his friendship with Frankie. Besides Violet, Frankie had two other sisters. Edie, who at eight, was the Runt's age and his former classmate. But then there was seventeen-year-old Irene. It was slender Irene, with her lovely tanned complexion and pale-blue eyes accented by straight, raven-black hair down to her shoulders, who had held the young boy's fancy for some time. She was the embodiment of this particular young boy's crush on an older woman as he always kept an eye out for any glimpse of her.

Tragically, the flickering glow of his puppy-love feelings for the sultry Irene were soon snuffed like the flame of a windblown candle. The end came a few weeks later when his Aunt Betty became embroiled in a nasty disagreement with Irene Manning. A flurry of feminine slapping and scratching suddenly erupted, yet quickly ended as tall, strong Betty grabbed a shocked Irene by her aforementioned raven hair, swung her around a few times and unceremoniously dumped her up against two clattering refuse cans. Needless to say, Irene stopped talking to Betty and to the Runt from that day on. As it is with most young boys' crushes, there was minimal pain, accompanied by a recovery time of hours.

With the advent of Fall, neighborhood children formed up for Sunday School classes once more, and all of the pupils in Sister Esther's class kept their promise by returning. To their disappointment however, Sister Esther was notably absent, her class taken by Sister Ruth. The Runt asked Sister Ruth why she was teaching their class and if she knew where their teacher could be. He was told that the teachers had been informed that Sister Esther wouldn't be returning after all. The disappointed boy felt that if he and all of her other pupils had kept their promises by returning, then Sister Esther should also have kept her promise to return. Not letting well enough alone, he persisted in wanting to know why Sister Esther wasn't coming back. He was crushed by Sister Ruth's soft-spoken reply that his beloved teacher had died during the past summer.

In a tear-filled daze the shocked little boy tried to remain for the class but asked to be excused and left the Sunday School, crying as he hurried home where he went to his aunt Maybelle. She had known how much he adored his tragically-lost teacher and could only try to console him. He couldn't understand, and asked "Why did such a good woman like her have to die. Why did God punish her?"

"We all have to die someday, Honey," answered Aunt Maybelle, "God didn't punish Sister Esther, he probably loved her so much that he wanted her to come to Heaven earlier."

"But she's gone forever."

"Yes, but at least you got the chance to know her and learn from her. I'll bet she wouldn't want you to be sad for her. She'd want you to be happy for her. So try not to be sad."

Since Chick was away in the Army, the Runt now often turned to his aunts in times of doubt and sorrow, or for solace and understanding. After his uncle Les enlisted, his aunt Etta joined their extended household, staying with Maybelle in the little house on the back of the lot. Etta, like Maybelle, had a quiet gentleness when dealing with her nephew and he loved her almost as much as Maybelle. His aunts' gentle presence and their guidance, made the years of being away from his mother and brothers so much more endurable. Even though he would one day move away and grow up, their loving, gentle kindness toward him in those times when a boy needed someone to talk to would always be remembered.

This gentle manner was evident even when they reprimanded him for filching candy bars at the grocery store. After Sister Esther's loss, it seems that the little boy began stopping in at the neighborhood grocery store a few doors from the mission and when the grocer looked the other way, the boy picked up a Butterfinger bar and dropped it into his pocket. Not knowing why he had done so, he continued to steal a few times until one day the grocer mentioned it to Etta. While Grandmaw Kelly had fire in her eyes, Maybelle and Etta calmly explained that what he had been doing was wrong and that he should never do it again. Someday he could be sent to reform school if he continued taking things that didn't belong to him. They reinforced his grasp of "right and wrong" and he learned this "refresher lesson" quickly.

The weeks following Sister Esther's death had been a confusing time of sadness and recovery. Before the Runt knew it, Christmas of 1942 was approaching. After rigorous training at Camp Grant, his uncle Chick was temporarily assigned to a replacement unit at Fort Sheridan, Illinois. Stationed just about twenty miles north of Chicago, Chick was able to come home for the holiday. Kathleen was Chick's oldest sister, and they had always been close as kids and he would still do anything for her. So many times, he had gone out of his way to help her and that Christmas Day was a prime example. Chick drove into Chicago, picked up Helen, Kathleen and the Runt, who had spent Christmas Eve at Kathleen's, drove them over to the Home where they picked up Bobby and Davey, then drove to the Christmas celebration at Grandmaw and Grandpaw Kelly's home.

Perhaps it was simply seeing Christmas through a child's eyes, but his grandparents' home was where the entire family had always celebrated Christmas together, in a festive way that the Runt wouldn't see matched anywhere else or in any other time. Either Chick's wife Helen, or Clay's wife, Anita, played the piano while everyone else, including restless kids, gathered around to sing Christmas carols until Santa Claus finally made his grand entrance, shouting, "Ho! Ho! Ho! Merry Christmas!" The Runt thought it was strange that none of the little kids ever noticed that as long as Santa was present, one of the uncles or in-laws was missing.

When all too quickly, the festive occasion came to an end, Chick loaded everyone back into his car and drove out to the Home where the wonderful and magical spell of childhood Christmas was broken, as Bobby and Davey were dropped off at the main entrance. The somber-looking, blue Christmas lights that lit up the spruce trees outside the main entrance cast a lonely, melancholy moment upon the Runt, making his parting from his brothers seem even sadder. Because of that lasting, sorrowful impression, in years to come, with a family of his own, the Runt would never decorate a Christmas tree in his home with blue lights only.

Their uncle Chick then drove back to Kathleen's place, where he dropped her and the Runt off and drove back to the Kelly home where he picked up Helen, and returned to their home. That completed his last favor for his sister and nephews, for what was to be a long time. He had orders to ship out with the 33rd Division, the Illinois Division. Only told that their destination was somewhere out on the Pacific Ocean, the rest was a military secret, a new term with which everyone would become familiar over the next few years.

Surprisingly, Chick's first stopover was in Hawaii, which by then had become a staging area for large troop movements and war materiel. He sent several pictures home and the Runt's favorite photo was that of his uncle dressed in summer khakis, hands thrust into his pockets, leaning up against a palm tree with a flowered-lei around his neck.

World War II's island-hopping Pacific Campaign embroiled Chick's unit in several major battles in the Solomons and the Philippines that made the newspapers, but he somehow managed to write an occasional, very welcome letter to his parents and his nephew. Those little V-Mail letters were like a small part of Chick arriving in the mail. While he was never able to divulge where he was, Chick's photocopied, reduced letters were always on the bright side, never complaining but reflecting a GI's wry humor.

It wasn't long after Chick's departure that Les, his aunt Maybelle's husband, who had enlisted in the Army Air Corps was also going overseas. His letters to Aunt Maybelle were usually of a more personal nature, so her nephew never learned too much about what was happening with Les. The Runt had learned that the greater the number of missions that a plane crew flew, the closer they felt they were to danger, and they were required to fly twenty-five missions before they could be transferred out of the combat theatre. The Runt never learned how many missions Les would eventually fly, since he didn't return to Maybelle. Their marriage, like many others, didn't survive the strain of war's danger, distance, and long separations.

On a bleak, fateful January day in 1943, the dream that Kathleen shared with her sons ended, when a long-overdue letter arrived for Kathleen from Don, one which would crush her spirit for months. Only words put down on paper, they stabbed her as painfully as a knife:

I've decided that I don't want to be tied down to a woman with three kids. I feel that I am too young to settle down with a ready-made family and I really feel that it would be best for both of us if we didn't write to each other anymore. I'm calling off our engagement and letting you know that you shouldn't keep waiting for me. Before I close I want to tell you that you may keep the engagement ring, since I had given it to you out of love.

Goodbye Kathleen,
Don

Reading the final phrase, Kathleen took the small diamond solitaire from her hand, shoved open the front window and with all of her might, threw the sparkling love-token out into the biting wind, where it plummeted into a snowdrift along Irving Park Road. Her indescribable pain was followed by a momentous anger brought on by suddenly being cut out of Don's life because she had three children, a condition that he had originally accepted from the very beginning. The pain and anger were in time, replaced by a lasting bitterness directed toward blotting out his memory.

Weeks later, Davey and the Runt prattled on about a particularly wonderful time they had enjoyed with Don.

Davey's nostalgia caused him to tell the Runt, "I remember how scared you were when you came across that snake up at the state park and how Don just grabbed it behind the neck and carried it away from you."

"He was so brave and good. I really miss him," replied his kid brother.

"You boys are not to mention Don's name anymore," Kathleen sharply scolded, "and you are to forget him."

Countless relationships ended by long separations had far-reaching consequences, often affecting all members of a family or families that might have been. Although his uncle Chick was the soldier he missed most, the Runt often missed Don, the man who would've been his new dad, intensely. Yet he wouldn't mention it to his grandparents and felt he couldn't tell his mother.

Pleasant memories of past times with Don had been too tightly woven into his young, impressionable thoughts, especially memories recalled when he heard "Maria Elena" on the radio. It had been Don's favorite song, one which Don had hummed and whistled often during their family outings. Missing his mother and brothers, plus Chick, and Don, could sometimes be a lot of missing for a seven-year-old boy to bear.

Chapter 7

The Homefront

Just as the moon's shadow can eclipse the sun, World War II cast into uncertain darkness the bright hopes and dreams of millions by taking their loved ones away. For those who had been left behind by a close relative, spouse, or sweetheart who had answered their country's call, it was a sad, terrible time; years of uncertainty while being separated. Seemingly, every American home had sent one of its own to serve Uncle Sam, as shown proudly in the curtained windows of homes, where small flags were displayed, each flag having one or more blue stars on a field of white within a red border. Each star had signified a loved one in the service. Solemn moments were often observed in one's mind when they passed the home of a family whose flag contained a gold star. A gold star proclaimed in mute evidence, that a loved one had lost their life in the service of their country.

Blackness fell occasionally on designated neighborhoods within the city as Civil Defense initiated practice "blackouts." Shouting block captains served as wardens during air raid drills and blackouts, demanding that all that lights be extinguished or opaque black curtains be drawn. There were always the few grumpy citizens who complained about bothersome drills, forgetting that there were people in war-torn countries filled with homeless refugees who were experiencing real air raids and having their homes obliterated by enemy bombs. Fortunately, the drills designed to prepare them for a real bombing raid proved unnecessary for Americans, who never knew the stark terror of bombs falling on their homes.

In each neighborhood, usually in a conspicuous spot on a busy corner, a large, wooden display case known as the "Honor Roll" was erected to honor all of the service men and women called away to serve. Decorated in red, white, and blue, and having a clear glass front, it contained snapshots of faces belonging to the cream of the neighborhood's youth, some in their late teens who would grow up quickly under enemy fire. Awards for valor were posted on the Honor Roll, along with all noteworthy news about any of the honorees.

In addition to sending their men and women off to war, civilians on the homefront made other sacrifices in giving up many old comforts and necessities. Meatless Tuesdays became common, as did making a set of rubber tires last longer. Women did without silk stockings, used less shortening and sugar, saved cooking fats, and smashed tin cans for recycling into the war effort. Automobile owners stretched their gas mileage to stay within their ration of gasoline, purchased with ration coupons that each car owner was allotted. Spare parts and gadgets heretofore made of now-scarce metal were becoming available once more, fabricated from a new substance named, plastic.

Under orders of another kind, the Runt did most of his grandmaw's grocery shopping, gaining first-hand his own memories of the use of the blue and red ration stamps and tokens issued by the Federal government in an effort to fairly and effectively ration food and meat in short supply. He learned also the extent and degree of his grandmaw's frugality and was reminded each time he returned from the store.

After unbagging all of the groceries and placing them on their large, round, kitchen table, he crossed his fingers as his grandmaw checked off each item against the prices on the register receipt and woe be unto any clerk who may have made an error of a more than a few pennies. For a few pennies, she sent her grandson back to get the error corrected but in the case of a more severe shortage, she went along and proceeded to embarrass the store clerk, manager, and her grandson, by inferring very strongly, that the shortage was deliberately caused by the clerk and sometimes even the manager himself! The Runt dreaded to hear, "C'mon, we're going back up there and get them crooks to give us the c'rect change back!"

Butter was a very scarce commodity and also very high-priced, since most real, creamery butter was being diverted to the Armed Forces. Civilians on the homefront learned to accept oleomargarine as a substitute. Known simply as "oleo," this synthesized butter replacement was sold in the same type of package as butter. The natural color of oleo was white, not yellow like creamery butter, and was about as appealing to the senses as a bowl of lard. In order to give the oleo a more esthetic appeal to the consumer's eyes and taste buds, a packet of yellow food coloring powder was included inside the package. Each week found the Runt expertly adding in the dry powder and kneading it into the oleomargarine in a bowl with a table knife. After about a half-hour, he had thoroughly mixed another batch of ersatz butter for his grandmaw's approval.

Lights and machines were never shut off in the many defense plants which aided the war effort by shifting into round-the-clock production. More and more women were hired by those factories, replacing their men who had been called into the armed forces. As more working mothers left their children with their grandparents, the Runt would come to see that he wasn't the only kid in that boat. Soon, many other children would go home to lunch at their grandma's, or bring report cards back signed by a grandparent instead of a parent.

Life back home continued on, affirmed in the green rebirth of nature in the spring of 1943, when Kathleen could tell two of her sons some good news. She had been able to rent another room, at her apartment house where she had previously rented a kitchenette apartment on Irving Park Road, just east of Sheridan Road. The two rooms were down the hall from each other so Bobby (now called Bob) and Davey would share a room of their own. Since they were in school all day and wouldn't be home alone, Kathleen was allowed to take them out of the Home. It was the Runt's bad break, that there still wasn't quite enough space for him to join them.

Already a freshman at Lake View High School, Bob had graduated from his elementary school as Class Valedictorian. At his graduation, he had also been awarded the American Legion award for being the most outstanding student exhibiting leadership. As pointed out earlier, Bob had established a reputation since his early years for being dependable and responsible, but he would one day pay a dear price for growing up so soon. Almost in punishment, childhood years of carefree play that most normal children enjoyed had never been an alternative for Bob. Unfortunately for him, those years had been stolen from him by adult responsibilities which he had assumed as his own, for his Mom and his brothers. The oldest son in an Irish family, he had always been the "shock-absorber" of Kathleen's sons, the first to face life's difficulties, learn from his experience and pass his hard-learned knowledge on to his younger siblings so they wouldn't have to undergo the same pain or trial. It hadn't been possible for him to allow himself to enjoy a boy's childhood, since he had worn the mantle of "Man of the house" during too many of his childhood years. To just be a little boy, like everyone else, had never been an option open to him.

As a young adult later in life, when his youngest brother would thank him, praising him for always having set such a good example for them, Bob would vent pent-up feelings to his brother of eighteen, that he didn't want to be the example to follow anymore. He didn't want to have that yoke of responsibility around his neck any longer and for a change, he wanted the opportunity to just live for himself. Tragically and unfairly, Bob was the son whose personal life would suffer most from the years of a broken home, because he had willingly taken on the heaviest burden. It was a burden that shouldn't have been his in the first place.

Kathleen's place on Irving Park had now become the setting for their semi-monthly get-togethers, since the older two boys were staying there. These occasions were still limited to every other Sunday for reasons that were known only to Grandmaw Kelly who wouldn't allow the Runt to make the trip every Sunday, even though he had learned how to make the trip by himself. It could have been possible that she harbored some jealousy toward Kathleen, because it was apparent to her that her grandson loved his mother very deeply and not his grandmaw, with whom he stayed all of the time. She may have overlooked the fact, that her grandson never had any choice, in the matter of coming to live with her.

Going to his mom's place was always a happy event for the Runt, to which he looked forward, from the moment he bid them goodbye on the previous visiting Sunday. Each visit was an adventure for him because of the new sights and sounds in the different world he found on the southern edge of the Uptown area.

A furnished one-room kitchenette with a shared bathroom down the hall, Kathleen's room was equipped with a small gas stove and sink in one corner which she closed off by drawing a curtain. Her small cupboard held a set of four plates, cups, and saucers of deep red, ruby glass. How her youngest son loved eating off those clear, red plates, never failing to hold his empty plate up to the light from the window and see the world in red. Other "depression" glassware consisted of "bubble" bowls of various translucent colors of glass, their smooth surfaces blistered with bubbles, with scalloped edges. At times when he didn't seem to be hungry, the frequent and pleasant smell of fresh coffee brewing could awaken hunger pangs in his stomach.

Even the bed in his mom's place was different. He would learn later on that it was called a Murphy bed. If Kathleen needed the space in her room, she could simply lift the end of the bed and it would rise vertically, stashing away in a wall compartment. Not extraordinary to most people but it held the Runt's rapt attention, as did all new gadgets and innovations. Not having a telephone of her own, if Kathleen needed to make a phone call, she simply opened the hall door, dropped her nickel into the pay slot of the public phone hanging on the wall there and placed her call. Conversely, if she were waiting for a call, it was convenient. However, that phone could be a bothersome nuisance when the calls weren't for her or when she didn't expect a call and the phone continued to ring.

Adult eyes might have viewed Kathleen's furnished room more realistically, as a slightly run-down furnished room, where an occasional roach might leave its hiding place within the walls and be seen. But to the little boy, it was just a warm, wonderful, cozy place that was the closest thing to Heaven, for his mother lived there.

Countless other memories he'd always carry with him, were collected outside, on the streets and sidewalks of Sheridan and Irving Park Roads, which intersected a few blocks north of Wrigley Field. Formed by a third-floor-front window-view, those memories included simple everyday street scenes. From his panoramic window to the world, a child's eyes took in the shops, bars, and stores along Irving Park Road. Each establishment trumpeted its presence through their brightly-colored neon signs - brilliant, glorious images to his eyes. Broadcasting their messages out into the darkness, the signs were magnified into glowing auras by the gloomy mist of rainy nights, only to be quickly devoured by the all-consuming darkness.

Surveying his pauper prince's kingdom early on a summer Sunday evening, he looked down across the street, then over to the Avalon Cafe. Its savory, meaty aromas mixed with the scents of the night, rising above the still warm pavement, permeating the sultry air wafting through the window. The night scene below yielded noises of a bygone era, no longer heard in Chicago, sounds such as the earth-shaking rumble of steel-wheeled streetcars that punctuated the night with clanging of warning bells, accompanied by the melodic reverberation of early model Ford V8's motoring by. Raucous sounds which served as a noisy counterpoint to the friendly chatter of people strolling by on the sidewalk below.

Pleasant hours had flown on the wings of evening and soon it was time for the Runt to leave for his grandmaw's house. In leaving, he would say goodbye to everyone except Bob, who always escorted him, riding the streetcar with him to the transfer point at Southport and Irving Park. There, Bob would wait with him until the right streetcar came, making certain that his little brother was safely on his way home. One late afternoon of a very cold Sunday soon to come, wouldn't be forgotten by the Runt. It would be the time when Bob damp-combed his hair into a pompadour, fashionable at the time, before catching the westbound Irving Park streetcar at the stop across the street with his little brother. At the Southport transfer point, they waited a long time in the cold for a streetcar to come. Locked in the Runt's memories was the sight he beheld when he looked up at his big brother as the streetcar arrived and saw that Bob's hair had frozen into an ice-covered mound.

Climbing up the high steps of the red-and-cream-colored, rail-bound juggernaut, he paid the conductor his half-fare of four cents and found an empty window seat. The electric underseat heater's warmth enveloped his butt like a warm blanket as he sat down on one of the firm, wide, woven-straw seats. Looking out the window and waving goodbye to Bob, he became troubled because his caring, guardian big brother was huddled in a frigid doorway, waiting now for the eastbound Irving Park streetcar to take him back home.

As Winter rolled into Spring, then Summer, those golden summer months of 1943 brought the Runt his greatest time of all those six years away. That Summer, he was allowed to spend two glorious weeks of his school vacation with his Mom and brothers. Somehow it seemed to make up for a few of the many lost "in-between" Sundays.

On one very muggy, hot, July day during those two weeks, Kathleen had worked late at the defense plant and was too worn out to make dinner. All four of them went down to the Thompson's Restaurant that stood at the corner. There, the boys felt like princes of the realm, as they dined on the cold plate special, an exquisite, if not euphemistic, term for a plate of cold lunch meat!

In that bygone era, as it still is today, an underprivileged kid's neighborhood playground consisted of the network of streets, alleys and the vacant land under the "El" tracks. How could the Runt forget the fearsome din of an elevated train thundering overhead when he heard it for the first time as a wide-eyed kid? Under the "El" tracks! An open, littered thoroughfare belonging to the city, where no crabby neighbors could run them off. What a fantastic place for two young boys to conduct their important explorations!

Teeming with relics of "civilization," the castoff bits and pieces of everyday activities ranged from empty olive-drab Lucky Strike cigarette packs to an occasional, used condom. Some of the litter, especially under the "El" platform, was a profusion of potential keepsakes that only young boys could deem valuable. Except, when one hot sunny day, in the shade of the "El" tracks, their scavenging yielded M-O-N-E-Y. Davey brought over a damp, dirty, wrinkled dollar bill which he had found and the two young prospectors scurried home to salt it away.

"What are we going to do with it?" asked the Runt of his bigger brother.

Davey responded with, "We? I found it so I'm going to give it to Mom because she always works so hard for whatever we have."

Leaving the soggy bill to dry in a sunny window, they strolled back out into the blast furnace of a sun-scorched concrete alley on a hot summer afternoon in Chicago.

The Runt had been inspired! He told Davey "If you can find a dollar, so can I!"

So, back under the "El" tracks they hurried, where they began searching around for no one knows how long, since watches were only for rich kids who could afford them. After defending the length of their search for the umpteenth time, the Runt struck paydirt, coming up with a matching damp, dirty, dollar bill!

"What are you gonna do with the dollar?" asked Davey.

"I'm giving mine to Mom, too! One dollar isn't much but two's a lot!" replied his little brother.

Again, the two money-gathering scavengers hurried home and added it to the stash in the window. Surprising their mom was more fun than arguing over how they would have spent it anyway. All they had to do was clam up and not blow the surprise when she got home!

"Remember, mum's the word!" whispered Davey.

Upon Kathleen's long-awaited arrival, the mischievous looks on the faces of her two youngest offspring begged her question, "And what did you two boys do today?"

When presented with the dollar bills, she began to cry, puzzling her sons who muttered, "We didn't mean to make you sad."

She wiped her tears and replied, "I'm crying only because I'm happy.

Even more perplexed, her sons thought their mom had a funny way of being happy.

Not much in today's monetary terms, during those early war years, Kathleen worked the better part of a day in a hot, grimy, defense plant, to earn two dollars. An extra two dollars in the house had given her a real lift. For her sons, just to see the joy in their mom's eyes, had made their time and effort worthwhile.

Each vacation day at his mom's was a series of boyhood adventures for the Runt and his brother-sidekick Davey, young explorers of the long-charted areas of Lakeview and Uptown. Wherever they went, each new sight or event formed a lasting memory in the impressionable mind of a kid who almost never got to venture out on his own from his grandmaw's backyard, except to go to school.

Even trying to spend the gift of a found, shiny, silver-colored penny was an adventure. Minted in 1943, Zinc-based pennies had a distinctive color of their own, but to the boys' chagrin, those pennies wouldn't work in a gumball machine, candy machine, or any corner vending machine. Unless they could work out an exchange with a friendly grocer, the "lead-pennies" of 1943 had no practical value for these latchkey, street kids, who snacked out of penny vending machines!

Walking south on Sheridan Road one gorgeous summer afternoon, the roar of the crowd at the baseball game reached its crescendo as they approached Wrigley Field, overwhelming the Runt, listening with a child's ears. His young eyes took in its awesome structure, with the big "CHICAGO CUBS" sign painted on the back side of the five-story high scoreboard wall. The ballpark was the most enormous thing he had ever seen and quite a thrill for a scrawny kid. In a couple of years he would attend his first game and while roaming the ramps, catwalks, and concession areas he would fall in love with the place and the team, becoming a Cub fan for life.

On one of those bright, clear vacation days, either the fleet had arrived in port, or the Great Lakes Naval Training Center had given liberty to everyone on base. By the hundreds, sailors in summer whites turned the corner of Sheridan and Irving Park into a sea of white as they hopped streetcars, hailed cabs, or anything on wheels, in order to get into downtown Chicago. Kathleen sought to preserve the sight of that mass of red-blooded American naval manpower in white bell-bottoms by busily snapping pictures from the front window, with her big, Kodak box camera, pictures that would still generate conversation years later.

Davey and the Runt usually went to the movies on Saturdays or during the days of summer vacation, having their choice of either of two fine theatres on Sheridan Road. Most of the movies they saw during that time were a mix of patriotic musicals such as "Yankee Doodle Dandy" and the grade "B" war movies churned out by Hollywood. Films such as "Guadalcanal Diary," "Bataan," "Immortal Sergeant," and "Marine Raiders" which were about war and leaving loved ones behind were heavy subject matter for two young boys.

Watching the films, they would often think of Don off at war, for in spite of Kathleen's admonition to forget him, they still remembered his gentle shepherding and fatherly interest in them as kids. Then, young boys' prattle would turn to their most fervent desire: that wonderful day when they might someday have a new dad. Despite loving and respecting their mom, they still longed to be part of a complete family like all of the other kids they knew. Without a dad, a part of their life always seemed to be missing. It was a need that would never be filled.

During the Summer, Davey liked to walk around barefooted and early one afternoon, as they strolled into the Mode' theatre, the manager asked them to turn around and leave, because "Nature Boy" had left his shoes at home. It wasn't much of a bother for them, since they were able to run home, get Davey to put his shoes on, dash out the back door of the apartment building, through the yard, over to Dakin Street and back again at the Mode' theatre in just minutes. Somehow, the theatre manager didn't seem at all impressed by this nifty capability.

A bastion of film entertainment, standing a couple of blocks north of Irving Park Road was the Queen of Sheridan Road: the classic, cavernous Sheridan Theatre. It was owned by Chicago's most elite theatre chain, which for decades had owned the most elegant theatres in the Chicago area. The boys preferred the Sheridan, not only because their brother Bob worked there as an usher and could get them passes, but also because it was the closest thing to a palace that they had ever seen. Royalty exuded from its softly-lit oil paintings gracing the walls of the carpeted halls, mile-high ceilings trimmed in gold leaf, tapestried walls, marble facades, indirect lighting and an enormous auditorium. To a short, runty kid, the building looked to be a block long and a half-block high, with a sculpted cavalcade of horses, wagons, and people across its facade. Its interior, as in all of the finer theatres, was palatial, with a gorgeous architectural design throughout the auditorium, and carpeting in the lobby that was so thick and cushiony that it seemed to put extra spring in a kid's step, making him bounce when he walked.

Best of all reasons for going to a movie theatre was the feeling of cool relief the boys experienced on a hot, muggy, Chicago summer day, the kind of day when the sun-baked sidewalk burned hot through the holes in their shoes. What a relief it was to escape the oppressive heat by entering that gigantic igloo of welcome cool, dry air. It wasn't surprising that kids from the area would stay to see the show a second time. They had no qualms about prolonging their stay in order to put off having to go back outside, to be cut down by a death-ray of heat that seemed to suck the air right out of their lungs.

Movie theatres, however, weren't the only interesting places they found, since Lincoln Park wasn't all that far away and it was the home of the Zoo. The Runt wouldn't forget the blisters on his heels from the loose shoes he had worn. He had once again listened to Davey, who opined that his little brother's feet would be more comfortable without socks. Wrong again, Davey. Help him bust the blisters!

It was during this strange time - when a world was at war and two young boys were having the time of their lives - that another man finally came into Kathleen's lonely life. A nice, friendly, tall man who showed Kathleen that he really cared for her, his name was Tom Martin. About six feet tall, on the thin side, with hazel eyes and dark brown wavy hair, Tom had a quiet, gentle way about him. Dropping by a couple of evenings each week, Tom slowly became friends with Davey, who came to like him, as did the Runt, when he came out on his semi-monthly visits. Bob, however, was old enough to remember his dad, and pushing fifteen, was too old to accept a stepfather readily. He had also been the man in charge up until then and never really warmed up to Tom. Tom had been interested in Kathleen since the time when she was seeing Don. Classified as 4F, Tom hadn't had to serve in the military, so he was still around after Don joined the Army. Although Tom had always liked Kathleen, he didn't try asking out her out, since he felt it wasn't right to try and date a soldier's girl while he was away. Not only was Tom nice, he had social values and scruples, too. Eventually, he learned that Kathleen and Don's engagement had long been broken off and after a period of weeks, asked her out. They began seeing each other on Saturday nights and then on Sunday afternoons, too. Tom realized that when a man is interested in seeing a woman who has three sons, on Sundays, he had better plan outings which include those sons.

Demonstrating a keen knack for choosing the kinds of places where young boys like to go, Tom took them to see flying skaters being dumped over the rail at the Roller Derby in the old Coliseum on Wabash, the midway, roller coasters and space ship rides at Riverview Amusement Park, and Ringling Brothers, Barnum and Bailey's gigantic three-ring circus when it appeared at Chicago Stadium, among many other events. Kathleen and the boys loved the excitement of those events which they had never seen before, but were seeing with Tom. During the next year, Kathleen would slowly begin to learn to love and trust someone, once more.

Chapter 8

Her Name Was "Snoojie"

Needless to say, leaving the love of his mother and brothers and returning to his Grandmaw's home after two weeks away was coming back down to earth hard, like he had fallen out of a second floor window. It would take a few days to get back into the everyday routine of his chores and having little opportunity to express himself. He began looking forward to a new school year and the reconvening of Sunday School.

But first, in what seemed to be turning into an annual affair, the Runt had been scheduled for plastic surgery and due to a busy summer schedule, the hospital had pushed back his operation until late August again. Worried about the after effects of this surgery he didn't sleep well and on the day of surgery, was a scared little boy, hopefully waiting for his mother to come. Scheduled for 4:30 P. M., the hours passed quickly by, as he waited and worried. The clock in the hall said it was 4:25 and still no Mom. Dejected and nearing despair, he felt very alone, wondering why his mom didn't come to see him.

Outside, the shadows of late afternoon had begun lengthening and at precisely 4:30 P. M., as an orderly was wheeling in a gurney for her son, an out-of-breath Kathleen arrived, gasping between breaths that she'd had to work later than planned. As his mother's wonderful face smiled downward at him, all worry drained from him, such was his joy at seeing her. She then explained to him very quickly that he needn't worry since serious surgery wasn't going to be done after all but that the doctors were only going to remove his tonsils and adenoids, a simple operation. Gently, the orderly reminded him that it was time to go, whereupon the now cheerful little boy climbed onto the gurney and was wheeled down the hall to the elevator, which took them up to the familiar operating room floor.

For the first couple of days after the operation, his throat seemed to be raw flesh but the Runt would now learn that the rumor he heard was true: when kids had their tonsils out, they got to eat all of the ice cream they wanted. It certainly beat forcing down the mashed split peas a nurse had given him for lunch on the first morning after his operation which had felt as though he had been swallowing broken glass. After a few days however, he returned home and went about getting ready to go back to school. He hated to miss school because he enjoyed reading and learning. He'd fallen behind after his operation last year finding it very hard to come back and catch up with everyone else, but he had kept trying. Trying was what he had learned to do best of all the lessons learned in his young life.

As if to ease some of the little boy's concerns, Fate, in a small, feminine form, tapped him on the shoulder on a clear, September day. Turning quickly the Runt was smitten full in the face by the familiar elfin charms of Marjorie Cribbens, a classmate of his since first-grade. She asked him to help her because the red plaid school bag, a back-to-school gift which her parents had bought for her had just ripped open, allowing her books and papers to cascade to the floor.

"I just need a little help in carrying my books home. Could you please help me?"

Nearly too bashful to answer, he mewed a "Yes," before he bent down to pick up the last couple of books from the floor.

He then accompanied her home, the two youngsters walking the one block to her house. Leaving her at her door he walked westward, up Diversey toward Racine and then home. It's doubtful that his feet ever touched the ground.

The next day he asked her if he could carry her books home again and then halfway home she took his hand. Day after day for over a month, he carried her books for her and then for a reason that is lost in antiquity, the routine came to an end. Maybe it was the teasing she could have been taking from classmates, or perhaps her parents discouraged their familiarity, but the walking home together had ended. Unknown to her, he would still continue to have a puppy-love crush on young Marjorie all through elementary school.

Puppy love of another kind had come into his life a couple of years earlier when a chubby, squirming creature had been brought to Grandmaw Kelly's home by her son, Clay, who couldn't keep it. With his sad, brown eyes turned all the way up, Clay had asked his mother if she could give the puppy a good home. She took in the pup and would eventually name her "Snoojie." Snoojie was responsible for the Runt learning at eight years of age, that a pet dog offered pretty good protection for a home. Now two years old, the shepherd-collie mix was a sweet, playful companion, who possessed the tucked-over ears of a collie and silky, black and tan fur. She was also was one of the best watchdogs one could own.

On a dark and moonless night in November, all of the adults and Betty had gone over to the movies at the nearby East theatre on Lincoln Avenue to attend a Dinnerware night. Theatres at that time, in order to attract crowds on off-nights like Tuesday, would give away a dinnerware piece to each lady on Tuesday night. Since Grandmaw Kelly wanted her dinnerware set completed as soon as possible, she had suggested that the other distaff family members go with her; four women: four dinnerware pieces. Everyone, even his grandpaw, had gone to the show except the Runt, who, having a bad cold was advised to stay home. His grandmaw asked, "Do you want Betty to stay home with you?"

One glance past his grandmaw's shoulder into Betty's glowering face told him what his answer better be.

"No Grandmaw, I'll be alright. Don't anyone worry about me. No, I won't open the door for anybody; I'll stay right here."

"Okay. We'll be back in a couple of hours. Bye."

"Bye Bye."

"So long, twerp!"

"Be good now."

"Bye son."

Slam.

So there he was in the kitchen, huddled between the gas range and the wood-burning stove, easily the warmest spot in the house. It wasn't just coincidental that he was in the center of the room where no one could sneak up on him. An intruder would have had to get past Snoojie to get to him because scrunched into that small area with him was the noble dog, whom he had coaxed close to him for protection. For over an hour they remained there, her dozing at his feet while he stood reading a book laid upon the edge of the gas range.

Suddenly, Snoojie's ears perked up and a fierce growl began deep in her throat. She trotted to the kitchen door, barking fiercely at something out there in the night that only she detected. The fur on her back was up and the sight of her all ready for danger, caused the hair on the back of the Runt's neck to stand up and goosebumps formed on his arms.

Believing that Snoojie would chase off any prowler, he imprudently opened the back door, and the furiously growling dog charged headlong out into the night. He ran after her as she raced wildly around the darkened back of the house and up their gangway. By the time the little boy caught up to her in the front yard, she was straining at the gate, barking ferociously at fast-fading footsteps running away in the darkness. Calling her after him, the Runt and the dog hurried back to the warmth and safety of the house.

Later, when the rest of the family returned from the movies, the Runt had never been more glad to see grown-ups in his young life. Even in the safe environs of a home full of people, he couldn't stop thinking to himself: what might have happened to him, if Snoojie hadn't been there to chase away the prowler? Snoojie and he had been pretty close friends before but from that night on, he tried to take her with him whenever he went. Gaining a sense of protected security by having a dog around, he would also want to keep a dog throughout his adult years, too.

Her name? Yes, it was unusual, wasn't it? It was a moniker borrowed by Grandmaw Kelly from an old "B" movie of the '40's. A year or so earlier, when Snoojie was still unnamed, his Grandmaw and Aunts Etta, Maybelle, and Betty went to the East Theatre to see a movie with Melvyn Douglas. In one part of this particular movie, as told scene by scene to the Runt by Betty, Melvyn Douglas and a rival suitor were arguing over the affections of their female co-star. Suddenly, Melvyn Douglas slugged his rival, and to his surprise the woman hurried over to the aid of the prostrate, semi-conscious fellow and knelt down cooing, "Oh, Snoojie." Whereupon Melvyn Douglas roared, "Snoojie?" Like glue onto wood, the name stuck in Grandmaw Kelly's mind and when she got back home, she announced that the little ball of fur they had been calling "Puppy," finally had a name.

During World War II, before the movie began, a patriotic short trailer was shown. Sometimes the theatre management would show an additional promotion for one of the war bond drives, or a charity collection such as a Red Cross solicitation would take place as the house lights came up. However, the show always began with the showing of patriotic trailer, a film clip of "America The Beautiful" or "The Star-Spangled Banner," the strains of which would accompany a colored scene of Old Glory flying from a flagpole, during which everyone stood. Most people would sing, while others stood in reverent silence. At the close of the patriotic anthem, the movie would begin.

As November faded into December and into the hard months of winter, the Runt dutifully performed winter chores for his grandmaw, which included supplying their kitchen and dining room stoves with a sufficient amount of coal. Every evening, at her beckoning, the little boy would carry the empty coal scuttles out to the coal shed near the back of the lot. Working in the dark, he used a small shovel to fill the scuttles, then carried one scuttle back to the big house. Not very robust, the skinny kid felt that the scuttles were just the correct weight for him to lift when they were empty. Carrying each of the two full coal scuttles with two hands, on separate trips, he held the load of coal close to him, causing it to sway and bump his bony knees with every step back to the house, leaving an intermittent trail of coal behind him as he trudged along.

On doubly-dark nights when no snow covered the ground and deep shadows swallowed up all light, the Runt's vivid imagination never failed to exercise itself vigorously, when, except for Snoojie, he was out alone in the dark. In just moments, he could churn up the image of a slavering, yellow-eyed, lupine creature stalking him from behind the bushes and he fearfully staggered to the house with the scuttle a little faster. Wrestling the heavy scuttle inside the porch door, he then made sure that Snoojie was still around and with his dark little eyes darting back and forth, he scurried back to the coal shed for the second scuttle, hauling it back to the house in the same fearful manner.

When snow covered the ground on cold winter nights, an eerie half-light reflected off the snow outlining the stark, black limbs of several trees in the yard, swaying in the wind and seeming to grope for him. In evading their grasp one night he looked around, wide-eyed, to see a gray, menacing figure off to the side in the middle of the yard. After making sure that it hadn't moved, he realized that it was only the snow woman that he and Betty had created during the last snowfall.

Winter nights brightened by a full moon's light allowed his imagination, with a nudge from the crack of a twig, to easily fabricate the possibility of a snarling wolfman hiding in the shadows, vulnerable only to a silver bullet, waiting for the boy's protective dog to wander off! More than once, he wondered if his Uncle Chick had ever kept any silver bullets for his old .22 rifle.

The young boy's imagination worked outside the world of his yard, too. Often, while walking down Lincoln Avenue on the way to the store, his young imagination might start him racing up the sidewalk, his opponent being a streetcar coming up the street behind him. Imagining that if it caught up to him, he would expire or suffer some other dire fate worse than death, he was spurred to run faster. If little boys of that era could have stashed away a portion of their imagination for later endeavors in life, the world might have possessed an overabundance of inventors and mystery writers when those same boys became men.

In fourth grade, his imagination came to fore when assigned to write compositions and stories. His mind often voyaged out among the stars during class and if allowed to compose a fictional story, would draw colorful ideas from his daydreams. Joy Regan, the friendly brown-haired girl with glasses, sitting at the desk in front of him complimented him once, after he had read one of his stories aloud. In Joy, he would find a fellow star-voyager who, after becoming good friends, confessed to dwelling upon the future in a time of space ships and how awe-inspiring it would be to travel out among the stars, light-years apart.

At the desk on his left sat a very poised and prim, Ruth Perlman, a black-haired, lovely girl with the brightest China-blue eyes. Ruth had written an absorbing tale about the Middle East in ancient times and the Runt was quite spellbound as she unfolded her story. History and Geography, and the ties between them, were subjects of great interest to him and conflicts in a far-off land thousands of years ago gripped his interest. Later on, he, Ruth, and Joy would be assigned to work together as a committee to write a combined story about the origin of civilization, a dream project for them. In doing the story, each of the three not only had enjoyed the project and received a good grade but also had made two new friends.

It was also during the fourth grade, that the Runt encountered his first male teacher, Mr. Ray Harger. An accomplished and interesting science teacher, Mr. Harger conducted classes which held the Runt's interest and inspired his initiative, especially those lessons about the human body. Soaking up the information like a sponge absorbs water, the Runt quickly learned and committed to memory, the names of all of the human body's principal muscles and bones. Rapidly finishing his assignments, the young boy was given a small book to read by Mr. Harger, in order that he might keep learning so near the end of the semester.

A physiology primer the book held the Runt's interest so profoundly, that he asked Mr. Harger if he could take it home with him. After receiving permission, he read it on the way home, and except for suppertime didn't put it down until he finished it that evening. He truly loved learning and science was always his favorite subject. The Runt returned the book to Mr. Harger the next day.

The teacher asked his young student, "Have you ever thought of becoming a doctor someday?"

The Runt replied, "Yes, many times I've thought of becoming a doctor."

With that, Mr. Harger opened the book and wrote a dedication of good wishes to "young Doctor Ryan," and returned the book to his student saying, "Keep the book and good luck!"

Fascinated with the physiology of the human body, the Runt found that other kids were intrigued by the human body but in a different, more ghoulish sort of way. It was on a close, very warm June night that he was to learn more about human nature, beginning out in the huge, triangular alley behind his grandmother's house. Bounded by homes and businesses along Lincoln Avenue, Diversey Parkway, and Lakewood Avenue, the concrete alley was the neighborhood recreation center for adults to meet and talk, in addition, it was also home to an endless variety of juvenile games and a hard surface for the volleying of tennis balls by young adults.

On this particular night the alley had been taken over by a kids' ballgame. Involving at least a dozen kids of all ages, the game came to an abrupt halt when a light went on in the back window of the Westlake Funeral Home as it must have on countless other occasions. But tonight would be different because a couple of the older boys, including big Roger Kellman wanted to go over and see what was going on inside. "Oh! Awful!" commented a couple of the younger girls who fled for home at the idea. Lest they be thought "chicken" the smaller boys stuck around, only because the big guys were there to take care of them or call them "cowards" or "sissies" if they didn't stay.

The yellow-light of the window shone down from about eight feet up the wall of the funeral home, much too high to look in but Roger was big and resourceful. Opening up the parking lot's back gate and swinging it over by the wall, Roger had been able to climb up on the gate where he stood on his tiptoes to get a peek.

"Whaddayasee?" asked Donnie Allers, Roger's friend.

"Whaddayasee?" prompted another big kid.

"Shaddup! Nobody's in there!" came the word from above. "Shh!" again from above. Then in a forced whisper, Roger began his commentary, "Shh! Somebody's coming in! Can't quite see who they are." Moments passed, then, "Wait!" Then more moments passed.

"Whaddayasee?"

"Geez, they're bringing in a stiff!"

"Yeh? What's it like?"

"They got it covered with a sheet, stupid."

Moments later, "They've got bottles of something. Moments passed. "Ohhhhhh God!" And with that last statement Roger quickly turned, jumped off the gate and vomited onto the sidewalk.

"What'd you see?" asked Roger's buddy.

"What happened?" asked the others but Roger was beyond words at the moment and wanted only to get away from there.

Those whose taste for the macabre had been easily sated began drifting away, retreating to the relative safety and normalcy of the alley proper. Others, the older, morbidly curious, remained; searching among their number for another staunch, brave soul who might scale the gate, another who might see and report those events meant to be kept from their knowledge. Whatever it was that Roger Kellman had seen during that embalmment, neither the Runt nor his young friends ever found out.

That night had occurred during the Summer that marked nearly five years that the Runt had lived at his grandmaw's. He had been cared for and loved by his Aunt Maybelle for most of those years and soon he was going to have the opportunity to repay her.

When Maybelle's baby boy Roy had come to be five years old, she, like millions of women, went to work in place of the men who were off to war. Strangely, this time Grandmaw Kelly could watch Roy while Maybelle went to work. Of course, Grandmaw Kelly had the Runt to help her out and so it became his job to watch his little cousin, Roy, no matter where he went. Most of the time it wasn't so bad, when Roy played together with his older cousin.

There were other times though, when Roy didn't want to play anymore and wandered back into the house. Roy, at that time of his young life, often had a problem with truth, for he and truth were strangers. Several times when their grandmaw asked him where his cousin was, Roy replied falsely, that his cousin didn't want to play with him and had left him by himself. Instantly, her Irish was up, and she stormed out of the house looking for her other grandson, the good-for-nothing one.

For the first time or two, the Runt was unaware of how much Roy had stretched the truth and when he saw his grandmaw slam the gate shut and come storming toward him, he wondered why the ground was shaking under her feet as she approached him. Oh! Oh! Why was her other hand behind her? She's got the belt! Not the belt again! Grandmaw Kelly always believed Roy's fibs, and his cousin got the long end of it, the belt that is. For most offenses she applied punishment with the belt, but for other, more grievous offenses, atonement could be gained by other methods, one of which is soon to be described.

At his worst, Roy could annoy the Runt past all endurance, goading him with an expertise that belied his tender years. Reaching a point where he would have punched anyone else, the Runt held back and held back until he finally said it. He called Roy that word that he had overheard in the schoolyard, without having had it first explained by his buddy, Billy Immenhauser, who knew what all of those dirty words meant. Strangely enough, Roy knew the word's meaning and it sent him running into the yard, screaming for their grandmaw. Finally, the Runt was rid of the little pest! He didn't know it but he had just traded a small problem for a much larger one, when in just moments, using no stealth, no Invisible Man technique, Grandmaw Kelly came bursting out of the yard like Whirlaway out of the starting gate, yet with a new kind of fury. But she had forgotten the belt! Ha! She didn't have the belt with her! How bad could the punishment be this time?

Suddenly she was in her older grandson's face and her fingers of steel nearly tore off his ear as she pulled him alongside her, his feet slipping, stumbling, barely touching the ground, back into the house. In livid, yet total silence, she shoved her grandson in front of the kitchen sink where she took a washcloth, held it under the running faucet, then rubbed a lot of soap on it and forced that foul-tasting cloth all around the inside of his mouth. Off in the corner of the kitchen, Roy grinned smugly as his older cousin tried very hard not to retch.

It wasn't an entirely hopeless situation though, since his aunt Maybelle always believed that there were two sides to every story, believing the Runt's as easily as she believed Roy. Maybelle knew that sometimes Roy could be devilish, so she calmly took the time to take the Runt aside, after he had called her son that nasty name and explained to her nephew the meaning of the word.

Then she ended with, "And now that you know what it means, I'm sure that you won't use it again, will you?"

The Runt told her, "No, I won't use it again."

And he didn't! The next time he remembered to use a different word, yet ended up in the kitchen again and was accorded the same ghastly punishment! Within a few months, the Runt knew each soap, not only by its fragrant bouquet but also by its taste. The absolutely worst taste of all, in his humble, yet very experienced opinion, was that famous red-colored bar of soap that was advertised to prevent body-odor. It won "gag me" honors, hands down.

After several infractions, Fate offered the Runt sweet revenge one fateful day when all he needed to do, was turn his back and walk slowly away. Along about mid-afternoon, Roy and the Runt were playing along the railroad tracks but Roy was quickly sinking into one of his uncooperative moods. Roy decided that he wanted to walk along between the tracks and when asked to get out of there by his cousin-guardian, Roy decided not to listen.

Ding! Ding! Ding! The crossing signal's bell suddenly began ringing and its lights started flashing on and off! A switch-train was coming down the track, about two blocks away. The Runt shouted, "Roy, get out of there!"

Roy's response was a pouty "Hmmf."

Again a shout, "Roy, the train is coming!"

Again a "Hmmf."

When the train was a block away, the Runt yelled, "Roy, get off the tracks!" and pulled him off but his stubborn little cousin stepped right back onto the tracks.

The Runt thought desperately, then ran into the yard calling for his aunt Maybelle just home from work, who hurried out of the house to see what the commotion was. Her frantic nephew only had time to shout it once, "Roy won't get off the tracks and a train is coming!"

Racing up the alley and out in front of the house, they got to the tracks just as the steadily-approaching switch locomotive was less than fifty feet from Roy, who staunchly continued walking along the ties, between the tracks. Aunt Maybelle ran out onto the tracks and snatched her son from in front of the locomotive, just as the engineer turned in his chair, saw them, and applied the brakes.

Maybelle had saved her son's life, for braking by the train would have been too late. Nearly in shock, she tearfully asked her only child, "Are you alright?"

"Yes Mother, I'm okay."

Maybelle then proceeded to set his pants on fire with a well-deserved spanking all the way back into the yard and presumably into the house!

As he watched his cousin getting his just desserts, the Runt thought aloud, "Sometimes, life can be good."

One might wonder here, after the bum raps and undeserved punishment, why the Runt would bother to tell his aunt, let alone hurry, instead of walking slower. The Runt knew right from wrong and in spite of any sibling differences between them, he still loved his cousin and playmate, who would someday be like a little brother to him. Perhaps it was because both of their mothers were working and therefore each of them knew a little boy's loneliness for his absent mother. But the most likely and overpowering reason of all could have been that while the Runt was devoted to his mother, he also felt a deep affection and loyalty toward his Aunt Maybelle.

Always gentle and loving toward him, Maybelle had been like a surrogate mother to him, genuinely concerned about him and who treated him with infinite kindness over the years he spent away from his mother and brothers. When it had become necessary to correct his behavior, she never raised her voice or scolded but spoke to him as she would to another adult. She must have understood the unending loneliness that the Runt felt for his mother and had filled in for her as much as she could. As long as he would live, her nephew would owe his aunt Maybelle a debt he could never repay.

Chapter 9

Together Again

"School's out, school's out, teacher has let the monkeys out!" was the refrain sung by school-aged children whose school year had ended earlier in the day. But the Runt had better news on June 22nd, 1944. The long-awaited day for which he had prayed every night during those six long years had finally arrived. Shadows of late afternoon had barely begun to lengthen as the nine-and-a-half-year-old boy gathered his few belongings. He was getting ready to leave Grandmaw Kelly's home, 'cause he was going home!

Kathleen, after months of combing the North Side, had rented a six-room apartment over on George Street, in the heart of the meat-packing area, a block away from Grandmaw and Grandpaw Kelly. She and his brothers had already been living there for two weeks, and now he would be joining them to complete their family.

Welcoming the prospect of her daughter living close by, Grandmaw Kelly had been less than thrilled when she realized, as part of Kathleen's setting up a household for her sons and herself, her grandson would be leaving her. As the moment approached for her grandson to leave, Grandmaw Kelly asked him a question, the answer to which she should have already known.

She asked, "Who do you love most, your mother or me?"

Taken aback, he hesitated. While he loved and respected his grandparents, he adored his mother above anyone else in the world. His response, the most honest, natural one for him was, "I love my mother most of all."

Upon hearing his reply, his grandmaw became angry, seething at first but then escalating quickly into a full-blown rage. She screamed, "How can you do this to me, when y'all know Ah have a bad heart?"

"I didn't mean to make you feel bad."

"Y'all git out of this house and don't you ever come back again!"

Departing moments later, her grandson left crying and carrying an awesome load of guilt upon his young shoulders. While it was true that she might once have suffered an attack of angina, Grandmaw Kelly had not yet celebrated her fiftieth birthday and would live on well into her eighties.

As her emotionally-torn grandson trudged north towards George Street, he felt that if his grandmaw's heart failed, it would be his fault. Several minutes later, he arrived, disconsolate, at Kathleen's front door, still in tears. His mother, concerned that he would be sad on this occasion, asked him, "What's wrong, don't you want to come and live with us?"

Feeling that he would burst, her son blurted out, "I waited so long and prayed for this day, but it seems like I might be wrong for leaving my grandmaw."

"Why do you feel that way, Honey?"

Then he slowly proceeded to tell her about the farewell scene, after which, Kathleen told him, "You needn't cry. I promise you that Grandmaw will be alright and she certainly won't die because of your leaving."

It just might have been, that Grandmaw had sung that same tune to Kathleen some time before.

Going upstairs where Davey was setting the table, the three of them waited until Bob returned from the store, then gathered at the supper table to say a prayer, thanking God for bringing them back together again.

Together. What a joyous, overwhelming feeling it was for a them as they ate a hearty home-cooked meal, the first in their own home, after six lonely years. As darkness finally fell on that Midsummer's night, they sat by the eerie glow of a kerosene lamp brought with them from Texas, because the electricity hadn't been turned on yet.

Putting her two younger sons to bed that night, Kathleen carried the kerosene lamp with her into their room. Her youngest son would always recall the lamp's pale light flickering on his mother's loving face, as she bade them goodnight. Cast onto the wall by the lamp's gentle glow, her dark shadow followed eerily behind her like a specter, as she left their room, ending the happiest day of the Runt's young life.

Sunbeams pierced the Runt's eyes through the gap between the window frame and the window shade, and in moments, his first day in their new home began. After breakfast, Kathleen and Bob went off to work, leaving the two younger boys to clean up the house. After their chores were done, Davey, already a veteran of several forays into the neighborhood, led his younger brother on a tour of their environs. An adult might tend to disparage what the Runt saw, but they were surrounded by a young boy's delight.

Their house on George Street was a two-flat, frame building with tan imitation-brick siding, having a full attic and wooden back porches, complete with bannisters for young boys to slide down. Situated on the front of a deep lot, their house shared the lot with the still-standing remains of a burned-out frame cottage on the back of the lot. In the mind of young boys it was an archeological find! Entry into the old burned house proved to be pretty risky, since no front porch existed, and the rear porch stairway had been completely burned away.

No matter to them. Stepping carefully around the charred carcass of an unfortunate feline victim of the fire, they climbed like mountain goats up the empty stairway and into the entry-way, crusted with charcoal. As vital as the tomb of Ramses II to these fledgling, unlearned archaeologists, the structure's stale air reeked of the heavy odor of smoke, which only enhanced its mystic ambience. While it was the Runt's most exciting exploration, it would only be the first of many expeditions that they would conduct into that old hulk of a pyramid, until its complete demolition, two years hence by a new owner.

Back at the house, if the two adventurers had liked the light from the kerosene lamps, they would learn to love it during the next two weeks, another two weeks without electricity. Reinstated recently from the city's condemned buildings list, the house also lacked window screens, a central furnace or space heater, a concrete basement, and locks that worked. But they were all together in their home, and there were ways to work around minor inconveniences. Fortunately, the summer temperatures allowed them to forestall the purchase of a heating stove until early Fall.

Some necessities wouldn't wait and had to be addressed immediately, such as refrigeration. Iceboxes predated refrigerators, but their purpose was the same: to keep food cold. Whether Kathleen lacked the funds or was waiting for a good deal on one, they immediately needed something that would keep milk, meat, and butter cold.

Enter boyhood resourcefulness. Davey and the Runt found the solution, while out the first afternoon. Living in the heart of a meat-packing area gave them ready access to large quantities of frozen carbon dioxide or "dry-ice." It was in every alleyway, dumped from trucks and firms that used it for temporary cooling of perishable shipments. The boys had found a coolant, but needed something to keep it in. Finding a clean, tall, round, cardboard tube with a top that could be removed and replaced easily, they packed the dry ice in its bottom, and placed some salvaged excelsior on top of the ice. Voila! An icebox!

Arriving home first, Bob, older and much wiser, did approve the idea, with one small change; he cut a small vent hole in the container, to relieve any gas pressure that might build up. When Kathleen got home, she was thrilled at her sons' ingenuity, and the practical nature of a tube of dry-ice. A month later, Kathleen purchased an icebox, because an electric refrigerator was still too expensive for her limited budget.

Although more acceptable than dry-ice, the icebox needed a drip pan under it to catch the melted ice-water, which needed to be dumped once or twice a day. To forget to dump it, meant be prepared to mop the floor later on when a pool of water would serve as a reminder. Ice was a reasonable, though very temporary coolant and during Summer's scorching days, experienced a very short life span. Replacement ice wasn't too hard to come by, since several ice-vendors known simply as "icemen" plied their trade in the free market of neighborhood streets.

Ice-vending was usually a summer business done by coal and fuel oil companies in the area. Each iceman handed out free cards, about nine by twelve inches in size, to prospective customers. Those cards contained the company name in the center but on each of its edges was printed one of four numbers: 25, 50, 75, or 100. When ice was needed, a customer placed the card in their front window with the appropriate numbered edge on top. If they needed fifty pounds of ice, they left the "50" on top. Sometime during the day, the iceman would troll the neighborhood in his truck and spotting the sign, stopped his truck. Ambling back to the tailgate of the truck, the iceman would then lay a protective pad of leather or canvas over his shoulder, hoist a fifty-pound block of ice onto that same shoulder and haul it up the stairs to the customer's door. Returning to his truck, the iceman's canvas pad was by now water-soaked and water had begun trickling down the back of his shirt.

Often on those scorching days, the Ryan brothers and other neighborhood kids who didn't have much money, waited for the iceman to stop, in order to bum some welcome, thirst-quenching ice-chips from him. Sometimes the brothers had received enough ice to mix up a pitcher of ice-water but usually they, like their friends, just sat on their porch or somebody else's porch, sucking on the quickly melting, cold, refreshing ice.

With their house situated between two other similar two-flats, their outside world began at the edge of their yard. The meat-packing establishments began two doors west, filling both sides of George Street, beginning with a two-story brick building which housed a poultry company, the stench of whose operation permeated the neighborhood. Live chickens, delivered at one large dock door could be processed and shipped out another door the same day. Strangely enough, the noses of neighborhood residents somehow got accustomed to some of the odor but the stench continued to assail the noses of any visitors!

All the well-known meat-packing companies such as Swift, Armour, and Wilson lined both sides of the street, and their trucks and those of affiliated vendors, filled its pavement. Living and playing on that street, demanded that Davey and his kid brother learn how to safely play in and out among the omnipresent trucks, tractors and semi-trailers.

Miraculously, no neighborhood kid was ever a traffic statistic, although the Runt once gave it a really good try! Barreling out of the alley one day, on a borrowed bike, he was riding too fast to make the turn into the street quickly enough and grazed a passing car. Losing control, he fell off the bike, bumping his head on the pavement. Near panic, the tall, young meat-packer who had been driving the car, walked the Runt home, where he told the story to Kathleen and offered to pay for any medical expenses as he drove them to his company's doctor. The kid's scalp wound only took one little stitch, but it taught him an indelible lesson, because he never again rode out of an alley too quickly.

A worse time of the year could not have been chosen by Fate to inflict a case of "shingles," medically known as Herpes Zoster or Herpes type III on the young Runt. Consisting of several clusters of irritating, itching blisters near his right armpit and chest, the rash made the Runt miserable. A trip to the doctor resulted in a prescription that eased some of the itch. Concurrent with the incubation of his ailment, another incubation had been taking place since Kathleen set up housekeeping a couple of weeks earlier.

A shortage of funds had made it necessary for her to purchase second-hand furniture and in the case of bedding, also the mattress for Davey and his younger brother. Having inspected the mattress very carefully, for telltale stains or any signs of vermin, Kathleen had concluded that the mattress was acceptable and she brought it home for use.

One night, a very warm night, the Runt awoke in severe discomfort, feeling as though his rash was acting up in biting pain. He called his mother who first thought that perhaps he was being a bit of a baby with the pain of his rash.

"I'm feeling pain too, Mom," admitted Davey.

Whipping back the covers in the light, horror filled Kathleen's eyes as she screamed, "Oh my God! Bedbugs! Get up quickly! Both of you take a bath, now!" Swooping up the sheet and bedspread, she threw them on the back porch, and soon followed with the mattress.

Apparently a few of the bugs had been hidden deep inside the old mattress at the time of purchase and after a fortnight of warm incubation had multiplied into a severe infestation. After spraying every inch of their bedroom, she later told her two youngsters, "Go sleep in my bed, I'll sleep on the sofa for a few days, until I can get you a good mattress."

Within a week the two boys had a new mattress and the Runt was saying goodbye to the last of his shingles blisters, ready to go exploring again with Davey. Ever-expanding their street playground, the two boys were walking along the tracks near Lincoln Avenue by the produce market, when one of its employees spotted them. Recognizing the Runt from the many grocery trips he made there for his grandmaw, the employee asked them if they would like to go with one of the drivers on the delivery truck and help him deliver produce. Asking what was in it for them, they were told that they could earn a dollar each plus all the fruit they could eat on the way. A dollar each and free fruit? It sounded good to them!

Davey had chosen to ride up front in the cab to talk to the driver, probably learning how to shift gears, while his kid brother rode in back with the produce. Who enjoyed the most berries and grapes? The kid in back, of course! The driver's route supplied several restaurants along Michigan Avenue and other Loop thoroughfares. By making his stops quickly, they were back early in the afternoon, each of them a dollar richer. It had been the Runt's first tour of the downtown area and he had enjoyed his short venture into another part of the big city of Chicago that he would come to love.

On a sultry, rainy day in late June, when yard and street play were curtailed, Davey and the Runt had other ways to spend the hours. Next door to them, on their left, was the two-flat that housed the Farr family. The Ryan boys were over there, hanging around with Billy and Jerry Farr, who were the same age as they. It was to be a day of daring-do for Davey, who had the courageous heart to attempt the unthinkable, the foolhardiness to follow through, and the good fortune of avoiding injury in the performance of the feat.

As the rain fell, they played on the stairway landing between the Farr's second floor and the attic, Davey observed that the roof of the commercial parking garage east of them, was level with the landing, and that they could probably jump across the gap which was about four feet. The Runt replied "Not me!" His sentiments were echoed by the Farr brothers, who thought it was too far, and wanted no part of being reduced to a crumpled heap of twisted limbs, nearly three stories below.

Undaunted by their refusals, or the yawning chasm between the two buildings, Davey, who was pushing twelve years of age, scrambled over the railing, poised on the landing's edge, and vaulted off into space. Sailing over the portion of the brick wall that extended about two feet above the garage roof, he landed on the garage's sloping roof where he couldn't roll off. A few seconds later, his kid brother resumed breathing. Eventually, Davey coaxed Billy Farr into duplicating his feat, and Billy also made it. The two younger boys still refused, preferring to remain live "chickens."

What Davey and Billy hadn't thought through was that once they made it to the top of the garage roof, how would they get back? The top of the garage wall's extension was covered with slick, rain-splattered, sloping tile plates and to stand on them was to invite slipping off and plummeting three stories straight down. As the two older boys sat pondering their return leap, the Runt thought, "I suppose we'll have to call out the fire department! The police will be here and they'll tell MOM." In those days, the police could instill more fear in kids by threatening to tell their Mom or Dad about their infractions, than if they had threatened them with being thrown into the slammer. The Runt had once heard some "tough-guy" blubbering to a cop, "Don't tell my Dad! Don't tell my Dad!" No punishment was more dreaded by a kid, than retribution meted out by the kid's own parents!

Davey's little brother needn't have worried. Showing no fear, Davey stepped up on the wall's tile, and like a frog off a lily-pad, sprang across the gap, caught a push from God and grabbed the railing as the arc of his jump dipped downward. He pulled himself up and climbed over the railing, sporting a smug grin. Then he turned and told Billy, "It's easier than it looks, go ahead and jump." God must have helped Billy too, as he leaped across the void and managed to catch the railing, which fortunately for both of the boys had been in good condition. While they proved that the feat was possible, for reasons known only to Davey, it would be the last time he attempted jumping across their gangway.

Boyhood experiences such as their's that day, weren't the kind of things young boys told their mothers about after they'd been working all day, and had come home looking for a little peace and quiet. In fact, neither of the boys would ever think to tell Kathleen about it until after they were grown at which time her response was, "I'm so glad I didn't know about such things going on, back then."

Something in Davey's nature was revealed by the day's events that his kid brother would always admire and envy in his bigger brother. Davey didn't know the meaning of fear and lived for the excitement that hazardous feats brought him. This daredevil bent caused him to live his teens and young adult years, "On the edge."

Davey also had a devil-may-care compadre living next door to them on the other side of their house. On that lot stood another two-flat which housed the Kowalczyk family. Ronnie Kowalczyk was a tall, dark, good-looking kid, just a year younger than Davey. Ronnie for several years would be their best friend on the block, sharing countless boyhood adventures with them.

One adventure buried in memory began on the morning of the "Coffee Table Incident" in late June of that year. Davey and Ronnie were upstairs in the apartment's living room, probably sneaking a smoke while the Runt was out on the sidewalk downstairs, enjoying the sunshine. Suddenly a frenzy of shouting by Davey, more shouting by Ronnie, and the worrisome sound of crashing glass, interrupted the Runt's sunny interlude.

Two at a time the Runt dashed upstairs, to see what had happened. His eyes opened wide in shock when he arrived in the living room. He saw Kathleen's pride and joy, a lovely, maple coffee-table topped with a blue mirror, de-topped! When the Runt asked what happened, Davey and Ronnie both stammered, explaining what had transpired in just seconds. A hornet had flown into the apartment and they both decided to give chase with rolled-up newspapers to do it in. Running along the sofa chasing the wasp, Davey in his excitement, stepped off the sofa and onto the blue-mirrored top. The chase ended as the glass shattered under the weight of his foot. Ronnie suddenly remembered that he had an errand to run, leaving the scene of the crime to the Ryan brothers, who wondered what their mom would say when she got home. Thinking desperately, the possibility of disguising the damage was suggested, then dropped quickly, as a viable alternative. They were trapped like rats! As their hours dwindled down to minutes, no solution came to mind, and the condemned young prisoners of their own consciences, waited for their mom to come home. When Kathleen got home, they didn't have to wait long to found out what she would say. It was the first time either of them had ever seen her really lose her temper. She was so upset that she told them both to "Get out of the house and don't come back! I don't want to see you again!"

Making it as far as next door, the two intrepid travelers camped out on Ronnie's front porch, but without Ronnie. They hadn't thought it strange, that Ronnie still hadn't gotten back yet from that errand he had to run. Their ingenious young minds were too involved with the choices of what they should do: stick around or leave home. If they were going to run away, they had to get back into the house first, getting past a furious Mom, in order to pack some clothes and food for the long trip.

Nearly an hour after they were thrown out of the house, Kathleen called them in. She apologized for losing her temper but explained that the table had meant a lot to her. She said that they could help make amends by going around to hardware stores and glass stores, to see how much it would cost to put a new glass in the table. They nearly fell over each other, volunteering to check out prices the very next day. Whew! What a relief it was to see that she was being her old self again.

Two weeks later, a new blue mirror would adorn the coffee table and no one would have ever known that it had been broken. Well, almost no one. What a humorous sight it might have otherwise been two weeks earlier, the sight of two boys, ten and twelve, leaving home and walking down the road with their belongings tied up in bandanas on sticks over their shoulders.

It hadn't been a good week for Kathleen who welcomed the following Saturday as a chance to catch up on housework and some rest. She may have been on the blue side of her emotions while Davey was at the peak of feeling devilish. Beginning with little feigned refusals to help out, Davey then teased his mother to the point where Kathleen had just about enough, saying, "One more peep and I'll take the broom to you!"

Of course, Davey responded with, "Peep."

Kathleen snatched her straw broom from its position in the corner of the kitchen, grabbed it and cocked her hands at her side with the broom up in the air, looking for all the world like Stan Musial waiting for a high inside fastball. She chased Davey and caught up to him. With all her pent-up fury, she delivered a southpaw swing of the broom across Davey's backside. Thwack! The impact of the broom forcefully drove Davey forward onto the floor as the broom handle itself broke just above the straw portion. From the sound of it, the Runt thought his mom could have gotten three bases with that blast.

Davey was unhurt but very amused and started laughing when he saw his mother clutching the broken, empty handle in her hands, at which Kathleen just sat down and cried in frustration. On top of her bad morning, Kathleen now needed a new broom. Then out of the sheer silliness of it all, she looked at the useless broom handle and her grinning son and began laughing herself. She then tempered it by chortling, "See how funny it is, Davey, when you want to go to the movies and I tell you I bought a new broom with the money!"

Thus ended another typical Saturday in the Ryan home on George Street.

Chapter 10

"George Street Flyers"

In mid-July, shortly after busting the broom with his butt, Davey's penchant for tempting Fate would backfire but he wasn't the one who suffered injury. On a beautiful, outdoor kind of day in Chicago, Davey and his kid brother were still inside the house after lunch. Davey, who'd been inspired by a trapeze act he'd seen in the movies, began telling his younger brother about his plan for a trapeze act.

"I've got a great idea for an exciting act that could become famous but it will take a lot of practice to get it right."

The Runt asked, "Who's gonna be in the act?"

"You and me at first, then we can bring Ronnie next door if he wants to join up too."

"What's gonna be the name of the act?"

"The George Street Flyers!"

"Sounds like a dumb name. What are 'Flyers'?"

"Trapeze performers. You know, the guys who swing on trapezes way up at the top of the circus tent."

"The guys that let go and somersault through space hoping their partner will catch them?"

"Yeh, now you've got it!"

"What if I don't wanta be in it?"

"Well, you start small with simple stuff, y'know, just to improve your balance. C'mon, I'll show you, there's nothing to it."

With that he told the Runt to climb up on his shoulders and the dumb kid complied. Then Davey told him to get to his feet and stand on his shoulders which the trusting Runt did.

In that stance, Davey started slowly, carefully, walking

through the dining room and things went fine, until they approached the doorway. So that his brother could clear the door, Davey leaned forward to duck down rather than bending his knees and lowering his body. As Davey leaned forward, the Runt lost his balance and fell straight to the wooden floor, landing on his right forearm.

Snap! With that sickening sound, the Runt's wrist broke under him. When the Runt looked at his forearm, it was bent in a "U" shape halfway up the forearm, with the sharp end of the bone jutting out through the skin, what he would later hear described as a compound fracture. Suddenly he felt strange, dizzy, and disoriented, as if he weren't there but off to the side watching this happen. Davey knew that the arm was broken and pulled the bones back together. He also realized that his little brother was getting dizzy and very pale: signs of shock, and he had better get him to bed fast.

Lying in bed the Runt worried about what their mom would say. He knew if it was broken, she'd worry, so maybe he could convince her that it was only sprained. He worried so much about how she would react when she got home, that it had diverted his thoughts from some of the severe pain. When Kathleen came home, fatigued and exhausted from the heat, Davey met her at the door to ease her fears.

"Don't worry Mom. You shouldn't worry. Mom, don't worry."

It really didn't take much of that routine to make her worry about what she shouldn't be worried about! Impatiently, Kathleen asked Davey, "What's wrong?"

Davey replied that the Runt was hurt. "He's broken his arm."

In their bedroom, the younger brother heard Davey and muttered, "Broken his arm? As if I did it by myself!"

But then Kathleen asked probingly, "How did it happen? You'd better tell me the truth."

Davey then changed his story, admitting, "It was my idea and I guess I'd have to say it was all my fault."

Kathleen hurried into the boys' bedroom where her injured son lay in obvious pain, but when he saw her, he quickly rolled over onto his side, holding the broken arm away from her, so she couldn't see it. He repeatedly protested, "It isn't broken! It's only sprained!"

When Kathleen saw the arm, she said, "Your arm is definitely broken and you and I are going to Children's Memorial Hospital to have it set properly."

It wasn't just through intuition that she, as a mother, knew just where to take her sons for first aid and medical attention. She had been given many of these valuable tips by women at work, who also had healthy sons that they were trying to raise to adulthood.

By then the scorching afternoon heat had rolled into a hot July evening and the on-call medical staff at Children's Memorial had already had a long day, when in walked Kathleen and her son with the broken wing. The doctor and nurse in charge showed considerable patience in setting the bone back together through the use of a fluoroscope, which dazzled the Runt. It was so neat that he exclaimed, "My brother Davey ought to see this!" He was able to see the bones as they were being painfully set, but fortunately for him, the device had held him awestruck to the point of allowing his mind to focus on something other than the pain.

After mixing a batch of plaster for the cast, they applied it over the layers of gauze they had wrapped around his skinny, wounded forearm. When that was finished, they put a sling around the back of his neck to support the arm. With the sling in place, it had suddenly dawned on him that this was how his good arm was going to be for the next six weeks. Six long weeks! That meant that the rest of summer vacation was going to be spent keeping the cast dry and the arm immobile; no swimming, no biking, no orange-crate scooter racing, no nothing. Mulling over those prospects caused him to sink slowly into the dumps. Kathleen saw her son's spirits ebb as she took her injured young warrior home and after dinner, as a treat, allowed he and Davey to go to the movies with the admonition that if the Runt began to feel badly, then they should come home right away.

Arriving at the East Theatre, they learned that it was Vaudeville Night. In another wartime effort to boost attendance, the theatre's management had revived the idea of vaudeville amateur acts performing between movies of a double feature. The Runt thoroughly enjoyed the first act which was a very young, dark-haired girl dancer who kept his attention throughout her act. The additional acts were enough of a distraction to the kid with one good arm that he only thought of his broken arm when an act finished and he couldn't applaud.

Somehow, the broken bone ends failed to knit properly, as detected in a follow-up examination ten days later. The Runt was scheduled for surgery at the end of July, when under a general anesthetic, doctors broke the wristbone again and reset it. The six-week clock for healing time was pushed back two weeks and it appeared that as part of his Back to School look, the Runt would be wearing a plaster cast.

After a few weeks, oxygen deprivation caused the outer layer of skin on his cast-covered forearm to die, peel, and itch. The itching combined with the summer heat nearly drove him nuts. Being unable to reach inside the cast and scratch the itch is a torment known to cast-wearers throughout the world. Minimal relief was obtained with a straightened coat-hanger which offered some scratching capability but the device could only reach so far.

He passed the remainder of the Summer by learning to throw a ball, fence (with wooden swords), chop wood, and eat, with his left hand, becoming proficient enough with his left hand to remain somewhat ambidextrous all of his life. He wondered of course, why his mom always worried that one of her boys could poke an eye out while playing with wooden swords. Weeks of itching inside the cast ended on the Friday before Labor Day, when a doctor at Children's Memorial Hospital had mercifully removed the cast, and jokingly told the eager young boy not to pitch for a while. His enjoyment of the Labor Day weekend had been heightened by the sudden freedom from that heavy cast, scrubbing the dead skin from the arm, feeling the air upon it once more, and lots of long overdue scratching.

Going back to school on the Tuesday after Labor Day would be different from all of the other back-to-school days the Runt had experienced, because for the first time, his brother Davey was going with him. Heretofore, Davey had always gone to school near the Home or near Kathleen's apartment on Irving Park Road, but finally, living in the same home, they could now attend the same school. Because of his transfer from another school, Davey was held back one semester and was starting the second semester of the sixth grade. His little brother was starting the second semester of the fourth grade, in the same home room with Ronnie Kowalczyk from next door. Having one of his best friends in class boosted the Runt's spirits and Ron was pleased because his little neighbor could help him with his studies.

It was going to be a great school year, thought the Runt but it would be even better than he anticipated!. Marjorie Cribbens, the girl he had a crush on since the second grade had just caught up to him by skipping a grade into his class. This class was taught by Miss Callahan, a genteel lady with beautiful white hair, who emphasized music and social skills, combining both with periodic sessions of students dancing around the perimeter of the room.

Over the next few months, the Runt would have several opportunities to step all over the feet of the girl whose books he carried three years before. He thought it strange that he and some of the boys actually seemed to enjoy asking certain girls to dance, when Miss Callahan announced that it was "dance time." Sometimes, two or more boys would ask the same girl, as was the case with little Marjorie. The taller girls in class had a harder time of it since the slower-maturing boys were usually shorter than they and unfairly, were reluctant to ask the taller girls to dance. The older, taller guys naturally had the widest choice of dance partners.

Back at home, on the evening of the first day of school, Davey asked his kid brother, "Who's the toughest guy in school?"

Curious about his reasons for asking, the younger brother asked, "Why do you want to know? Are you in trouble?"

"Naw, I'm just curious."

With that, the Runt said, "I don't know about the whole school, but the toughest kid I know of, is a sixth grader named John Tully. He doesn't look for fights but he has beaten up most of the other tough guys."

"Oh, Okay. Just curious, that's all," muttered Davey, who then just sauntered away.

A few days later, a fight broke out in the schoolyard at recess. Naturally it drew a crowd of boys; some out of curiosity and some who were glad that it wasn't them. One of the first of the latter group to arrive was the Runt. Surprise, then understanding filled his face when he recognized who the combatants were. Flailing away at each other within the circle of onlookers were his brother Davey and Tiger John Tully.

Although it was over in a short time, the fight had a surprise finish. Davey had won the fight handily and afterwards, shook hands with John, who also bore no hard feelings. The two of them became good friends for the rest of their days at Agassiz School. The Runt had surmised that being a new kid in school, his brother had to establish his own reputation. Could it be that Davey hadn't wanted to fight any preliminary bouts, starting at the bottom and working his way up, but established his credentials by trouncing one of the toughest scrappers in their school?

The Runt then asked Davey, "Did you pick the fight with John?"

"Why?"

"Because you always told me to never start a fight."

"But what else did I tell you?"

"You also told me to be ready if one comes your way; don't be caught off-guard! Then fight back as hard as you can."

Dave's response to his kid brother continued, "I know it looks that way, but I didn't start the fight. We were playing football and I played just as rough as Tully did. Instead of backing down from him, I blocked him just as hard as he blocked me. But when Tully took a poke at me that's when the fight started."

Throughout the days of Fall, the Runt regained the strength in his right arm and was once again able to do all of his daily chores. He was also quickly put back in the after-supper lineup by Bob and Davey as first-string dishwasher. Neither Bob nor Davey had ever been fond of washing dishes. Now the lineup was back to normal. The old Cubs' double-play combination of Tinker to Evers to Chance had nothing on the combination of these three boys when it came to getting the dishes done.

Flawless though her sons may have been, Kathleen, by seeing

them in action one time had been driven back into the dining room with her hands over her eyes. The sight that greeted her eyes when she walked into the kitchen was her youngest son washing dishes and her son Davey drying the dishes. Then her heart stopped as Davey tossed the dried dish to Bob standing in the pantry doorway where he caught the dish and stacked it on the shelf. Afterwards, needless to say, she remained in the living room until the dishes were done. What she didn't see wouldn't bother her.

One day, the Runt decided to take on another chore which would be a labor of love, love for their mom who had done so much for them. That day had been extra long and tiring for Kathleen. As she began preparing dinner, she wished aloud that it would be so nice, if just once, she could just come home and not have to make dinner. She hadn't known that during her plaintive soliloquy, her youngest son had walked in through the front door and overheard her. Upon hearing his hard-working mom's fervent wish, it became imperative to him that her wish come true, by having dinner ready for her when she came home from work.

Having watched the preparation of a meal many times, the next afternoon found Kathleen's youngest son opening up cans and making hamburger patties. Then came the big moment: firing up the gas range and getting everything started. Nervous sweat made his shortening-greased palms even slicker, causing him to nearly lose his grip on the frying pan, but he thought of his mom, how much he loved her, and managed to begin putting together a meal for the four of them.

The frying hamburgers emitted a tantalizing aroma that filled the house and teased Davey's nose just enough for him to follow the scent into the kitchen where his younger sibling was scurrying about.

"What are you doing, Runt?"

"I'm making supper."

"Oh crud! I hope you don't poison us."

"Okay. Then you try your hand at cooking, so Mom doesn't have to cook when she gets home."

"Uh, uh! But I will set the table and stuff! Hey, how did you learn to cook?"

"I watched her lots of times."

Bob couldn't be there to help for he had already taken a job working after school. When Kathleen came home, she was pleasantly surprised and overjoyed to see the table set and a meal on the stove. Then she sat down and wept. Feeling sorry for their mom, the two boys put their hands on her shoulders, to which she responded by touching each hand and telling them, "I'm not sad, I'm crying because I'm happy!" She would one day become accustomed to coming home and having dinner already on the table, for the Runt and Davey made it their obligation to set the table and make dinner as often as they could on weekdays afterwards.

Menu choices were many, if not frugal, in those budget-strapped days. Anything the Runt made for dinner, he had already seen Kathleen make often. One of them had been a post-Depression and wartime-era favorite which consisted of a bowl of heated canned tomatoes and broken pieces of bread, lightly sprinkled with sugar. In lieu of salad dressing, sugar could be sprinkled lightly on the lettuce of a salad. And they would not forget the breakfast fare of that era, such as corn meal mush or the 10 pack boxes of cereals made in Battle Creek, or broken pieces of bread in a bowl of milk, sprinkled with sugar.

If one wonders about the consequences of the large part raw sugar played in the diet of poor children of that era, sugar's effects during that time can be seen in the mouths of most adults whose childhood spanned those same years. Blackened silver dental fillings present in a majority of adult molars offer silent testimony to the destructive combination of sugar, candy, and poor dental hygiene practiced then, a combination which must have allowed many a dentist to pay for his children's college tuition.

Shopping for groceries was a task which fell to the two younger sons who went to the corner store frequently since, in those days, iceboxes required that meat be bought fresh each day. Brand names of stores and supermarkets among canned foods were, Royal Blue, Monarch, Natco, and Ann Page. Along with staples they shopped for laundry and dishwashing soaps, among which were brand names such as: Rinso, Duz, Ivory Snow, Dreft, Surf, Gold Dust and Silver Dust. Among the brand name cleansers were Kitchen Klenzer, Old Dutch, Bon Ami, and Bab-O. Most of those brand names would, in a few years, follow horse-drawn carts into antiquity.

Soon their first long summer together had passed and the odor of soft-coal smoke wafting on cool breezes accompanied October's end, as the spirit of Halloween pervaded the air. Customarily, various civic groups arranged huge parties in the playgrounds of their neighborhood schools and Agassiz was never left out. Like most of the kids who couldn't afford store-bought costumes and simply improvised their own, Davey dressed up as a woman in one of Kathleen's old dresses and high-heeled shoes, while his kid brother went as himself.

The Runt had known for a long time that his big brother could really pick 'em up and lay 'em down in a footrace but seeing Davey in high-heels, the younger brother would've probably put his money on someone else, preferably someone wearing flats.

When the race for twelve-year-old boys was announced over the loud speaker, Davey pulled off the high-heeled shoes and lined up on his mark, barefooted. Unabashedly holding the shoes, one in each hand, Davey exploded off the starting line, the hem of his dress trailing behind in the breeze as his bare feet went spat-spat-spat-spat, barely touching the gravel. He won his heat by five yards, beating out seven other hard-running boys. His blazing speed, total lack of fear, and fine swimming ability made Davey an amazing older brother and irreplaceable sidekick to have. His kid brother idolized him, yet envied his qualities at the same time.

That golden Summer of 1944, back with his family, was filled with enough new experiences for the Runt that in remembering back, it would seem as long in duration as three other summers. It was that summer which served as the resumption point of their life together for Kathleen and her sons.

Chapter 11

Kathleen Remarries

Throughout 1944, during its sizzling Summer and continuing on into its cool, colorful Autumn, Tom Martin had regularly visited with Kathleen at the house a couple of evenings during the week and on Saturdays and Sundays, in his efforts to court her. Quite often they went dancing on their Saturday nights out. Davey and the Runt were always glad to see Tom but they usually were asked by Kathleen to play outside or were given money to go see a movie. It seemed that of late they had been seeing a lot of movies! Seems like Bob wasn't usually around when Tom came over, since he worked quite often during the evenings and on the weekends was too busy with his own dating plans.

Tom's courtship of Kathleen had crept along for what seemed like years when in reality, it was closer to a year and a half. He had proposed and given her an engagement ring on her birthday back in February, gaining her agreement to getting married this year. Kathleen's boys hoped that maybe this time it would be the real thing for all of them.

Yet, as the once colorful leaves of fall were blown around in tiny whirlwinds by November's chilly winds, the boys realized there wasn't going to be any wedding in time for Turkey Day. Hope then sprang anew, thinking that their Mom's wedding day would be in time for Christmas, the greatest event of the year for kids, but it too, came and went. On Friday the 29th, the boys resigned themselves to "maybe next year" since Sunday would be New Year's Eve and this year was nearly over.

December 30th dawned on a cold Saturday morning which found Kathleen waking her sons early. What? Getting up early on

Saturday? This better be worth it! Something's up. Their mother was all dressed up; crying, nervous and happy, all at once! Then she told them, "Tom and I are getting married today! We decided while we were out last night we would go downtown to City Hall and be married in a civil ceremony. Hurry up and get dressed, I have to leave very soon."

After their mother left, a tornado of housecleaning activity helped pass the late morning hours for the three brothers. Whenever the boys cleaned, each of them had certain tasks which they had chosen, and dusting was one of the Runt's tasks. In dusting off his mother's prized, three-mirrored vanity, he had first removed all of his mother's bottles of toilet water and cologne. As always, he paused for a moment, opened one of the bottles of the sweet-smelling flasks, and in his mind, was whisked back to a visit at his mother's small flat on Irving Park Road, years before.

He had opened the bottle knowing how certain melodies and scents can be associated with events that have been imprinted on one's memory. In these few moments, the memory which he had recalled was how dearly he had loved his mother and how much it once meant to him, just to visit with her for a day. Today, he had been reminded of his love for her and was very happy for her.

While the two younger boys gleefully anticipated a stepfather and looked forward to the grown-ups' return, Bob said he would wait to see how things turned out. Being older than his siblings and therefore more reserved in his enthusiasm, he appeared to be skeptical. Not letting their older brother's pessimistic attitude deflate the party balloon of their excitement, the younger boys happily greeted their mom and new stepfather at the door when they returned.

Eagerly they asked Tom, "What do you want us to call you?"

He replied, "Just call me Tom," unaware that his response had disappointed the two younger boys whose boyhood hopes had for so long, centered around the chance to call someone "Dad."

Within a few weeks Tom began dictating changes in their behavior as part of instituting his own rules, in order, he explained, to cultivate better manners among the boys. He'd never complained about their manners before he became their stepfather and when Kathleen asked why he was starting now, Tom replied that it was for their own good. For a month the changes went along with little friction as he slowly began to be accepted by the two younger boys.

Until one worrisome, dismal Friday night, when Tom had failed to come from work. Not knowing what had happened to him, Kathleen was fraught with worry. Friday night rolled into Saturday morning, then Saturday evening and still no Tom. Bob wasn't at home for he had just gone out on a date when Tom staggered home, disheveled and reeking of liquor. Tom proceeded to argue drunkenly with Kathleen and repeatedly harangued Davey and the Runt, shouting that he was the man of the house, and they had better stay out of it. At ten and twelve years of age, they didn't pose much of a threat to him. Any challenge to his claim of being the man of the house would have been issued by Bob, whom Tom may have perceived as a threat to his dominance over the family. As the minutes crawled by, Tom became menacingly abusive toward Kathleen, remaining so until demon whiskey clouded his mind so badly, that he lost his balance and like a felled tree, toppled to the floor, where he lay in a drunken stupor.

At that point, Davey ran to get the clothesline and he and the Runt hurriedly tied Tom up with it, after which, Kathleen sent Davey running to a pay phone in order to call Tom's older brother Frank, asking him to hurry over and intercede. Frank, a kind and decent man, came over quickly and shook his head when he saw what situation had developed. Untying Tom, he then led him out, telling his now mutely docile brother that he couldn't come back until he sobered up and promised to apologize to everyone.

All during their courtship, Tom had hidden his alcoholic bent and its emergence devastated Kathleen. She had left the father of her sons because of years of drunken abuse and now she had married another drunkard. In addition, Tom couldn't stop finding fault with her sons, the same boys he seemed to care so much about before they were married. The kind, wonderful man she thought she was married to, had turned Mr. Hyde-like, into some- one she didn't know. She had been frightened to a point where she just didn't know what to think or do and began to blame herself.

On Monday, Tom returned in tearful apologies to Kathleen and the boys who, all but Bob, felt sorry for him. They cried with him and forgave him, because he had promised never to do it again. Little did they know then, that over the next twenty-five years, they would come to learn that the most heartfelt promise of a sobered-up drunkard is empty and without meaning, so long as he refuses to admit that he has a drinking problem.

Two weeks later the sound of shattered glass awakened the Runt, followed by the sound of arguing but then he fell back into deep sleep. On their way to Sunday School the next morning, cold, wet raindrops splattered them as Davey and the Runt came upon their family's table-model radio, lying broken in the gravel lining the sidewalk. It lay where it had fallen after being thrown through the dining-room window by their enraged stepfather, just hours earlier. They were astonished and a little afraid. Afraid when they thought of the anger and violence that led to the mute, shattered radio lying in their path, in the rain.

Nearly every weekend afterwards was to be a "lost weekend," going on for years. Instead of helping in the support of their family as he had promised, the bulk of his paycheck went toward the maintenance and support of local taverns. The loving home life they once knew now seemed to have been taken over by Dr. Jekyll and Mr. Hyde who had taken up residence with them, when Tom's outlook changed from quiet and moody, to ranting and irrational arguing.

Conversely, on several occasions, the boys had seen how Tom's nasty, alcohol-induced mood could instantly change to one of patronizing charm, when another woman such as a neighbor lady or Aunt Etta or Aunt Maybelle stopped by. Aunt Etta never seemed to catch on to his act, or maybe she did and didn't want to antagonize him.

The cycle of drinking and sobering-up served to drive wedges between he and the boys that would never be fully resolved, and they were now glad that they didn't call him "Dad."

Fortunately, lost weekends were offset by the warmth of week nights at home and the closeness that the boys felt for each other and their mom. Forced to return to work, Kathleen had accepted a night shift job at the candy factory, and in order to keep up their household, she did her housework in the early evening right after supper, before she went to work. Tuesday evenings saw her and the younger two boys hanging up the wash, fluff-dried by the laundry who delivered it that afternoon. The Runt made up his own games around the semi-wet clothes, especially sheets which made great tents when they were opened up and hung from two lines.

On Tuesday evenings visitors would find a home filled with moisture from the drying clothes, which steamed up the windows, and they would find the radio tuned to the "Suppertime Frolic," the country and western program on station WJJD. Although it seemed that most Chicagoans despised "Hillbilly Music," Kathleen enjoyed the singing of artists like Eddy Arnold, Bob Atcher, and Red Foley, passing on her affection for the music to her sons by listening to it every evening. It was a blessing, that being originally from Tennessee, Tom didn't object to country music. An hour or so after sundown, WJJD would go off the air and the radio would then be tuned to one of the networks for an evening of great radio comedy entertainment.

On Kathleen's paycheck, combined with some help from Bob's part-time work after school, they managed to survive but until the boys became old enough to work full-time, theirs would always be a meager existence, without extras or any improvement in their standard of living. Often, on Friday night, while Kathleen was at work, Tom would come home drunk and for no particular reason, spank the two younger boys who were home alone.

By March of 1945, Tom had evolved from being a tolerant new stepfather with the potential of endearing himself to three stepsons, into an insecure overlord who, even when sober during the week, would not tolerate any conversation at the dinner table, and who demanded quiet during the evenings. School friends were not allowed to visit nor were after-school activities encouraged. For the two younger boys it was a terribly disappointing end to their long hoped wish for a loving stepfather. Bob who had held back caring, would come to despise the stepfather that he felt had been forced on them.

Weeks later, in May, millions of families rejoiced in the news that the war against Nazi Germany in Europe was over; the day would be remembered as VE-Day and it meant that the war was half-over! The Runt learned that no one would be coming home yet, since occupation duty was necessary in Europe and all other Allied forces' military efforts were to be shifted to the Pacific Campaign against Imperial Japan.

Soon after Nazi Germany's unconditional surrender, newspapers began publishing vivid pictures in their editions back home. Horrifying pictures they were, even for adult eyes to see as they documented the inhumanity of human beings against their own kind. The young boy read how spearheading United States Army units had been the first to enter and liberate Nazi concentration camps.

These were the death camps where millions of European Jews and people who were members of other groups who didn't fit into Hitler's "Herrenvolk" scheme of an Aryan "master race" had been systematically gassed, and their bodies burned in crematorium ovens. Looking through page after ghastly page of revealing photographs, the Runt saw ovens full of ashes and human bones and dead bodies in ovens that hadn't yet been ignited when the liberating forces arrived. Those pictures were not faked, nor were the stories inspired by fantasy. In the Runt's own heart and mind, he prayed that this would never happen again to anyone else.

A few weeks later, on a balmy evening in June, perhaps as a welcome respite from the mugginess of an early Summer, Kathleen had arranged for Bob to go along with his kid brothers and a few of their friends, to the Lincoln theatre, to see "Cobra Woman." Designated as the troop leader, Bob shepherded all of them during the trip to the show, during the movie, and the trip back. But he seemed to really enjoy the responsibility.

Despite Bob's fraternal care, he couldn't protect his kid brother completely, for during the movie the Runt fell in love with the female lead. A beautiful, exotic, French actress named Maria Montez had played the title role and was truly beautiful and deadly. It was the second film the Runt had seen her in, the first one being "Ali Baba and the Forty Thieves." Too late, for as they left the movie after seeing the end twice, the Runt floated out with wings on his feet. Luckily, his infatuation lasted about two weeks.

In mid-July, good news drifted down from Grandpaw Kelly's. The three puppies that Snoojie had whelped on Memorial Day, were weaned and ready for new homes. With that, all of Kathleen's sons set up a united front. They wanted one of the pups very badly and besides, he would make a good watchdog! How Kathleen was ever able to persuade Tom to allow them to bring a puppy home, would remain a mystery. One can only guess that it may have been due to a twinge of conscience on Tom's part.

The Runt and Davey were lucky enough to get to pick out the chubby, squirming puppy they wanted and felt they had made a great choice. He was the cutest and smartest pup of the litter, and most resembled a shepherd-collie mix. The two younger boys wanted to name their new pup, "Teddy Bear" because he looked so much like one but Bob favored "Bosco," which his siblings thought was a dumb name for their dog. Eventually, majority rule prevailed, and "Teddy Bear" became the newest member of their family, his name soon being shortened to just "Teddy."

Teddy's first few nights were memorable in that he never stopped howling until after two in the morning, because he missed his mother and litter-mates. Not big on dogs anyway, Tom gave Teddy one more night, then he would have to go back to Grandpaw Kelly's. Whether Teddy understood Tom or three nights happened to be the magic number, he didn't howl afterwards, and was allowed to stay with them. After a week of keeping him in a big box up on the attic landing, the boys pleaded with Kathleen to let them keep Teddy in the house. Saying no at first, she relented when told of their fears that the rats they had seen in the basement might kill their puppy. From then on, Teddy slept in the house.

Doted on by all three of the boys, Teddy was loved most by the Runt who became his master. What made this so was the loving care he gave his dog over the years as he fed the dog, walked the dog, and brushed the dog. They became inseparable in years to come, so much so that whenever Kathleen needed her youngest son to come home, she simply told Teddy to go find him. Many times, the Runt would be dismayed to find his street ballgame interrupted as Teddy came running up, sometimes with a note attached to his collar telling his master to bring home a loaf of bread or quart of milk.

During those carefree, childhood late Spring and Summer days, the boys still didn't own a bike. Each weekend, they would ask for and receive a quarter each from their mom and rent bikes from the bike shop on the south side of Lincoln Avenue, just west of Lakewood and George. A shiny quarter each bought them one fleeting hour on the bikes of their choice and how furiously their legs pedaled for that hour!

One Sunday, just hanging around on the sidewalk brought them a chance to earn some money. The hot, afternoon sun burned fiercely in their eyes when the owner of the poultry company came outside of the plant and spotted the two younger Ryan brothers leaning up against a lamppost. Approaching them, he asked if they would like to come in and cool off, help him out, and earn some money by chasing chickens for him. Like a donkey following a carrot, they were interested, although he must have already known that they had experience chasing chickens around the neighborhood. During the next hour they went through the air-cooled plant and gathered up all of the loose chickens they found, turning them over to the shift foreman. While there, the Runt had been able to see the whole processing line from start to finish. Not a pretty process but it seemed efficient.

On the first floor, a chicken's legs were shackled by a worker, to a rod hanging from a conveyor line. Hoisted upward to the second floor, the next area was the killing floor where a razor was used to cut the chicken's throat by hand and the belt carried the chicken onward, leaving a trail of blood below it. The boy looked up into the eyes of the large, black man, who had been assigned the task of killing the chickens, and saw sadness in them. Moving on, the Runt watched the chickens being carried along toward the scald vat in which the now-expired chickens were immersed in order to loosen their feathers. Further down the line, feathers were plucked by hand, chickens were eviscerated by hand, then ran through another scald vat followed by a cold vat, then packed, by hand. The process didn't take more than minutes.

Emerging from the poultry house of death, the boys walked out into the warmth of the bright afternoon sun, having earned enough change for the movies and maybe some popcorn. While they didn't feel much like eating at that particular moment, they were feeling especially glad to be alive.

A few evenings later, on a clear, summer night when all should have been well with the world, the Runt looked for and found, trouble. Perhaps it was due to cockiness felt after having won all of the fights that had been forced upon him, but he had allowed his resentment of a newcomer to fester too long, and the Runt picked a fight. He fought with neighbor and friend, Woody Fleck's cousin Rich, who had just come up from Kentucky. After several seconds of swinging and scuffling, Rich had the Runt pinned down until his antagonist said he gave up. After holding out for what seemed to be ten minutes, the Runt capitulated and Rich Fleck released him.

Before he could walk away, the Runt was confronted by his brother who said, "Now go over and shake hands with Rich!"

"No! Don't wanna!"

Then Davey clarified his position, "You better do it before I beat you up too!"

Relenting, his kid brother said, "Oh, alright, but why should I? Where were you when I needed help? You once said you'd come if I needed help and you just stood around!"

Responding, Davey told him, "You shake hands with Rich, to show that there are no hard feelings so that you'll remain friends," he explained. "But you want to know why I didn't help you?" Davey asked. "First of all, it was a fair fight; you and Rich were evenly matched and you were losing all by yourself. Second, you started the fight!" Then he shouted the question, "Didn't I tell you never to start a fight?" Continuing, Davey said, "Since I told you never start a fight I wasn't going to help you anyhow. I hope you learned a lesson from it."

It was the first and last fight his kid brother ever started.

Chapter 12

George Street Paper Boys

During that Summer, seeing his family strapped, Davey felt the need to contribute financially to his family's needs and went to the circulation office of a local neighborhood newspaper and signed on for one of the paper routes. Arriving home flushed from running all the way, Davey blurted the news to his mom that the paper route would pay him one-half of whatever he collected. Kathleen, pleased at the prospect of additional income, was hopeful that a few more dollars might offset the drain on her husband's paycheck caused by his drinking.

In hearing about the route, an excited kid brother volunteered to help Davey, by sharing the route with him. Davey welcomed the help because when he had been assigned the paper route he didn't realize that it was one of the paper's largest routes with over 200 paying customers. Bounded on the North by Melrose Street and on the South by Lincoln Avenue, the route's eastern and western boundaries were Southport and Greenview. The route comprised several blocks of the west side of Southport, and the 1400 block of Barry, Fletcher, Belmont, and one side of Melrose.

When her sons brought home their first pay of $3.00 each, Kathleen stressed the idea of savings, whereby each of them would save a dollar in the bank, keep a dollar for spending, and contribute one dollar to the household, an arrangement with which they agreed. None of her sons would have ever thought of not helping out financially. Over the next year, two paper deliveries and three collection trips weekly, would be faithfully performed by the two enterprising young boys and in a few cases, with a lot of help from their mom.

All paper boys having routes in Davey's and the Runt's district always picked up their bundles of papers at an unsheltered dropoff point, open to the elements, behind a little shoe-shine stand located on Wellington just east of Southport. It was operated by a crusty, loquacious old Greek who, depending on his mood, had considered the boys coming there as a nuisance to be disdained or friendly ears to hear his verbose chatter.

On one greenish-gray Sunday morning, after the skies had opened up and drenched the North Side, Davey and his brother found that all of the newspaper bundles had been completely soaked by the torrential rain. Seeing that the papers shouldn't be delivered in their soggy condition, the resourceful boys hauled them home and with Kathleen's help, managed to dry them out, several papers at a time in the oven throughout the day. By three o'clock, the two busy brothers were heading out to the route where the salvaged papers were delivered late but readable.

Paper boys still collected personally from their customers back in those days and during a bout with the flu which took down both boys simultaneously, Kathleen did the collections in their place. She asked each of them to jot down the names and addresses of their customers who hadn't yet paid. Upon receiving the list, she then struck out for their route. Returning home, she seemed to have enjoyed being out meeting people and explaining to their customers why she was collecting. She had received tips from some customers who usually tipped and the boys told her to keep them, for she had collected the money.

The boys were still sick two days later on Sunday. Having no car, Kathleen took their handwritten route books and wagon, picked up the bundles of papers with their route number and delivered the papers by herself. Being a mother who loved her family, Kathleen had determination and believed in fulfilling commitments, traits which she endeavored all through their childhood, to instill in her sons.

As the Runt resumed delivering his papers on Sunday mornings, he could hear the pealing of Saint Alphonsus' bells, calling its many faithful to Mass. Going northward from house to house along Southport, he was passed by crowds of churchgoers on their way South toward Saint Alphonsus on Wellington, which drew its parishioners all the way from around Addison Street. He always felt guilty since the crowds of worshipers served to remind him that he hadn't gone to Sunday School since he began working the paper route.

On a warm May Sunday, when the April rains had given way to sunshine, the Ryan boys came into a monetary windfall. Across Greenview, the street that marked their paper route's western boundary, sat their newspaper's circulation office which usually opened around nine o'clock but not this Sunday. This they discovered upon reaching the corner of Fletcher and Greenview from where they could see that the office was besieged by impatient customers, anxious to buy a copy of the newspaper.

Suddenly they were spotted by the crowd, which one by one, began hurrying toward them. "Hey kid! You wanta sell one of those papers?" shouted a large, portly, sweating man who was upon them with a quarter in his hand. Not waiting for his fifteen cents change, he charged off, as the space he had corpulently occupied was instantly filled by a flurry of outstretched hands offering them coins. When it was over, the boys had been enriched by a $4.25 bonanza. Quite a haul when one considers that they generally collected $12.00 per week, receiving their 50% netted them only $6.00. Needless to say, they were chastised by their manager for doing so but they argued that at least the customers had been able to buy their papers! As usual, the lecture they received had gone in one ear and out the other.

This wasn't the first time a difference of opinion arose between the circulation manager and the boys. Davey and the Runt had confirmed on the route map that theirs was one of the biggest routes on the paper. There was an awareness on both sides that with over 200 paying customers, their route had one of the highest collections in the district. They usually chose to ignore their manager's instructions to deliver papers to everyone on the route whether they paid or not.

Strictly out of principle, the boys delivered only to those customers who paid, since they believed it wasn't fair for everyone to receive the paper but only make some suckers pay. It didn't make sense, for if the paying customers protested and stopped paying, the boys would be delivering papers for nothing! They always had extra papers, since they always received 350 copies and would sell spare copies if asked. The Ryan brothers always kept an eye out for the circulation manager's car and when sighted, they would deliver to each doorway but only until he drove off. Often one of them would spot his light gray car parked down a side street across from their route. It became an enjoyable game of cat and mouse to them.

After a year, Davey was able to get a different part-time job working as a delivery boy at one of the grocery stores and the Runt took responsibility for the whole route for the succeeding four years. He used a wagon to haul the papers in Summer and in Winter, depending on the amount of snow cover, often used his four-foot sled in the snow. Frozen toes were an occupational hazard for a young boy out in sub-zero weather, yet how often friendly customers would allow him to come in and warm up, to the end of giving him hot cocoa and cookies.

A standing Sunday morning wakeup call existed in the first floor rear apartment on the odd-numbered side of the 1400 block of Fletcher. The mother of an attractive daughter in her twenties was to waken her when he came by. She had taken a liking to the Runt and would rise from a warm bed to join him at the kitchen table just to talk and get her hands coated with ink from the newsprint, rolling newspapers. Originally, she and her mother allowed him to come in and roll papers in the warmth of their kitchen until the young lady asked him to teach her how to roll newspapers. It somehow baffled the Runt that such a nice woman would get up early on Sunday just to talk and roll papers but he appreciated her company.

Giving wasn't one-sided however, for the Runt often did favors for the elderly on his route, such as running to the corner store for a lady customer on crutches. It seemed that older people were just happy to have someone come by and talk with them. One older woman, Mrs. Spies, whose gregarious, retired-policeman husband had passed away months earlier, once advised the Runt, "Don't speak so softly, for I can't always hear you."

Replying, he said,"I speak softly because I am ashamed of how I sound."

Saintly Mrs. Spies gave him a piece of advice which he took and remembered, "Don't be ashamed of the way you speak, but if you don't speak up, then more people may not hear you or understand you as easily, and that would be a shame."

A very sweet and very old lady customer named Mrs. Langer, who lived in the basement flat of a two-story building on Belmont Avenue usually asked him if he could fill up her coal scuttle from a coal shed out back. She lived alone and he was glad to help out by doing such a small favor. Heck, he used to haul two coal scuttles when his grandmaw had sent him out to the shed for coal. When Mrs. Langer invited him to come in and warm up by the fire in her small stove, the young boy wondered how she managed to stay warm. Since his elderly customer couldn't afford to pay for the paper, the Runt always left her a free one, one of the many extra copies he had.

After a year or so, there came a day when Mrs. Langer didn't answer when he knocked at her door, so he just left the paper. She didn't answer his knock at her door the next time, nor during that week. Two weeks later, his knock was answered by a young couple who had moved into the apartment. When inquiring if they would like the paper delivered, he asked, "Can you tell me what happened to Mrs. Langer?"

He was saddened by their reply, "She passed away."

Over the five years during which the Runt was to work his paper route, he would lose many of the elderly people who had become his friends.

Owners and bartenders working the taverns located along the paper route were always kind to and protective of this young newspaper boy. On many stifling summer days when the Runt brought their copy of the paper into the tavern and asked for a glass of cold water, he was given a glass of cola or orange juice instead. In collecting for the newspaper, the pockets of his blue jeans would bulge with loose change, for which the bartenders or owners would gladly exchange dollar bills after he and they counted it out on the bar. During the Winter, the tavern-keepers always offered him the chance to warm up for a few minutes. The kid didn't notice how smoke-filled the taverns were until he stepped back outside, coughing when the blast of cold air reached his lungs and tasting the pungent smoke.

Most neighborhood taverns back then, were decent, respectable places, having two entrances, the usual front entrance and a side entrance known as the "Family Entrance." Often the young boy saw an elderly man and sometimes, an elderly woman, going out of the side door, carrying a small, covered, tin bucket, brimming with foamy draft beer. Those small buckets of beer may well have been the forebears of the six-pack of draft beer. The friendly taverns would soon be where he first got to see his beloved Cubs play ball on television, that miracle of home entertainment. Although television was a marvel, it was available at a marvelous price - too high for most consumers. The better taverns found that in order to compete, they had to have a television set for their customers to watch as they sat at the bar.

On a humid, cloudy afternoon about four-thirty, the television set in a Belmont Avenue tavern was turned up loud for a ballgame on Channel 9, when the Runt opened the tavern door to deliver the paper. The game featured the White Sox against Boston's Red Sox and Ted Williams was coming up to bat. Pausing for a moment, only to watch the American League's greatest all-around hitter, the boy watched as the Splendid Splinter swung from the heels on a low outside pitch. The hometown announcer's calm, biased narrative belied the unusual nature of the event taking place, reluctantly reporting, "It's going back, back, back; it's in the seats. A home run by Ted Williams has just put the Red Sox out in front." While White Sox fans at Comiskey Park may not have been thrilled by Williams' feat nor its timing, the Runt had never seen a low outside pitch get turned into an opposite-field home run by a left-handed batter up into the left-field seats. For the Runt, it only reinforced what he already believed about Ted Williams, that he was one of the two greatest hitters alive, the other being Stan Musial of the National League's St. Louis Cardinals.

On days when he didn't need to tend his paper route, there were plenty of things for curious young boys to do around the neighborhood. It was no problem for he and Davey to get a bone for their dog, not with a Darling Rendering Company truck stopping everyday across the street. After asking its driver for a bone, they were given a couple of beef leg bones that were nearly as big as Teddy.

If bored, they sometimes moseyed down the street past the poultry place, past Swift & Company to the railroad siding situated alongside a cold-storage warehouse branch of Wilson & Company. On a good day a crew would be unloading a refrigerator car that had been dropped off at Wilson's railroad spur. To kids, the men all seemed tall and they wore knee-length, white, denim coats which sometimes had bloodstains on them.

Each of the warehouse workers carried a nasty-looking thick meat-hook. The end of the hook was sharp and with it, a worker hooked a side of beef and pulled it toward him, hoisted it onto his shoulder and carried it out of the refrigerator car. One really neat thing they had, was this steel rail mounted from the ceiling of the dock, along which pulleys were pushed back and forth. As a side of beef was taken from a refrigerator car, the worker hung the tied legs of the side of beef over the pointed end of an S-shaped hook as the rounded end of the hook hung over the pulley. This done, he simply pushed the side of beef along the rail into the icy air of the warehouse.

Try as they might, the boys never got to follow the workers inside and enjoy the cool air for long since they were rousted out every time a worker found them inside.

Living two doors away from the poultry place, it wasn't unusual for an occasional chicken to be seen strutting through a neighborhood yard. A big mistake for the chicken, since it usually meant Sunday chicken dinner for someone. On the "Day of the Chickens," however, there were chicken dinners for everyone who had the old get up and go!

To fully appreciate the chaos that resulted that hot, mid-Summer day in 1945, one would have needed to be there. The midday sun glared hot through his windshield as an impatient, sweaty driver attempted to back his straight rig into the dock of the poultry place. Cutting his sweat-covered steering wheel too sharply, his back wheel missed the poultry place's driveway and headed toward the curb instead. When the truck's back wheel bounced up and back down from the curb, the sudden impact jostled its overload of crated chickens. In addition, the load of crates hadn't been too well-secured and the drop from the curb caused a large crate to dislodge, teeter back and forth precariously on the edge of the tailgate for what seemed an eternity, until at last, it crashed to the pavement. Upon impact, the old wooden crate disintegrated, setting free at least a hundred chickens.

Standing not more than ten feet away, watching this dream moment frozen in time, were the two younger Ryan brothers. Within moments they were up to their knees in frantic poultry fleeing helter-skelter past them! Recovering from their momentary shock the two boys split up and chased chickens in and out of every yard in the neighborhood, alerting their neighbors as they ran through.

Soon it seemed that all of their friends and neighbors were involved in what would be remembered as the "Great Chicken Chase," competing against workers from the poultry place. What a melee it was: dozens of grown people, both residents and poultry workers, shamelessly chasing chickens over a quarter-mile square area. The tally for the Ryan family was chicken dinner for two Sundays, but only after the Runt, standing outside their ground level basement swore to the poultry workers who had come by that he hadn't caught any chickens, as Davey kept two chickens quiet inside the basement door. The unwritten rule of the neighborhood was, if a chicken was found walking around free, it belonged to its finder.

Speaking of their basement, it was an eerie place to be on a rainy day when outside activities were curtailed. Having only a dirt floor and few windows, it reminded the Runt of the Roman catacombs he saw pictured in an encyclopedia, except that they hadn't found any skulls or bones, yet. Damp, musty air assailed their young noses when they opened its door, welcoming them to the nether world. On good days, or bad, depending on one's perspective, they might hear the skittering of tiny clawed feet as the rats scurried away to safer places.

It was late afternoon on a nothing-to-do kind of day in the basement, when Davey, chasing out a rat, suddenly fell to one knee, painfully holding his leg.

All he said was, "Get Bob! Get Bob!"

His kid brother dashed up the stairs, yelling for Bob as he ran, shouting "Davey's been hurt!"

Hurrying in the opposite direction, Bob blew past the Runt above the first floor, running down the stairs two at a time. By the time the little brother caught up to the oldest, Bob was already carrying Davey in his arms back up the stairs. Catching up to them at the second floor, the Runt found out that in the dim light of the basement, Davey had stepped down close to a post having a rusty nail protruding from it, which had ripped a three-inch gash to the bone of his calf.

When she got home, Kathleen took Davey to the Alexian Brothers Hospital where three stitches were needed to close the wound. Throughout those painful moments, Davey never cried. He didn't have to, for his little brother was still at home, where he cried for Davey until he was brought home. At the hospital, Davey was told that for several days, he was to rest the leg and cut back on some his strenuous activities. Good luck with that advice, Doc! The kid was hobbling around after the second day; too many things to do and too many places to see to let a few stitches cramp his style.

Davey's leg healed just in time for him and his little brother to welcome their new neighbors, the Gentrys to their building. For the year that the Ryans had lived in the second floor flat, the first floor flat had been vacant, and they welcomed the company. Friendly as all-getout, the Gentry's were from Tennessee and while Davey and his brother thought it wasn't quite as good as Texas, they allowed that Will, a moon-faced, chubby kid, close to their age, was an okay guy and they became friends. Kathleen and Tom also welcomed the idea of having a family occupying the flat downstairs, if only for security reasons.

Now, with the addition of Will, the three musketeers, Davey, Ronnie, and the Runt, had become four. Over the next year or so, they would become good friends, finding enough interesting things to do while managing to stay out of trouble. Ignorant of the ancient teenage taboo against dating older girls, the Runt always wondered why big brother Bob wasn't interested in Norma Jean Gentry, the pretty girl downstairs, who was only two years older than Bob. The Runt himself became the target of matchmakers Davey and Will, who, because it made him blush three shades of red, adopted the habit of teasing the Runt about Will's younger sister Lizabeth.

The Gentry's arrival led to the occasional playing of country music on their back porch during the warm evenings. A special treat was enjoyed when their cousin Betty Lou Gentry came over and sat in with her amplified Hawaiian guitar. It was hard for Davey's little brother to figure out: whether Davey liked Betty Lou's guitar-playing or Betty Lou the most.

The Runt noticed the beginning of strange changes in his brother's behavior which he couldn't explain. Unaware that the actions he detected were puberty's early effects on his older brother, who had become much more interested in girls than in playing ball or kicking the can. Baffled, the younger brother wondered how any girl could be more interesting than a good game of "One Caught - All Caught" or repeatedly ringing the doorbell of the powerhouse across the street until the night watchman would wake up, furiously throw open the door, and chase them down the street to no avail.

Following the Gentrys in taking up residence on George Street, the Towers family, a family of seven also from Tennessee, arrived with little fanfare. Moving in up at the corner on the other side of the street, the Towers' were friends of the Gentrys. Tall, thin, and amiable, Josh Towers was a friend of Will's and was placed in the Runt's class at school, while Josh's blue-eyed, honey-blonde sister Marsha would someday become a girlfriend of thirteen-year-old Davey. Although the Runt was too young to care at the time, the Gentry and Towers families seemed to present evidence that Tennessee could be known for its pretty girls, because each of the two families had produced several lovely girls.

Invited to several of the birthday parties celebrated at the Gentry's and Towers' homes, the two brothers found that these pretty, genteel, and refined girls from the South seemed to favor kissing games. That was all well and fine with Davey and Will but Davey's little brother of ten-and-a-half thought that such games were silly and you were bound to get germs from them. After one party where, upon leaving, he got cornered by Tara Mae Towers, the seventeen-year-old yet very pretty sister who thought the Runt was so-o-o-o-o cute and planted a wet kiss right on his young, inexperienced lips. So firm was he in his belief of germs that he tore himself out of her clutches and ran all the way home where he hastily began to gargle a well-known antiseptic for five minutes. Little did he know then that years later, at the advanced age of eighteen, he would daydream about the possibility of encountering Tara Mae again.

Throughout that gorgeous Summer, all four of the boys went to the park, the beaches, and to that dangerous off-limits place that the Ryan boys' parents dreaded: "the Rocks." The Rocks were huge, quarried, cubic rocks at least eight by eight by ten feet in size, piled against the shore of Lake Michigan to prevent erosion of the shoreline. Because of the slippery nature of the submerged rocks and a strong undertow, swimming and diving were prohibited, as the Park District life guards did not patrol the Rocks. Self-destructive swimmers and divers usually reduced their own numbers by a few each Summer when they ignored the warnings, giving the Rocks an unwarranted reputation.

The boys liked to go there only to feel the cool lake wind in their faces on a hot, humid day, and to hear the crashing of the waves against the unyielding rocks beneath them. They weren't crazy enough to try swimming there but still didn't tell any of the adults that they visited the Rocks since their parents would only worry after the fact. It wasn't that they were thoughtful, they just didn't want to give their stepfather any reason to punish them.

If the beach wasn't a good idea on a particular day, then while at Lincoln Park, the boys could always stop and visit its Zoo. The Runt always liked to stop and visit the "Eagle," a replica of a Viking ocean-going ship with its many oars and shields above the oars. Within a matter of seconds, the young boy's imagination had taken him aboard a sea-going dragon ship, transformed into a brawny, battle-hardened Norseman, the chief of a hardy, boisterous crew on the lookout for other ships and lands to plunder.

Chicago was blessed with many Park District pools, distributed among the city's neighborhoods. Our heroes' favorite spa was Hamlin Pool on the North Side, where one could find them on those days when the asphalt was scorched into softness on the city's streets and the beach seemed too far away. A Godsend to underprivileged kids who enjoyed its clean, cold water, the pool, was patrolled by Park District life guards who tolerated no horseplay in the pool area. Scheduled on alternate days, boys enjoyed the pool on different days than the girls.

After working up a tremendous appetite during an afternoon of swimming and baking in the sun, if any of them had enough change, they went over to the Ma and Pa grocery store across the street from the pool and bought some candy, potato chips, or shoestring potatoes. What a great treat it was for a ten-year-old, to chomp down a bag of salty, greasy shoestrings in order to quash the hunger pangs brought on by an afternoon of vigorous swimming in cold water and have the energy to walk back home. An exhilarating, refreshing way to spend a hot, humid day! A really great way to spend a childhood Summer during the war, a war that would soon end.

Chapter 13

The War Is Over!

As if in anger, the August sun burned hot in the western sky, its rays spearing under the window shade and scorching the kitchen floor as the Runt's family sat around the table having dinner. However, the early evening of Tuesday, August 14th would not be remembered for its humidity.

Several articles had appeared in the newspapers lately which reported that a secret weapon had been used against the Japanese. Called an "Atomic Bomb," two of them had been dropped on two of Japan's major cities, Hiroshima and Nagasaki. Neighborhood kids had been talking about what such a bomb could have been like and imagining what a terrible force it must have had in order to destroy a city. Up until then, the biggest bomb any of them had ever heard of had been called a "blockbuster." Kids and grownups alike seemed to be waiting for the next move of the Japanese.

Like wailing banshees, the screams of air raid sirens suddenly split the sultry air, drowning out all other early evening sounds. Moments later, blaring automobile horns added to the tumult. At a loss to explain why sirens and horns should be sounding, they rushed to turn on the radio, and it warmed just in time for them to hear a voice on the radio repeating a news bulletin: "Imperial Japan has agreed to unconditional surrender! The war is over!"

A holiday feeling of joy washed over the boys who asked to go outside and celebrate with everyone else but Tom told them, no, they had to finish their dinner. Later they were allowed to go out but not until after most of the pandemonium had subsided.

Occurring two weeks later, a most historic event transpired half a world away in Tokyo Harbor, on the battleship, USS Missouri. After the terms of surrender were signed by Japanese officials, all across America, Sunday, the 2nd of September, 1945 would come to be known as "VJ-Day." It signaled the end of one era but the beginning of another, the "Atomic Age."

After the previous days's events Labor Day seemed anti-climactic, and the traditional end of summer vacation passed quietly, until the realization struck home in Davey's mind. "Is vacation really over?" he asked rhetorically on Labor Day night, as he stared in mock disbelief at the calendar. Each semester, Davey faced the first day of school with a sense of dread his kid brother couldn't fathom, since the Runt accepted schools as readily as he accepted the changes in the seasons; a result of his mother's encouragement.

The need for schooling and studying hard had been emphasized by Kathleen since they first began school. She stressed their need for an education in order to better their lot in life, prodding them with, "You may have been born poor, but with an education you won't always have to be poor." She extolled honesty as a virtue, having only contempt for those who didn't have, yet took what they needed from others, saying, "Being poor don't give us the right to steal from someone else!"

Settling down at his desk on the first day of school, the Runt looked around the classroom and saw that the old, pendulum-driven, wooden Seth Thomas clocks which occupied a spot near the door of every classroom had been replaced by modern, round, electric clocks with second hands that clicked off the seconds. He also saw that he had been separated from most of his old classmates, including Marjorie Cribbens. Making new friends would require time and lots of effort but he had done it before and felt confident that he could make new friends in this class.

Marjorie, however, was in the same class with his downstairs neighbor and friend, Will Gentry. Perhaps it was the euphoria that everyone still felt from the ending of the war but it was at this time that Will played a cruel joke on the Runt by setting him up. Will had manipulated the Runt into thinking that his friend Marjorie was very interested in going to the show with him. Naturally, since the Runt was shy, Will volunteered to act as his go-between.

The appointed Sunday afternoon was an early fall delight, with warm, dry weather and bright sunshine into mid-afternoon, when the young patsy told his mom he was going to the show. At the designated time, he appeared at the rendezvous point in his blue slacks, white shirt, and red pullover. There he waited fruitlessly for an hour but Marjorie didn't show. Embarrassed, he went into the theatre, losing himself and his red face in the crowd.

The Runt was much too embarrassed to approach Marjorie for nearly two weeks and finally one day he asked her if Will had ever mentioned going to the movies. Marjorie answered that Will Gentry had never discussed anything like that with her. Feeling very foolish over the incident, the Runt felt too ashamed to speak with Marjorie afterwards and for the rest of his time at Agassiz, would feel awkward around her, and avoided talking with her. When he asked Will why he lied, Will just explained it all away as a joke. The Runt had liked Marjorie since the first grade and being embarrassed by his friend Will caused his friendship with him to cool.

As days went by, he couldn't help but notice the effects of the war's end that were beginning to be felt in his neighborhood. Ronnie Kowalczk's brother Jim arrived home from serving in Europe with the Army Air Corps, and soon his other brother John, who had won the Silver Star and Purple Heart, came home. Other neighbors and relatives began coming home one or two at a time, bringing happiness to homes throughout the neighborhood. More and more, one could see uniforms or parts of uniforms being worn everywhere. One also saw the other heroes, men who had also been badly wounded during the war and returned horribly burned, paralyzed, or missing limbs.

Months passed into December and Christmas was "just around the corner." For the first time since Pearl Harbor, the Yuletide spirit could truly be felt in the air once more. Christmas cheer permeated the night air as a light snow fell on Chicago that evening when Tom and his youngest stepson went shopping in the Lincoln-Belmont shopping area. In buying all their gifts for Kathleen and the others, they had trudged in and out of one store after another traveling several blocks up Lincoln Avenue, having a good time just talking together and laughing.

On this shopping trip, the Runt had seen how Tom had been fun to be with once more, almost like during the days before his mom and Tom were married. He remembered the times when Tom took him to the clinic when his mom couldn't. Tom had been there when he panicked while confronted with a monster X-ray machine and had talked him back down to calmness once more. Too many operations or treatments had caused the Runt to lose the courage that had enabled him to willingly climb onto operating room gurneys. For a while he had been just another scared little boy who wouldn't go near the machine.

Tom seemed to get along with the Runt best, of his stepsons, perhaps because he was the youngest and still most adaptive to a new stepfather. In complimenting the Runt on his "smartness" and his ability to hold on to money, he said that money didn't burn a hole in his pocket like it did with Davey. Too bad Tom didn't realize his silly mistake in complimenting the youngest boy while putting down the brother he loved, in the next breath. Nearly every night, the Runt prayed for a way that God could leave the good in Tom but take away the nastiness that accompanied his drinking and the mindless tirades which followed.

Having finished their shopping at Belmont Avenue, they paused to put down their huge bags full of packages, to let the blood back into their fingers. Tom quickly dug out a cigarette and began fumbling for a book of matches.

From near the curb along Belmont a voice shouted, "Hey buddy! Got a light?"

Turning in the direction of the voice, they saw a man kneeling on a board at the curb, selling pencils. Lighting a match, Tom replied, "Here you go, pal," and within cupped hands reached out and held the glowing match to the man's cigarette.

"Thanks buddy. Merry Christmas!"

The Runt saw the man's young face, and realized that he couldn't be much older than his brother Bob. Looking down, he noticed that the young man wasn't kneeling; he just had no legs from the knees down. The young man's board had casters attached to its base in order for him to push himself about as he sat on the board. Spotting his "Ruptured Duck" veteran's pin, the Runt believed that the young veteran had lost his legs in the war.

143

Overcome with a feeling that it was so unfair, the Runt suddenly felt a tightness in his throat and his eyes began to burn. Not wanting to give in to tears, the boy looked east on Belmont, above and beyond the veteran, and in the distance through the falling snow, his eyes dimly made out the image of the large, red neon cross on St. Luke's steeple. Staring at the cross through tears in his eyes, he felt momentary religious doubt. Questions formed in his mind asking if there really was a God, why did He allow human beings to have wars, and where was He when this young man lost his legs? It seemed as if, for this night, the Christmas spirit had left the boy and he asked Tom if they could go home.

Fortunately, the majority of returning veterans had avoided serious injuries while in harm's way but did not escape injury altogether. Every one who came back and all who had waited at home, had been affected personally in some way, even Maybelle's ex-husband, Lee, who after his discharge, returned to his hometown but found a new life apart from Maybelle and their son, Roy, since their divorce had long since become final. He was one of the fortunate ones who had come back alive and in one piece, yet one whose personal life had been changed for all time by the war.

Even though the war ended in September of 1945, it would be New Year's Eve before Chick could return home. Christmas had been celebrated at the Runt's home, with he and Davey getting a new Schwinn bike which they were to share. However, Christmas at their grandparents had been postponed until Chick's homecoming, when he could share the holiday with them. For once in the Runt's life, something was more important than Christmas: the anticipation of seeing his good old Uncle Chick again.

Upon his arrival, most of Chick's family noticed a change in him that war had visited upon many who had endured its pain and horror. More quiet and reserved than could be remembered, Chick seemed somewhat distant for a year or so. Even in years to come, Chick still never told any of the boys of his war experiences nor the carnage behind his battle stars. His war years were put behind him, while he, like millions of other ex-GI's, tried to put his life back together. In time he would once again become the fun-loving uncle that his nephews had known long ago.

Fate hadn't always been so generous with the many sons and fathers she had called away to war. Often, the Runt remembered back to the bright autumn sun of an unforgettable September afternoon back in 1943, when he learned of one boy who wasn't coming back. The beneficent sun couldn't brighten the tragic news that accompanied the Runt's distraught aunts when they had arrived, weeping, at the Kelly home. He had been off in the dining room, playing, when he heard them come into the kitchen and the door was closed between the kitchen and the dining room.

Hearing the women weeping, the Runt felt the sadness that carved its way through the door which separated them from him, yet not knowing why. Then he heard the name, Earl. An invisible, solemn pall of grief filled the room as he slid open the door and cautiously sidled in where everyone had gathered. He asked what was wrong but no one answered him. Finally, his Aunt Maybelle, who always had that little extra internal strength, called him to her. Tears began to well in his eyes as she tearfully told him that cousin Earl, the gentle boy from Missouri had been killed in action during the invasion of Italy, on the beach at a place called Salerno.

As some men and women came home from military service others went away. Now it came to be Bob's turn to go off to faraway places. Wanting to avoid further, more serious altercations with his stepfather, Bob enlisted in the Navy at the end of January, not even thirty days since his Uncle Chick's return. Just seventeen, he was able to sign up for only two years with Kathleen's permission. Devastated by his decision, Kathleen allowed him to go knowing that she would again be separated from him, while his younger brothers would find a big emptiness in the house without his reassuring presence.

If he had to enlist it was a good time for Bob to join up, since the war was over and Chicago was in the grip of another dreaded Midwestern Winter. Sent first to Memphis, Tennessee where the weather was a lot milder and the girls were supposed to be friendly, Bob was scheduled into Boot Camp for a good six weeks. Whether the local girls were friendly or not, Bob never got a chance to find out, since he wrote that he hadn't been able to get off the base!

Whenever a void is formed in nature it somehow becomes filled before long. Having seen his oldest brother go off to the Navy, the Runt was just a little down when at the end of the semester Miss Callahan gave him a double-promotion, his second, putting him in the second semester of the sixth grade. There he would be competing with kids who were generally a year older than he and where the void in his life would be filled somewhat. Showing up in his new room the next Monday, he looked around to see another roomful of strangers and for an introverted kid, the challenge of making new friends.

One of the girls wasn't such a stranger to him though, having seen her often in the halls and the playground but she had always been a grade ahead of him. A kid who had just turned eleven in a roomful of twelve and thirteen-year-olds, he soon got his chance to meet this girl who seemed to glide along when she walked, not needing to take steps. It was while studying shared maps of the Southwestern United States, that he would get to know the exquisite Carolyn Puente.

A stroke of good fortune had prompted Miss Monahan to suggest that they work together sharing the last map. Luxuriant, auburn hair framed her lovely, oval face but her eyes were her most compelling feature; almond-shaped, deep-set azure eyes. Eyes that made him feel a strange sensation somewhere deep inside him, leaving him a little woozy, they screamed for his attention as she took her seat next to him.

Tongue-tied in awe, he studied the map of the Southwest with her and thought about what he could say to her. A deep love for his native Texas had been instilled in him by his mother and often he had read and reread stories telling of the history of Texas, the Alamo, Stephen Austin, and Sam Houston. He felt some pride in knowing that his native county had been named after Jim Bowie, who had been lost in the Battle of the Alamo.

In an effort to promote conversation, he offered quietly that he was born in Texas. Responding with a flutter of her lovely twelve-year-old lashes, Carolyn asked, "What city?"

"Texarkana. Where were you born?"

"In the state of Coahuila, in Mexico," she replied.

"Why don't you show me where it is on the map," he offered, sliding the map and himself just a bit closer to her.

As they perused the map, crossing the border between Texas and Mexico, they found Coahuila, south of the state of Chihuahua. Carolyn told him that her family was from Mexico and that she had been born in Saltillo, its capital, and smiled. Gee, it was nice to see her smile and she had such pretty white teeth. It began what would be a semester-long friendship between them.

Several weeks later, after floating home on a cloud of fantasy, the Runt found a letter from Bob. He had graduated from "boot" and was being sent to the fixed-wing aircraft mechanics school at Jacksonville, Florida. Sent to another nice warm place, he was to learn how to repair soon-to-be-obsolete, propeller warplanes. As always, he ended by saying that he sure loved to get their letters! Bob had become a regular letter-writer, which pleased Kathleen and his kid brothers, knowing that he was adapting to Navy life and keeping in touch.

A sense of humor pervaded all of his hurriedly scrawled letters which his youngest brother pored over repeatedly. Teasing his youngest brother when he scored high on Navy exams or proficiency tests, Bob told him he wasn't the only smart one in the family. Bob wasn't aware that his kid brother always held a high regard for Bob, believing Bob to be the one who had the looks and the brains in the family, while Davey had the heart of a lion. No matter what grades he might receive, the kid brother felt that his oldest brother could always outdo him anytime.

Before the Runt knew it, it was late June and the school-year of 1945-46 was suddenly over. The apparent brevity of the previous semester may have been due in part to the fleetness with which the classroom hours next to Carolyn had passed. Report cards were handed out, revealing good news and bad news. Constituting the good news were good grades but the bad news was that Carolyn and the Runt were being separated by assignment to different rooms. They would never share another class during their remaining time at Agassiz.

In most cases, a boy might keep in touch with a pretty girl who affected him so deeply, but except for sending her a valentine the following February, he didn't try to stay in contact with her. Even though he would have liked to have Carolyn for a girl friend someday, he never thought to pursue her because he felt that she was too far above him, in looks, poise, age, and class. Due to the many put-downs and taunts by a minority of kids in earlier times, a feeling of inferiority in some areas had developed which the Runt carried inside him.

For the next couple of years he kept a clipping from a magazine perfume ad in the back corner of his dresser drawer. The ad featured the portrait of an attractive model who bore a striking resemblance to Carolyn, for whose picture he would have been too embarrassed to ask. Despite being different, he could still dream like any other boy and feel affection for a lovely girl. The young boy had been enchanted by the charms of lovely Carolyn and would always remember her.

As the Runt completed another school year, his brother Bob finished the Aircraft Mechanic schooling course and in his next letter related the following events. Assigned to a ship upon graduation, he was cooling his heels in Norfolk Naval base, waiting for his ship to come into port. Managing off-base passes, he and a buddy hopped the bus to Washington, D.C., which to any patriotic kid was a very impressive city to see. He had joined the Navy to see the world and he had already covered a good portion of the Southeastern part of the country.

Back at Norfolk, the aircraft carrier "Valley Forge," CV-45, had put into port while he was on pass. When Bob first saw the incredible ship upon returning, she so amazed him with her size that his jaw just dropped. He hadn't seen a carrier except in the movies and she was awesome to behold! The grand lady would be his home and duty station for the balance of his hitch.

Late June brought an ironic twist of Fate to Kathleen, not too long after she had married Tom Martin, when she encountered another returned soldier to whom she had once given her heart. This soldier had been one of the first to dutifully answer his country's call, yet like so many others, had his hopes and dreams forfeited in return.

On a day too sweltering to have been out looking for a new

job, Kathleen, while walking home, suddenly felt as if she had seen a ghost. Squinting to see more clearly through shimmering heat waves rising from the sun-baked cobblestone pavement of Lincoln Avenue, she saw someone up ahead on the other side of the street. He resembled her old love, Don Averill. Not able to see for certain that it was really him, and because this man walked with a cane, Kathleen was still in doubt. Throwing propriety and caution to the wind, she just had to know if this was the man who had broken her heart all those months before.

With her heart pounding, Kathleen hurried along to gain on the slowly walking man across the street, in an effort to see his face. Yes! It was the still-handsome face of the man she had once loved with all her heart, but she pretended not to see him when he spotted her and waved. Turning away out of embarrassment and in a last ditch effort to ignore him, Kathleen felt her heart would burst as she heard her name called once again by his voice.

Relenting, she slowly turned to face the man who discarded her love years before. Still burning inside her was the hateful bitterness that she carried as a shield against the pain he had caused her. Needing to speak to him, at least to find out how he had been crippled to the point of needing a cane to get about, she dodged several cars as she hurriedly crossed the street.

Awkwardly, they struck up a conversation and then, only too late, did she learn that Don, while serving as a combat engineer, had been blown off a bridge by shrapnel from a Japanese shell burst, suffering a spinal fracture. Several doctors at a military hospital told him that he had been paralyzed and their prognosis had been that he would never walk again.

Concerned that he might always be a cripple, Don didn't want to become a burden to anyone, most of all to Kathleen, for he had loved her too much. Don felt that Kathleen would love him despite his paralysis, yet in the belief that she and the boys would be better off without him, he had written the letter to discourage her from waiting for him.

Don then said, "In one small way, the Lord has smiled upon me, for through His help and months of physical therapy, I was able to walk again. Who knows, maybe someday I might even be able to throw away this cane."

"Maybe," Kathleen replied.

Spotting the wedding ring on her finger, a frown chased the smile from Don's face and an old suitor's questions followed, "How long have you been married? Are you happy? Is it someone I know?"

Not wanting him to know that she was married to another alcoholic, Kathleen stretched the truth by answering, "Yes, I'm happily married, but I don't believe that you know him."

"I'm glad to know that you're happy. I wondered for so long, how you had fared."

All the while they talked, in her heart Kathleen wished that those years hadn't passed, that Don hadn't been wounded, and even that she hadn't remarried. While Don's deep blue eyes searched hers for some hint of the truth in the words he was hearing, a silent scream protested inside her against this cruelest of all jokes, that Fate had played on them.

Holding back her tears, she mentally tore herself away as she ended their conversation with, "I'm glad to know the truth, for it helps me to finally understand what happened to you."

"I'm relieved that you understand what happened," said Don.

"I'm sorry but I do have to be on my way. I wish you the best of luck, Don. It's been good to see you again. Goodbye."

"Goodbye, Kathleen."

They then walked away from each other in opposite directions, both physically and literally, for their paths would never again cross. As Kathleen turned her back to the most wonderful man she had ever known, allowing him to go out of her life for the last time, an overpowering flood of emotions washed over her. Long-overdue, unchecked tears of loss streamed down her cheeks, as she continued walking. Within those final, bittersweet, cathartic moments, she was at last able to put away her bitterness, and allow beautiful memories of times they once shared, to return to her heart.

She knew at last, that Don had loved her truly and faithfully after all.

Chapter 14

Put Up Your Dukes!

A light rain blanketed the North Side on that warm, gray Saturday morning in late June of 1946, as Davey and the Runt trekked with their stepfather along the train tracks along Lakewood, up to Wrigley Field, seven blocks away. Neither of the boys had ever been inside the park, let alone actually seen a real major league baseball game, so Tom figured it was about time. The Phillies were in town and despite the rain tapering off to a light mist, ominous gray clouds continued to dwarf the stadium all through the game. Never raining hard enough for the game to be called, the misting persisted as they kept three seats dry on a bleacher bench in right-field. When the game was over the Cubs had not only won 5 to 4 on a Marv Rickert home run but had also won a fan for life.

While Davey had only been slightly impressed by this one demonstration of the National Pastime, his kid brother was already singing the praises of their hometown team that had won the National League pennant during the previous season. The Runt couldn't know then that he would grow to be an old man without having ever watching his beloved Cubs win another pennant. Though a baseball fan for life, his youthful memories would be of the great teams of other cities and many great players who spent most of their careers with mediocre teams, like the Cubs' own Andy Pafko, the Pirates' home run king, Ralph Kiner, and Reds' hard-throwing right-hander, Ewell Blackwell.

Summer of '46 brought pleasant warm evenings and great weather for school playground activities like playing on the slides, the rings, or softball and basketball. Playground equipment could be borrowed at the fieldhouse by any neighborhood kid with just a deposit, and his name and address. School playgrounds were managed like city parks and during school semesters you could find them open after school up until 9 o'clock at night. Closing time was always indicated by a short interruption of the playground lights at 8:55 and total darkness at nine. The school playground and its equipment were supervised by an attendant who only asserted his authority when the fracas or commotion reached a point to where it was brought into the fieldhouse.

Most of the conflicts between boys were resolved by the boys themselves and usually resulted in only minor cuts, bruises, or a bloody nose. Boys were competitive and even their non-contact sports gave them ample opportunity to defend their possessions and/or reputations. Rites of passage in those days dictated that a young man fight back and defend himself if someone punched him. If he didn't, then not only had he lost that fight but if others heard that he wouldn't fight back, then they would beat on him whenever the notion struck them. The harder a kid fought back, the fewer times he needed to defend himself.

The Runt had begun defending himself several years earlier and boys his age who knew him, didn't bother him anymore. Bigger kids were sometimes a different story, as he found out one hot, dusty evening while playing a pickup game of basketball on the dry, gritty, dirt and gravel court. Several bigger guys were playing with the younger boys and Tom Stuckey, an oversized galoot who had come along and inserted himself into the other team kept bumping into the Runt, pushing and fouling him, then finally slamming him onto the dusty ground.

Climbing back onto his feet, the Runt spat the dirt out of his mouth and called Tom a dirty player, getting punched in return for his unsolicited opinion. Stuckey had been looking for a fight and the Runt didn't have much choice but to give him one, taking several punches before realizing that the bully had a longer reach and was stronger. Suddenly the Runt was shoved aside like a sack of potatoes and there taking his place was his brother Davey who asked the bruiser, "Why don't you pick on somebody your own size, Stuckey?"

Davey wasn't much closer to this lunkhead's size either but his lion's heart didn't care! The customary volley of insults and threats ensued and finally Stuckey swung and missed a ducking Davey who then rattled Stuckey's teeth with a lightning straight-to-the-mouth left-jab. That only made the bully mad and the two of them fought furiously against each other. Although Davey was smaller than Stuckey, he was quicker and he could take a punch. Minutes later, Stuckey was down on one knee, spittin' blood, and mumbling that he'd had enough. The fight was over.

It was the only time that the Runt had known Davey not to reach out to an opponent and offer to shake his hand afterwards. He wondered about it as he followed his brother to the water fountain. Giving Davey time to run cold water over the cuts and bruises received in his place, the kid brother then faced him and asked, "How badly did you get hurt?" Davey brusquely turned away from him and hurriedly walked around the school building to the playground's other side. Saddened by his big brother's snub, he thought Davey was angry with him; maybe Davey had thought that he had started that fight with the bigger kid.

Only years later, during a Sunday afternoon phone call when his kid brother would ask Dave if he still cared about him would a grown-up Dave tell him about that walk around the building.

"You just asked me if I still cared about you. Kiddo, I've always cared about you."

"Sometimes I wonder, because you don't ever come over to my house to visit."

"Do you remember, years ago, when I fought Tom Stuckey that night at Agassiz?"

"I never forgot it. But afterwards, you just walked away from me, like you were mad at me. I didn't start that fight."

"I know you didn't. Oh kid, I wasn't mad at you! That fight against Stuckey was the worst fight I'd ever been in. But I would do it again for you."

But why did you walk away from me?"

"I went around behind the school building that night, to find a deserted place, so nobody could see me cry. I didn't cry because of the pain from the bruises and cuts on me."

"So why would you cry, then? You were a tough kid."

Dave went on, "I cried because Stuckey had picked on you only because he thought you talked funny. I cried because I had realized for the first time, how hard life must have been for you. I cried for my little brother who had been persecuted for just having something wrong with him, something he couldn't help and which would never go away."

Davey who had always loved and protected his kid brother, on that night back in the school yard had taken his brother's place, in the toughest fight he would ever have and had proved his brotherly love for all time.

Like most of Chicago's public schools in those times, the Near North Side's Agassiz School drew its students from its surrounding area which was a veritable melting pot of ethnic groups. No nationality or race had been left out of the composition of the student body, and yet the kids made no class or ethnic distinctions between names like Andyulis, Immelhauser, Li, Hladazy, Cermak, Rossi, Cohen, Petros, Martinez, Jackson, or O'Rourke. It seemed they were all just kids in the same school boat together, and the playground was their social and athletic center.

The only segregation encountered in their school was in the separation of the school's playground into boys' and girls' sides. While at recess or during lunch, boys were prohibited from playing on the girls' side of the playground. Teachers and patrol-boys monitored this separation and violators were kept after school.

For better or worse, spending a lot of time at the playground promoted association with all kids, even those who could be headed down the wrong road in life. One evening while his folks thought he was safe at the playground, the Runt was there alone, and nearly took a turn down the wrong road in life. Yet, how easy it could have been to take such a turn. Alex Macaluse, one of the eighth-grade boys, had always treated the Runt as a pal. A dark, coarse-featured Italian kid, Alex was feared by a lot of the kids but not by the Runt who looked up to him.

Since school was out for the summer and the fieldhouse wasn't open, there were no lights in the playground but Alex and a couple of other tough kids mentioned it was nine o'clock and were deciding where to go next, since it was still early, for them. Overhearing the conversation of the other three, the Runt learned that all three of them had juvenile rap sheets and when asked by Alex, the Runt quickly assented to the fact that he had gotten in trouble at the Julian theatre (they took his name for jumping over a railing). He didn't want to go home yet and just wanted to hang around with his buddy Alex for a little while longer.

When Alex asked the other two if they had any money, neither of them did, so they decided that the first thing they had to do was find a place where they could pick up some money the easy way, by stealing it. Suddenly the Runt felt an uneasiness within his stomach and remembered '53', the squad car that carried him to school and the shotgun in its back seat. Alex and the boys had decided to rob a grocery store a few blocks away and were heading off in its direction with the Runt tentatively trailing behind.

After letting him fall further behind for nearly a block, Alex suddenly stopped and turned toward the little guy bringing up the rear. Turning on his most menacing stare, Alex looked the Runt in the eye and said, "No crap now! Tell me straight, kid! You got a record or not?"

Hesitating, the Runt answered, "No, I don't."

With that, the towering Alex did the Runt the greatest favor of his young life by telling him, "Look kid, me and these two guys have been in scrapes with the law before and we're going to pull a job where we could buy some more trouble. If we get nabbed, we'll do time in reform school, but we already got records; you don't!"

"But I just wanted to stick around with you, Alex."

Then the last thing Alex ever said to him was, "You got a clean slate, kid. G'wan home! Stay outta trouble or you'll wind up bein' a loser like me."

Turning around, the younger boy trudged slowly homeward. As strange as it may seem, the Runt felt badly on the way home, having been rejected by his friend. But he also thought of what would have happened to him if he had gone with those guys? Arriving home late, he had no answer for a worried Mom who asked why he was late and why did he look so sad? His mind was troubled by being told to go home by one of his playground heroes and that he might so easily have gotten into serious trouble, letting his mother down. He went to bed that night, glad that he hadn't been a disappointment to his mother and glad that Alex had shown himself to care about him and be a real friend.

The last word he had of Alex Macaluse was that Alex had wound up in reform school from where he may have graduated to a life of crime. While the Runt never saw Alex again, he wouldn't forget him and would one day be ever grateful to him. On that night, the goodness that remained in Alex had caused him to reach out to an innocent boy, turn him around and put him back on the right path in life. Even though Alex called himself a "loser," he won big that night.

A week later, one of the greatest tragedies a boy can know, struck the Runt's household: their one-year-old dog, Teddy, was lost! Somehow, when they let him out into the yard, he had just wandered away. Kathleen's sons looked everywhere for him and enlisting the help of all of the neighborhood kids still resulted in not one clue. Heartbreaking days passed during which they heard nothing and saw nothing of their little friend. Asking old classmates from school if they had seen or heard of a dog resembling theirs also had turned up no new leads. Poor Teddy had just vanished from their world.

Two weeks passed and hope dwindled as denial slowly evolved into a reluctant acceptance of fact. Teddy was gone and more than likely he wasn't able to come back. Their friends still asked about him, causing the pain to sharpen during those moments. Then one neighbor kid mentioned that a friend of his, named Ray Nash, had mentioned lately that his sister just loved the new dog that they had found a couple of weeks before.

Talking to Ray Nash, the Runt asked about his sister's new dog and Ray told him, "It's a male, medium-sized, brown Shepherd-mix."

It sounded a lot like Teddy to the Runt whose hopes were quickly raised, causing him to blurt out his thoughts all at once, "He sounds like our dog. Can we come over and take a look at him? We lost our dog two weeks ago. Maybe your dog is really our dog."

156

"I don't know, he could be another dog entirely. Besides, my sister really loves her new dog. But I'll ask my folks if you can see him. At least you'll know he's not yours."

The next day, Ray came by and said, "My mom and dad said you can come by and look at him, just so you know he's not your dog. Don't get your hopes up because my mom promised my sister that she wouldn't let anybody take the dog if they couldn't prove absolutely that he was theirs."

"Yeh, I understand. But at least we'll eliminate one possibility."

"Yeh, we'll accomplish that."

The next day, the two brothers walked with Ray to his house up on Lincoln Avenue. Climbing up the back porch stairs, they overheard Ray's sister crying and Ray's mother telling her, "He had to be someone else's dog before he came to us, but we'll just make sure that the dog is theirs before we give him up."

The Runt then turned to Davey. "What if he is Teddy? How are we gonna prove he's our dog? We don't have any papers on him."

"I dunno!" was his older brother's less than helpful answer.

Meeting the boys at the top of the stairs, Ray's mother said, "He's a very friendly dog and he'll go to anybody. Ray, you go in the front bedroom where Annie has him and you hold the door closed until he's called."

"Okay, Mom."

To the Ryan brothers, Ray's mother said, "You stay here at the kitchen door and call him by the name you gave him. If he doesn't answer to the name you call he's not your dog. See if he answers to the name."

Davey said to his kid brother, "We're only getting one chance. If it's him you better be the one to call him. He was always with you."

With his knees buckling, the Runt said a silent prayer in his heart and called out. He called out for the little canine friend he had come to love so much, "Here Teddy! Teddy!"

Instantly a brown flash bolted from the front of the house, its claws slipping on the linoleum floor, racing toward them, and wagging its tail furiously. Jumping into the Runt's open arms, Teddy licked the tear-stained cheeks of his young master's face.

"Teddy. Oh Teddy."

Ray's mother could barely hold back her own tears, saying, "Oh Lord! He's your dog, alright, I can see that. Take him home with you! We'll find another dog for Annie that she'll learn to love even more."

Our heroes took their furry little friend home with them, never to lose him again until, as an old dog many years later, when he would breathe his last on a Christmas morning at home. As for Ray Nash, he became a good friend of the two brothers, while his sister, Annie, did get a dog of her own, that she loved even more, just as her mother predicted.

As August of '46 burned on, its steamy temperatures seemed to promote light-headedness in some adults who weren't quite as young as they thought they were. This fact came to light to at least one adult, on a hot Saturday afternoon when their aunt Maybelle's new husband Lew Frye dropped over to see the boys. Also coming along with their new uncle was an old uncle, their uncle Clay and their six-year-old cousin, Bucky. In addition to having brown eyes as warm as his heart, a friendly smile and devilish wit, Clay also possessed the heart of a six-foot-four, 220 pounder in his five-foot-seven, 140 pound body. Sharing the same St. John's Day birthday with his uncle, whom he resembled, the Runt admired his uncle for his fun-loving, humorous, down-to-earth attitude. He also wondered how such sad, brown eyes could belong to such a light-hearted man.

Standing six-foot-one and weighing about 180 pounds, Lew had once been a contending amateur middleweight boxer during his Navy days. Apparently he'd been a good one, since his handsome face hadn't a mark on it. Blue-eyed with very blond hair, and having a strong jaw line, it was easy to see why Maybelle had fallen in love with him. Lew often visited the Ryan boys, and sometimes brought his eight-ounce boxing gloves along for his new nephews to try on and spar with, while he taught them fundamentals of the "Manly Art of Self-Defense." The easy rapport he developed with them may have stemmed from his boyhood days which he and his brother Al also spent in an orphanage.

Bob, home on leave from the Navy, was seventeen at that time and he and his uncle Clay were bobcats having the same height and build. This apparent equality inspired Clay to challenge his nephew to go a couple of rounds with him. Clay made a grand gesture of saying that he would go easy on Bob because he was a kid. Referring to his uncle's greater years, Bob declined. Having his virility thus impugned, Clay hinted a bit too emphatically, that perhaps his nephew thought his old uncle might be too much for him. He got his match when Bob said, "Okay old man. You're on!" They put on the eight-ouncers and put 'em up.

With Lew acting as referee, the two boxers tapped gloves and squared off. That tap was the only contact Clay's gloves made with any part of Bob's anatomy. One, two, three, four successive left jabs were landed by Bob, who held back his right hand, while "good ole uncle" Clay nearly fell down trying to back-pedal quickly enough. The bout was over and everyone had a good laugh, especially their uncle Clay, who admitted that somehow, his oldest nephew had become a man while he must not have noticed that he himself was getting older. "And slower!" quipped his nephew, Bob.

The next day, Sunday, saw one of the first of many family picnics over the years which found everyone gathered in Lincoln Park, just west of Montrose Beach and the Horseshoe. Every family picnic the Kelly clan enjoyed over the years took place in that same location. Each year, at least one or two of the holidays were observed with a family picnic to which many family friends were also invited.

It was upon occasions such as these, that the majority of family members customarily got their first look at one's new girl friend or new beau. Unlike meeting everyone in the dreaded, formal atmosphere of a family wedding, a family picnic was a great environment for the introduction of that special person, who could then mingle with so many relatives much more readily. Snapshots taken at picnics were usually the earliest pictures taken of those who had married into the family. Having a shutterbug around also resulted in embarrassing pictures of old flames who might have attended just one picnic, years before but it sometimes took years to track down and dispose of those old, incriminating pictures.

The Runt, Bob, and Dave cooling off at Montrose Beach during a family picnic at the same old spot near the Horseshoe.

For all of the young bucks or old bucks who still thought young, picnics were also a forum for periodic tests of their manhood. Having grown another 10 pounds heavier, would one cousin try again this year and wrestle his previously victorious cousin to the ground? To the surprise of everyone, the scrawny kid who last year couldn't swing a bat might pick up a bat this year and drive a screaming line-drive past a doubting, ducking uncle's head.

Lady-like behavior was frequently tossed aside like a wet towel during the heat of competition because the Kelly women also played to win, often using their wiles to compete against the stronger men. Once during a touch football game, a teenaged would-be receiver, intent on going out for a long pass, was tripped and sent sprawling onto the unyielding turf by an aunt who claimed ignorance of rules against tripping. She was just as effective as a burly linebacker, since after that trip she could slow the kid down with just a nasty glare every time he came through her zone.

To the wonder of the youngsters who deemed it humorous, family members who were no longer kids always suffered aches and pains from stiff joints over the next few days, groaning each time they bent or stretched, while limber youngsters scoffed. Only after the inevitable passing of years and sweet, precious youth would those same scoffers experience their own painful picnic aftermath.

Chapter 15

Recreation

It was mid-morning, the day after that first picnic, and the Runt roamed anxiously through their apartment sniffing the air, trying to identify the pungent odor wafting through their windows. Unlike the usual unpleasant fumes of their neighborhood, this odor nearly took his breath away. Curiosity won out over his usual caution as he went down the front stairs and out onto the sidewalk in front of their house. Stronger here, the odor made him cough when he breathed, and he saw the wilted blooms of the flowers along their gangway, blooms which had been fresh the day before.

Seeing Mrs. Brown, his neighbor lady from next door with a wet hankie over her face, he asked, "What's that awful smell?"

"Ammonia," she replied, "It's killing my flowers!" Whatever ammonia was, the Runt didn't want to breathe any more of it than he could help.

Soon, firemen from a nearby engine company arrived, going into one of the packing company's buildings. A short time later he was able to find out that one of the company's freezing units had developed a gas leak of minor proportion. Had it been major leak, casualties might have included humans as well as flowers, and the entire area would have been evacuated. Wandering around just up George Street that night, Ronnie Kowalczyk and the Runt stopped by to talk with the night watchman sitting on a chair outside the door of the building where the leak had occurred.

Strong traces of the gas were still present but the two boys felt heroic under the cloak of youthful invincibility. Who else had been brave enough to go there and stand guard outside while the watchman made his rounds.

The old watchman's parting words were "If I'm not back in ten minutes, come and get me!"

Fortunately, he was back in the allotted time. It might have been better for all if his instructions were to call for help if he hadn't been back in ten minutes. Later, the Runt thought about what might have happened if they had been forced to go into the building to retrieve the old man and all of them were overcome by the gas? His feelings of invincibility faded quickly and the scrawny, scared, would-be hero ran home to safety.

Awakened days later by a chorus of hammers pounding and squealing nails being pulled from old wood, the boys ran to their back porch in time to see the beginning of the end for their old archaeological dig. Demolition Day had arrived for the old burned-out cottage on the back of the lot. The real estate agency which managed the property had finally sold it to a new owner who was having the unsafe old hulk taken down and removed.

While tearing down the structure resulted in a lot more yard space and a considerable number of artifacts discovered in its rubble, they would miss the sense of adventure found in the hulk's smoky environs. Poking around in its rubble like prospectors one brilliantly sunny day, Davey bent down and extricated a rusty old golf club, an old seven-iron, from the debris.

Absorbed in his find he took his stance, addressed an imaginary dimpled ball then threw his whole skinny body into a mighty backswing. Coming off the top of his backswing he skulled his kid brother who had been behind him, still intently poring over the rubble. A galaxy of first-magnitude stars replaced the bright sunlight in the Runt's consciousness as a shock wave of intense pain flooded his skull. Fortunately, it was merely a flesh wound as they used to say in the movies, and the Runt was back to normal a few minutes later. Once again the younger brother had survived one of his brother's devil-may-care moments. It was one experience that Davey wouldn't learn from, for in years to come, Davey was never able to hit a good seven-iron.

Speaking of movies, the two boys managed to go to the movies on Fridays, Saturdays, and Sundays. When boys worked a paper route and got a buck a week for themselves, they could afford to see movies that often, at ten cents per admission. Theirs was the good fortune of living equi-distant from several movie theatres. East of them on Lincoln Avenue, stood the East theatre, to the west on Lincoln were the City and Lincoln theatres. The B & K Belmont was on Belmont Avenue just west of Ashland and Lincoln. The B & K (Balaban & Katz) theatres were the showplaces of the city. North of them and farthest away, near Belmont and Sheffield, were the Vic and the Julian theatres.

The Lincoln, the Vic on Sheffield, and the East were good theatres showing contemporary movies of general interest. Musicals such as "I Wonder Who's Kissing Her Now?," "Tin Pan Alley," or "Three Little Words" were very popular at the time and introduced young moviegoers of the 40's and 50's to musical biographies of composers such as Joe Howard or Gus Kahn, or teams like Bert Kalmar and Harry Ruby who wrote music that had been popular before these kids were born.

The closest theatre was the City, on Lincoln just west of Southport, which showed old movies from the early 30's and into the 40's, usually as a triple feature. Three movies! Picture it! Kids with butts of iron could sit watching movies filmed before their birth, for four to six hours; a duration of time that would force most adults to squirm uneasily in their chairs, before finally giving up and leaving. The City theatre had unknowingly offered an education in older films and an introduction to film stars most kids would have only read about in movie histories. Every Laurel and Hardy movie had put in an appearance at the City theatre and the boys had seen them all, twice!

Most unique of all however, was the Julian theatre on Belmont, east of the Sheffield "El" which showed only Westerns. Its entire motif was Early Cowboy, manned by ushers in black, Western garb, with saddles, ropes, wagon-wheels, and leather trappings decorating the lobby and the stairways. Also decorating the lobby were still photos of many of the cowboy stars of that era, cactus heroes like Gene Autry, Tom Mix, William "Hopalong Cassidy" Boyd, Charles Starrett, or Al "Lash" LaRue. They appeared in black and white movies churned out by movie studios named Republic, Monogram, PRC, and RKO.

The Julian was where the two boys first saw their future cowboy hero, in an old movie named "Throw a Saddle On a Star." Starring Dick Foran, it featured a scene in which appeared a western band named the "Sons of the Pioneers," led by a skinny, smiling young buckaroo named Leonard Slye, who had already begun gaining worldwide renown as Roy Rogers.

An additional reason for going to the Julian, when a difficult choice had to be made, was the Julian's close proximity to a shooting gallery just west of the Sheffield "El." An authentic old-time shooting gallery with real pellet rifles, it had all types of games such as a submarine periscope, machine gun, dive bomber, and many electrically operated guns. They learned over a few years how to aim and shoot more accurately. They also learned that a kid could drop a lot of change in a place like the shooting gallery.

Whatever choice they made of theatres to go to, it didn't matter much during most of the year during fair weather. It mattered a lot though, in the wintertime when walking to the show always seemed to be a long trek, during which Winter's icy blasts managed to penetrate right through the fibers of their thick woolen coats, and chill them to the bone.

A strange incident occurred during a movie at the Lincoln Theatre which the Runt wouldn't understand until a few more years passed. Arriving at the show with his brother Davey and Will from downstairs, the latter two chose to sit together a few rows back from Davey's kid brother like they usually did. Their reasoning was probably so they could talk about girls and other things about which they didn't want the Runt to hear. After one tense, dramatic moment in the movie, which the audience reacted to with a sense of relief, an older kid came over to sit down next to the Runt. Striking up a conversation about the previous intense scene with the younger boy, he seemed to be very friendly and the Runt was eager to gain gain a new friend.

Quietly, Davey appeared at their row and told his brother, "Okay, this is where we came in. Let's go!"

His kid brother started to remind him that the show was only half over, saying, "But the show's . . . . ."

"I said let's go, we've got to get home!"

Reluctantly getting up, the Runt followed his older brother up the dark aisle muttering, "Why are we leaving early?"

Davey found Will in a row much farther back and abruptly sat down in the row, pulling his kid brother in with them. "I had to get you out of there!" Davey said. "There's something different about that guy and I don't want you around him. Stay back here with us!"

Not until later in life when he caught a ride while hitchhiking at seventeen and the driver, a grown man, tried to put his hand on his knee, did the Runt realize why Davey had hauled him out of that theatre seat.

Ever-vigilant Davey came down with a malady in late August which afflicted him with lethargy and pains in his extremities. Deeply troubled, Kathleen took Davey to the doctor who diagnosed his condition as "heart flu."

The doctor had chastised Kathleen for bringing such a sick boy to him on the streetcar saying, "This boy could've died on the way over here. "

"Oh my God! Is it that serious?"

"You've got to get him home," replied the doctor, "and be certain that he gets plenty of bed rest."

Taking a cab home with her sick boy, Kathleen followed the doctor's orders, putting Davey to bed immediately and then while he rested, hurried back out into the sultry night air to get Davey's prescription filled.

While she waited for the prescription at the drugstore, she went to a phone booth. Looking up the number of the American Red Cross in the phone book she called them, explaining the situation to a sympathetic representative. She was told not to worry, that the Red Cross would notify the commander at Norfolk Naval Base, home port of Bob's ship, the "Valley Forge." Relieved, Kathleen hurriedly returned home to her son whom she believed to be near death. It didn't look good for the kid, while the Runt wondered how his brother could have faded so quickly.

Fortunately, Bob's ship was returning from her "shakedown cruise" in the Caribbean and it only took a day or so to notify him that he had received an emergency leave in order to hurry home and visit his gravely-ill brother. Nearly three days had elapsed by the time the tired, worried seaman arrived home in Chicago.

Meanwhile, unknown to Bob, Davey's illness had been misdiagnosed by the first doctor and a second, more-trusted physician diagnosed Davey's condition as an easily remedied form of anemia and prescribed an iron tonic. Davey was up and out of bed feeling great, two days later. The third day he had been resurrected enough to be playing softball out in the street with the neighborhood boys.

One would have to be there to envision a poor, travel-weary Bob as he turned the triangular corner of Lincoln Avenue and George Street. Fearful that he might not have been able to get home in time to see his younger brother before he died, he was nearly knocked down in a collision with that same brother chasing a fly-ball. "Mixed emotions" serves as only a lukewarm description of Bob's train of thought in those moments: suspension of disbelief seeing a dying brother racing after a softball; had it been a joke played on him; what if the Navy found out and thought it was a ruse; what the hell was going on here?

Bob was at the same time, overjoyed at seeing Davey alive yet angry because he wasn't sick! While enroute he'd worried that Davey could be dead already. Bob's emotions ran the gamut with anger winning at first.

Wondering why Bob didn't seem to be glad he was home, the Runt hesitated to ask for he saw the withering look that Bob gave Davey. Not until Kathleen explained what the doctor had said did Bob lighten up. Later on he confessed that he was glad that Davey was well again, and agreed that he might as well enjoy being home as long as he was there. The story of his younger brother's speedy recovery from near death's door was one he would tell for years but never without a smile.

September's blue skies saw Bob off to Norfolk for the rest of his two year hitch and his two brothers back to school for their education. Accosted one day, across the street from school by a well-dressed man, they were given brochures offering lessons for different musical instruments. Taking the literature home to Kathleen, they all agreed that they should take the trial course of Hawaiian Guitar lessons for thirty weeks.

Dutifully at first, the two boys practiced for the prescribed one hour daily but since the poor quality of their playing would have set hounds a'baying, they began to lose interest. Perhaps it was the acoustic student guitar they got with the lessons but their efforts never sounded like their instructor's when he played his beautiful electric model. For some reason, perhaps that same poor quality of play, he never offered to let them play his guitar. It might have made a difference to the boys, in influencing their decision to continue on but after thirty lessons they quit playing. Much to the delight of several long-suffering neighbors.

A few weeks after returning to school, the Runt and his classmates were informed that Ronald Gehrman's mother had passed away. Ronald, a really good kid, hadn't been in school for a couple of days and the Runt's young heart went out to Ronald, for he could not imagine how he would feel if it had been his mom who died for he loved her so much. Later in the day, as a chilly downpour washed down the streets, the Runt walked to his paper route to make his collections. In passing the funeral home on Southport just north of Wellington, he saw Ronald Gehrman sitting in the outer waiting room. Feeling that he should go in, he did.

Getting up from his chair, Ronald walked toward the Runt, and offered, "You're the only classmate who has come, so far."

"I'm sure that there's gonna be a lot more, Ron."

Ronald and he talked briefly and then Ronald ushered him into the room where Mrs. Gehrman was laid out. "She died of cancer," said Ronald.

The Runt said nothing. He could only imagine the pain that his classmate felt, the same pain that he would feel if it were his beloved Mom. Finally he whispered, "I'm so sorry Ronald, that your mother passed away," and left.

All that afternoon he felt sad for his classmate's pain and finally he made his way home. Coming out of the chilly rain into his own warm home, he walked up to his unsuspecting Mom and gave her a special hug.

"What brought this on, son?"

Unable to speak at first, tears welled in his eyes, and then he quietly said, "I love you Mom."

168

"What's wrong, son?"

"I'm glad I've still got you, Mom."

Then seeing the puzzlement on her face, he told her of Ronald's loss and in hearing, Kathleen understood.

A few weeks later Fall was really upon them with its brisk winds and shorter days. The grapevine brought word of a great place where kids could go every night for sports, games, movies, and crafts. It was called the Sheffield Boys Club, the local chapter of the Chicago Boys Clubs and it would cost each kid a buck a year but it was worth it. Not too thrilled by the prospect of having her sons out of sight at some place she never heard of, Kathleen relented when she learned the Boys Club was located upstairs of the Sheffield police station and next door to the fire house

A great place to spend an evening, the Boys Club was off the streets, out of the cold, and drew many neighborhood kids and school classmates, even to the point of accepting girls as members too. As previously mentioned, the Club was located above the police station and while its entrance was only on the second floor, it was the highest second floor the short-legged Runt ever saw. Worried about nosebleed, he pondered that a kid had to be healthy just to make the climb up that long flight of stairs. In icy winters to come, danger and challenges to the Runt's footing were issued when packed snow and glazed ice coated "The Stairway Without End."

Administered with an iron hand by the director and his counselors, no foul language or violence was ever tolerated inside the Boy's Club. If a scuffle broke out, the combatants were taken aside and talked to. Disputes not settled by verbal agreements and a handshake were arduously worked out in the gym wearing boxing gloves and the proceedings were always supervised by a counselor or the director. If they stopped a fight to declare a winner, the dispute was over. If a defeated combatant still carried a grudge, they were ordered to leave and told not to come back.

The Club's second floor had been partially filled with long tables, best suited for all of the numerous board games that younger kids played. Ping-pong tables and pool tables were also present for the older kids. At the back end of the second floor, near the steam-pipes was the gym. It never took long to work up a sweat in a gym that probably gave some entrepreneurial young lad the inspiration for the marketing of saunas one day. The gym's minimal equipment included medicine balls, Indian Clubs, parallel bars, a horizontal bar, boxing gloves, and a window facing a brick wall which no one could ever open anyhow. It did however, offer a challenge to one's strength and although not known for certain, may have been responsible for a hernia or two.

Friday night was free movie night at the Boys Club, featuring comedies, newsreels, or older movies, oriented to the movie tastes of young kids and were shown up in the third floor crafts area. On nights other than Fridays, the crafts area was dedicated to the teaching of various handicrafts, chief among which were woodworking and ornamental metal. As one entered the area, their sense of smell was always treated to the scent of fresh pine. In addition to the challenge of learning craftsmanship, the Runt was tested constantly by the tools, struggling to prevent the slicing of his fingers by a chisel, saw, or any of several other dangerous implements that needed no encouragement to suddenly slip and gouge him.

The highlight of the year was the annual Boys Club Christmas party, which the director always endeavored to keep as an exciting, interesting time for underprivileged kids. After an evening of games and entertainment, he played the part of Santa Claus without donning the customary red suit and white beard. Through the charity of Boys Clubs' supporters and donors, he was able to give out gifts to everyone who was there. The really great thing about it was that the kids didn't have to buy a present in return.

In retrospect, every boy and girl, who during that era, had the good fortune to attend the Sheffield Boys Club, owed a big debt to its counselors and especially to the director who did such a remarkable job. The director whose real name won't be disclosed here, was addressed by everyone simply as, "Nick." Not a big guy in stature, being short and bald, Nick was a giant with the kids. His warm, welcoming smile and sincere, no-nonsense manner made a kid feel safe, as though he had a home away from home. And all of them did.

Chapter 16

Life Changes

Flipping the calendar over to 1947 ushered in a series of unusual events; the first coming in January, as sort of a post-birthday remembrance for Betty. The Runt's youngest aunt and pal from Grandmaw Kelly's household, had suffered an attack of acute appendicitis. Surviving post-op complications as well as the surgeon's knife, she would recuperate within a short while, much to everyone's relief.

Early February brought an improbable event: Davey, wanting to be called, Dave, was finally graduating from Agassiz! Big brother Bob, who, after the emergency leave fiasco, was finally able to pull some leave time again in order to attend. It was a bone-chilling day in February, a bad time for mid-year commencement exercises. Looking the complete gentleman in his blue suit topped with a two-tone jacket, dapper Dave accepted his diploma gladly.

After the ceremonies, Kathleen beamed in approval, saying how handsome he had looked. Then they were all off to the photographer lest the star of the festivities get mussed up before his picture could be taken. At the studio, Bob quickly intervened to prevent a scuffle that nearly ensued when his youngest brother repeated Kathleen's compliment to Dave, emphasizing that Dave had looked "So handsome." The altercation may have signaled the point at which brother Dave began to leave boyhood and the Corsican Brothers affinity he and his kid brother had shared, behind him. In the younger brother's mind, it would seem that his best friend, Davey the boy, was left somewhere behind at Agassiz, as Dave the young man, continued on to high school to form new friendships and ties, and in the process appear to slowly distance himself from his kid brother.

While Dave had excelled in running, climbing, and self-defense in his boyhood years, he seemed unconcerned about the need to learn, in order to become truly educated. Not caring at the time that the education he was being given had been intended to better prepare him for life, he put off planning ahead and hadn't determined what he was going to need to get ahead in life.

After graduation, Dave would attend Waller High School for nearly a year, failing badly in the curriculum. Eventually, he transferred to Washburne Trade School, where dropouts were sent, and where he intermittently attended the obligatory one day a week and then finally dropped out completely. Dave's cavalier attitude toward school was disappointing although he himself was never a disappointment to his family who continued to encourage him to resume his studies.

A few weeks after Dave's graduation, on a snowy night in early March, not fit for humans to venture out in, Tom escorted his youngest stepson to the various bicycle and auto supply stores on the near North Side to purchase a new bike. A new bike would soon be necessary in the spring days to come, on the paper route, since Dave had taken over and nearly wrecked their shared bike from two Christmases before. Having saved enough money on his paper route, the Runt wanted to purchase the new bike by himself, for himself. Tom had believed that the Runt was too young and naive to send out into the world alone, with a forty dollar fortune in his pocket to spend all at once. Apparently he had forgotten that the "naive" little kid had spent two years out on his paper paper route, and at Christmas time had handled upwards of $70 in tips bulging in his pockets.

After a second night visiting bike shops, and transferring streetcars in a sudden snow storm, they hadn't even seen a Schwinn.

Tom questioned his stepson with some urgency, "Why does it have to be a Schwinn?"

The Runt expressed his own heartfelt opinion calmly by saying, "I think Schwinn is the best and I don't want to buy anything else!"

172

Then, just when Tom's patience was nearly exhausted, they found "The Bike." As they passed by the auto supply store just two blocks from home, he saw several new bikes inside which were the new shipment that he'd heard about for weeks.

One solitary bike called out silently to the boy through the store's glass front door. They fell in love with each other at first sight, he a lonely boy in need of a constant companion and it, a red Schwinn Royal, trimmed in white, needing a good home. Equipped with the usual extras it had whitewall tires, the encased horn, a carrier on the back fender, and a light on the front fender. Their love affair would continue for nearly four years. Wherever he went, the Runt would ride his bike, on the paper route or out to play in the evenings. His own bike gave him his first real mobility and the freedom to range far beyond his own neighborhood.

His new-found mobility and freedom didn't keep the Runt from continuing with his studies which increasingly required him to look up items in reference books. An enterprising encyclopedia salesman struck it rich one cold, clear Saturday when he knocked on their door. Selling sets of Encyclopedia Britannica, his timely arrival and selling pitch to Kathleen and the Runt netted him a sale, while the Runt gained a set of bright red, leather-bound encyclopedias. The financial arrangements were all his too, since the Runt was to pay seven dollars a week for the next year, from his paper route earnings.

As soon as the set of encyclopedias arrived, the kid started with volume "A," reading through each volume until he had read the entire set. At the time of his life when his mind was a sponge for soaking up knowledge and retaining most of what he read, there he was, reading encyclopedias. It would prove to be one of the most valuable and timely purchases of his life.

Like all seventh graders, the Runt had undergone Chicago's standard battery of reading and math proficiency tests and along with a few classmates, had reading scores that were nearly college level. In spelling ability, he ranked as one of the top two in his class. This ability was to bring him anguish instead of pride in another of that year's memorable events.

In classroom spelling-bees, preliminary to the school-wide competition, he worked hard to be rated as the best of the boys in the most proficient seventh-grade class and he looked forward to the forthcoming championship spelling bee. Seventh-grade teachers were allowed to designate two representatives, a girl and a boy from each class. The Runt's teacher, Miss Bertram, came to him and explained that while he was the best of her boys, she was designating another boy in his place. Her reason was that during competition, he might be misunderstood because of his speech defect. Emphasizing that he had encountered no problem during their class spelling competitions, he pleaded with her to reconsider but she insisted that this was a different case.

Arriving home, the disappointed boy tried without success to hide his dejection from his mother. But mothers have been all-seeing and all-knowing since the dawn of our species and Kathleen immediately asked him, "What's wrong?"

"Nothing, Mom."

"Are you sure?"

"Nothing's wrong, Mom."

Only after several such replies, did her son tell her about Miss Bertram's spelling bee decision.

Consoling him as best she could, Kathleen told him, "Remember that you had been the best of the boys."

Keeping that in mind, he tried to put the matter behind him as best he could. Knowing he was the best and being able to prove it were two different things and he was reminded of this whenever any of his well-meaning classmates asked him why he wasn't representing their room in the competition. Only years later would he learn that his sadness was minor in comparison to the pain felt by his mother, who that night, had cried into her pillow for him and for his being different. Being raised in the old-fashioned mores of the rural South, Kathleen had somehow wrongly blamed herself for his birth defect thinking that her son had been punished for something that she might have done and when it caused him pain, she experienced his pain and more, for in her mind, it was her fault.

Within a week, as his disappointment slowly subsided, the

spelling competition was held and a new school spelling champion had been declared. Upon hearing the news the Runt asked offhandedly who had won. His dejection then became deep resentment when he learned that the boy who replaced him had lost to the winner, Ray Christianson, a seventh-grader who stuttered badly.

As the end of April, 1947, approached, drastic changes were in order for Kathleen, Tom, and the two younger boys during the "Spring of the New Bike," starting when their new landlords, Mr. and Mrs. Landrum, began exerting their ownership rights with an iron fist.

Prior to moving in downstairs, the Landrums had first evicted the Gentrys who moved to a home they bought a block away, over on Wolfram Street. The Landrums soon established limits on the boys' use of the back yard. Co-existence with the Landrums was barely a peaceful one although their son Wilbur, who had just returned from the service, was much more agreeable. Sandy-haired, blue-eyed, and slight of build, Wilbur was a friendly, personable young man. He was quite different from his parents, always taking time to talk with the Ryan kids.

Answering the doorbell one sunny day, Kathleen was confronted by a stern-looking man announcing he was a health department inspector. Shocked when greeted by a friendly Teddy wagging his tail, the man asked, "Is this the vicious dog?" He apologized to Kathleen but said that a complaint had been filed and he had been ordered to deliver a warning to the dog's owners, which directed them to muzzle their vicious dog and keep him on a leash.

Buying a leather muzzle that afternoon, the Runt fitted it onto his trusting little friend's face. The cruel, unyielding leather of the muzzle chafed against poor Teddy's nose and cheeks but the muzzle had to remain. Countless times the tormented dog would try to paw the muzzle off yet couldn't, breaking his young master's heart when he looked up whimpering, asking for help in the only way he could. Teddy, who had done nothing to deserve the "vicious" designation continued to suffer for a false complaint that the Landrums had filed.

Weeks later on a humid, sweltering afternoon, Wilbur happened to come home from work earlier than was customary and encountered the Runt walking Teddy near the house and stopped to say hello. Spotting the muzzle on Teddy's snout and seeing his obvious discomfort, Wilbur asked, "Gene, why is Teddy wearing a muzzle?"

To this the little boy could only steel himself and mutter, "The health department had received a complaint that Teddy was a vicious dog."

"He's not a vicious dog! He's such a friendly little dog." Wilbur replied.

"I know."

Then, wondering aloud, Wilbur asked, "Who would do such a thing?"

The Runt, choking back a tear, then replied, "They said the complaint was filed by the people downstairs."

"Don't you worry Gene, he won't have to wear it for long," snapped Wilbur who then went up the stairs and into his front door.

Ten days later, the same health department inspector stopped by once more. Smiling as Kathleen opened the door, he offered that he was happy to tell her that for some reason, the complaint had been withdrawn and they need not muzzle their dog anymore. Once again Teddy was free of the torturous device and Wilbur had the Runt's undying admiration.

Despite having a dog, a new bike, and new encyclopedias, the Runt was still left with an emptiness which his brothers had filled for so long. Bob was still away in the Navy and high-school-aged Dave was home less often in the evenings now, his time occupied by his new friends and girls. While it was normal for a kid Dave's age, it was a difficult adjustment for his younger brother, still in the late stages of boyhood.

Fate took a hand a few months later in her strange way, by bringing the Runt's aunt Etta to stay with them for a while. Having had, like Betty, an attack of acute appendicitis, her appendix had burst, causing peritonitis to set in. Needing someone to take care of her, Kathleen offered sailor-son Bob's room just off the living room to her sister. As an extra precaution, Kathleen offered that the Runt could sleep on the couch where he could hear Etta, should she need help in the night.

Resigned to sleeping on the couch, the kid had found earlier that it wasn't so bad, since he was short and skinny enough to fit into it. Sleeping on the couch allowed him an added benefit: not having to go to sleep until after everyone else went to bed. Bob's Navy hitch had given the Runt experience sleeping on the couch, when Bob was home on leave and had brought along his lifelong buddy Rob Scruggs, who joined the Navy with him.

Each night the Runt lay between the two sides of a folded set of blankets, while the street light in front of the poultry place projected some light into the otherwise darkened living room. Often, as cars passed by in front on the street below, their lights would move across the ceiling in the opposite direction of the car's travel. Surpassing any street light or car lights however, was the flash of the circling Lindbergh Light atop the Palmolive Building downtown. Its bright beacon passed through the North Side sky about every thirty-five seconds and he was lulled to sleep during the waiting interval many times.

Etta was bedridden for over a month, during which Kathleen and the Runt brought meals to her and tended to her needs. Despite her prolonged recovery, she could be fun to have around, a change in everyday routine. It was easy to see that she was getting better, when she started up with her wisecracks again. Like the time she looked in a hand mirror, saw her pallor, induced by illness and cracked, "Too bad it isn't Halloween yet, I'm looking at the makings of a realistic witch in this mirror."

Although the illness had really incapacitated her, Etta would soon recover her health and good looks. It was the middle of September when she decided to celebrate her recovery and thank her nephews for their help, by treating the Runt and Dave to a movie. In no condition to walk the mile to the Lincoln theatre, she also paid for the streetcar ride. Not flush enough to buy boxes of popcorn and candy, she had earlier bought a package of cheese and made a bunch of cheese and cracker sandwiches which everybody munched during the movie. It was fortunate that they would be taking the streetcar, since the streets were awash with a soaking, wind-driven rain. Unfortunately, they had to cross Ashland, then Belmont to get to the streetcar stop. As if in answer to someone's unspoken prayer, the rain eased up and they managed to stay dry while waiting for the Red Rocket to arrive.

Arriving home, the boys noticed an exuberance about Etta that had been missing from her persona all along. It may have been because she had at long last, been out of the house. She had realized that she was really well; the real Etta was back! It was early October when she returned to her own place, restored and ready to be on her own again but her company and her sense of humor would be sorely missed for awhile.

Moisture-laden clouds and moderate temperatures were dumping heaps of moist, "good-packing" snow as Thanksgiving Day found the younger Ryan boys rising late. Debating whether to get snow-soaked to the skin by going outside, or staying dry until they all walked around the corner to turkey dinner at Grandmaw Kelly's was quickly decided in favor of enjoying the snow. The unexpected appearance of Uncles Clay and Lew, and Etta's new beau, Pat, coming down the street from Grandmaw Kelly's resulted in a sudden, prolonged snowball fight during which everyone got pasted and peppered by several snowballs. Instead of only two younger snow-soaked boys messing up her house, five snow-covered boys came into Kathleen's clean hallway to warm up and dry off, the older three having decided to chance Kathleen's mild reprimand for "bringing in all of that snow" than to face Grandmaw Kelly's ire.

A short while later, after the three visitors dried off and had a warmer-upper drink with Tom, they left to get back to Grandmaw's, turning to yell a warning to Kathleen's family that they'd better hurry or there wouldn't be anything left of the turkey when they got there.

As always, Thanksgiving had been the precursor of the Christmas holidays. The annual school Christmas pageant was prepared for well in advance at school through the teachers' diligent supervision of speaking-part rehearsals and choral practice of included carols and music. The few non-Christian students were understandably excused from having to participate in an event which might have borne little meaning to them.

Although each year's theme was the same the pageant's musical treatment could vary somewhat. One re-enactment that never changed was the entry of "The Three Kings" portrayed by three of the tallest boys who entered through three separate doors at the back of the auditorium. Each in turn would sing their particular verse as they walked their long aisle up to the stage. This had to be a tough act since not only was each boy singing solo, he was off by himself in a different part of the auditorium. Since each "King" was usually an older, taller boy, they normally sang the bass part of classroom music selections and having to sing the melody of the "Three Kings" solo was a vocal exercise to which they weren't accustomed.

One pleasant difference in this year's pageant was that several classes had been combined into a large, four-part chorus which had been given the opportunity to perform the "Hallelujah Chorus" of Handel's Messiah, an inspired piece that gave the Runt goose-pimples whenever he heard it. The other difference in this year's pageant, was that it would be the last Christmas pageant he would see performed at Agassiz. Next year, he would by then have graduated.

As the holidays passed, the Runt reverted to fending for himself like he did while living at his grandmaw's, relying more on classmates and other friends from the neighborhood for companionship and activities. Strangely enough, when many of his male friends and classmates were born, the name William had been a favorite for he had several friends named "Billy."

There had always been Billy Milford, a smart, nice-looking kid, who lived on Diversey in an apartment building with his widowed mother. While he and the Runt weren't close friends, they were buddies who had fought against each other and played together since the Runt lived with his grandmaw down the alley from Billy. Billy's mom was nice but quiet and she seemed to be very business-like. They had a nice, neatly-kept apartment and Billy had his own room. Often he would invite the Runt over after school for a short while and show him all of his Indian artifacts and other stuff he got at Camp Owassipi. In the wintertime, the two of them often took their ice skates over to the flooded schoolyard and joined the other hundred kids skating after school.

Another favorite buddy in school was Billy Immelhauser, whom he teamed up with a lot in class, in gym and out in the schoolyard at recess. Billy I. was a friendly, good-looking kid, with chiseled Teutonic features topped by nearly white, blond hair. It was helpful to know Billy because he had always known the meanings to all those new swear words and strange dirty words that the Runt would occasionally hear. He could ask Billy what the word meant and Billy wouldn't laugh at him for not knowing. Billy was at a disadvantage like the Runt, having an older brother in the same school, who hadn't exactly reached academic heights. It was somewhat unfair that their teachers treated the Runt and Billy with disdain, until the younger brothers demonstrated that they were better motivated than their sibling predecessors. It was unfortunate that honor student and class-president, brother Bob, hadn't preceded Davey and the Runt at Agassiz.

A new classmate, Billy Roder, who had moved from Battle Creek, Michigan became the Runt's very good friend, remaining so all the way through high school. Easygoing, just a bit taller and heavier, Billy R. had a grin that made you like him right away. Sometimes, on the coldest days, Billy would come along on the paper route with the Runt, helping him deliver papers.

Although the Ryan boys were still prohibited by Tom from inviting their friends over to the house, at least their friends could invite them. Often, Billy Roder invited the youngest Ryan over to his house on Magnolia near Diversey to play games and do homework together. It may have been an illusion but Billy R.'s house always seemed to be brighter and warmer.

Surprised when Billy told him that he also had a stepfather, the Runt envied how Billy's stepdad took an interest in his stepson's studies and endeavors, and wished that Tom could have been less strict and more like Billy's stepdad. Since Billy Milford and Billy Roder lived less than a block apart, one might think that they would be good friends but during the few times that the Runt was together with them, they didn't seem hit it off very well. Liking both of them, the Runt would only get together with one of them at a time after that.

Billy Roder didn't belong to the Boys Club, perhaps because

his folks would rather he stayed close to home on cold winter evenings. On club nights the Runt would usually get together with another classmate and friend, Ernie Adolphus, who lived down George Street at the corner of Racine, and walked the five blocks with him. On frigid nights it didn't seem as far having a friend along to take one's mind off the long, cold walk home.

With their clothes still warm from the Boys Club, they'd trudge for the first block between Sheffield and Seminary, up the brightly-lit alley alongside the police station, behind other buildings on Diversey which offered protection from the Hawk until they arrived at Wesley Methodist Church on Seminary. Then they'd traverse the long vacant lot west of the church, trudging parallel to Diversey where the Hawk-like wind caught them full force.

Pretending at first that the bush-covered berms they climbed along the southern boundary of the lot were English moors, they made a game of crossing the wind-raked prairie. Of course as soon as these young, movie-going kids of that era thought of "moors," they associated it with the phrase "A howling on the moors," and it followed that they would think of werewolves. Upon the mention of those terrible creatures, the two boys then ran like Hell's hounds were after them, not because of any old werewolf story mind you, but just to keep warm and get home quicker. Among the things that time changed were the "moors," which were destroyed a couple of years later during the construction of a new car dealership.

A tall kid, Ernie always had rosy cheeks, a slight overbite, and a high, squeaky voice, which belied the fact that he was strong and tough as nails. Ernie and the Runt had the distinction of being the only two boys in their class whose voices hadn't yet changed. Being "left behind" by all the other guys, being the last two boy sopranos was a distinction they shared, although that status was less appreciated by the Runt each week.

Since Ernie had the paper route adjacent to his, the two boys also shared the common experience of working a paper route through all kinds of weather in order to help make ends meet at home. Their paper routes shared the two sides of Melrose Street where each of them finished. Often they would finish up on Melrose together, racing to finish first, then stopping for a soft drink in the grocery store at Greenview, before hauling their wagons home together.

It was a Friday night in mid-January as the winter of '47-'48 locked the Midwest in its icy grip but it was movie night at the Boys Club, an event that mere cold usually wouldn't keep the Runt and Ernie away from. Answering a knock, Ernie opened the door only to hear that the Runt wasn't going after all. Oldest brother Bob had just been discharged from the Navy and the whole family was getting together for the welcome home party. Poor Bob enjoyed the party but he had a problem, in that he couldn't seem to get warm enough. His tour of duty had been spent in the Southeast and the sub-tropical area of the Caribbean. It would be several weeks before he re-acclimated to cold temperatures of the Midwest again.

As winter slowly became spring, Bob's return had been beneficial to Kathleen and her efforts to straighten out Dave. Bob was a good influence on his younger brother and when necessary, could give Dave a solid nudge in the right direction. Dave caught another nudge, which came sharply and suddenly from his younger brother, on a Saturday in late March. Opening up the kitchen window to let in the fresh, warm southwestern breeze, Bob saw his younger brothers hauling trash out to the garbage cans. Shoving a full garbage can out of the way, Dave teased the Runt, saying, "I'd better move these cans for you. A runt like you might hurt himself shoving them around."

It had been the last straw for the youngest Ryan who had long been weary of that name. Walking up behind his older brother, he whispered, "Dave," and when Dave turned around, brought him to his knees with a punch in the stomach. The kid had put his whole being into the hardest punch he could throw. As Dave cursed him, moaning on his knees, his younger brother grabbed his brother's arm forcing it into a half-Nelson, and shoved his brother's face into the dust of the alley.

Then through clenched teeth, he hissed, "My name is Gene, not kid, not Runt, but Gene! I don't want you calling me Runt anymore, do you hear me?"

Grimacing in pain, Dave replied, "Okay, okay, for now, but I'll get you later."

Witnessing the event from start to finish, Bob later reminded Dave that their little brother was right and Bob settled the issue once and for all by adding, "Let's you and me both call him Gene, from now on! We'll humor him for a while."

Finally, just as Bobby had become Bob and Davey had grown into Dave, it was time for the Runt to become Gene.

Later, on April 1st, the Martin-Ryans received papers in the mail giving them thirty days notice of eviction, charging numerous misdemeanors on the part of the tenants who kept a vicious dog who habitually urinated on their doorstep, and other lies. In truth, the Landrums needed the apartment for their son Wilbur and that should have been reason enough by itself, without resorting to falsehoods.

Eviction posed a serious problem for the Martin-Ryans. In addition to Tom being out of work, the postwar housing shortage still affected renters everywhere who lacked the means to purchase a home of their own. For the Martin-Ryans, eviction meant that decisions had to be made, in splitting up their family among relatives once more, since there wouldn't be time to find an apartment.

Gene had a decision to make at this time, too, one that would have a definite bearing on his occupation or further schooling after high school. He had already discussed going to college and medical school which got a quick and final no vote from his stepfather, who told him that they didn't have the money to send him to college, and he should plan on learning a trade so that he could help out at home. His long-time dream of being a doctor had now been quashed. When he thought of going to one of the city colleges, he worried that most of the college prep course required three or more years of high-school math. When he had received his second double-promotion, he skipped the grade in which many basic math concepts were taught and he was now having math troubles.

A counselor scheduled him for an essential math course when he got to Lane which would remedy his math deficiencies. In talking with several of his classmates, he found that Billy Milford was taking a Commercial Art course which would only require two years of math. Because he liked art and drawing, Gene mistakenly thought it might be an ideal course for him and reserved it as his major. It was unfortunate that a very important decision such as what he wanted to do for the rest of his life had to be made with little help, when he was only thirteen years old.

May 1st, moving day, had arrived and they were down to the wire, all packed and ready to leave. Moving meant the end of their loving home on George Street; the home where they had been reunited after years of separation, and where they made so many friends in the neighborhood and in school. The four years they had lived there were awash with unforgettable memories which would cause those fulfilling years to remembered as the richest years of their lives.

Kathleen and Gene, along with his dog, Teddy, went to stay with Grandmaw and Grandpaw Kelly in their home which they bought the year before, on Altgeld Street near Western Avenue. Located on the city's Northwest Side, they were living in the Logan Square district. Meanwhile, Tom had managed to find a furnished room near Riverview, where he was able to find a temporary summer job as a ride operator of the Blue Streak roller coaster. For a short time, Bob and Dave shared a room at the Rex Hotel over on Ashland and Belmont but it had cost too much for them to stay long. Eventually Bob moved in with Etta and her new husband, uncle Pat, while Dave found temporary quarters with their uncle Chick and aunt Helen.

This split-up would last four months, the first two of which posed difficulties for Gene who still attended classes at Agassiz over two miles away. When it rained he rode the bus to school while he rode his bike on fair days. The hard part was delivering his paper route after school. His old neighbor Will still lived in the old neighborhood and Will's folks allowed him to keep his wagon in their shed. Even so, Gene usually wouldn't get home until early evening. Soon graduation would ease some of that!

Late June may have come quickly for some but not for the class of June, 1948, who grew anxious for their graduation. For months they had sung their graduation anthem and for days they had marched down the aisle. Gene was considered to be the short-est boy and was designated to lead off the commencement march. The only nice part about being the first boy in the procession was that his girl counterpart was little blue-eyed, blonde Doris Apple-white, who was absolutely one of the cutest girls in school.

The day before graduation however, the class party for all of three graduating home-rooms was held in the gymnasium. It was a last chance to mingle with the students from the other two gradu-ating home-rooms, many of whom Gene had shared classes with in earlier years.

One girl, Joy Regan, a good friend since fourth grade, stopped to talk with him as the music began. She asked him if he was going to dance but all flustered he replied that he didn't know how to dance. Laughing it off she led him by the hand out to the dance floor where she graciously allowed him to step all over her feet for five minutes until the music mercifully ended. Joy was a very nice girl but she had undergone some obvious changes since they had studied together. To put it succinctly, Joy was fourteen going on twenty, wearing a straight, black skirt that seemed to be sprayed on her; clingy, peach satin blouse, with stockings and heels. Joy was already a woman, Gene thought, while he was still a boy. Even after the party was over, the smell of her perfume permeated his thoughts.

Finally, Graduation Day came around! Whew, it was hot! Why not? It was the 24th of June. Posted by Miss Hanrahan at the rear door of the auditorium, hair all slicked down, Gene could feel his knees knocking as he looked out over the crowd, some of whom were already looking back to see when the march was going to start. Off to his far right, at the other rear door, he could imagine Miss Monaghan lining up the girls, led by little Doris, who seemed to be losing it when he saw her during lineup five minutes before. What's that? Oh no! The music is starting!

Suddenly surrounded by the majestic sound of "Pomp and Circumstance," he heard Miss Hanrahan's voice urging him, "Go! Go!" He stepped through the doorway into the auditorium and miraculously, out of the corner of his eye, he saw Doris stepping off at the same time. Why don't these people turn around and face the front? It makes a guy nervous when they all turn and stare, he thought. There they are! Mom, Bob, and Dave, all grinning from ear to ear. It wasn't so bad, he pondered, at least no one was in front of him to block his view of the audience and stage.

For all of the practice and preparation that went into commencement exercises, it seemed that the day itself was a blur of voices, talking, singing, laughing and crying. For most of the graduates it was the last time they would see each other since they were all off to different high schools. Many of the qualifying boys however, would simply meet again in September at Lane Tech and begin the next phase of their education.

While his seventh-grade reading and arithmetic scores qualified him, and he had applied, Gene was still not certain that he would be joining his friends at Lane. Still unsettled was the question of where Gene and his family would be living when he began high school in the fall. His stay at his grandmaw's was only temporary and to attend Lane Tech he had to have a permanent residence north of North Avenue. Each time an apartment possibility was discussed by Kathleen and Tom, Gene would ask if it was north of North Avenue which, after several inquiries became an annoyance to them due to its lower position on their list of priorities. Some of the possibilities weren't north of North Avenue and he worried as much about that as finding an apartment where he would be allowed to keep his dog, Teddy.

Staying with his grandmaw would be different this time. For one reason, his mom had moved in along with him. For another, the new neighborhood was far removed from the Lake View district he had grown up in and offered a decided change of scenery with considerably more hustle and bustle on its streets and sidewalks. Once again, as on Lakewood, Gene found himself living in a triangular neighborhood, this one bounded on the South by Fullerton Avenue, on the West by Western Avenue and on the East and North by Station Street which was less than a half-mile long and ran diagonally northwest, from Leavitt Street and Fullerton to Western and Logan Boulevard. A perfect right-triangle, Gene called it, "The Brimstone Triangle." It was a name which he thought appropriate, since Station Street also paralleled the Milwaukee Road's Northwest line, "The Route of the 400's," and a sniff of the ambient air always yielded traces of sulfurous smoke fumes.

Along this right-of-way, especially around rush hour, faint traces of smoke gave way to rolling, cumulo-nimbus clouds created by gushing steam and coal-smoke erupting skyward from the blackened stacks of the awesome, nearly terrifying, steam-locomotives which thundered along the rails. It took a lot of guts for a kid to stand on or near the embankment as one of those ironclad monsters, having driver-wheels taller than a man, thundered past at sixty miles per, belching its fire and brimstone up into the urban sky, and shaking the ground so badly that the tremors began even before the train approached.

Like late-Jurassic dinosaurs, these monsters also were soon to be extinct, driven off the rails by the newer, cleaner, Diesel locomotives, which were slowly replacing them. The experience of hearing the loud, spine-tingling "chugga-chugga-chugga" of exhaust stacks and seeing the madly reciprocating steam-driven pistons of a steam-locomotive at high-speed was replaced by the muffled rumble of Diesels. While he would still be awed by the tremendous power and rumble of a Diesel locomotive under way, the unforgettable sound of the iron horses remained with at least one kid, who once had the pleasure of witnessing those magnificent, black, steel beasts. To Gene, no other rolling invention of human hands would ever be as earth-shaking and earsplitting as a steam-locomotive, and he would miss them as he would any other creature gone extinct.

After getting accustomed to the noise and smoke of their neighborhood, Gene felt less a stranger, as his cousin, Roy, who shared the room with him, introduced him to the rest of the neighborhood's younger populace. Roy, now nine, was staying with Grandmaw Kelly since Maybelle and Lew had been traveling extensively, following Lew's work into the Great Plains states. Roy, needing to go to school regularly had remained in Chicago. Except for the hassle of still going back over to his old neighborhood to work his paper route, Gene was finding each day of this summer vacation to be exciting.

Gene and Roy spent a lot of time playing in the neighborhood with the other kids and occasionally went to see a movie at the Rogers up on Fullerton, the Oak down at Western and Armitage, or maybe all the way to the Congress theatre on Milwaukee Avenue.

Each night, Gene would lie in bed and gaze out the window of his room at the warm pink, flashing neon star of the Star Cleaners building just a block away. The flickering star cast a rosy glow in the sky around it, generating a sense of warmth and comfort within Gene. He enjoyed living in this area and felt that it wasn't a bad neighborhood to live in, if his family could just find a place to stay permanently.

Chapter 17

A Period of Adjustment

Independence Day was upon them and it was to be an extra-special Fourth, because Aunt Maybelle and Uncle Lew returned from their extended trip out west and had come over to the Kelly's home to share the holiday. The Kelly clan and the majority of their neighbors sat on their porch stoops or stood in front of their porches talking while the kids surreptitiously went about setting off their illegal firecrackers. In spite of their being illegal in Illinois, fireworks were sold under the counter in many of the Ma and Pa stores. One only needed to ask around to find out which stores.

While firecrackers created a little excitement by themselves, the big show didn't begin until 9:30 when Riverview Amusement Park, a mile away, ignited their fireworks setup. Family and neighbors simply walked the half block up to Western Avenue where they could watch the fireworks while leaning against one of the commercial buildings at the corner of Altgeld and Western.

Due to the distance from Riverview, conversations, and other ambient noise, the booming of the fireworks couldn't be heard too well but spectacular starbursts filling the sky were worth the watching. Certainly all of the youngsters' eyes were fixed on that point above the northern horizon where occasional man-made star showers would cascade down to the ground. Occasionally a Green Hornet streetcar rolled past, emitting its unique steel-wheeled whir, then slowing to a halt at the Altgeld stop's safety island just across the street.

H-o-n-k! H-o-n-k! A car's horn screamed for the crowd's attention and split seconds later, the terrible wail of auto tires braked in a panic stop and the sight of a man lurching off the safety island into the oncoming car's path were frozen in time. It was horrifying for Gene to see disaster a moment away and be helpless to prevent it. Bam! The car struck the man and he was catapulted up and over the hood, along the left fender and with a sickening thud, he fell onto the cobblestone pavement not far from the crowd.

Rushing out into the street, several of the crowd tried to help the injured man as another neighbor called for an ambulance. Near shock, the prostrate man mumbled incoherently and the smell of whiskey was heavy all around him; perhaps a blessing in disguise since some of his pain was being numbed. The driver of the car who hadn't had a prayer of stopping his vehicle in time, was beside himself, feeling guilty that he had inflicted such pain on another human being. Within minutes police cars and an ambulance arrived, the injured man who had by then gone into shock was taken away with a compound fracture of the thigh. After questioning witnesses, accident reports were written up and the scene on Western gradually returned to normal.

During times of mutual concern or shock, people will often turn to total strangers and start talking with them. During all of the excitement, Gene had done that, striking up a conversation with another boy who also seemed very concerned about the injured man. A lovely girl about Gene's age had been standing next to the boy and as Gene started walking down his street, they walked along with him. Pleased with the company, Gene asked the boy where he lived and learned that he lived just three doors from Gene's grandparents. The boy had been away on vacation at his parents' summer house during June and that's why Gene had never met him.

Gene began the introductions and the boy introduced himself as Brad von Held yet failed to mention the quiet, cute blonde girl walking next to him.

As Gene arrived in front of his grandmaw's house, he stopped, telling them this is where he was staying and told Brad, "I didn't catch your girlfriend's name."

Laughing in feigned embarrassment, the mystery beauty exclaimed, "Oh please, I was just waiting for my ignorant brother to introduce me! I'm Eileen and it was so nice meeting you. Maybe we'll see you again since you live so close by. Goodnight."

"Goodnight Eileen. So long Brad."

Climbing the porch stairs, Gene encountered his grandpaw, holding down his favorite chair on the porch.

"Is that your girlfriend, son?"

"No, Grandpaw," blushed his teenaged grandson, who continued, "but I sure wouldn't mind if she was."

"You never know what's going to happen, son."

Tossing in his bed that night, unable to drop off to sleep right away Gene remembered Eileen's words, and sent a mental response to her, as if she could receive it, "I certainly hope to see you again, Eileen."

The next day, Gene watched from his bedroom window for signs of Eileen in her yard but only saw her mother and learned where Eileen got her pleasant looks. Eventually Brad came out into their yard and Gene called him, and after talking across two yards, the two of them decided to go play catch at the schoolyard.

Grandmaw Kelly didn't like Gene associating with his new friend, since it cut back on the time that Gene spent with his cousin Roy. Gene found out too, that his grandmaw once had words with Brad's dad over some minor neighbors' dispute and since then she had held a grudge like a miser holds his money. She had a problem with Gene hanging around the von Held kids. Like a one-armed juggler with six Indian clubs, Gene found himself juggling his time with Roy, Brad, and Eileen throughout July, without making his grandmaw too unhappy.

In the next couple of weeks Brad and Gene would become pals and one high-sky morning when the sun was high with not a cloud in sight, Gene said, "Hey! Let's go to the Cubs game!"

At first Brad said, "No, I don't want to watch those losers."

Responding with "C'mon, the Dodgers are in town and they're the defending National League champs," Gene got an "Okay, but let's get there early" from Brad.

An hour later they were in the ticket line at Wrigley Field. Paying for grandstand seats, they pushed carefully past the triple turnstile bars, the kind that rotate upward with a sudden flip. Gene thought bars like that could geld a careless young man or at least bring him to his knees. Running up the cavernous ramps and finding seats on the third base side of the grandstand they found wall to wall people! It wasn't as empty as they had expected it to be. What was up? Why the crowd? Finding suitable seats away from a post, Brad and Gene sat down and looked over the lineups. Then it struck them. After having lost the 1947 World Series to the Yankees the Dodgers found themselves struggling, but had been drawing large crowds since last season with Jackie Robinson, a Negro player.

Having player problems at first base, Leo Durocher, their manager, had moved second-baseman Robinson back over to first base where he won Rookie of the Year honors the year before. Gene suggested, "Maybe we should go over and sit on the first base side."

Brad's reply was, "No, this is close enough!"

As the game got under way, the two boys followed the action closely, cheering the Cubs and booing the Dodgers. Brad soon became part of the crowd, as they fell into booing Jackie Robinson whenever he came to bat.

"Why are you booing Robinson more than the other Dodgers?" Gene asked of his friend.

"Cause he's a jig!" snarled Brad.

Hearing the persistent shouts of racial derision and being his all-tolerant grandpaw's grandson, Gene was troubled by the crowd's and Brad's reaction. As far as Gene could see Robinson played as well as anyone else; even better when one considered the taunts and prejudice he must have endured in silence, down on the field.

In the bottom of the sixth inning, the crowd's hostile attitude toward Robinson underwent a dramatic change. With two Cubs on base and only one out, a screaming line-drive destined for extra bases was speared by Robinson in a fantastic diving catch fairly deep behind first base. He sprang to his feet, took a step and a half and with cat-like quickness, dove for the bag, doubling-up the Cub runner trying to get back. Suddenly the grandstand shook with a tumultuous roar as the 37,000 people filling Wrigley Field applauded and shouted their approval.

The top of the seventh inning saw the first two other Dodgers hit long, noisy outs. The next batter up was Jackie Robinson. As he climbed the steps out of the dugout, the crowd, including Brad, was on its feet giving him a standing ovation. They applauded, not because he was Jackie Robinson, the first Negro baseball player to play in the major leagues but because he had become just another player to them like anybody else, who had made a tremendous play. The cheering people may have, in their fallible, human hearts, also been trying to make amends for their earlier pre-judgment of him. For whatever reason, Gene Ryan would always be glad he had attended that ballgame, seeing so many people experience a change of heart on a bright, early July day in 1948.

As they walked to the bus and while going home on the bus, Gene was heartened by the turnabout in Brad's attitude as he repeatedly mentioned how Robinson was better than he thought and that he also was surprised at what a good hitter Robinson was. Hearing Brad's glowing praise, it seemed to Gene that perhaps Brad had finally gone color-blind.

While Brad was a lot of fun and a good friend, his sister Eileen was a very cute, honey-blonde with the warmest smile, blue eyes that sparkled and a wonderful personality. Only thirteen years old, like Gene, at five feet one inch, they were the same height. While puberty hadn't yet struck Gene, he was beginning to understand his brother Dave just a bit more.

He began to comprehend why Dave didn't really want to play street games with him over on George Street as long as Marsha Towers was around. There really were other interests in life besides sports and games. Kept busy by his paper route and his grandmaw's many chores, Gene found that he hadn't much time left to socialize. In spite of his schedule, he managed to spend just enough time around the lovely creature and her brother, while their parents worked.

Eileen was a very bright girl, able to discuss seriously, a variety of subjects with Gene, even to the point where they quizzed each other on their general knowledge. Eileen was a smart cookie. She and Gene had also found many unimportant things to talk about, more than he could ever talk about with any other girl. Yet it wasn't a case of puppy-love, as it seemed to be more of a case of "puppy-like." What he really fell in love with was the taste of rich, cool, frothy, chocolate milk which their family always kept in their refrigerator, having at least one, sometimes two glasses offered to him during a visit. Eileen was such a gracious host!

As always, the good things in life too quickly come to an end and Gene would soon be moving away from Eileen, and Brad. It was mid-July when the long-awaited news came that after all of their searching and negotiating, Kathleen and Tom had at last found an apartment for all of them, even their dog. They were able to sign a one-year lease on a seven-room apartment on the Near North Side, on Newport Street between Lakewood and Southport. Not only would Gene be able to keep his dog, Teddy, but the location was north of North Avenue, which meant being able to attend Lane Tech, his first choice. As an added extra, the apartment in question was only four blocks from Gene's revered Wrigley Field, home of his beloved Cubs and Bears. Gene was going back home to the North Side!

Like doomsday heralded by Gabriel's trumpet, moving day was announced by their uncle Chick laying on the horn as he pulled up in the rented moving van. As if anyone might still be sleeping at nine o'clock in the morning at Grandmaw Kelly's! Lights had burned late into the evening the night before, as Kathleen and Gene packed, making sure that they would be all ready to go when the van arrived. In jubilant anticipation of getting back her full-time bathroom privileges, Betty had even lent them a hand in packing. It was a moving day to be unlike any other, since their furniture and appliances that had been stored in several places when the family had split apart in April, now had to be retrieved and moved.

Within minutes, other cars arrived with the rest of the moving crew. Counting uncles Chick, Clay, and Pat, plus Tom and the three Ryan boys, there were enough able bodies to manage all of the lifting and carrying that soon got underway. Grandpaw Kelly, having only one leg and unable to perform the physical moving tasks, wasn't going to be left out. He made up for it by giving the active movers all of the instructions they needed and even some that weren't. Grandpaw Kelly enjoyed it because of the camaraderie. It also got him out of the house and away from Grandmaw Kelly, who always had her own list of jobs for him.

After loading up furniture and appliances from two locations, the crew was off to the new apartment, some riding in a chase car, the others riding in the moving van's cab and in the back of the van. Hanging on to the side rails of the van as he rode with the load, Gene at times felt as if he was on board a ship at sea. Maybe that's what he should do when he was eighteen, he thought; join the Navy like Bob did. Only he didn't want to serve on some gigantic aircraft carrier. No, he wanted destroyer duty on one of those fast little ships that hunted submarines. That's it! And boy, those Navy whites were so neat-looking! Yeh, it sounded pretty intriguing to him.

Approaching the house on Newport, Gene liked what he saw: nice one and two-story brick or stone homes on both sides of the street. As he and Dave hauled one of the rugs up the stairs and into the apartment, he saw that the apartment was pretty big. Later, by asking in which rooms they should put their beds, Dave and Gene were told to put their beds in the same room. They would still share the same bedroom, while Bob got a room of his own.

"Must be nice to be the oldest brother and get a room of your own," groused Dave, enviously.

Bob would even have room to set up his desk which his youngest brother mentally noted as a potential reason to be able to use his oldest brother's room.

Adding up the rooms, Dave and Gene both arrived at the conclusion that there was still a bedroom available. Looking at each other they thought aloud, "Why isn't one of us getting that room?"

Approaching Kathleen, they asked her, "Why isn't one of us getting the extra room?"

She answered them saying, "I understand why you are asking,

but someone else is coming to stay with us and that room will belong to her." Then she closed the discussion with, "Shouldn't you boys get back to moving furniture?"

The young protesters shuffled back outside into the stifling humidity of late July, wondering who "her" was? While they both liked mysteries, "her" was a mystery that would torment them as back and forth they went, from the truck to the house until the truck was empty.

Then Chick hollered out, "Everybody get aboard! Got to go back to get another load!"

Load, drive, unload; another trip, Load, drive, unload; another trip. Long before the end of the day, the thought would occur to Gene, that June 22nd, the summer solstice, hadn't been the longest day. This July 31st was the longest day!

Finally, around 8 o'clock that night, everything was moved in and all of their furnishings were in place. Kathleen then uttered those beautiful words, "Come and get it!" as she served a long overdue dinner to her brood and anyone of the movers who wanted to stay. After dinner, Bob, the eligible bachelor, didn't bother going out, but retired early, as did everyone else. The first day of August dawned the next morning and at breakfast, no one had complained about not being able to sleep.

Kathleen then explained the agreement that she and Tom had made with their new landlord, Mr. Anderson. It seems that Mr. and Mrs. Anderson had an elderly woman friend named Mae Waltzer who had been staying with them but now their son would be coming home from the Navy to stay and so they asked Kathleen and Tom if they would take Miss Waltzer in as a boarder. In return, they would reduce the usual rent and Kathleen and Tom could also keep Teddy. Without the extra money from boarding and the cut in the rent, Kathleen and Tom might not have been able to afford such a large apartment, so they had agreed to Mr. Anderson's terms in accepting the apartment. The spare room was to be used by Miss Waltzer, whom they would be meeting when she came downstairs to join them later that afternoon.

After breakfast, needing reinforcement of his festering protest, Dave buttonholed Gene, asking him, "What do you think of that? A stranger is coming to live with us and we never had a thing to say about it!"

Gene just said, "I know, but I guess we'll have to let it go. I wondered if they'd taken in a boarder if it wasn't necessary. At least we get to keep Teddy don't we?" Then Gene continued, "Look at the size of this place! Seven rooms and we get to use the yard, too. It could have been a lot worse."

"Yeh, I guess there might be reasons." Having failed to gain support for his argument, Dave went out, after telling Kathleen he'd be back later.

An hour later, Gene was champing at the bit to walk around and see what the neighborhood had to offer. The photoflash of a bright midday sun nearly blinded him as he stepped outside the apartment. He walked up to the drugstore at Southport and Roscoe to check it out, coming away with a cursory opinion of their fountain service: great cherry-cokes. Fred, the soda-jerk behind the fountain, informed him that the Music Box was the only movie theatre within blocks, just up Southport near Grace Street, four blocks away. The only other nearby theatres were back in his old George Street neighborhood, nearly a mile away. Heat waves shimmered above the cobble-stoned pavement of Southport as Gene peered longingly south toward his old neighborhood and paper route. At least the streetcar was close and he could always ride his bike back to the old haunts and friends that he'd left behind.

At Roscoe, he crossed over to the other side of Southport. Walking along the other side, he noticed that they had taken up residence within a block of an elevated train tracks, just a block from the Southport station of the Ravenswood "El" line. Neat-looking shops and stores lined both sides of Southport, forming a neighborhood shopping strip, offering all the goods and services a family needed.

The graveyard stillness of the Sunday afternoon air was disquieting: lonely-looking streets too reminiscent of long ago Sundays. He would have welcomed the noise of an "El" train to shatter this stillness but being Sunday, the trains ran on a limited schedule and no train passed overhead. Crossing Southport again, he looked around and could just as well have been standing in the middle of the street in an old western ghost town. Ghost towns had nothing on this place as he thought to himself, where is everybody? Turning northward, he strolled back to Newport then down to their neat, solid, two-flat in gray stone. He had seen no other teenagers in the area; not a good sign for a teenager, new in the neighborhood.

Around four in the afternoon, the doorbell ring was answered by Tom, who was unexpectedly showered by sparks of outgoing friendliness from Miss Mae Waltzer. A plump person of size, her medium-brown hair speckled with gray was worn back in a bun, accenting a pale face that when young, must have always been protected by an ever present sun parasol and very lovely. At 65 years young, Mae's faltering steps and her use of a cane indicated a severe arthritic condition but she would demonstrate in days to come that her eyes and mind were clear and sharp.

Well-versed in a wide variety of subjects, her whole being opened like the petals of a rose when she was included in a conversation. Witty and quick to respond, she held her own in any give-and-take banter and over the four years she remained with them, would be accepted as one of the family, becoming a confidante of and advisor to each of the boys. Despite his vociferous protesting, Dave soon realized that Mae was "cool" in that she had kept up with the times and understood the present-day jargon. Hey! He could talk to her; she was okay!

Besides his family and its new foster member, Gene still had one other reference point in his young life that offered him continuity, in the midst of changing schools, friends, and neighborhoods. He still had his paper route and his customers, with whom he had developed a good rapport over the past four years. Some kids on the route had come to be his friends, inviting him to play in their ball games until time forced him to get back to delivering papers.

Gene's last month of vacation was spent keeping an eye out for kids his age but seeing none, would ride his bike over to George Street and then to the Agassiz schoolyard. Sometimes he encountered his old puppy-love, Marjorie Cribbens, but she was interested in Bob Brucken, another old friend of his. While his school friends would go on to other high schools in a few weeks, they had been the only friends he knew in the area and this was his last chance to be around them.

If the Cubs were playing at home, he usually bought a bleacher seat ticket for sixty cents and before noon, had his pick of any seat in the bleachers. On days when he found himself short on funds, he rode his bike to the ballpark and waited outside the left field wall on Waveland Avenue. Standing ready with his mitt, he waited with many others for a ball to be hit out of the park.

When the summer heat wending its way down Waveland parched his throat, he went over to the gas station at Sheffield and Waveland and opened up the soft-drink cooler. Always cold, the large metal container held cold, liquid treasures such as Coke, Pepsi, Double Cola, Kayo, Canada Dry, and several brands of assorted soda flavors such as Lasser's, Nehi, and Bireley's.

On evenings when he didn't ride over to his old school, hanging around Newport and Lakewood was boring since there wasn't much for Gene to do alone. In the midst of another solo performance, sitting on the front porch after dinner, Bob came out on the porch and sat down next to him.

His oldest brother asked,"What are you doing?"

"Nothin'," was Gene's bright response.

"Want to go for a bike ride?" asked Bob.

"You don't have a bike!"

Continuing on, Bob said, "No, but I'll ride yours and you can ride on the crossbars, or I can ride it by myself."

Since Bob was bigger and stronger than he was, Gene quickly saw the logic of Bob's reasoning and answered, "Let's go! I don't mind riding on the crossbars."

Hauling the bike from their first floor back porch to the front sidewalk was quickly done and the brothers rode off down Newport, heading East, wobbling on their way until Bob got his bicycle act together, and put the bike on a straight course. Young Gene felt honored in a way since his brother Bob was by far, the best looking guy on the block and because Gene was plain, felt a little better-looking around Bob.

Lately Bob, like Dave, had seemed too busy to pay attention to him, working and studying to get his high school diploma. His education had been interrupted by his Navy hitch. Yeh, he was glad that he and Bob were going someplace together, like two lifelong buddies. It had been a while. Gene had missed all of his friends and hadn't made any new ones. It could have been that his big brother noticed his predicament and thought it might be nice to pay some attention to his lonely kid brother.

As they rode along, Gene was having a lot more fun than Bob, since the older brother was doing all of the pedaling and most of the worrying about bicycle operation and navigation. Onward toward the lake they rode, coming to the concrete and glass canyons of high-rise apartments lining the lake shore's narrow streets. As they turned onto one very narrow street which looked more like an alley, backed-up traffic filled the street as impatient motorists waited for the traffic signal to change. Gene, worried about his bike, quickly assumed much of the worry of navigation and offered his brother bits of unheeded advice, such as "Look out! Look out!"

Gliding over to the right with just inches to spare on either side, Bob steered the bike between the parked cars and a line of cars stopped for the light. Squinting his eyes, Gene didn't want to see it coming as they rode toward a certain collision or bad scratch of someone's car, and those were his legs hanging off the right side of the bike. The loaded bike had nearly made it to the intersection and without a scratch, which mattered little to one woman passenger who saw how close Bob was to her companion's car. Incensed, she gave them a piece of her mind through the closed passenger side window. Unable to hear her, they read her lips shouting "You damned fools!" at them. Bob just laughed heartily, pedaled onward, and as the light changed they rode through the intersection.

Lake shore breezes cooled their perspiration as they approached Lincoln Park and entering its green expanse, rode up to and along the lakefront. What a beautiful city they lived in, thought Gene, taking in the breadth of the nearly-white sandy beach, sweeping south to Chicago's downtown skyline, then east past the cribs to the horizon, where the blue-green of the lake clashed with the reflected mauve sky of dusk. He felt that his mom couldn't have picked a lovelier city to settle in after they left Texas.

After cruising along North Avenue beach, they turned around for home, riding through another part of the park just as the street lights flicked on in one of its parking lots. At one of the softball games, they stopped to turn on the bike's lights, for it was getting dark. Gene wanted them to be seen by car drivers and besides, he liked the green and red taillights he had installed on the back hub.

A great benefit of living on Chicago's North Side, was that it only took ten or fifteen minutes to ride a bike to the lakefront. Alas, it also meant that their ride to the park would be over too soon since it had been quite an evening. Pulling up in front of their house, Bob admitted to his legs being tired from pedaling for two as Gene hauled the bike back onto the porch. While he neglected to tell his brother how much he appreciated his company, it was obvious to Bob and to Kathleen when Gene recounted their expedition at dinner the next evening.

As the carefree days of Summer grew shorter, with Labor Day fast approaching, Gene began preparations for his enrollment at Lane. Across from Lane he bought a mechanical drawing set at Riesz' school supplies and a Lane Tech T-shirt at McGovern's. He was ready for Lane, or so he thought.

Chapter 18

Off To A Rough Start

Freshmen, hundreds of pukey freshman milled around, as if a swarm of humanoid locusts had descended on Lane Tech, massing on the Addison Street side and buzzing all around the Administration Wing. A few dorky newcomers had been escorted by their parents; Geez, how embarrassing that must have been. Around the grounds they meandered; even treading on Lane's sacred lawn. They would soon learn, as all Laneites did, that the campus lawn was revered as if it were hallowed ground, no student or teacher was allowed to walk on it, let alone picnic on it. Within a week they would also learn that their beginning freshman class numbered 1,266 freshly-scrubbed faces.

At last, the doors opened up to the Auditorium Wing and the lowest of the low began filing in. Ablaze with light from its massive chandeliers, the auditorium seemed cathedral-like in its grandeur. Agassiz's auditorium could have fit in the balcony of this place. As the uninitiated settled in their seats, not knowing what to expect, the second-floor catwalk doors flew open and a crowd of older students hurried to positions along the catwalk in order to take a look at the latest crop of "freshies." Catcalls and general verbal abuse greeted the class of June, 1952, followed by the ceremonial flinging of pennies at the sitting-duck freshman body by the old guard from the high ground of their second floor vantage point.

After what seemed to be hours, a councilor stepped to the microphone and brought the assembled freshmen to order, beginning with questions and instructions based on the answers received. "Do you live south of North Avenue, if so, you must attend Crane Tech. If you graduated from a parochial school you might have to take additional tests. If you graduated from a public school, take your transfer voucher to your assigned division room teacher."

"What?" snapped Gene, who suddenly was fully alert. He then asked no one in particular, "What's a transfer voucher?"

His stomach turned over as the immense hall began emptying out, and looking lost and ignorant, he was approached by a councilor who listened to his problem, then told him that he should have gotten his transfer voucher from his elementary school on the last day of the semester.

"Oh, no!" exclaimed Gene, who hadn't gone to school that last day.

Kathleen had figured that since it was only for a half-day and he had already graduated, it wouldn't be worth the bus trip back to school the next day, so she said that he could stay home. But now he couldn't get into high school without a transfer voucher, so he had to go back to Agassiz and get one.

Taking two buses, Gene returned to Agassiz and found Miss Hanrahan in an inquisitive mood, well, maybe it was more like an Inquisition mood, since she seemed perturbed that he hadn't come to school that last day.

"Why didn't you come to school on the last day? All of my other students attended the last day. Did you think you were special? Did you think I could just stop teaching my class and write out a transfer for you?"

Gene felt that the thirty seconds required to fill out the form would have infringed upon less of her class time than the time consumed by her browbeating.

Finally, clutching the signed document in his sweaty hands, Gene made his way back to Lane Tech's campus where he was stopped at the entrance by a hallguard who wanted to take him down to the Discipline Office for being out of class without a pass. Gene wondered, how could he be out of class if he hadn't been able to get in the school yet? Who was this guy? What was the Discipline Office? Answers to those questions would come soon to Gene, the hard way.

Registering late at the admissions office, Gene was raked over the coals for not reporting at the time all incoming freshman were supposed to. At last, he was told to report to Mr. Michaels' division in room 305 which happened to be up on the third floor and he was already late. Finding a staircase, he ascended to the third floor and scanned the room numbers as he hurried along, 302, 304, 306, 308. Where was 305? For that matter, where were any of the odd-numbered rooms? He felt like a rat trapped in a maze without the cheese!

What the poor freshman slob didn't know, like every other "freshie" at Lane, was that an invisible line divided the school into odd and even sides. All odd-numbered rooms were on one side of the massive four-winged building while even-numbered rooms were on the other side. "Freshies" didn't know where the dividing line was and required days to get oriented to the layout of their building. Desperate for help, Gene asked a student slouched in a chair in the hall for directions. Instead of directions, the student who was another hallguard, asked Gene for his hall pass. After seeing Gene's registration form, the hallguard allowed Gene to resume his search after giving the harried "freshie" directions on how to find the missing Room 305.

Following the hallguard's instructions, Gene was getting close: 311, 309, 307, then in big, black numbers, there it was, 305! Entering the room, he found a drafting class in session and Mr. Michaels, a friendly-looking bespectacled older man took the time to accept his registration form and explain where Gene should be going next. Gene had arrived just in time for the ten minute division room or home room period during which he was brought up to date and met his fellow division room classmates. Following the division meeting was lunch period and just in time because Gene was starved and shaky.

By early afternoon, he had caught up with his classes and finished out the day without further incident. He had quite a story to regale his family with that night. Naturally, Bob and Dave took shots at him because he had chosen Lane Tech in the first place. But Gene, along with his classmates, had opted for Lane because it was the elite school of Chicago's Public high schools, offering specialized and technical courses of education. It also engendered a feeling of pride, as exhibited by Dave's longtime, smart buddy, Jack Gorr, who had often supported and encouraged Gene in his decision to attend Lane.

On only his second day, Gene was able find out everything he needed to know about the aforementioned Discipline Office. He learned that "Discipline" was Lane Tech's term for detention. This knowledge sprang from a unwanted encounter with a kid in freshman gym class. Sitting on the gym floor with 250 other boys, Gene listened to instructions from their coach. Next to Gene was Wilton Hartman, a guy from his division room, who had a marking pen, and was trying to mark Gene up with it. Hartman's actions and Gene's fending off of Hartman were spotted by the assistant coach, who summarily hauled their butts down to the Discipline Office.

Mr. Ruesselsheimer, the discipline administrator, asked, "What is the charge?"

The coach replied, "Disturbing 250 students in class!"

"Well," said the administrator, his eyes gaining a sudden sparkle and his sneer curling into a smile, "we can certainly teach them a lesson. You said 250 students, eh? Since you boys are new here, we'll go easy and start you off with five discipline periods, starting today."

That was it. No appeal, no concern that they might have after-school jobs. Five periods meant remaining after school for one period each day for five days.

Leaving the Discipline Office, Gene turned to Hartman and muttered, "Thanks a lot, jerk!"

At 3:30, Gene and Hartman entered the large classroom used for serving out discipline periods, found two desks about halfway back and slumped into them. The murmur of voices throughout the fully-occupied room was evidence that it had been a banner day for the Discipline Office. A room full of offenders waited for the bell to signal the start of the period.

The bell rang just as Gene turned around in his seat to ask Hartman, "What do we do now?

Hartman shook his head slightly, and looking past him, uttered, "Shhh!"

Turning back around, Gene's eyes met the cold stare of the disciplinarian standing next to him. She then began writing on a slip of paper. What she was writing was a "+2" slip for him, meaning that he had just picked up two additional periods for talking during Discipline.

Handing the +2 slip to him, she hissed, "Silence! No talking!"

As quickly as the old mousetrap snaps, Gene had learned that absolute silence was one of the main rules of discipline periods and two disciplinarians were there to enforce them.

At Lane, and possibly in other schools, many teachers and administrators possessed two names, their legal names and the monikers with which the student body tagged them. Mr. Ruesselsheimer was also known as "Mr. Ruthless," a name probably given him in recognition of the zealous manner in which he administered disciplinary action. An air of Prussian aristocracy which clung to him like a scarf to the "Red Baron" was augmented by his stiff, military bearing. Strong, angular, Teutonic features were complemented by close-cropped iron-gray hair, while the only thing missing from his stern countenance was the obligatory dueling scar and spiked helmet. He seemed perfect for the job!

Shortly after serving out his discipline periods, Gene got to learn first-hand about the Hallguard Roving Patrol, commonly known as the "Rovers," which consisted of several teams of hallguards who patrolled the outside areas of the school's campus. Spotting an infraction of campus rules, they took the offender back inside to the Discipline Office where Mr. Ruesselsheimer dealt with them. The Rovers listened to no explanation and when they stated charges against a student, had no qualms about stretching the truth or putting the offender in the worst light, as Gene would soon experience.

In pursuit of more pleasant activities, Gene heard in early October that football tryouts were being held. The football coach had scheduled a primo day for Frosh-Soph football tryouts which were taking place near the parking lot and bike racks. Temperatures were about 70 degrees and a sunny sky smiled down on the young hopefuls who were trying out for the first time. Wally

Herzog, one of Gene's classmates in gym had told him that he was trying out and Gene came over to watch. Since his bike was at the end of the rack nearest the tryouts, Gene sat down on its seat and took in the show. Gene envied Wally and the other guys trying out, who were heavier and taller than he. Wally may have been more than a foot taller than Gene but he was thin, so thin that if someone stood Wally in a lumberyard next to the fence posts, it would have been difficult to pick Wally out! Wally seemed to have good hands for catching the football however, and after seeing him run patterns Gene thought that Wally had shown good speed too.

"Hey! What are you doing there?"

Turning around, Gene saw four guys and he told them, "I'm watching the football tryouts."

"Never mind the tryouts." Failing to identify themselves, they asked him, "What are you doing with that bike?"

"It's my bike. I'm sitting on my bike, watching the tryouts. Why do you want to know?"

"We've got a wise guy here," sneered their leader who told Gene, "We're takin' you down to Discipline!"

Turns out they were part of the Roving Patrol! Taking Gene in, the Rovers informed Mr. Ruthless that they had found Gene tampering with a bicycle. It was his second offense in this young semester, for which Gene was penalized with fifteen periods of discipline. He had learned, as many Laneites did, why the Rovers and their Gestapo tactics were despised.

Recognizing the need for order and discipline, Gene couldn't understand why Lane's rules weren't explained to freshmen or why the offender's side of a story was never heard or that some form of appeal wasn't in place. The Discipline Office at best, seemed like a kangaroo court for students and was the personal reason most often given by his friends, for transferring out of Lane Tech to another high school. Freshman classes generally lost about half their number through failures or transfers during their four years at Lane.

Lane Tech wasn't intended to be an easy school, socially or scholastically, but that's where the pride came from. If students made it through Lane, they had been through the course in what was considered as the best and toughest of Chicago's high schools and could be proud of their achievement.

As the first few weeks went by, it was apparent that high school was going to be a lot tougher than grade school had ever been. School was quickly becoming much less fun than it used to be as Gene realized that his new classmates were no slouches and he really had to hustle to keep up with them. Science and English were still the easiest subjects for him while Algebra and Mechanical Drawing gave him the most trouble. Because the Essential Math class recommended by a counselor at Agassiz had filled up, Algebra had been substituted by a Lane advisor, and Gene was struggling to get up to speed. Gene had enrolled in the Commercial Art curriculum, and being interested in creative art, the rigid nature of mechanical drawing left him cold.

Since Lane was a technical high school, several four-year curricula were available to students interested in college preparatory work, a technical career such as Auto Mechanics, Aviation Mechanics, Machinists, and Printing, or a specialized career such as Architecture or Commercial Art.

Due to over-registration in the Commercial Art curriculum, Gene and several other students were transferred from Mr. Michaels' division to Mr. Walton's division, splitting them off from friends that they had already made. Usually a student's division room teacher was also a teacher of their major, so that the teachers knew more about their "home-room" students and had a stake in their development. Messrs. Michaels and Walton were drafting teachers who taught no Commercial Art students, yet each had a sprinkling of them in their division rooms comprised primarily of drafting students.

In essence, underclass Commercial Art students were orphans, reporting to begrudging division teachers who only tolerated the additional responsibility of recording attendance of and relaying communications to students whom they only saw ten minutes per day.

While their former division roommates were studying under Mrs. Berlansky, a highly-regarded art teacher, because of overcrowding in the Commercial Art classes, Mr. Walton's group of

Commercial Art students, found that their class schedules had been changed to include a different teacher for their Art class. Their first year of art instruction had been assigned to Mr. Kirkstat, a drafting teacher. Mr. Kirkstat, whose unofficial name was "Mr. Jerkstat," would base a good percentage of his grading on whether or not a student had bought certain supplies, for example: a 2H pencil sharpened no more than 7/8 of an inch. During their long first year, his students would learn very little in his Art class.

Gene's enthusiasm for Gym class, like he himself, started slowly and faded fast, since most of the guys were older than he was and he had never been all that healthy as a kid. Surgery to remove a pneumonia-damaged portion of his right lung as an infant had left him scrawny, short-winded, and a wimp in athletics despite riding his bike two miles to school every day. When gym classes mandated running outside around the campus, Gene found it hard to keep up, with his lungs afire, throat parched, and legs of lead. Running right after lunch was another problem for him as sometimes Gene got cramps in his side. He was beginning to feel like a physical mess!

His greatest embarrassment in Gym came very early in his high school career when their coach, who was also the varsity football coach, ordered everybody onto the quarter-mile track inside Lane Stadium. The class of 250 young boys had by now been divided into 12 teams for the sake of organization and competition. The coach had set up several heats of 440 yard races, each heat comprising members from each of the teams.

As the runners in his heat got on their marks at the starting line, Gene was a bundle of adrenaline-pumped nerves and the sandwich he had for lunch weighed heavy on his stomach. Bang! Like a herd of stampeding free-range mustangs the other runners galloped past him, kicking gravel in his face. At the 220 yard mark, he couldn't get his breath, his side was cramping, and he fell back but didn't quit. Wanting no one to see him double-up in pain, he stayed with it and kept shuffling along until he finished the race, dead last, taking over ninety seconds, a clocking he would never forget.

As he crossed the finish line, he heard the coach and most of the gym class laughing at him in amusement, because he was running so slowly. Wanting to just disappear, Gene's humiliation ignited a burning desire within him, an ambition that drove him through all the physical trials of the next four years. He promised himself that he would never physically fail at anything again.

That night, in his bedroom which he shared with Dave who wasn't home, Gene began what would become a nightly exercise routine for the next four years; a regimen of knee-bends, push-ups, and sit-ups, to strengthen his legs, arms, and stomach. He learned to his disappointment that he only stood five-feet-one and weighed 105 pounds, as he measured his height and weight for later comparison.

During that week, he began to run every chance he got, not for speed but to build up his stamina and endurance. Gene had psyched himself up to grow taller and get stronger because he had come to realize that it was getting to be a tough world out there and he seemed to be ill-prepared to meet it. Keeping his own council, he didn't let on to his family that he still felt like a Runt and might always be.

His teenaged spirits had also begun to flag because he hadn't yet found any friends in their neighborhood, a situation that was soon to change. Ruddy-faced and dark-haired, Hans Mauer walked into Gene's young life one cool afternoon, just as the late autumn sun was fading into the cold, gray horizon. Standing astride his bike in the street, Gene encountered a tall, lanky kid about his age crossing the street in front of his house. Striking up a conversation with him, Gene found out that Hans was only an eighth-grader who had been away at a soccer camp most of August. For several years Hans had played soccer for the North Side athletic club and had become very good in a sport which had never seemed to catch on the United States.

Tall, big-boned and lantern-jawed, Hans had a slight German accent, not unusual in their predominantly German neighborhood. While Hans had been born in the United States, his parents were first-generation German immigrants who spoke their native language at home. Hans also liked to play touch football and baseball and they agreed to get together the next evening. At last, Gene had found someone his age in Hans, who lived just across the street.

After talking for a while the next day, Hans decided to take Gene up to the west end of their block and introduced him to another tall, dark-haired guy named Jack Kramer, a thin, handsome kid who appeared somewhat aloof. Jack was a freshman at Lake View high, from where Gene's brother Bob had just gained his GED. Talking for a few minutes and getting acquainted, the three of them decided to go over to the drugstore where they had sodas and shakes over which they talked about sports and schools, while sitting in a booth.

A tumult which sounded like a fight erupted outside, but it was simply Himself making an entrance. His approach had been heard before he ever walked in the door, after baiting a couple of kids outside. How could a short, skinny kid be as vociferous as "Weasel"? Always brash, sometimes despicable, Fred "Weasel" Dolan was a red-haired, freckle-faced braggart who, saints preserve us, also happened to be Irish. With protruding ears he was as ugly as his friends Hans and Jack were handsome, and he had a personality to match. For better or worse this eighth-grader named Dolan would be the fourth member of the small group of which Gene would be a part, for the two years he would live on Newport.

Before the evening was over, they made plans to go bowling early that Saturday afternoon down on Broadway, where they could bowl for twenty cents per line as long as they finished before the four o'clock league began. Gene was looking forward to bowling but he had to do his homework Friday night and cover his paper route early on Saturday, in order to join his new friends at one o'clock.

Ring! Ring! The doorbell's ring roused Gene early Saturday morning, while brother Dave just rolled over in his bed. Gene awakened to hear his stepfather, Tom, welcoming their visitor. He heard the murmur of voices get louder then softer as he heard footsteps approaching their bedroom door. As the door slowly opened into their room, still early-morning dim, Gene recognized who the skulker was, in the subdued light from their window.

With his jacket collar turned up, hat brim turned down, and putting his forefinger to his nose, Gene's uncle Lew flashed a broad smile at him, as he moved quietly past Gene's bed with intentions of rousting Dave and scaring the bejabbers out of him. Reaching the edge of sleeping Dave's bed, Lew raised his arms in an exaggerated pouncing pose, when he himself was pounced upon.

Rowlff! Grrrr! Grrrr!

"Whoaaa! Hey!"

Suddenly Lew's pants leg was being ripped and savaged by a furious Teddy who, failing to recognize this stranger with his face covered, had followed him in then attacked to protect his friend Dave from apparent harm.

Instantly, Lew threw off his hat and quickly said, "Teddy, it's me, Lewie! Don't you know me, boy?"

Teddy responded by lowering his head and sheepishly wagging his tail.

Red-faced and shaking, Lew turned to Gene and said, "You've got some watchdog there!" while everybody else roared with laughter.

Gene didn't think much about it at the time but his uncle left earlier than he normally would have. Later, in retrospect, Gene realized that despite his being strong and tough, ex-boxer Lew might have left early because of a needed change of shorts.

That afternoon at the bowling alley, Jack, Hans, and Gene had made a pleasant series out of their games while Weasel's bragging and banter were just barely tolerable. Gene wondered what Jack and Hans saw in this jerk except that Hans and Dolan had attended the same grammar school together, but Gene appreciated their company enough to overlook Dolan's shortcomings. After five games each and more than that number of bowls of popcorn, they tallied up their lines and paid a dollar each for the afternoon. Not bad, since bowling usually cost thirty-five cents a line.

Asking if anyone wanted to take in a movie that night, Gene got negative responses from the good guys but Dolan said, "I'll go."

"Great ..."

"What show we gonna see?"

"There's a good movie at the Music Box!"

"I saw it!"

"Then let's go to the Lincoln."

"I saw that too!"

"Okay, Dolan, what movie haven't you seen?"

"The one at the Belmont!"

"Okay, we'll go to the Belmont!"

It would be the first of many times that the two peacefully co-existing enemies shared each other's company, going to carnivals, baseball games, and movies. Often, when Jack or Hans couldn't make it, the two played catch or visited the Lincoln-Belmont YMCA's gym and pool. Weasel Dolan was extremely self-confident, believing himself to be a potential Major League second-baseman and a great basketball player, when he was neither. Gene thought at times, that with his attitude Weasel would probably not live to be very old.

Columbus Day afforded all school kids a rainy day off, so Gene invited Jack and Dolan to stop by and maybe they could play some Rummy. Sitting down at the dining room table Gene asked Mae if she wanted to sit in as a fourth, an invitation which she quickly accepted. It was fun watching Dolan's eyes bulge when elderly Mae easily, expertly riffled and shuffled the cards ala Las Vegas. She was sharp and could remember every card that was played.

After the two boys went home, Mae later told Gene, "In my long life there have been very few people that I had met and didn't like, but Freddy Dolan is one of them." She asked Gene as did some of the neighborhood girls later on, "Why does a nice guy like you hang around with a creep like Fred Dolan?"

Gene replied, "I know how you feel! He can be so exasperating at times. But often he's the only guy around to hang out with, and sometimes, maybe even Dolan needs a friend."

A puzzle in himself, Jack Kramer could be great guy, as Gene found out when he and Jack had a lot to talk about during bowling by themselves or took in a Cub game. Jack was another avid Cub fan and they enjoyed basking in the bleachers together, especially on rare occasions when the Cubs scoreboard crew could hoist the blue flag with the white "W" after a game. While playing catch in the neighborhood, Gene observed that having long arms, Jack could really fire a ball and with his lanky body had the range of motion necessary for a good shortstop. While playing touch football, Gene learned that Jack was the best punter he knew, being able to boom forty-five-yard punts. But when Dolan was around and in one of his cheap shot moods, Jack, for some inexplicable reason would switch to another, offensive side of himself, and the two of them together were insufferable.

Hans Mauer was another story completely. There seemed to be some form of mutual respect between he and Gene. Gene also respected the strength in Hans' strong, long arms, that could have pummeled Gene to a pulp if they ever got into a physical disagreement. If a guy had troubles, Hans was there to help him out. In addition to being a good soccer player, Hans had a right arm that with practice and proper coaching might have gotten him a pitching tryout with a Major League farm club. A hard throw from shortstop by Hans could punish Gene's glove hand and after about an hour of practice, it was all Gene could do to keep from throwing in the towel.

Seeming to like people, Hans got along well with strangers. He didn't have any reservations about making friends with people easily, as long as those people weren't Jewish. As Brad von Held had seen only in black and white, Hans Mauer's only fault was that he only saw people as non-Jews and Jews. Hans spoke the word "Jew" contemptuously and could denigrate Jews with a biased passion that a white-clad Klansman would have admired.

His grandpaw's tolerance toward other races and religions had been absorbed by Gene during his early years and he couldn't agree with Hans on this issue. Since his dearest teacher, Mrs Kosterman and a good friend, Ruth Perlman at Agassiz were Jewish, and being helped out considerably by a Jewish classmate, Jake Kapp, in his first days at Lane, Gene despised Hans' bigoted comments. Attempts on Gene's part to get Hans to see Jews in a better light were met with biased resistance by Hans. Since he couldn't change the attitude that must have been instilled in Hans during his childhood, Gene began letting Hans' anti-Semitic comments run off his shoulders, accepting Hans, a bigot, as his friend, yet rejecting his bigoted comments when spoken.

With the painfully slow passing of his early freshman days, Gene had gained three classmate friends, Pat Decker, Joe Garth, and John Chavez, who day by day would earn his trust and friendship over the next four years of high school and for years afterwards. Fellow castoffs who were transferred out of the good art class and Mr. Michaels' division room, their friendship during Gene's early days at Lane had lifted his spirits and bolstered his flagging confidence.

The three were all taller, stronger, mesomorph types whom Gene worked closely with and he developed a sense of respect for them as they shared all of their classes and Mr. Walton's division room. Pat was Gene's locker partner and friend, sharing the same locker since there weren't enough to go around. Joe would be Gene's drawing bench partner during their two inglorious years of Jerkstat's art classes. John shared a drawing bench with Gene during their Mechanical Drawing class and also shared a common interest in Astronomy, joining the Astronomy Club together, which met after school.

As midterm grades came out in time to bring them home over the Thanksgiving holiday, his grades reflected Gene's mediocre first ten weeks at Lane, when except for a B in Algebra, he pulled C's across the board. Lane's grading system quickly made believers out its students. A score of 95-100 for an 'A' and 88-94 for a 'B', were really tough, while a student could rate a 'C' only if he scored 81-87. Failure was certain for any student scoring less than 75. Whether it was a lack of brains or a stiffer effort requirement, he wasn't doing as well as he thought he should be and over the holiday began to really think about his progress thus far. Except for Jerkstat, he had good teachers, so he figured correctly, it must have been him. Algebra was very tough for him, so he had worked extra hard and got a good grade. Why did he do worse in subjects that had always been easy for him? Could it have been a lack of concentration on his part during the first half of the semester.

Not having yet experienced the throes of puberty, Gene was

still able to appreciate a pretty face and two of his teachers qualified in that area, both teaching what should have been easy subjects for him. Mrs. Lauerson, a fairly young, smart and pretty blonde taught Science, his favorite subject, but he had pulled an average grade of C. English, which he aced in grade school, also resulted in a C. English was taught by Miss Berwyn, a substitute teacher who had followed two previous substitutes into this den of young lions. Not long out of college herself, Miss Berwyn was a slender, brown-haired, attractive young lady in her mid-twenties, with riveting blue eyes.

Bingo! Gene had established a correlation between pretty teachers, favorite subjects, and low grades. He had allowed these two teachers to become a distraction to him, and would have to work harder, although in the case of Miss Berwyn, he had plenty of company. It wasn't her fault she was young and pretty but she compensated for it by maintaining absolute control of her class. She was properly friendly but would tolerate no out-of-line remarks, double entendres, or innuendo, and she knew her subject cold which she taught well to those who paid attention.

Distractions such as this probably wouldn't have occurred in a coed high school, where pretty girls constituted an equivalent percentage of the class population. Also, since Lane was an elite school, its teachers were for a large part, those teachers with the greatest seniority, who had spent years in Chicago's educational system. It was an all-boys' school where the faculty probably consisted of fifty-percent women, but most of them were nearing retirement. Miss Berwyn couldn't help but be the daydream darling of freshmen English classes and foremost in the thoughts of nearly every boy who passed her in the hall.

Despite all of the freshmen being in the same academic boat, Commercial Art students remaining in Mr. Michaels' division seemed to develop an "us" and "them" attitude toward the students who had been split off into Mr. Walton's division. An old friend from Agassiz, Billy Milford, whose interest in Lane's Commercial Art had considerably influenced Gene's enrollment in the course, remained in Mr. Michaels' division, and became more aloof, even verbally abusive toward Gene, as if it wasn't "cool" to associate with a student you knew in grade school.

In addition to the academic challenges which he expected to face, Gene carried an additional burden that most kids never shouldered. Being different was a burden he had incurred at birth and he was always aware of it, being reminded of it each morning by the bathroom mirror. There would always be a minority of mental midgets who felt it was their duty to remind him that he was still different from them. Those reminders usually came from misguided kids who did poor imitations of Gene's speech from his first days at Lane, just as he had experienced at Agassiz.

Having anticipated more maturity in his high school classmates he soon realized to his disappointment, that the difference between taunts in grade school and taunts in high school, is simply in the physical size of the kids doing the taunting. The size of their mentalities had, however, remained small. Ignoring such remarks became more difficult and tiresome when they occurred on a daily basis. One might expect such abuse from ignorant strangers but hearing such remarks from guys he knew, like Stan Janowicz, who was in his classes from the beginning, troubled Gene much more. All he had wanted, was to be accepted.

It had already struck home in Gene's mind that there wasn't going to be "one more major corrective operation" to make everything better, nor was any miracle going to occur. These were part of his childhood hopes that many times were all that had kept him going. Now realizing that he would always look and sound different from everyone else, Gene was trying to accept it. What he had trouble accepting was the attendant intolerance on the part of a minority of others. Somehow, he needed to find a way to live with it. It wouldn't be easy.

Chapter 19

Learning The Ropes

After the Thanksgiving weekend, Gene went back to school determined to bring up his grades. Having spun their wheels much of the early weeks with substitutes and feeling bogged down by daily readings of Shakespeare's "MacBeth," Gene's English class was in for a literary treat. Miss Berwyn switched gears and began introducing her young charges to the delightful short stories of more contemporary authors such as Bret Harte and O. Henry. They read serious, touching sagas such as "Outcasts of Poker Flat," "Luck of Roaring Camp," and "Gift of the Magi," and the side-splitting humor of "Ransom of Red Chief." She led them down a new path into a valley of literary adventure that could be had by reading a book and allowing the author to paint his illustrations on the canvas of their mind.

In reading through "Outcasts of Poker Flat," one learned that chivalry had still been alive in the Old West. It shone in the person of Mr. Oakhurst, who was the strongest, yet in the end, was the weakest of a motley group of outcasts maintaining dignity in meeting their fate. O. Henry told of a Red Chief whose antics begged a paraphrasing of an old Latin caveat to "Let the kidnapers beware!" for Bill and Sam, two kidnapers who had earned every penny of the 250 dollars they paid Mr. Dorset, to take back his son from Hell.

Returning to his General Science class, Gene knuckled down and paid more attention than he had before, although to goof off in Mrs. Lauerson's class was like poking a stick in your own eye. Mrs. Lauerson was a pleasant-looking blonde woman but a dead serious teacher, and "Passing The Buck" was a game she always held in reserve for those in her classes who became unruly. If any student caused a disturbance serious enough to rile her, she identified the student by calling out the student's name, and telling him he had the "buck." The "buck" was a gift that kept on giving throughout the class period. Once a student was given the buck, he could only give it to someone else who subsequently acted up in class. As the bell rang at the end of the class, Mrs. Lauerson would ask, who had the buck, and the buck-holder would be given an additional assignment to be done that evening. Being left holding the buck was an unpleasant experience one didn't want repeated and "Passing The Buck" proved to be an effective tool, since the threat of its use often kept order in the class, even when not invoked.

Slowly, ever so slowly, the weeks passed until Christmas arrived, which was celebrated in the usual manner. A new Christmas song, "All I Want For Christmas Is My Two Front Teeth" performed by Spike Jones had its debut and by Christmas had driven everyone to distraction by its repeated radio play. One-of-a-kind snow crystals are some of Nature's most beautiful creations and she dumped four inches of her finest, overnight, on Christmas Eve, giving Chicagoans a white Christmas. Observing the giving of gifts on Christmas morning, everyone, including Mae, opened their gifts, accompanied by the usual comments and repartee. As the snow continued to fall later in the day, everyone left the house to spend Christmas elsewhere. As Mae waited for her nephew to pick her up, so she could spend the holiday with he and his wife, the remaining family members got into a taxicab, difficult to find on Christmas Day, for the ride over to Grandmaw and Grandpaw Kelly's home.

Christmases of the past few years had caused the women in Gene's family to be apprehensive about their men consuming too much liquor at Christmas gatherings. The guilty parties were Tom, Clay, Pat, and Lew, although Lew usually appeared to be the most sober of the group. The women had legitimate cause for concern since the two previous Christmas celebrations were dampened through excessive drinking by the men. They had unfortunately, not seen the worst of it. Before the day was over it was to be a Christmas not to be forgotten for years to come.

After the presents had been given out by the honorary Santa of the day, heated words were exchanged by Clay and one of the other drinkers, which led to Clay swinging with a drunken punch that never landed. His wrist had been grabbed by his older brother Chick's iron grasp for Chick had heard trouble brewing and anticipated his brother's action.

Clay didn't get a chance to throw another punch because Chick, who only wanted to keep the peace on the Lord's birthday, had wrapped his arms around his younger brother to restrain him until he calmed down. Clay resisted and became abusive to his brother who then wrestled him to the floor where he held him down for what seemed like an hour, until Clay cooled off. Surrounded by the anguish and weeping of their sisters, Clay at last agreed to behave. With that, Chick allowed his younger brother to get up and brush himself off.

Child-like contriteness filled Clay as he apologized to everyone, especially to his older brother whom he loved. Without a word, Chick turned away from his brother, took his coat from the hall closet and made ready to leave with Helen. Clay pleaded with his brother Chick to stay, and to forgive him, but Chick, for reasons which he felt were valid, quietly turned to their mother and said goodbye. Clay stood just off the hallway, crying, which moved Gene to tears in his eyes.

Yet, the most tragic sight of all to Gene, was when he turned to see his beloved grandpaw's big shoulders shaking as he sat sobbing on the stairway, his heart broken. Gene's hero, his strong, gentle grandpaw, who had never allowed pain to break him nor make him cry, was inconsolable because his cherished sons had fought and appeared to be splitting apart.

Grandmaw Kelly called her own doctor, asking him if he could come out and look her son Clay over. She had suspected that he wasn't healthy and his actions told her, as a mother, that something wasn't right with her younger son. A short time later the good doctor who came out on Christmas, arrived and examined Clay, diagnosing his condition as nervous exhaustion. The stress of his job, failing home life, and holiday drinking had brought him to where he was just short of a nervous breakdown. The doctor told him that he had to ease up, rest, and possibly get away from the sources of aggravation in his life.

A pall of gloom had enshrouded the living room since Chick left and it wasn't long after the doctor's departure that Kathleen called a cab for their trip home. Waiting for the cab, she pleaded with Tom to drink some coffee instead of more liquor but stubbornly, he refused. When the cab pulled up, Tom wasn't able to walk to the cab without falling down in the snow. Bob, who managed to leave when he sensed turmoil beginning, had taken his girlfriend home and wasn't there to help. Trying very hard, Kathleen's two youngest sons couldn't pick their stepfather up.

By now, thoroughly disgusted with the drinkers, Kathleen's Irish was up when she saw her brother-in-law Lew coming out of the house, and shouted at him, "You helped him to get like this, now help us put him in the cab!" Lew, ever the gentleman, responded and half-carried Tom to the cab where he dumped him into its back seat and apologized to Kathleen, to little avail, saying, "Tom did a lot of this to himself. I had suggested more than once that he should go easy on the liquor."

That holiday had been a harbinger of Christmases to come, since from that time on, the holidays were usually spoiled by Tom's drinking. It was a blessing that the Ryans had enjoyed their earlier Christmases before he came into their lives; at least they would always have them to remember.

Between Christmas and New Year's Eve Gene had a birthday, turning fourteen, but typical of most of his birthdays his family had been financially tapped by Christmas gift expenses. It hadn't been unusual to receive a Christmas gift and a gentle mention along with it, that it was to be his birthday present too. Gene believed that the only worst day of the year to have a birthday on was Christmas Day itself. Thinking of children that might someday be his, he hoped that their births would occur in the Summer.

New Year's Day, was a quiet day except for the late afternoon sounds of the Rose Bowl broadcast, on radio. The Western Conference or Big Nine was being represented by Northwestern while the Pacific Coast Conference's representative was the University of California. By listening to the game, Gene passed a few hours cheering for the hometown team as Northwestern's Wildcats and California's Golden Bears played a very close game. A photo of the controversial game-winning play would be plastered all over the papers and sports publications for days. The photo captured for all time, U. of C. defender Norm Pressley's painful grimace as he exerted every ounce of himself into a vain attempt to stop Northwestern's fullback, Art Murakowski, from carrying the ball over the goal-line for a touchdown. He succeeded in causing a fumble as NU's big back went over.

For what seemed to be a eternity. the officials debated whether Murakowski fumbled before or after he broke the plane of the goal-line. The picture told it all, showing Murakowski just after he crossed the goal-line, with the football beginning to float out of his hands as Northwestern won its first Rose Bowl game as a Big Nine representative by a score of 20 to 14. Sports were big in Gene's life, since they not only offered entertainment, but often the chance to participate at a much lower level, while sports had offered many a kid a great alternative to getting in trouble.

Having a lot of time on his hands and no homework during Christmas break, Gene got together with Hans, Jack, and Dolan to go bowling several times and managed to see a few movies. Walking along Broadway toward the bowling alley, they stopped at a few new car dealers to lust after some of the new 1949 cars displayed in their showrooms. Gene had already seen some of the cars cruising down the streets, but the showroom was where they got to see them up close before an irate salesman shagged their young butts back out onto the street. What nerve! Didn't he realize that they were car-buyers too, just a few years removed?

Interested in automobile design since he was a little boy drawing cars, Gene saw that Ford Motor Company and Chrysler Corporation had tooled-up for radical design changes, the first since before the war. Gone were the curved, humpback coupes and nearly torpedo-shaped sedans, replaced by a squared-off, boxy look throughout their lines. Mercury, which had always looked so much like Ford, for the first time, sported a far different look about it. Design of Mercurys previously done by the Ford Division had been assumed by Ford's Lincoln Division beginning in

222

the 1949 model year. From that year on, Mercurys would more resemble Lincolns than Fords.

General Motors had opted for less radical changes, in designing the 1949 models produced by its five divisions. Generally, their models retained some of the curves in their decks and fenders. While their line-leader, Cadillac had produced a very elegant sedan, the Buick division had upstaged them, producing a classic square-decked sedan in their Super and Roadmaster series.

The major design change was the elimination of fenders, a boon to body and fender shops everywhere. Where heretofore fenders had been bolted onto the body of the car, to be easily and economically replaced, fenders were now part of the body's design. Crumple a fender on one of these new babies and it meant big body and fender repair bucks! Big bucks? In Gene's case, how about NO bucks? Gene thought of his education first then a job. Any potential plans for buying a car were still years away for him.

Returning to school after the Christmas break meant there was only one month of Gene's "freshie" semester to go. Having long since put away his bike, Gene shivered while waiting for the bus to come by as the frigid winds whistled past the corner of Lakewood and Addison. While January blasts of arctic air could chill a person clear through their coats, a few minutes on that big, warm, luxurious bus were sufficient to bring one back to the realm of the warm people.

The Chicago Motor Coach Company operated the buses in those days before the Chicago Transit Authority came into being, when Chicago's transportation system was a patchwork of several privately-owned companies. Rail-bound streetcars were operated by Chicago Surface Lines and the elevated trains were owned by the Rapid Transit System. Transfers from one line to another were free and fortunately, were honored between the companies.

The huge, heavy, CMC buses were "Behemoths of the Boulevards" and a few other streets such as Sheridan Road and Addison Street. Slow and ponderous they expelled a noxious exhaust, but gave their riders a comfortable ride that was smooth as glass. Somehow, it seemed like a special occasion to go downtown on one of those buses in the Summer, riding it along boulevards through Lincoln Park and finally along Michigan Avenue, taking in the skyline and other sights.

Getting off the bus across from school one frigid morning Gene heard, as he did every day, the carillon bells pealing the school fight song "Go Lane, Go!" from the clock tower. Thinking he had time for a fast cherry-Pepsi, he hurried, quickly walking over to Riesz' school store, where once inside he bumped into his Agassiz pal, Billy Roder. They were both enjoying a cherry-Pepsi and a glazed doughnut when they agreed that it had been a long time since they went ice-skating and arranged to go that night. They planned to meet at the Fullerton Tennis Courts at Fullerton and Sheffield, which were flooded every Winter into a pay-per-visit ice-skating rink. When he met Billy Milford in the hall, Gene asked him if he wanted to go along, since they were also old skating buddies but Billy declined. It was the same old problem; he couldn't get the two Billys in the same place at the same time.

In order to get to the rink, Gene walked over to the Ravenswood line's Southport station where he caught the "El" which was the fastest way to get there. Gene always grabbed a window seat and watched the corners of buildings zip past, seeming to be inches from the window he was looking through. It gave him a thrill to stare out at the building walls that raced past and suddenly see open space as a long brick wall gave way to a vacant lot or street.

As the train neared snow-covered Wrigley Field at Clark, Addison, and Sheffield, its wheels swung into the usual ninety-degree right-turn to pick up the Sheffield line's tracks. As the cars entered the turn, the tortured squeal of steel wheels against steel rails filled the car; an awesome strain on the eardrums, but Gene loved the sound. Sparks cascading out from under the cars as the train intermittently made and lost contact with the third rail added to the excitement. Did he favor ice-skating or riding the "El" the most? It was an even bet.

Arriving at the rink, he and Billy skated around to loosen up, in anticipation of being allowed to join up in a pickup game of hockey. One of their primary hockey-player friends was Jimmy Wolf, the younger brother of Mac, a grade school classmate of

224

theirs. Jimmy and his family were originally from Canada and Jimmy was easily the best player on the ice. His fine skating, excellent puck-handling, and passing ability made him a natural center.

Jimmy told him the year before, "Hockey isn't only skill with a stick and skates; it requires using your head and staying cool in a very frustrating game. You get plenty mad but you get over it. Just don't carry a grudge or hard feelings when the game is over!"

Gene ran through his friend's bits of advice, trying to remember them all, because tonight he wanted to play.

A scrapper, Jimmy had also mentioned last year "If you or an opponent lose your cool and gotta fight, the cardinal rule is that if you're wearing hockey gloves, you gotta drop them first because those leather-covered gloves have steel-protected fingers."

So, Gene thought, that's where the term "Dropping the Gloves" which had the same connotation as "Meet me outside," came from. Because he didn't own a pair of hockey gloves, Gene just kept it in mind in case a combative opponent happened to be wearing a pair of them and wanted to mix it up in the future.

Gene had practiced carrying a puck and shooting a lot the year before but that was the only experience he had. He was barely good enough to play in a game and had never played in a hockey game. Tonight was different because Gene and Billy were picked to play on opposite sides and soon after, the faceoff started the game.

Surprised by how quickly he had begun perspiring, Gene realized that when he had practiced shots and stick-handling, he could quit when he got tired. Not so in a game without time outs except when the puck went into a snowdrift alongside the ice. He also realized what Jimmy meant in describing frustration as a part of the game.

Four times in a row Gene had managed to make his way up the ice with the puck, struggling past Billy and warding off other defenders with his elbows, only to be met with a teeth-rattling check, or a "now-you-see-it, now-you-don't" poke-check by Jimmy, who took the puck away for the fourth straight time. Seeing red Gene went after Jimmy but their scuffle was broken up before Jimmy could even get his second glove off. Moments later, Gene apologized to Jimmy but was told by his friend, "Don't worry about it, we're still friends! I told you this game makes you crazy enough to fight with your friends but just forget about it when the game is over."

When the players called it a night, Gene felt a pleasant kind of fatigue. He had accomplished something tonight, he learned a few more hockey techniques, and a variation of sportsmanship he hadn't been exposed to before. Now it was time to head over to the fieldhouse and get some exorbitantly-priced hot chocolate!

Despite being accustomed to the January cold through prolonged outdoor work on his paper route and ice-skating, Gene also liked to be at home where it was warm. The hissing and clanking of radiators as hot, vitalizing steam coursed through their pipes always seemed to have a comforting ring to it. As something of a peace offering, Tom appeared to have gone on the wagon since New Year's and had sprung for a new Muntz television set, their first TV.

Network television channels offered a ten-minute newscast at 10:00 P.M., then a five-minute weather forecast followed by feature programs at 10:15. Featured were variety programs, sports such as Roller Derby and pro wrestling, and even movies to be enjoyed in one's home. Movies required viewers at home to sit through an auto dealer's interminable commercials, during which it seemed viewers were shown the dealer's entire car inventory. As the dealer-host paused at one "beauty" after another, the TV lights reflected off the highly-polished cars into the camera's lens causing momentary "black spots" on the transmitted picture. A good memory was required on the viewer's part when the commercial break was finally, mercifully over, in order to remember what movie they had been watching and where they were in its plot!

The new television set was so neat, it even got bachelor Bob to stay home for a couple of weeks! One of Bob's favorite shows was "Kukla, Fran, and Ollie," just because he liked Ollie the dragon and Fletcher Rabbit. Gene really loved to hear his oldest brother's laugh and enjoyed his companionship because Bob was a lot of fun to be around. On rare occasions Gene overheard Bob singing a few lines of some popular song, not knowing that he had an audience. Bob's baritone voice handled "Somebody Else Has Taken My Place" with an easy, lyrical tone but he wouldn't hear of singing in front of anyone. Bob was too shy to share his voice with the world, when to the contrary, Dave, who only thought he had a singing voice, would gladly sing out for any audience of at least one.

Dinner was a time for conversation, news of the day, and learning. Often, the three brothers and their mother took turns asking the capitals of states and other geographical questions of each other, such as where were the White Mountains or Green Mountains located or what two rivers meet to form the Ohio River? Mae sometimes sparked the conversation by prodding the older boys for news of their dates. Knowing lots of jokes, the three boys offered many of the jokes traded around the kitchen table at dinner, especially if their stodgy stepfather was working the late-afternoon shift at a bakery.

January's end brought a warm glow to Gene that had nothing to do with the weather. It was Friday, the 28th, and the end of his first semester at Lane. He not only made it through his "Freshie" semester but managed to bring up his grades. Trading a B for a C in Algebra, he had improved his English grade to a B and his Science grade to an A! Unfortunately, his major, Commercial Art, still saw him swimming in mediocrity with a C. Speaking of swimming, which he had always enjoyed, and Gym, he netted grades of B and C, respectively.

So much for the good news. Mister Neville, the English teacher for whom Miss Berwyn had substituted all last semester, was back, and he wasn't happy. On their first class day, he came on like gangbusters, explaining that, "I'm not as healthy or pretty as your last teacher but if you work with me I'll work with you, but if you cross me up, I'll screw you over!"

Gene thought Nevlle's address was so tough and unwarranted, that it was almost comical. As the early days of February passed, Mr. Neville probably realized that his class really didn't comprise the "Dead End Kids," and began to ease up on his tough-guy impersonations.

Mr. Neville initiated a unique requirement of his own within his class; whereby each student would give a two-minute talk on any subject, once a week. No excuses were accepted! He set aside each Monday's entire class period, dedicating it to public speaking. It was a fantastic idea! Even though it set very large butterflies to flight in Gene's stomach, everyone had to go through it. It seemed that guys were hesitant to poke fun at someone else speaking, when their own turn was coming up soon. The talk requirement was a double-edged sword to Gene. Talks in front of the room made him less afraid to speak in public, giving him practice and confidence. The talks also let the other boys know what it felt like, to be on the spot talking, with everyone watching you. Gene would come to be grateful to Mr. Neville and his great innovation.

Gene usually listened to the third period of the Blackhawk games on WCFL every Sunday night, so he often talked about the previous night's game or the Blackhawks in general. Not fielding much of a team despite having players like Bill Mosienko, at center, and All-star wing, Roy Conacher, the Blackhawks were deeply mired in sixth place in a six-team league! In those days the Blackhawks didn't garner much of a following either. In fact, as Gene listened, the sound of a puck banging off the boards seemed to reverberate up to the rafters and echo throughout Chicago Stadium. It was never excessive crowd noise that drowned out Johnny Gottselig's play-by-play but more likely, the sound of their embattled goalie, Sugar Jim Henry, stopping shots, and bodies being slammed into the boards, sounds that rattled off the cold balcony walls and around the vast array of empty seats.

Gene made friends with one of his Art classmates who had been aloof until now, when his talks about the Blackhawks caused Rob Jonas, a Blackhawk fan, to strike up a conversation with him and get to know Gene.

Now that his second semester was under way and he wasn't a "freshie" anymore, he felt that he should perform some sort of civic duty to his school, so he went down to the Hallguard Office and offered his services as a hallguard. One gave up their study period in order to become a hallguard, although most of them could be seen studying at their posts since each post had a student desk. Accepted on the spot, he found himself being escorted to his post by one of the hallguard lieutenants for that period. Traversing the entire first floor, he and his leader then took the stairs, and as they ascended to and passed each floor, Gene thought, "Nope, not the second floor, nope, not the third floor. Must be the fourth floor." Bingo!

Arriving at the fourth floor, his leader couldn't find the hallguard post to which Gene was being assigned. "Some post," Gene thought, "this patrol lieutenant can't even find it! What do they call it, Little Siberia?" "Follow me!" said the lieutenant. "What have I been doing all this time?" thought Gene. Back down to the third floor and over to another quadrant of the building they went, then they ascended the stairs again to the fourth floor.

Pushing open the hallway door, the lieutenant said with a sigh of relief, "Here we are!" Gene's eyes took in a short, barren hall in the music wing which he would later learn, joined several rehearsal and practice rooms. "Little Siberia" may have been an appropriate name. Assuming his post, he felt at least it was a quiet post and he could get a lot of his studying done.

B-L-A-A-A-T! B-L-A-A-A-T! Suddenly his ears were assailed by sounds not unlike the trumpeting of an agonized elephant. The elephantine sounds wafted from one of the rooms nearby. From a room further down the hall came the screams of a tortured cat, or so it sounded to him. Through the weeks of February, as the musicians improved, Gene would begin to enjoy some of the classical pieces being rehearsed and his initial regrets would be forgotten.

That early February was a typically frigid kind of February in the Midwest, when Bob wearied quickly of freezing in his tracks while waiting in the frigid weather for buses. He up and decided it was time for him, as a man of means, to buy a car of his choice. So what kind of car did he buy in the dead of Winter? A convertible! Gene wondered why his twenty-year-old big brother had suddenly lost enough of his normal reasoning power to buy a convertible in the dead of Winter. It was a beautiful ragtop though, a used 1947 humpback Ford club-coupe, with a maroon paint-job and whitewall tires.

The car filled his youngest brother's heart with envy just as if Bob had acquired free box seats at the next World Series. Bob never explained how he was able to just start driving, when he hadn't used anyone else's car to practice. He said he learned to drive in the Navy. Sure. No one got to see him drive his car until he brought it home after the first week! Gene's thoughts ran the gamut of suspicions. Bob must have stashed the car somewhere else, so he could practice before he brought it home. That's it, he must have stashed it over at their uncle Chick's! Bob didn't want to look stupid in front of his younger brothers if he let the clutch out too quickly and killed the engine or didn't shift right and ground a pound of metal off the gear teeth! Gene never did find out for sure.

Only a couple of weeks elapsed before Bob took the newness out of his car by ramming a truck from behind. A losing proposition at best, since the left front fender of the Ford was caved in by the impact which left the truck unscathed. While still drivable, the Ford cruised with a rather cool effect, as its damaged left headlight pointed up to the left at about a 35-degree angle. Many an irate neighbor living in a second-floor apartment came to the window as Bob drove past, wondering who the hell was shining a spotlight through their window. Alas, Bob had the damage repaired by the end of February and both headlights again pointed the same way, normally.

Early in March the boxing world saw the end of its greatest heavyweight champion's reign, when Joe Louis hung up his gloves, leaving the heavyweight division with two claimants to his crown. Louis had defended his crown successfully twenty-five times over the twelve years since his 1937 knockout of James Braddock. In his professional career, Louis experienced only one loss, to Max Schmeling of Germany whom he later knocked out in the first round of their rematch. Joe had come along in an era when the general public was interested in boxing because it was honest, and the sport had plenty of good name fighters. After Louis' announcement, Ezzard Charles and Jersey Joe Wolcott, who both claimed Louis' crown eventually agreed to a bout in June to decide the new champion.

March also saw the "Sweet Sixteen" or Illinois State High School Basketball Championship Tournament downstate in Champaign-Urbana, bringing together sixteen of the best high school teams in Illinois. In those days, Chicago high school basketball was divided into Senior or varsity and Junior championships. Chicago's Public League champion Senior team represented the city in the state championship downstate, and in 1949 Chicago was represented by the Blue Devils of Tilden Tech.

Following the March Madness downstate, the High School Championship of Chicago game, pitting the Public League champions against the Catholic League champions was played at the Chicago Stadium. Since Public Junior champion Lane Tech was matched against Junior Catholic champion Leo in the preliminary game, Gene decided to go to the game. It was a long streetcar ride on an Ashland Avenue Red Rocket to Madison Street, and then a walk to the Stadium.

Staying in the game for three quarters, Lane's Juniors couldn't prevent Leo's Juniors from building up an insurmountable lead, eventually losing 47 to 33. Public League fans were disappointed on both ends of the double-header as Gene and thousands of other Public League fans then watched the Catholic League's powerful St. Patrick's squad edge Tilden Tech by a single point. Although the trip to the game had been long, for the losing Laneites it was an even longer trip going home.

April brought the first real signs of Spring to the North Side. A new baseball season had begun and Gene was already going over to the ballpark for weekend games. While most bleacher fans rushed for seats in the left-field or right-field bleachers, Gene favored the first row of the seats in dead center-field, right above the 400-foot sign. There he watched his favorite player, number 48, Andy Pakfo, back in center-field where he belonged, after moving to third-base the season before.

A strong ex-farmboy from Boyceville, Wisconsin, Andy Pafko, was a player who if he could have played for a contender, with other good hitters in the lineup, might have become as famous as Willie Mays or Joe DiMaggio. Probably one of the most underrated players of his time, Andy Pafko roamed center-field with easy, deceptive speed, had a rifle-arm that made opposing base-runners think twice about taking that extra base, and was also an exceptional hitter for average and power. Not exactly a young matinee-idol, when Andy occasionally turned around to acknowledge the crowd's appreciation, he still managed to flash a friendly, toothy, smile that was pure warmth.

This desire to play was fully evident to Gene who sat behind the 400-foot mark on that overcast Saturday, when rain threatened to wash out the game. It was the last day of April, the day when Andy Pafko made the play for which he and the umpire, Al Barlick, would always be remembered.

The St. Louis Cardinals were in town but the Cubs had a 3 to 2 lead in the top of the ninth inning, and there were two outs. One more out and everybody could go home. Don't worry about Nippy Jones, the runner on first, because the batter, a pinch-hitter named Rocky Nelson is gonna be the next out. Nelson ends up lining a sinking shot into shallow center-field, as Pafko is off at the crack of the bat, his legs churning like an egg-beater, he leans out and snatches it out of the air just above the grass! Pafko's got it! The game is over, the Cubs win!

Wait a minute! The Cardinal runners are still racing around the bases! Don't they know the game is over? Pafko's still running in, yelling that he's got it and holding the ball up for everyone to see! Then the Cub center-fielder realizes that the plate umpire didn't rule it a catch, and fires the ball to home-plate, too late. Jones and Nelson had both crossed the plate. One hellacious rhubarb now erupts on the field of play during which the scoreboard attendant hangs up a big yellow "2" in the top of the ninth for the Cardinals.

Everyone of the nearly 30,000 fans in the ballpark saw "Handy Andy" make the catch, but Al Barlick, the plate umpire, didn't see it that way and rules it a "trap," saying that the ball had hit the ground first. Perhaps a gust of Chicago wind had blown a speck of dust into his otherwise perfect eyes and he didn't see it at all. His decision stands and as the smoke of dissent clears, the runs count for St. Louis. Okay guys, you'll have to win it the hard way. Get two more runs in the bottom of the ninth and win it anyhow.

232

Alas, just as it was with so many other Cub games, victory was not to be theirs that day. The hometown boys failed in their half of the ninth and lost the game, 4 to 3, sending Gene home fuming. The play was written up in the sports pages and was the primary topic back at school the following Monday. Remembered by many fans as a catch, it would in years to come, be falsely referred to in baseball lore as "the Pafko Trap."

The remaining several weeks of Gene's freshman year passed by uneventfully, quickly, and mercifully. Two days before the end of school, when Gene arrived home, he thought to remind his family that the Charles-Wolcott fight was going to be on that night. They already knew about it. In those days everyone knew when a heavyweight championship bout was coming up, even Grandmaw Kelly. It had been written up in the paper and the fight was the most important topic in school. That night, a young Ezzard Charles outpointed an aging, sentimental favorite, Jersey Joe, in 15 rounds to become undisputed heavyweight champion of the world.

With school work winding down, the last week of school had been a snap, and suddenly it was the last day. Friday in late June, and school was out for this new sophomore. Receiving his course book, Gene was satisfied that his knuckling down had helped. His latest grades reflected that his work in Algebra class had improved enough to gain him a B, and he moved up to a C in Mechanical Drawing, while his other final grades remained the same as the first semester. Not exceptional grades but an improvement, which was its own reward for the increased effort on his part.

A turbulent weekend was in store and it began with the jubilation of being free for the Summer, while the early part of the weekend was spent by Gene and his brothers packing their clothes and getting Bob's car ready for a trip down to Southern Illinois. Planned since early June the trip began with an invitation from their uncle Clay, inviting them to his farm for a week!

Chapter 20

Down On The Farm

Only weeks after that tragic Christmas, Kathleen's brother Clay followed the doctor's advice and quit his stressful job. He, his wife Anita, and their son, Bucky, moved from Chicago to a small farm located in a southern Illinois pastoral setting near Newton, in Jasper County. In his letters to Kathleen, Clay wrote that he had returned to the farm life that had been instilled within him as a boy. City life, with all of its hustle and bustle and aggravation just hadn't been the life for him. Gene recalled that of all of his mother's siblings, it appeared to him that his Uncle Clay had more of the country boy left in him than the others.

Months later, near the end of the school year for Dave and Gene, Clay wrote to Kathleen asking if her sons would like to come down for a week, to spend some time on a farm, and help him out a little. She mentioned it to her three boys hoping that Bob would go, and drive all of them down. As one voice, all three were elated at the prospect. Bob then asked for his week's vacation from work early enough to coincide with the trip. They were all ready for a farm experience, one that these sons of a one-time farmer's wife hadn't had in a long time.

Rising bright and early that Saturday morning, the brothers drove to Cicero Avenue, then traveled straight south to the southern end of Chicago where they promptly got lost looking for the Dixie Highway, whatever that was. Stopping to get directions at a gas station, they continued south down U. S. 45 to Kankakee where their ride to fun and sun came to an unexpected halt.

Stalled in the middle of an intersection, their trusty Ford had overheated and was losing its water as it sat piddling onto the pavement. Telling their kid brother to get in and steer, Bob and Dave got behind and pushed the light car, easing it up the driveway of the nearest gas station where a grinning attendant awaited them.

Gene wondered if the attendant was smiling because he was glad to see them or because he thought they were three city-slicker suckers in trouble far from home, and getting them out of trouble might mean big money for him. Shame on you Gene! It turns out that the man was just being friendly. Fortunately for them, the hose was in stock and the mechanic was honest, as he just changed the top radiator hose within minutes and got them back on their way for a reasonable charge.

Flying down U. S. 45 in the light convertible, at the breakneck speed of sixty miles per hour, the wind roared past their heads, whipping their hair with the torque of a Mixmaster. They slowed to pass through small towns like Onarga, Loda, and Paxton, pushing to make it to Champaign-Urbana by lunchtime. A college town, Champaign-Urbana was the home of the University of Illinois, and the two older brothers mentioned that it would certainly be worth their while to stop there and check the town over.

Gene knew they really wanted to stop so as to have a chance to check the girls over. He understood, because at fourteen he too was starting to have those new, strange feelings about girls more often now, although he didn't tell his brothers. Who needed the additional grief of their needling?

Pulling over to the curb near a small diner in what appeared to be a college residential area, the three brothers got out and moseyed into the diner. A typical hamburger diner of that era, when the term "fast food" pertained to what one ate during Lent. The mouthwatering aroma of custom-fried hamburgers and onions permeated one's olfactory senses upon walking in. The diner looked clean, friendly, and to its further credit, a garish, bubbling, jukebox dominated one corner.

As they sat down at a table, the juke box filled the diner with the sound of a bouncy, infectious song called, "Piano Roll Blues," which going-on-seventeen Dave really got into, drumming his hands on the table in time with its rhythm.

Ordering up lunch, they settled in and when Bob got up to play the juke box, Dave called to his brother, "Hey Bob!"

"What do you want?"

"Play Riano Poll Blues!" He tried again, "I mean, Riano Poll Dues!"

"What is it that you're trying to tell me? One more time, Dave!"

"Piano Bowl Rues!"

Dave's mind might have been addled by too many hours spent with the wind whistling past his head and ears while riding with the top down but if it had meant saving his life, he couldn't get the correct title past his lips! Bob and Gene were doubled up with laughter, while others in the diner were enjoying a laugh too. Tripping over that song title must have formed some type of mental block within Dave, because for years, when family members kidded him about it, he usually ran into the same problem of mispronouncing it again.

Resuming their run downstate into the sun, Gene switched places with Dave taking his turn sitting in the back seat with the wind howling past his head. While he could still hear, his ears picked up the pleadings of his brother Dave.

"Hey Bob, how's about letting me drive for just a little while? C'mon, just for a while."

Gene hoped that Bob would keep driving because Dave had never gotten behind the wheel of any car, and Gene had a strong desire to continue living.

Shouting, "No! No!" into the wind howling over the back seat, Gene was unheard.

"C'mon Bob," implored Dave, "Lemme drive on the highway."

Bob finally, surprisingly said, "Not a chance, I want to get us there in one piece!"

Weary of listening to the roar of the onrushing wind, Gene curled up in the back seat with his jacket collar around his ears, and dozed off. Hours later, Bob had found his way through Mattoon, then Effingham, where they picked up Illinois Highway 33. The late afternoon sun had bronzed the fields near the clean, sleepy town of Newton, when they pulled into a Deep Rock gas station where they got directions to their uncle Clay's farm.

Ten minutes later, they were rolling downhill on a road alongside a farm, when Bob honked the horn wildly as they spotted their affable uncle waving at them in the distance. While the Ford was a sharp-looking car, it hadn't been built for a long highway ride. Pulling up in a cloud of dust, they all got out and limped around to stretch their legs and get the feeling back in their butts. Everyone was delighted to see each other again as backs were slapped and hugs exchanged. They had arrived at their uncle's farm safely and felt really welcome.

A short time later, their aunt Anita called them all in for supper, shouting, "Come and get it or I'll feed it to the pigs!" – an old, familiar, Kelly family put-on, when calling a crowd of relatives to dinner, but these Kellys really owned pigs to feed it to! Anita outdid herself for she was a great cook, and the long trip had made the boys hungry. The taste of fresh, warm farm milk right out of the cow took a little getting used to, but after a meal or two Gene learned to like it. The milk was rich, and contained all of the creamy butterfat Nature intended, unlike dairy milk in the city where the butterfat had been removed and sold separately as cream.

After supper, feeling stuffed, they all walked out around the pasture and barn just to get familiar with the place, while their irrepressible uncle kept the mood light with some of his best off-color jokes. It was heartwarming to see their uncle's good humor back and that he seemed to have regained his old self again. As they walked, Shep, Clay's very friendly, black and brown Setter-Collie dog trailed along behind them.

Dave asked, "Hey Unc, how about watching some television?"

Dave swallowed hard when his uncle responded with, "Since y'all will be gettin' up at four-thirty in the mornin', it'd be a better idea for y'all to get a good night's sleep."

As much of a shock as it was to their systems for city-dwelling young men to get ready for bed at nine o'clock, it was to be a greater shock when they arose in the middle of the night at four-thirty. The early summer sun appeared to be a huge ball of burnished gold when it sank below the horizon just a little while before and now night was already upon them.

All of the bedrooms were upstairs and Bob and Dave were given the spare bedroom, while Gene was given the downstairs couch to sleep on. Again, the couch! If Gene had any experience of note in his young life, it was sleeping on couches. He figured that since he had so much couch time back at home, his hosts must have assumed he had a preference for it. Soon the last light switch clicked off and it was as if someone had thrown a black cloak over Gene's head. Darkness in the country was total blackness everywhere. Only the stars offered any light but it took a while for his eyes to adjust to starlight. Past the open window out there in the dark, a lone whip-poor-will repeatedly called out, and although unseen had made its presence known to all hearing creatures about.

Morning comes early on the farm, especially for the farmer's wife as their aunt Anita was up at four, getting breakfast for the five others in the house. The aroma of fresh coffee and the sound of sizzling bacon caused Gene to stir and struggle to keep his eyes open. Finally wrenching himself free of the warm, comfortable couch he staggered, squinting into the brightly-lit kitchen. "Well, well, an early riser!" said his aunt, chuckling at her nephew's disorientation. "If yore lookin' for the washroom, you'll recall we told you it was straight out back," she added, good-naturedly.

Fully awake now, Gene thought he would keep her company. As he sat talking to her, he thought of how kind the years had been to her farm girl features. Gene always admired his aunt Anita and thought her to be a quite a lovely lady with dark blonde hair, very clear, engaging blue eyes, and a warm smile set off by pearly white teeth. He remembered how pretty she had looked way back when she and Clay had come over for lunch during the time he stayed with his grandmaw in the Kelly's home at Fullerton and Southport.

A few minutes later, his uncle Clay came downstairs followed by Bucky, and Clay asked Gene, "Did the howling of the wolves bother you during the night?"

Gene, sensing another put-on, remarked, "I didn't think there were any wolves here in Illinois. In fact, I believe that the closest four-legged wolves are up in Minnesota!"

Finally, the remaining two Ryan visitors found their bleary-eyed way downstairs and sat down at the kitchen table.

Bob, being the oldest, asked, "What are the plans for today, since you asked us to come down to help?"

Clay replied, "We'll probably spend most of the week buildin' a pen. A place to keep the livestock in outside of the barn."

"Doesn't sound so hard to me!" interjected Dave.

His uncle reminded him that, "In order to build a pen, y'all got to dig post-holes!"

Later in the morning, as Bob and Dave became familiar with the mechanics of using a pull-apart post-hole digger, they realized that their week on the farm wasn't going to be a week off from work. They didn't really care, since they enjoyed the camaraderie with their uncle Clay who probably still worked harder than anyone else.

In assigning duties to everyone, Clay delegated the lighter work of carrying tools, wire, dirt and other things back and forth, to the younger boys, Gene and Bucky. Most of the time though, they found that there wasn't all that much work for them to do on that first day, so they managed to find a way to get back into the house and coax a few more cookies and a glass of cool, thirst-quenching lemonade from Anita.

Farm life wasn't so bad, thought Gene, as he sat, drink in hand, in the shade of the porch roof with his ten-year-old cousin, peering through the blazing heat waves of late morning, watching his older brothers work. Seeing his sweating siblings taking turns thrusting the post-hole digger into the unyielding, sun-baked soil, Gene figured that he should probably go over to help them.

He thought better of it when his ears picked up the sounds of his brothers grunting and cursing when the digger hit bottom, then they had to pull its handles apart and lift out a heavy scoop of clinging, damp, clay soil. Hearing them hiss the word "blister" a few times, Gene figured that he'd better follow his uncle's instructions and keep out of the way. Maybe instead of helping them, he could take them some ice-water or some of this great lemonade their aunt Anita made, if there was any was left. He wouldn't get blisters on his hands by taking them lemonade.

Earlier, Gene overheard his brothers make plans to go into Newton that night and check out some of the town's female residents. After a great supper cooked by Anita, Gene looked for his brothers, finally going up to the spare room. Expecting to find them all slicked-up for their foray into town, it seemed to Gene that he'd walked into a morgue. Bob and Dave who had probably just stretched out after supper, were both snoring away dead to the world. Shaking his head, Gene muttered, "Looks like a couple of hotshots aren't going anywhere tonight!" and he slipped back out of their room.

Steamy vapor rose from the ground in the humid, 90-plus degree heat of midday which clued their uncle Clay into cutting Tuesday's work day a little shorter than the day before.

"It ain't smart to kill off yore help in the first couple days," he told his nephews at their noon dinner. "Ah might want a hired-hand someday," he continued, "and hearin' that Ah'd worked a couple of young men to death might make prospective hands a mite leery." He went on, "Instead of workin' this afternoon, we'll scare up a couple of rabbits for dinner. How does rabbits sound to you, Shep?"

With that, the dozing dog jumped to his feet, started jumping around in circles and scratched at the back door!

"You boys think this dog likes to rabbit-hunt?" Clay asked.

After lunch, the small hunting expedition trekked to a level spot near the woods where their uncle halted them and said, "Just watch and don't make any noise."

As his uncle loaded two shells into the shotgun, Gene wondered about Shep, and asked, "Where's Shep?"

Whispering, Clay replied, "Shep has already gone out ahead of us and is out there lookin' for a rabbit. When he comes across the scent of one he'll work his way behind it, and drive it back up towards us."

Shep had been raised by someone else and Clay took Shep in when his former owner moved to Colorado. Shep trotted with a limp because his former owner had taken him rabbit-hunting, and one time had fired too late, winging Shep's back leg with a piece of buckshot.

In a few minutes, a dog was heard barking back in the woods. "Hot damn! He's got one and he's runnin' it back this way!" shouted Clay. "Watch and see!"

Old Shep's barking was getting louder alright, which meant he was coming their way. Suddenly a cottontail broke out of the brush into the clearing, heading right into Clay's line of fire as the dog stopped dead at the edge of the clearing. Blam! One blast from the old twelve-gauge hit the mark, killing the rabbit instantly.

Gene wasn't a hunter but since the rabbit was food for the table he could understand the necessity, as long as it was a clean, quick kill which caused no suffering to the animal. Although the outcome was somewhat sad to him, it had been interesting to watch: an intelligent dog finding the quarry, making his way behind it, and driving it back toward his master, then stopping in time to avoid being shot himself. Sending Shep back out, the dog repeated his performance and a second shot felled another rabbit.

Clay told Gene to pick up the rabbits and bring them along because they had to take them back to the house and clean them. Picking up the two still-warm bodies, Gene felt a strange pricking of sorrow again. While the whole process didn't seem pretty, it had been humane, and Gene tried to consider it as part of life in a rural setting.

Having eaten rabbit and squirrel meat for supper at his grandparents, after his uncle Chick's occasional hunting trips, Gene didn't mind. Rabbit was quite a bit like chicken with the only concern being that he didn't bite down on a piece of buckshot that might have been overlooked in the cleaning process by his uncle.

After working half a day the next day, Wednesday, Bob and uncle Clay decided to drive into town for some fencing, but before they left, Dave asked for and was allowed to take Clay's shotgun. Going out into the woods with Shep, he spent the entire afternoon hunting and came home empty-handed.

"No luck today," Dave admitted to Gene and Bucky, who remained safely behind, "a couple of rabbits got away before I could fire, and I missed two others."

"Thank God," said Gene, "At least you managed to miss the dog too!"

On Thursday afternoon, Gene, in a moment of sheer boredom, agreed to accompany Dave on yet another rabbit hunt. Gene carried the BB gun. Why? He had no idea. Anyway, after they combed the brush for what seemed like hours, they began making their way back. Near the farm, Dave thought he might have seen a rabbit run under an old chamber pot lying in the brush. Coming back to the house empty-handed, the hunters were asked if they had bagged anything and Dave replied, "Nope, I didn't get a thing."

Whereupon, Gene contradicted his brother, saying, "C'mon Dave, you're too modest! You're forgetting how you put a blast right through the middle of that old metal pot!"

Their uncle grinned and said, "I thought that shotgun blast I heard had a tinny ring to it!"

Having finished the pen on Thursday, at Friday's breakfast they asked what was left to be done. Their uncle replied that, "There's only one thing to do today. Jest put the livestock in the pen where they won't roam all over anymore."

"That's it?" asked Dave. "Hey I guess we're going into town this afternoon, huh Bob?"

Seeing his uncle's Cheshire Cat grin, Bob offered, "It's not going to be that easy, is it Unc?"

"We'll jest have to see how much work it can be to round up two half-growed litters of pigs!" replied their roguish uncle.

What would be remembered among the brothers as "Roundup Day" was about to get under way. Making sure that the new pen's gates were closed, they began leading in the livestock. First the docile livestock such as the cow, the horses, the goat, and then a few minutes of the "Chicken Run," trying to get the hens and chicks in without stepping on any of them.

"No problem!" yelled Dave as he hauled in the remainder of the chickens, holding them by their feet.

Ducks?

"No problem" said Dave as he headed them off at the pass so Gene and Bucky could grab them.

No one was going to try grabbing the goose or her gander for fear of having one of those mean, vise-like bills clamp down on some tender body part. Instead, the two geese were herded in by closing in on them from both sides and from behind. Reluctantly, they began waddling along, staying just ahead of the pincer movement.

The sows? "You want me to get the sows in the pen? I thought you were going to take care of them, Unc!" said Dave, who suddenly had a problem!

Those big babies weighed a couple hundred pounds each and had long, sharp teeth that could clean an ear of corn in seconds.

"Uh, just how did you say we were going to do this, Unc?" asked Bob.

Having had his laugh, Clay picked up a long stick and walked over beside one of the sows and tapped her on the flanks while shooing her in the right direction. Way ahead of him was Bucky who ran and opened the gate. After a couple of short detours the old sow was safely in the pen.

Bravado returning, Dave yelled, "I'll get the other sow, Unc!"

Quickly responding, their uncle shouted, "No you don't! Leave her alone 'cause she's got nursin' piglets with her and she'll go for you!"

"Say no more!" said Dave, breathing an audible sigh of relief.

Instead, Clay instructed that they would move her piglets to the pen first, then drive the sow over. The little pigs gathered near their mother and the pig-chasers were forced to quickly reach in next to her back leg and snatch away a piglet. With ten little piglets, it took time. When only one of the smaller litter was left, it huddled under its mother's belly where no rational person was going to reach!

Dave, in a moment divided between bravado and madness, climbed over the rail fence attached to the barn and confronted the sow, holding a long stick like a bat in his hand. Sensing an attack, the sow grunted at Dave and pawed the ground. Dropping the stick, Dave was up and over the fence before the falling stick hit the ground! In that moment of diversion, Bucky groped through the fence and snatched away her last piglet. Clay then moved this sow, now anxious to rejoin her piglets, by prodding her gently along with a stick, as he had done with the other sow.

Now all that remained to be done was to round up the weaned litter of eight larger pigs, who were on their own and running loose. The Ryan boys had no idea that the "Great Pig Chase" would go on for hours. Nothing is faster, wilier, and squirmier than a scared young pig who doesn't want to be caught. After twenty minutes of being outrun by some pigs and out-maneuvered by many others, the pig-chasers were starting to realize that these curly-tailed squinty-eyed pigs from Hell couldn't be caught by chasing them one on one. That was a hopeless technique. Marshaling their forces, the humans decided to split up into two teams and were more successful when each team concentrated on one pig at a time. After nearly an hour, the last pig had finally been apprehended and put into the right section of the pen.

The roundup could have been over sooner but when a fifth pig had been caught earlier, Gene had swung the gate open too far. The pig and its four captive litter-mates escaped once more, forcing the pig-chasers to catch the same five pigs all over again.

It was late Friday when they were finished with the pen and the roundup, but Bob and Dave again were too worn out to strike out for town after supper.

Stopping by their room, their uncle asked, "Why haven't you jumped into the Ford and high-tailed it to town already?"

They just shook their heads.

Eyes half-closed, Bob asked their uncle, "How do farmers and cowboys who do this all of the time, have enough energy left to go carousing at the end of the day?"

Clay laughed and responded with, "Them ole boys wait until Saturday night! And it takes time to get used to hard, heavy work, when you haven't done it lately. If y'all want to get used to it, Ah'll let you stick around for another month!"

Bob and Dave sleepily deferred.

Early Saturday morning saw a heavy rain fall from overcast skies, but Gene enjoyed the sound of rainfall spattering the leaves of the fully-leaved trees. He appreciated the freshness of warm, moist air and the stillness of early morning in the country, not realizing until nearly his last day there that his mind had been reliving his days as an infant, when he walked along the cotton rows of his parents' farm. Enjoying each morning that week, by easing out onto the porch to hear early-rising birds and fill his lungs with the fresh morning air, Gene was enjoying his temporary return to nature and the country. Now in his own mind, Gene was able to answer the question he had once wanted to ask his uncle about moving back to the country. The calm serenity of country mornings not available to city boys had helped him understand why his uncle had opted to return to the country life.

After a leisurely breakfast, unusual on a farm, Saturday's plans were discussed and a well-deserved night on the town was arranged for the evening. Ah, but first, their uncle suggested that Dave take Shep and the shotgun over into Rabbitland and see if he could bring something home for Sunday dinner this time.

Having distracted Dave's attention with rabbit-hunting, Clay then said he needed to go into town and asked Bob if he wanted to go along. Clever ruse, thought up by Clay, the old rascal; divert the kid who was just seventeen, then take the twenty-one-year-old into town, and not without an ulterior motive.

Saying they would be right back, with a wink to Bucky and Gene, Clay and Bob drove off. The Ford convertible quickly disappeared over the top of the hill and on toward town. Not wanting to wait until evening, the old fox's plan was to go into town to have a few drinks and be back in the afternoon.

Just to pass the rest of the morning, Gene went along with Bucky, who had stopped to picked up his BB gun at the house. The two then went into the woods behind the farmhouse, where they took turns taking potshots at old cans and bottles. The breeze blowing down through the trees brought the sound of a beautiful bird call to their ears.

"What kind of bird is that?" asked Gene.

"It's just a cardinal, you'll find them all over around here." replied his cousin.

"The cardinal's my favorite bird," said Gene "but living in the city, I've never really seen or heard one."

Gene was horrified as Bucky then took aim up into the tree, where they both saw the bright red bird.

"No Bucky!" shouted Gene.

"Bting!" The BB gun went off.

Aghast, Gene saw the first live cardinal that he had ever seen, falling in a death spiral to the ground near them. Although dazed, the bird got to its feet and seemed otherwise unharmed.

Controlling the urge to throttle his younger cousin, Gene asked, "Why the hell did you do that?"

"I don't know," retorted Bucky, slightly dazed himself. "I just sighted in on it out of habit, and never thought that I could actually hit it. It sure is a pretty bird, up close, when you get a chance to look at its face, like its wearing a black velvet mask. I'm glad I didn't kill it."

Gene said, "Think twice next time and maybe you won't be so quick to squeeze the trigger on a gun."

Late afternoon shadows stalked the western wall of the farm-house, when a tired, dusty, and empty-handed Dave trudged up the road a quarter-mile behind Shep and still no return of Clay or Bob. As the next hour passed, understandably, the cookstove of their aunt's temper began a slow burn. After supper, she became concerned that their cow hadn't been milked and her spouse was the only one who knew how. Dave gave it a good try but no milk was forthcoming. Asking why it was important, Bucky told Gene that a milking cow must be milked twice a day, otherwise, she endures severe pain from holding her weighty milk if you miss a milking. As a last resort, Anita called her brother Larry, who came from ten miles away, arriving just before dark, to milk the cow.

Their aunt's slow burn now had been supplanted by a main burner kicking on and the two Ryan brothers went into silent mode, not wanting to ask any dumb questions. Their aunt was on the warpath and she was putting on her warpaint! As she finished her light makeup, she snapped, "Bucky, you get the car out of the garage!" Taken aback by her statement, Gene was aghast. Their cousin was only ten years old and he drove a car? This, Gene had to see, as he headed for the door. Whoops, his brother Dave nearly knocked him down while rushing for the door to get a look too! There he was, their little squirt of a cousin backing that big, shiny Chrysler down the driveway to the house, where Bucky parked it, shut off the engine, opened the door and with a twirl of the key chain, dropped the keys in his pocket.

"Okay, you little squirt, when did you learn to drive?" asked non-driver Dave as he accosted his cousin near the car.

"Oh hell, I get to drive all over this farm but they won't let me drive on the highway, yet!" replied his grinning cousin.

Bam! The back door had slammed shut behind Anita, all gussied up, ready to go into town and remind her spouse that it wasn't nice to leave his wife and three kids (well, so what if two were nephews?) at home while he stayed in town all day! Taking charge like a hardened platoon leader in some war movie, she snapped off orders with a crisp efficiency that would have made General Patton proud. Looking at the three boys, she said, "Bucky, you go put Shep in his run! One of you other two go double-check the gate on the pen to make sure it's properly latched!" Then to all within earshot, "Soon's you get back, everybody git in the car, 'cause we're goin' to town!" she snapped.

Arriving in Newton after setting a new elapsed time record for the farm-to-Newton run, Anita parked the big Chrysler in the teeming, brightly-lit town square. It looked like most everybody in Jasper County must have driven in for their Saturday night on the town; well at least every one of the 2350 residents of Newton! Leaving the boys in the car, Anita began checking out a few of the watering holes and found her long-missing husband and nephew in one of the best-known bars. Coming back to the car, Anita asked the boys if they wanted to go to the movies and sent Bucky and her two younger nephews off to the show.

With only the Star Theatre in town, the choice of movies was limited to the John Wayne movie, "Sands Of Iwo Jima" which hadn't been around to Chicago's neighborhood theatres yet. Dave and Gene hadn't seen it before and enjoyed the film but poor Bucky already had and was bored out of his skull. Going back to the car after the movie, Dave, being the oldest, strolled maturely into the bar to let his aunt and uncle know that they were back and to his surprise, was sent right back outside. Seems they had strict rules about under-aged young people being in places where alcoholic beverages were sold.

Shortly afterwards, Gene's aunt, uncle, and oldest brother came out of the bar and despite their uncle wanting to continue on, Anita said that it was time for them to head back to the farm. Since Bob looked sleepy, his uncle said he would drive Bob's Ford and the two of them were off down the street while Anita was waiting to back out into traffic in the town square. At last able to swing out into traffic, she drove toward the road back to the farm, when she saw the Ford suddenly turn off into the opposite direction of the farm. The chase was on!

Any hopes that Clay might have entertained of leaving his wife behind were poorly founded, since their Chrysler, unlike the Ford, was built for the highway! By keeping the pedal to the metal, Anita easily kept the once-fading taillights of the Ford in sight as her spouse took various shortcuts, perhaps in efforts to elude her. He must have forgotten that she had grown up in this area and knew all the back roads better than he did!

Now they were really clipping along, on a straight, black-topped road, into and right straight out of, the town of Wheeler. Soon they were in the next county, approaching a section of road repairs outside the town of Dieterich. Suddenly the Ford was braked hard but still had not avoided some rough railroad tracks in the road which it hit at too high a speed, bouncing off course like a rubber ball from the impact! At that point, their uncle knew the game was over and turned slowly into Dieterich, pulling over in front of a tavern with which they were familiar.

Catching up to her husband Anita played it very cool and acted as though this wasn't unusual. She treated it as though it had been a game and started up with a normal conversation as they examined the Ford for any damage. Bob who had been sleeping on the back seat prior to the impact, had been jolted to being wide-awake and unhurt. In passing, their uncle Clay touched his wife's cheek and mentioned that he just thought the night was still young and had a sudden impulse to drive over to Dieterich. Watching them, Gene believed that the love at first sight which had stricken them so many years earlier was still very strong between them.

After going inside for a nightcap and lingering for several minutes, the two spouses returned to the cars and drove their

Chrysler back to the farm. Bob, of course drove his own car back, with younger brother Dave riding shotgun. Needless to say, everyone retired quickly to bed, upon their late arrival at the farmhouse.

The next sensation Gene felt after falling asleep was being shaken by his uncle, rousing him from sleep. The bright, morning sun beamed brightly into Gene's eyes as he saw his uncle put his finger to his nose, imploring silence as he beckoned Gene to follow him. Getting out of bed, Gene quickly threw on his jeans and shirt and now immensely curious, followed his finagling uncle onto the porch.

Stepping onto the porch, Gene saw his uncle loading two bright red shells into the shotgun. Breaking into that broad, devilish grin of his, Clay piqued his nephew's curiosity a bit more by signaling again for silence, and sneaked under the open window of the spare bedroom where his other nephews remained asleep. After he pointed the weapon skyward, the morning air was split by a deafening roar as Clay yanked each of the two triggers in succession. Instantly the curtains of the upper window flew aside as Bob and Dave poked their wide-eyed heads out to see what happened! "Now that you boys are up, you might want to get ready for breakfast," chided their impish uncle. The day had begun.

Their last meal on the farm was another great country breakfast of flapjacks, bacon, sausage, fried eggs, toast, and coffee. Just the sort of heavy, high-calorie meal to keep them awake on the road. After breakfast, the Ryan boys went about packing up their gear for the return trip home. By midday they had loaded their belongings and the several additional items received from their aunt and uncle including a crate of eggs, which they had wanted to send to Kathleen and Tom.

It was with no small amount of sadness that the three boys bade their aunt, uncle, and cousin, goodbye, for no one wanted to leave, but Kathleen had advised them not to overstay their welcome. Gene had to tear himself away from the farm and Shep, for in that short week, he had found his roots, was already regressing into being a country boy and had already become attached to the friendly, handsome dog.

Finally, when everyone's goodbyes were said, Bob started up the Ford and as late morning's misty haze rose toward the bright sun, the top-down Ford, carrying its three young passengers, rumbled up the road, topped the hill and disappeared.

As the evening dropped its curtain of darkness on the sprawling, boisterous city of Chicago, the trusty, maroon Ford rag-top, despite the bouncing around it took the night before, delivered its cargo of three sleepy young men safely to Chicago's North Side, after a long, uneventful trip back home.

Chapter 21

Wrigleyville

Following his week of rural adventure on the farm, Gene whiled away the rest of the summer of 1949 playing softball, going to Wrigley Field for most of the Cub home games, and hanging around on cool, concrete porches during the idyllic summer evenings. Organized baseball games were scarce, so Gene played a lot of "Catch" with different combinations of his three new friends, Hans Mauer, Jack Kramer, and "Weasel" Dolan. For some reason, it seemed that all of his three friends rarely made an appearance together, so he'd get together with Hans and Weasel, Jack and Weasel, or Hans and Jack.

Usually they would grab a softball and bat, go up to the parking lots behind the stores adjacent to the "El" tracks, on Southport and just hit out balls until the batter made three outs. With Kramer really able to belt the ball, they needed as much of an outfield space as they could get! By a benevolent stroke of fortune, they were all right-handed batters, eliminating the need to shift over for a left-handed batter, allowing these would-be All-stars to consistently play "Right Field Out" in all of their games.

A "pickup" baseball game was one of those rare occasions when they were able to get more guys together for a ballgame on an open field or vacant lot, of which there were many at that time. Using a smashed milk carton for home plate, an old board for first base, a brown-paper bag for second and just an idea where it was for third base, kids played with a baseball that must have weighed at least eight ounces instead of just over five, due to the layers of tape wrapped around it. The bats they used were old, often cracked and taped or had chipped handles.

Equipment was but a secondary consideration, for to a boy the essence of baseball was the joy of playing it. In that time, many a kid's dream was to someday be a Major League ballplayer, and it mattered not at all that he might be paid to play baseball since he would have played for nothing.

For variety, they'd sometimes wander go over to the produce store on the corner of Newport at Southport to play a game known by hundreds of names in the hundreds of Chicago neighborhoods in which it was played. "Squoosh," as it was often known required only an inexpensive ball. The game consisted of throwing a tennis ball or other hollow, rubber ball against the corner of any horizontal ledge of a building. Any base hits were determined by whether the ball was caught on one or two bounces or judged to be a home run if it hit high off the wall of the building across the street.

After night fell, the warm summer evenings were often whiled away by sitting on one of their porches or the porch of a friend. Next to Jack Kramer's house was one of their favorite friends' porches on which they hung around. It belonged to the family of Alvina Schmidt, a very nice, interesting and friendly girl who was a sophomore at Alvernia, a Catholic all-girls' school. Often Alvina's junior girlfriends would stop by. Carolyn Arndt, a comely, short blonde, and Gloria Hensel, a lovely, statuesque brunette who, being shy, seldom said more than two words around the boys, rounded out the porch-steps gathering.

Alvina came to be good friend of at least three of the guys, while Dolan usually stayed away, having become persona non grata with Alvina who had asked him to leave one evening, after his mouth had gotten too big for his face. On occasion, Alvina would impugn the sanity of the other three guys for hanging around with Dolan, to which the boys often replied that they were probably the only friends Dolan had.

Porch conversations covered a wide range of subjects, from movies to sports, music, current events, and even different religions. Gene was learning once again, how nice and enjoyable it could be, just talking and socializing with girls once more. He had realized early-on that the lack of feminine classmates was a major drawback of attending an all-boys school. It may have been that way with the Alvernia girls too, since they always seemed to have a good time bantering back and forth with the boys.

One evening as nubile Carolyn sat quietly next to Gene on the porch swing, her upper arm inadvertently happened to touch against his. The warmth of her skin and the subtle perfume she wore caused him to regret being so bashful and wish that he were a couple of years older. Alas, nothing remotely related to romance would ever materialize between the mature Miss Arndt and the bumbling fourteen-year-old who admired her from a distance.

While his working mom wasn't home during the day, to ask about the glazed-look seen in his eyes after encountering Carolyn walking by his house, Mae Waltzer certainly had sharp enough eyes to spot love in bloom and never lacked the nerve to ask if he had a sweetheart. Naturally all he could do was stammer a bit and quickly change the subject by saying that she of all people must remember how things were when she was young and the belle of the ball. It worked every time, for Mae had enjoyed quite a full, enjoyable life of parties and dancing in her younger days and loved to recount her tales to anyone who would listen. Often like a live-in aunt that they never had, Mae, who was long-retired, had nothing but spare time and was a ready ear to listen when things were going badly for one of the Ryan boys. She was a source of friendly advice if it were requested, and one felt that Mae had been there and understood how life's ups and downs could trouble a young adult or adolescent. She was by then, just like one of the family.

On those days when none of the guys was around, Gene took his league ball and mitt over under the "El" tracks where he had chalked a strike zone on the bricks of the rear-wall of one of the storage buildings. Over the next two years he would spend many hours trying to perfect his fastball, a non-existent curve, and a pretend knuckle-ball which only he deemed to actually be floating in on wind currents. The pitch he worked hardest at next to his fastball, was the knuckle-ball. Influenced by the Cub's old knuckle-baller, Dutch Leonard and Cleveland's 20-game winner, Gene Bearden, it was probably best that he concentrated on a knuckler, since his fastball would've been more accurately described as a rapid "change-up."

But for a look at real baseball, Gene only had to walk those four blocks up the old Milwaukee switch line's tracks to the ballpark on any day the Cubs were playing at home. Generally though, he tried to save his money by buying bleacher seat tickets for double-header games. What's that? No, a lot of people can't endure the pain of sitting that long, but a young kid could sit on those petrified-plank, bleacher seats without backrests for six or seven hours with no problem!

In that year the Cubs had, for once in the annals of baseball, appeared to have gotten the better deal in a trade. A last-minute, four-player trade of outfielders on June 15th had brought Hank Sauer and Frankie Baumholtz from the Cincinnati Reds for an old Cub favorite, Harry "Peanuts" Lowry and Harry "The Hat" Walker. The trade came when Sauer was still finding out how to use the power that he had gotten from recently switching to a 40-ounce bat and became immensely popular with Cub fans when he began pounding the cover off the ball for the Wrigley Field crowd.

Despite having power-hitters like Sauer and Andy Pafko in the middle of their batting order, the North Siders would still finish the season dead-last but before the last crack of the bat in late September, they would bring their die-hard fans an abundance of late-inning rallies that fell short, proving to be an exciting last-place team!

From his front row seat in dead center-field, Gene studied Andy Pafko and the center-fielders from the visiting teams, in a time when there were several fleet-footed ball-hawks who nevertheless carried anemic batting averages. Gene wasn't watching them for batting tips but for the way they played balls hit to the outfield. The Phillies' Richie Ashburn, the Braves' Sam Jethroe, and the Reds' Lloyd Merriman were all speed-burners while the Dodgers' Duke Snider and the Giants' Bobby Thomson were power-hitters. Of course purists might argue against "The Flying Scot," since the right-handed hitting Thomson had played his home games in New York's Polo Grounds. The left and right field fences were only a short 250-feet from home plate in the old "Grounds" but Thomson had broken Gene's heart too often, by belting the ball out of Wrigley Field, with other Giants on base.

Gene especially would study Sam Jethroe, who had played for years in the Negro leagues before he got his major league break after Jackie Robinson broke the color barrier. As the fleet-footed ball-hawk roamed the outfield during batting practice, Gene heard many flyballs pop as they fell into the wiry outfielder's glove as he played them perfectly. It was how Jethroe played line drives and ground balls that really impressed him. No one charged the ball like Sam Jethroe, who had a unique style of racing in for a ball hit to the outfield, then picking the ball up, stepping onto his left foot and firing the ball into the infield, all in one quick, fluid motion. A runner who challenged Jethroe's arm on a base hit to the outfield was usually an exciting out.

One day when Boston's Braves came to town for a double-header, Gene and Dolan went out to the ballpark and after watching baseball all afternoon, the two boys came home, got their gloves out and played catch. Jethroe's performance had stuck in Gene's mind as he asked Dolan to keep throwing him grounders. Gene then tried emulating Jethroe's quick pickup and release motions, drawing disdainful remarks from Doyle as to why Gene was acting so weird. In telling Dolan what he was doing, Dolan cracked, "Why are you trying to imitate a Negro player?" "Shut up and throw the ball!" was Gene's quick response.

Practicing over the rest of the summer, Gene was able to coordinate the separate actions into one continuous motion as he had seen Jethroe do. In games which Gene would play in the years to come, that split-second saving in time was to be the reason why many opposing runners were out trying to make two bases out of a single, or trying to go from first to third on a ball to the outfield and sliding into a surprise tag at third.

Because he was a class glove-man in a game which demanded class hitters, Sam Jethroe would be out of the majors within a few seasons and most baseball fans would forget him, but he was never forgotten by one skinny kid in Chicago who virtually lived in the center-field bleachers of Wrigley Field. A kid who learned to love playing the outfield simply because it offered the greatest challenges to a quick-release of the ball and one's throwing arm.

Baseball however, wasn't all that Gene and his friends were

beginning to think about. Nothing brought this so poignantly to mind as a quick walk-through along the neighborhood sidewalk by the stupefyingly lovely Iris Woodward. A senior and cheerleader at Lake View High, Iris was athletic, auburn-haired, vivacious and she only lived four doors down from Gene. It made their day if one of them greeted her with a "Hello" and this older vision of elegance deigned to acknowledge their existence. Exuding a class which was several notches above their greatest aspirations, Iris was simply someone that dorks such as they might only daydream about.

With the Summer's end his sophomore year would soon begin, a year Gene would come to remember as his worst year, academically and socially. In looking over his schedule, he looked forward to returning to school, anticipating a much better year than his freshman year since he had the Lane routine down pat by now. The kid was in for a series of disappointments.

His first disappointment, a big one, came when his Commercial Art class, scheduled to be taught by the esteemed Mrs. Berlansky was again rescheduled, to be taught again, by Mr. Kirkstat! Gene and many of his classmates felt that their first year had been a waste of time and deeply resented this turn of events. In their second year of art study, the closest they got to meaningful art training would be when they were allowed to do charcoal sketching from life. Many of these students who had enrolled in the four-year Commercial Art curriculum were staking their future on a career in Commercial Art. Sadly, some of the students who were bogged down in Mr. Kirkstat's class would come up short in practical art and technique training, and would in later years ultimately be forced to find other vocations.

Other disappointments followed which appeared to Gene, to hinge on the fact, mentioned before, that Lane was an elite school which seemed to draw teachers with the most years of seniority in the Chicago school system. This appeared to be very apparent in Gene's sophomore schedule, since his Geometry, Biology, and English teachers were all near retirement. In fact, all three of them would opt for retirement during the next year, one year too late, as Gene would feel, when he heard the news.

Trying very hard he wasn't able to grasp Geometry's concept as it was taught, getting a C for the semester. English which had always been interesting was stifling, in his particular class, and he merited only a C. He prided himself on his love for Science, yet achieved only a C in Biology, despite intense effort on his part.

That intense effort became necessary on Gene's part in Biology, since that dark day when a classmate threw something at the teacher, Mr. Kerley, as he left the room and Mr. Kerley wheeled around in the doorway, pointed his bony finger toward Gene in the back of the room and shouted, "You did that!" Looking up, Gene had no idea what old man Kerley was talking about and denied knowledge of anyone throwing anything, but for the rest of that semester, Gene suffered this teacher's suspicion, ridicule, and bias. Chuck Sherson, the guy sitting next to Gene knew he didn't do it but Mr. Kerley had never trusted Chuck either. Three days after this semester of persecution would end, Mr. Kerley retired.

Print Shop which gained Gene a B, was the bright academic spot that semester. His composing room bench partner was Pat Decker, his friend with whom he shared a locker. Pat and Gene got along great and Pat helped Gene out when he ran into typesetting problems. Yet even a good, learning experience was marred by the overbearing presence of one oversized, and over-aged motor-mouth in his Print Shop class.

His name was Marstrom, and each day he would ride Gene loudly and unmercifully about his speech and looks. In itself, that was just bearable but the unnerving part was that some of the others in class went along with Marstrom and emulated his persecution of Gene, in order to curry favor with Marstrom. One day, coming out of a diner across the street from school, one antagonistic member of Gene's division made fun of Gene when no one was around. He must have thought that since Gene put up with Marstrom, he was afraid. Gene flattened him then walked away.

Later when early February ushered in the second semester, Gene couldn't help but notice Motor-Mouth Marstrom's very conspicuous absence. While rumor would have it that his antagonist had been arrested, the rumor was offset by a half-joking story that he had been expelled because he had finally become old enough to vote. In either case, Gene would be relieved to know that at least one insensitive bastard wouldn't be around anymore. Later updates would confirm the story that, in fact, Marstrom had been arrested, sentenced, and was doing jail time.

This long, discouraging year would be the year to nearly drive Gene to drop out of high school but he dreaded the thought that he would have to go to a continuation school one day a week until he turned seventeen. Again, he had kept his problems to himself, for his mom had enough problems with his stepfather, and his brothers wouldn't be able to help him in school anyhow. He felt that he had to handle this by himself. Maybe by continuing to study hard he might catch a better break next semester.

On the horns of a dilemma, he confided in his friend, Pat Decker, at lunch one day. After hearing Gene out, one of Pat's bushy eyebrows lifted as he pondered a solution. Looking Gene in the eye, Pat's cool gray eyes fixed Gene's concentration as he reminded Gene that if he could only stick it out and continue his studies at Lane, he would graduate at nearly seventeen-and-a-half. "You sure don't want to go to continuation school with those hard cases, Ryan," advised his friend. "If you thought Marstrom was bad, think of a bunch of Marstroms in every class at continuation school." Shuddering at the thought of such a possibility, Gene thanked Pat for his advice and agreed that maybe he should continue to tough it out at Lane.

Aiding him in his efforts to persevere during this time were the effects of puberty. In addition to the strength he gained from his 12 month regimen of nightly exercising, he had begun to get taller and heavier, growing to five-feet-eight from five-feet-one, and gaining twenty pounds, up to 125 in the last twelve months. Back in February of 1949, he had begun measuring his height and weighing himself on the 15th of every month, so he had visible proof just by looking at the marks on the wall and the scale. Some things were working out for him, although he was still a long way from his goal of six-feet, 180 pounds like his boxing mentor and uncle, Lew.

More frequently now, Gene spent evenings at the Lincoln-Belmont YMCA with Dolan, sometimes playing basketball, but usually Gene spent his time lifting weights, running laps on the track, and working on the boxing bags and pulleys. By finishing up the evening with an hour in the pool, he learned how to stay underwater longer and deeper, until he became a fair diver and a better breather. He was hanging out with Dolan a little more than he might have preferred, only because his friendship with Jack Kramer had experienced a rough spot or two of late.

An example of their touch and go friendship was demonstrated when Jack wouldn't speak to Gene for two weeks after one evening outside the drugstore, when Dolan and Jack had double-teamed Gene verbally while Gene bantered back. Jack then took the low road and got in a final, cheap shot that caused Gene to lose it. Not caring how tall Jack was, Gene cocked back his right fist and with his left hand, grabbed Jack by the front of his gabardine jacket hard enough that he ripped the jacket down the front. Dolan stood mute with his mouth agape, while Jack was livid, spouting profanity at Gene; yet all his fight must have been in his mouth, for he turned and sulked away from his smaller antagonist. Gene did come away from the fight that never was with one bright thought: it looked like all of the previous year's exercise was beginning to work for him.

The cold nights of this winter were beginning to seem longer since Gene longed to play hockey but had refrained lately from doing so. Just a few weeks ago, when he had been putting into practice the important things about hockey's techniques and its proprieties, that he had picked up the year before, he was to play his last hockey game. On a cold February night, perfect for starting a rush up the ice, he was engaged in a friendly game with Billy Roder and a few others, including a couple of strangers, two strapping guys he hadn't met before.

While Gene was in close to the net someone else had taken a shot on goal that was kicked out and the rebound came Gene's way. Slapping at the loose puck, his skate blade slipped as he followed through, and his stick came backwards very hard. He would never forget the sickening thud of stick against skull. One of the strangers, the bigger one, had been behind him and was skulled by Gene's stick on the backswing. As if shot through the head the guy fell in a heap onto the ice and Gene thought he had killed him.

While the kneeling players ministered to the prostrate body they saw that he was still breathing.

Worried sick, Gene told the guy's friend, "Geez, I didn't mean to hit him. I slipped on the ice."

The stranger said, "I know you didn't and I'll tell him, but he's got a lousy temper and he's startin' to come around, so it might be better if you weren't here when he comes to."

Reluctantly, Gene then left the rink per the kid's advice but the feeling that he might have killed someone never left him and he would never play hockey again.

Ice skating remained Gene's favorite winter sport but he left his hockey stick at home from then on, and concentrated on racing instead. Finding times when the ice wasn't crowded, it was a thrill for him to skate all out, learning to take the turns at high speed, and building up his endurance. While his high-speed turns weren't fast enough to make the team at school like Billy Milford did, he was just as fast as Billy on the straightaways. If he had sold his hockey skates and bought a pair of racers instead, he probably could have made the team. But he had gotten them from his mom for Christmas just the year before, had finally broken the uppers in, and didn't want to give them up.

Gene still got an occasional chance to hang around with his brother Dave, like the cold, snowy Friday night Dave and his best friend, Gene's fellow Laneite, Jack Gorr, allowed the younger Gene to wander along with them to the Century theatre over on Clark near Broadway. Walking to and from the theatre nearly two miles away in the middle of February, they kept warm laughing at the spontaneous antics of Dave and Jack.

Jack started it off as they walked through what seemed like a blizzard, by staggering with eyes closed and arms outstretched, shouting in a clipped British accent, "Snow! Snow!" cracking the brothers up. Jack had a great sense of humor and treated his buddy's kid brother as an equal, while Gene thought highly of Jack. The trio laughed and kidded back and forth all the way to the show. It was only with extreme self-control that they were able to contain themselves during some of the more serious, perhaps corny, scenes during the showing of the movie "Jolson Sings Again," a sequel to "The Jolson Story."

Both movies starred Larry Parks as Jolson and had given a new generation the opportunity to watch and learn about a popular singer from an earlier time. Gene did wonder why the great Al Jolson had performed in blackface since he wasn't part of any minstrel show. The movie exposure however, brought Jolson a temporary resurgence of popularity, so much so, that U. S. Army troops whom he would entertain during USO shows in the next few years, would thoroughly appreciate his showmanship and dynamism.

The next Monday at lunch period, Gene and Jack Gorr were standing in Riesz's school store were they had just finished rehashing their Friday evening at the movies over hamburgers and Pepsi. Jack suddenly remembered that he had a meeting with a counselor to talk about a class change; new semesters were always like that.

Gulping down his Pepsi, Jack left with a quick "See you later!" and exited in a blur of motion.

Watching through the glass window, Gene held his breath as he saw his brother's best friend race across the street dodging horn-blowing cars like a Bear halfback eluding tacklers until he reached the other side of the street.

"Jack, you're a good-looking guy," Gene muttered, then went on, "but keep doing that and you'll just be a handsome corpse!"

Finishing his Pepsi, Gene stepped out into the clear, cold air and coughed some of the second-hand smoke out of his lungs.

"Do you have a cold?" asked a familiar, feminine voice from behind him.

Turning around, he saw just the woman he expected to see, a vivacious, blue-eyed, strawberry blonde about five-feet-two.

"What are you doing here?" he asked the second most important woman in his life.

"I work right over there in that building," she explained, pointing to one of the one-story light industry businesses across from Lane. "Been there for two weeks now!" she said.

As they stood talking for about five minutes, a few classmates of Gene's began filing past, on their way back to afternoon classes. As the guys went by they all seemed to slow down, slowly appraising this lovely female talking to an ugly kid they thought was a dork. They had no way of knowing that she was his aunt Maybelle, who was only on her lunch break. Although she was married and the mother of ten-year-old Roy, Maybelle had retained her figure and possessed a cute, young face, passing for eighteen or younger in the eyes of many Lane students.

Arriving back in class, Stan Janowicz was the first of many to bombard Gene with queries of "Who was that girl? Is she your girlfriend? How did you get a girl like her?" While many questions were asked, no answers were given, save a sly smile on Gene's face. Gene wasn't going to spoil the impression that his friends and enemies had by telling them who she really was. Somehow though, as Gene and his aunt would occasionally meet on the sidewalk, a few of the guys seemed to develop a higher opinion of him, even to the point of relative strangers striking up conversations with him.

As February rolled into March, the weather took a turn to the warmer side. It was just after dinner, on one of those unseasonably warm, March evenings, when Jack Kramer and Gene ran into Tommy Rourke who was home on spring break from military school. Gene had seen him around a few times during the last year and a half but never really got to know his name until Jack introduced them this evening. Of medium height and stocky build, Tommy, a reddish-haired kid, was cheerful, loquacious, and the kind of guy you wanted to be friends with from the beginning. After talking for a while, the trio decided that since it was such a pleasant evening, they would take a walk down to Broadway.

They hadn't gone two blocks when they encountered three scruffy-looking guys who Gene later learned were from a gang on Henderson Street. As the two punks were passing, one of them flipped his glowing cigarette at Tommy's face. Although it fell short and hit him in the chest the glowing sparks burned into Tommy's new, brown, leather jacket. Tommy was steamed and he was going to take them on.

Turning around, he shouted to the three, "You guys think you're wise?"

As the punks turned toward Tommy, Gene, and Jack, one of them drew a knife to keep Tommy's attention while the second suddenly sucker-punched Tommy in his solar-plexus, doubling him up.

As Gene moved to intervene, he came face-to-face with a butcher knife pulled by the third punk, who said, "I'll gut you if you move!"

Jack, of little help had been right behind Gene. The two of them were held at bay, prevented from doing anything to help Tommy. Quickly the three punks were off and running into a nearby gangway. Coughing until he regained his breath, Tommy swore that there would be another time when he would get even with the pasty-faced, ugly-toothed misfit who suckered him.

Continuing on their way, they walked down to Broadway, then up to Addison Street, then westward past Sheffield and alongside the darkened, deserted temple of Chicago baseball and football. Passing Wrigley Field's main gate at Clark Street, Gene gazed in awe at the brightly-glaring neon and incandescent sign which announced that Opening Day of the 1950 baseball season wasn't far off. Despite last-place finishes by their team in 1948 and 1949, the trio of true Cub fans was excited at the prospect of returning to the ballpark when the season began in the third week in April.

April came and the Cubs began the season by showing that last place finishers don't improve much in their next season. First or last, a great time could always be had watching a game, since the great teams still came to town, and the Cubs still had the best-looking ballpark in the Majors. Ballparks unfortunately, don't win ball games and April ended with the Cubs showing signs of being mediocre once more.

May opened with several beautiful evenings and on one of them, wondrous Riverview beckoned to Gene, Jack Kramer, Tommy Rourke, and Weasel Dolan and they couldn't pass up the chance to go and enjoy the rides and Midway. For just five cents each, they were in the gate, walking past the Silver Flash, taking in the sights and sounds. By the time they walked along the Midway to the Comet, three of them were eager to ride a roller-coaster. Gene had ridden it before, but tonight he might have deferred but then Tommy talked him into it. Once they were over the first hill, it was like riding a bicycle and the exhilaration was back! The evening hours slipped away as they rode several of the rides and enjoyed seeing many other attractions, including lots of high-school girls.

Exiting through the main gate, the four guys turned north and walked toward the Roscoe streetcar stop, when who should pass them from the other direction but a familiar face that belonged to a scruffy guy walking alone. Tommy immediately recognized the ugly-toothed punk and knew that the time and place to get even had arrived.

Doing an about face and leaving his friends behind, Tommy caught up to the punk, and blocked his path, confronting him with, "Hey, remember me?"

Either amnesia-stricken or playing dumb, the punk answered "No. "

Tommy then asked him, "How good are you in a fair fight?"

The punk responded with the first word of a two-word obscenity but the second word was muffled by Tommy's fist. Then Tommy followed with a one-two combination that took him down.

As he prepared to leave his adversary lying there in the dust of a grassless vacant lot, Tommy told him, "I'd better never see your ugly face again!"

Hurrying to catch up with his friends, Tommy allowed the matter to close without further comment.

Spring's beautiful weather continued through early June, when late on a Saturday afternoon, Bob Ryan approached his kid brother and asked him, "Hey, Jocko, want to go to the show with me?"

Pleasantly surprised, Gene said, "You bet! What show are we going to?"

"The Century," answered Bob, "so we'll be taking the streetcar. The car's still in the shop. "

"That's okay with me. It's beautiful outside. "

Walking down Newport the few blocks to Clark Street, Gene was elated, because he enjoyed being in the company of his big brother who again seemed to be taking an interest in him.

264

His brother's added interest might have been spurred by an earlier conversation that the two of them had in the morning. Gene asked Bob if he could use the desk in his room for some drawings and in giving his consent, Bob had asked Gene how he was doing in school.

Looking around to see if anyone else could hear, Gene replied, "Remember last semester, when I said my grades couldn't get much worse?" He continued, "They're gonna be worse and I feel like I'm going to be a disappointment to Mom."

Bob then heard some of the background behind his brother's unusually poor grades and consoled his kid brother, saying, "Don't worry about it, Jocko! The semester will be over soon and next year you'll get a fresh start. Remember this too, you could never be a disappointment to Mom or your brothers."

How that one phrase from his learned brother's lips lifted Gene's sagging spirits. It had been a relief to share his problem with someone else, older and much wiser, and have his self-induced burden lightened.

Getting on the streetcar, Gene reveled in the fact that Clark Street was one of the trolley lines that ran the Green Hornets, just like Western Avenue. Green and cream in color, these streetcars were the new generation of motor cars which rolled smoothly and speedily along their rails, quickly accelerating and decelerating at stops along the way. Windows open on a pleasant evening, a cooling breeze washed through the chrome-plated bars on the windows, blowing Gene's straw-like hair all over his face. Not Bob's though. Bob was too cool to have his thick, dark, wavy hair blow around, although his hair's tendency to remain in place may have been assisted by a heavy application of some greasy kid stuff.

In no time, the streetcar ride was over and they were deposited at the intersection of Diversey and Clark, right in front of the majestic Century Theatre. As they strode up to the box-office, Gene, standing behind Bob in line, reached in his pocket for the price of admission.

Bob said to the cashier, "Two, please!"

Gene said, "Thanks!"

"For what? You're buying the popcorn and soft drinks, Jocko."

The title of the movie they came to see is of little consequence at this point, but the two brothers had a great time watching it and bonding. A simple evening of movie-going with Bob was a great occasion for Gene who filed it away among his treasured memories. It may be coincidence but as Dave had begun dating and seemed to have no time for his younger brother, Bob appeared to be taking over as sidekick for a while. Gene didn't mind at all.

A few weeks later his sophomore year at last, came to an end on a long awaited Friday. As he had predicted, his final grades were worse than the first semester, his C's in English and Geometry degrading down to D's, the lowest passing grade. By remembering his talk with Bob earlier in the month, Gene didn't dread bringing home his course book, which was the permanent log of all of his grades for all four years. Naturally, his stepfather chastised him for lower grades than before but Gene just kept thinking, that next year was going to be better.

Up early the next day, the last Saturday in June, a gorgeously sunny but hot day, Gene was completing the remaining collections on his route, finishing up on Melrose at Greenview. He then stopped in at Pfeffer's grocery store on the corner to cool off with a cold soft drink. It was the end of the route and the end of the week. Now all he needed to do was to turn in his receipts at the circulation office just down Greenview. While he was savoring the cold beverage, his eyes caught the late newspaper headlines in the newspaper rack.

What's that? South Korea was invaded by North Korean troops early this morning? Where were North and South Korea? Moving closer, Gene saw that a small drawn map accompanied the article and he stared at it. Oh yes, it's that peninsula south of China, just west of Japan, across the Sea of Japan. The article said that South Korea had been invaded early on June 25th. But today's only June 24th! Forgot! They're a day ahead of us in the Far East.

It began for many people that same way; just a headline in the paper about an event halfway around the world. On June 27th, the United Nations Security Council approved a U. S. resolution to intervene in the Korean conflict. By June 29th, Seoul, the capital of South Korea had fallen to the North Koreans. On July 1st, the first U. S. troops arrived in South Korea as the advance party of the U. N. forces. Considered a "police action" by the federal government, the conflict would become a major war effort of over three years duration and would cost the lives of 250,000 U. N. troops. Of that quarter of a million war dead, over 54,000 of them would be American boys. "Police action?" It seemed like a war to everyone else.

The Korean War's effects would be felt in Gene's family and millions of others, as World War II "retreads" were called back to active duty and the number of men called up by the draft each month was increased. The United States was mobilizing once more, to engage in a far-off war, this time in an alliance with numerous other U. N. members who were also sending troops.

As the days passed, it became customary for the newspapers to publish a map of Korea each day, with a line showing the territory held by the U. N. forces. It soon became obvious that the U. N. forces were being pushed further southward until finally the North Koreans held most of South Korea.

Worried that his brothers might be eligible for the draft and liable for service in Korea, Gene asked and learned that Bob stood a chance of being called up, despite his having already served a hitch in the Navy. Dave, at seventeen, who had always talked about joining the Marines, was still too young for the draft but talking like he was ready to go when the time came. Gene hoped that the time wouldn't come, for either of them.

Chapter 22

Homeowners At Last

The late morning calm of an early July Saturday was interrupted by the deep-throated rumble of a large truck engine coming from in front of the house. Looking out the huge center window of their living room, Gene saw the all-too-familiar sight of a moving van parked in a large space that had been vacated by two cars. The new owners who had recently bought out the Andersons were taking possession of the apartment upstairs. Relations with the Andersons had always been tenuous at best but lately had eroded into several heated discussions between a drunken Mr. Anderson and anyone he encountered from Gene's family. The Ryan boys hadn't been disappointed in the least, to hear that the Andersons were selling the building and were glad to see them move out.

As Gene watched the new owners moving in, he beheld a lovely, red-haired girl, perhaps a year or two older than he, helping to carry in boxes. Fine-featured and slender, she had a pleasant voice which he overheard in conversation with a woman who was probably her mother and who, at one point called the girl Valerie. He later learned that the new owner, Mr. Riley, was a fireman who had been transferred to a local engine company from the Gage Park neighborhood on Chicago's Southwest Side. So her full name was Valerie Riley. What a nice name, Valerie Riley. It seemed to have an Irish lilt to it. In days to come he concocted ways to "spontaneously" bump into her as she left the house or returned from a trip to the store. He was still too shy to say anything more than "Hi!" when he did meet her after lying in wait and turned two shades darker red, blushing as he said it.

Just as Gene was getting adjusted to this Lakeview neighborhood, now comfortable with his new friends and the young Titian-haired Valerie's presence boding well of things to come, Gene learned that it would soon be time to move again. Mister Riley had given Gene's folks thirty days to move, since he needed the first floor apartment for his brother's family. With time so short, Kathleen and Tom were hard-pressed to find an apartment which fit their needs.

In talking her parents, Kathleen received advice and a promise of some financial help if she and Tom were to buy their own home. Coincidentally, there was a two-story, Georgian-type home on Montana, the next street over from Gene's grandmaw and grandpaw. Upon seeing the house, Kathleen and Tom began negotiations to buy it, eventually closing a deal giving them possession on August 1st, when their thirty day notice was up.

Throughout the remaining days of July, Gene passed the time playing ball, delivering his paper-route, going to as many Cub games as he could, and devising ways of encountering the soon to be left behind Valerie. A week before they were to move, Gene worked his route for the last time, telling some of his customers of five years that he would be moving away and that he would miss them. They had given him many memories that he would always keep with him, especially the lovely young woman living on Fletcher Street who used to roll newspapers with him on Sunday mornings. It felt so strange for him to be turning his route over to the circulation office in order that it could be assigned to someone else.

A few days before their family was to move, Gene and Dave were "invited" by Bob to drive over with him and see the new house. Since they were told to wear old clothes, it sounded like this was going to be more of a command performance. Seems they were needed to do some quick and dirty work over at their "new" house before moving in. On their way over, Gene gave himself a mental pep talk about not forming negative impressions from a first glance. He needn't have bothered. As they approached the address, his entire positive mental attitude collapsed into a slag-heap of disappointment when he saw the house.

His first thought was to ask Bob, "You sure we've got the right address?"

"Yep, this is it!"

In a sorry state of disrepair, the house on Montana Street, east of Western Avenue was easily the shabbiest-looking building on the block. An eyesore of a wooden porch was its most prominent feature with enough of its canopy remaining, to pose a hazard to the life and limb of anyone who ventured under it. Its common brick facade had been made ugly by uncounted changes of seasons and weather. An old wire fence, serving no useful purpose, meandered haphazardly along the sidewalk. A sad-looking hulk of a structure, the house seemed even uglier when compared to its well maintained twin, a few doors east. What the boys had seen so far were the house's good points.

As the three brothers ventured into the house through the side door, Gene hesitatingly entered last and felt justified in doing so when Dave, going in ahead of him, started up the stairway in the darkened hallway. Dave's foot thrust through the opening where a step should have been and he stopped just short of the floor when his amazing body control enabled him to break his fall with his chin. Cursing, he extricated his leg, struggled to his feet, and shoved the door open wide to get some outside light on the subject. Then they saw that there was no stair tread to cover the offending riser.

Coming back to see what happened, Bob said, "Oh yeh, I forgot to tell you that Mom mentioned there were some bad stairs. Watch your head Gene!"

His warning to Gene was just in time as his youngest brother nearly skulled himself on an old two-by-four jutting out from the stairway ceiling.

"Darn," muttered Gene, to no one in particular, "two of us have nearly fallen through the stairs and been decapitated and we're not even out of the hallway!"

"Stop belly-aching," came Bob's response.

Poking through the house like spelunkers exploring a cave, they first entered a tiny, yet very grimy kitchen, just big enough to cook in, then around a discarded cabinet blocking the doorway to a small dining-room that looked too small for their dining room table. Like a small octopus, wires protruded from an opening in the ceiling where a long-removed light fixture used to be. Passing through the average-sized living-room, which screamed its need for redecorating, then up another stairway having a broken tread, they arrived at the second floor.

There they found two small bedrooms and one of medium size. In nearly every room they found holes in the plaster walls, electric wires hanging out, sagging, water-damaged ceilings, broken window cranks, and in all cases, a crying need for wallpaper replacement or painting. It was approaching darkness and they tried the lights, some of which didn't work at all.

It was fortunate for Kathleen that Bob was in charge of this detail, otherwise the two younger brothers would have surely bolted and left the building as it was, just like its previous owner. He had allowed a building to deteriorate so badly that Bob thought the old coot should have been charged with a felony. Small wonder that when moving day rolled around, neighbors from all over the block would stop to say hello to the new owners. It was a cinch that they believed the new owners couldn't do any more damage to the place; it had to get better if new people moved in!

Taking charge of things as he always had, Bob said, "I'll go and get a 2 x 10 and replace the missing stair treads. Dave, find a hammer or crowbar and rip down that rickety, wooden porch!"

"That's right up my alley!"

"Gene, you grab a broom and dustpan and start sweeping up this trash lying everywhere!"

"Okay."

Dave who had a knack for wrecking things, attacked his job with relish, climbing up on the porch hangers and demolishing the decrepit, rotten boards until all that was left was a pile of wooden rubble littering the concrete base. He then shoved all of it off into a garbage can and rolled the can out to the back alley for pickup. Bob got back and began replacing the missing stair treads while Gene gave him a hand.

Finished for the evening, they piled back into the Ford and drove off down the darkened street. As he stared back at their "new" home, Gene anticipated with dread, moving into this "Ramshackle Inn" in a few more days.

Bob had put the top down and turned the radio up. As they drove along, Gene, in the back seat thought what a nice night it was to be riding in a convertible. As the Ford rolled North along Damen Avenue, then up along the railyard overpass, Bob and Dave talked in the front seats. A movie theme-song came over the radio that for some strange reason was currently topping the Hit Parade. "The Third Man Theme," a smash hit all over the country with its unusual sound of a zither as lead instrument, was airing. Gene was amazed that a song that couldn't be sung or danced to was becoming a million seller.

A few days later, just about two years since they had moved the last time, Moving Day arrived again, as did several aunts and uncles to help out. The house on Montana had been emptied out and cleaned up as well as possible and at least there was room in which to put everything. In making the move, Bob would be giving up a room of his own since the three brothers were to share the back bedroom, the biggest bedroom, where two bunk beds and a single bed would fit well enough. Making the move with them was good old Mae, who was given one of the two front bedrooms.

Closet space was limited to a very small closet in each bedroom plus the hall closet near the front door, downstairs. No problem. This family had moved so often that they were accustomed to traveling light. Several of the windows wouldn't open and those that did had no screens. Many a bee or wasp met eternity in the form of a rolled-up newspaper during this summer of transition. There were some pluses to be considered, however. One was that they had their own fenced-in yard in which to let their dog, Teddy, run free any time he wanted to. The second plus was the garage which Bob would take advantage of by getting his convertible off the street where it would have been susceptible to knife slashes.

A new residence required a lot of work and that August was filled with a multitude of tasks: tuckpointing of the brickwork by any and all hands, painting of the bedrooms done by Kathleen and a conscripted "volunteer," Gene, who disdained the smell of paint thinner, yet it would be some time before the production of latex-based paints. After tuck-pointing, the brickwork was given two coats of brick-red paint with white windows and trim, to transform the old ruin into a house that looked lived-in! A new aluminum awning in matching colors was installed and now the old house once again looked like one of the grand dames of the block.

The painting job seemed more like a party when their aunt Maybelle, uncle Lew, and cousin Roy showed up, bringing their own ladder. Everyone took a different area to paint. Maybelle, Lew, and Roy took the side of the house, Kathleen and Tom kept to the ground level of the front, while Dave and Gene went up the high ladder to the roof where they painted the inside and outside of the gutters with thin aluminum paint.

Taking away their ladder, Bob chose to paint the high facade below the area where his siblings were working. Crossing the house going left as he worked, he passed right under his brothers who had started by going right as they worked. Needless to say, Bob received a few splatters of aluminum paint in passing. Splatters begat sputters and threats which scared no one, although fear would rear its ugly head a short time later.

After they finished painting the gutters, Dave and Gene wandered around the roof, seeing the neighborhood from thirty feet up. Gene was particularly interested in looking over toward the back of the house on the next block where Eileen von Held, his pretty friend from two years before, lived. Finally, having seen enough and needed for other tasks, they decided to come down from the roof.

Seeing no ladder below helped to set Gene's nerves on edge but even after Bob moved the ladder back to the roof's downslope where they had ascended the roof, fifteen-year-old Gene froze in fear when he approached the edge of the roof. In climbing up on the roof, Gene had no trouble leaving the ladder but the thought of reaching out into space for the ladder froze him with fear when he approached the roof's edge to get down to the ladder. Very quiet now, he didn't budge.

Dave asked him, "What's wrong?"

"Nothing."

Dave tried again, "Are you scared?"

Gene assented by nodding his head but clung to the roof's

edge. Dave felt that if he didn't get Gene off the roof soon, he might never get him down.

Calming his kid brother, Dave told him, "Move back from the edge of the roof and let me go first. Then I'll help you get down." Allowing Dave to descend the ladder, Gene felt a sense of relief when his fearless brother's helping hand reached up above the roof's edge.

He then heard Dave's reassuring voice say, "Okay, put your foot over. I've got a good grip and I'll hold onto you. You won't fall."

As in earlier times, Gene still trusted in his brother and his fear began to subside. Once again, Dave had been there and he was going to be okay.

Later in life Gene would, with experience, learn to stifle the numbing sense of fear before it took hold of him, sometimes just by talking to himself. He had to work very hard at learning to control his fears. Unlike Gene, his brother, Dave, had never known what fear was.

During that Summer with all the countless repairs to be done, welcome help arrived quite often in the form of their aunt Maybelle and uncle Lew, whose presence and helping hands always made work more pleasant. One job that former Navy seaman, Lew took upon himself was that of chief electrician. A house painter by trade, Lew had little experience with electricity, although it was more than anyone else had, so the job was his by default!

It was during one early evening, a sultry one in late August, when Lew tackled the rewiring of the dining room light that didn't light. Lack of self-confidence had never been one of this ex-boxer's problems and after unscrewing the fuse downstairs, he came back up and went about the task of sorting out the can of wire worms he was opening in the ceiling. After nearly an hour of alternately scratching his head and scratching his butt, good old Lew had completed the rewiring. Sending someone down to screw the fuse back in, a grinning uncle leaned back a bit on the ladder, proudly reviewing his work and waiting for the fuse to allow electric to flow properly through the wires, into the bulbs, illuminating the room.

274

Bzzzt! Sfzzzt! Sfzzzt! Those are the closest descriptions one could accord the sounds which emanated from the ceiling box, but visually, the sparks, flames, and smoke were beautiful; somewhat reminiscent of July 4th's fireworks. "Shut it off! Shut it off!" shouted a startled Lew, but it wasn't necessary to unscrew the fuse since it had blown shortly after the smoke and fire began.

Gene thought that if he had known it was going to be this exciting, he would've asked a few of his friends to come over. As the smoke cleared, Gene thought better of asking his uncle what he was going to do for an encore. It followed, that a short time later, in early September, a licensed electrician was contracted by Kathleen and Tom to rewire the entire house. It seemed like an idea whose time had come!

Even though they had already moved in, the basement had been unusable due to the piles of debris and cinders which had simply been dumped on the floor over a period of years by the previous owner. Bob and Gene attended to this together when the two of them worked all day hauling out the heavier items.

As they each carried one end of a heavy cast-iron stove, taking it out, Gene spotted a black spider huge enough to swallow Rhode Island, slowly crawling along the side of the stove toward his hand. Dropping his end of the stove, Gene stabbed at the spider with his shoe, snuffing the huge arachnid with a crunch.

Bob, having the entire weight of the stove suddenly fall into his hands, thought that his kid brother picked a lousy time to screw around and yelled, "Why the hell did you drop it?"

"I saw a spider!"

"Are you afraid of a little spider?"

"You call a tarantula a little spider?"

"We don't have tarantulas around here!"

"Not anymore!" said Gene, ending their dialog by picking up his end of the stove once more.

After filling four garbage cans with cinders and dumping a truckload of old paper and junk at the alley, the basement was swept out, hosed down and made ready for storage of their stuff. Later that week, as Gene dumped other trash in the garbage cans, he looked at the pile of old newspapers and started reading some of them.

One bunch of papers had been published during the late thirties and chronicled the events of Pope Pius XII's election to the papacy by the Vatican's College of Cardinals. It proved to be interesting reading since it was a day by day report of a historic event which he had been too young to remember. In so doing he learned of the Vatican tradition of white smoke and black smoke, signifying whether or not a new pontiff had been selected. Accounts of prewar events continued to be read each day as long as the garbage hadn't been picked up. It was ironic that papers which should have been discarded long ago were still conveying information, imparting to Gene more knowledge about the history of the world in which he lived.

It was stinking hot that afternoon when while putting out a can of debris, Gene listened intently, for he heard a soft cry upon the thick afternoon air. A kitten, it sounded like a kitten, and the mewing emanated from under the debris in the concrete garbage bin. As he removed the trash from the bin, the mewing became louder, until finally, he was right on top of the helpless creature. An old bucket containing a residue of roofing tar lay right above the point from which the mewing came.

Removing the bucket, Gene saw not one kitten but three, covered with the melted tar. Running into the house, he told his mother what he had found and she hurried back to the alley with him. Slowly extricating the hapless, abandoned kittens from their tar-covered den, they took care that no hardened tar would pull out fur or flesh. Bringing them into the house, Mae offered that it would be better for the kittens if they were drowned but the Ryans would never do anything like that. On the contrary, they would try to do everything in their power to keep the kittens alive.

Within minutes, Grandmaw Kelly, the lover of warm, furry creatures who seemed to be able to talk to animals, arrived and lent a hand in attempting to slowly remove the hardened tar from around the eyes and ears of the kittens whose eyes fortunately hadn't opened yet. Painstaking hours were spent over the next few days, carefully removing the tar with diluted turpentine and soap and water from the three kittens. Maybelle had heard what happened and took the female, the weakest of the kittens, home to attend it. The nursing kittens were fed milk with eyedroppers, in an effort to sustain them until they could get healthy.

During the next few weeks, the weaker kitten died but the two surviving kittens could be heard mewing in their towel-lined cardboard box where they were kept as they got fatter and healthier. Their mewing bothered Mae, who had rarely complained before, saying that while they were cute, she wished that their constant mewing would stop. One day, when Gene came home for lunch, the overwhelming quiet made him wonder why the kittens weren't mewing. He looked in on them, in their box and thought it strange that they weren't on top of the towels as always, seeing that they were under the cover of the towels. As Gene lifted the towels, the teenager saw that the two remaining, cuddly kittens were lying still, in death. He saw them and began to cry. He cried for all of their suffering, then their getting better, only to smother in their towels.

Then Gene realized, that during the many days in their box, the kittens had never crawled under the towels which he had found snugly over them and against them. From that moment on, he suspected that Mae had come downstairs and smothered them while no one else was home. He despised the thought that anyone could do so and would become distant from her and remained so for the next two years that she resided with them.

It would be fall before Gene got over the kittens' deaths but the hard work of cleaning and fixing up the house helped take his mind off the tragedy. Even his grandpaw got into the family project of renovating the old house. In his extreme negligence of the house, the former owner had removed the basement entry door at one time and possibly thinking it wasn't necessary, had failed to put it back. The door was nowhere to be found and that's why Grandpaw Kelly had showed up bright and early, to give his grandson a carpentry lesson, first sending Gene back over to his grandpaw's house to bring over a door that he had set out in the yard. Soon the teenager returned with the door.

While small, the door didn't fit the opening very well. In the course of the next few hours Gene saw his grandpaw get vexed, almost enough to swear, but still he didn't. There was a man with will power! After sending Gene on several trips back over to ask Grandmaw Kelly for various tools and lots of reworking, Grandpaw Kelly had gotten the door to fit, even though the door was no longer square. Who cared? At least it fit into the jamb, saving the cost of a custom new door.

As the summer of 1950 passed, the local hardware store owner grew richer with each trip made by members of Gene's family, each becoming known by their first name to the proprietor. It seemed every day required another trip for lumber, plaster board, trim, tools, tile, paint, paint thinner, tile cement, and more paint thinner.

Early October greeted the new homeowners with brisk, fall temperatures that coerced their aged, tired, coal-burning furnace into giving up its ghost. A call to the nearest heating contractor resulted in quick response and an even quicker estimate of how much better a new furnace and all-new ductwork would function and just how costly it would be.

"Lucky for you folks it happened during October and not in January!" said the contractor, attempting to salve their financial pain as Kathleen and Tom reviewed the heating contract.

Indoor temperatures had fallen while the furnace was down, and Bob out of consideration for his kid brother asked if he was getting chilled. Remembering that as a kid Gene had been susceptible to colds, Bob was making sure that his younger brother stayed healthy, suggesting to him that he put on a sweater. Although Bob was just being the big brother, his kid brother was glad for his concern.

The new furnace would percolate perfectly in the icy winter months that were to come. There were many reasons why it would have to. The old, drafty, ill-fitting windows of the house allowed heat to escape nearly as fast as it was generated by the new oil-fired unit. Expedience dictated that openings around the window frames be stuffed with whatever scrap cloth was available. The old front door with a large glass pane had fit so badly in its jamb that it was soon sealed-up with a layer of plastic to keep out the drafts. This resulted in the phenomenon of the door's plastic envelope inflating and deflating as if breathing when the winter winds blew; an eerie sight and sound to catch the attention of an unsuspecting visitor. There wasn't much fear of carbon monoxide fumes, however, since fresh air and ventilation were never in short supply in this house.

Setbacks such as these were taken in stride since this family had always been at the mercy of landlords and now, for the first time in their city-dwelling lives they were the owners of the house. They were the landlords for a change!

Becoming first-time homeowners had been a very expensive initiation for Gene's folks, who between August, 1950, when they moved in, and the roofing job done in May, 1951, would incur the expenses of: completely rewiring the house, a new heating system and ductwork, a new water heater, new wooden windows for the entire house, and a new roof. This little fixer-upper would be a once in a lifetime experience for them, fortunately.

Chapter 23

An Upperclassman

Gene had been so busy working on their home during the late Summer and early Fall, that he barely had time to follow the pennant races. The Philadelphia Phillies, began their run for the National League flag early in the season and had been dubbed, "The Whiz Kids" by hyperbole-infected sportswriters. Faltering in September, they still won the pennant on the reliable arms of two great, young, starting pitchers. They were a right-hander named Robin Roberts, who had trouble winning number 20 and a southpaw named Curt Simmons who commuted back and forth from his activated National Guard outfit, one of many units that had been activated since the United States sent troops into Korea back on July 1st.

School was once more in session, calling Gene back for his Junior year, which would prove to be one of his two best high school years. Now he would be riding his bike up Western Avenue to Lane Tech, still only a mile and a half away. Having quit his paper route, he was between engagements jobwise, and once again, had to depend on his folks for an allowance. It helped that he could travel to school on his bike, saving the carfare.

While riding his bike home one golden, September afternoon, he rode through the alley east of Western Avenue, crossing Altgeld, when he heard a soft feminine voice call his name. Hitting his brakes hard, he spun the bike around in the gravel, ending up face to face with Eileen von Held. She was the lovely girl who lived a few doors away from his grandmaw, whom he had formed a friendship with just two years before. "Gosh, she's a lovely girl!" he thought, as they talked about some of the things that happened since he left the neighborhood. He once again got that feeling that he experienced while dancing with Joy Regan at their graduation party; the feeling that he was still a kid while Eileen had become a sophisticated young lady.

In mid-September, Gene was troubled by the news that the U. N. forces in Korea had been nearly pushed back to the beaches at Pusan and it appeared that they were going to be pushed into the sea. Then on September 15th came the news that General MacArthur, in a masterful stroke of military genius, had ordered his forces to launch an invasion at Inchon Harbor above the North Korean main forces. The invasion allowed U. N. forces to slash North Korean supply lines and cut the enemy off from their main force. Eventually the U. N. forces drove the North Koreans northward above the 38th parallel. It was wonderful news for all Americans and especially for the families of American soldiers and marines who had faced annihilation at Pusan.

Adding to Gene's consternation was his brother Dave's registration for the draft on his eighteenth birthday. Now Dave was eligible for the draft and a shooting war was on. Having anticipated, even looked forward to military service since he was a young boy, Dave didn't seem worried. Again his kid brother did enough worrying for both of them.

As days passed in his old neighborhood now being revisited, Gene slowly renewed old friendships with boys and girls he had known before. The girls all seemed to be very nice, lovely, young ladies, who two years before, had been skinny adolescents; most of whom had not been remotely interested in the opposite sex. Being new to a neighborhood where most of the kids were of Polish descent, Gene had difficulty learning the last names of his neighborhood friends, finding their spelling and pronunciation to be difficult for him.

The number one interest in Gene's young life at this time was touch-football. Every day after school, except Fridays, the neighborhood boys would gather on Oakley between Montana and Altgeld for touch-football games in the street that continued until enough of them had been called home for dinner that play would cease. By now, equally proficient at throwing a spiral pass or catching a long one, Gene enjoyed both. Defending against passes on defense inspired him, in that one was expected to outthink the receiver who knew where the ball was going and needed to shake the defender. His hard work in exercising and running for the previous two years now paid him dividends. He had gotten faster, could run sprints all day, and for a slender kid, could throw a football fifty yards.

When going out for passes, he had practiced concentrating on the ball in flight, rarely failing to catch any pass that touched his hands. This high degree of concentration was detrimental to his health one cool afternoon, as he raced out for a long one. Running full speed between the curb and the center of the street, he had the ball in sight, and was reaching up to haul it in. BAM!!! The crashing noise was accompanied by a searing flash of pain in his upper left leg. When he could see past the pain, he saw that he had been taken out of the play by a heavy old Buick parked at the curb. He had blocked the parked car out of his mind.

The impact had bruised his left thigh severely and left him limping for days while it only put a small dent in the base of the Buick's fender. Gene realized that he could have easily broken his leg but someone up there must have been watching over him. While it only took two weeks to get over the physical impact, the mental impact would cause the rest of the season to pass before Gene could forget about parked vehicles and get his concentration back.

Having developed his skills, he yearned to play for his school, but beginning his Junior year now, it was much too late for Gene to tryout for his high school team. Destined not to hear the cheers of spectators nor the roar of the crowd when a touchdown was scored, the busy side streets and Logan Boulevard's parkways in their Logan Square neighborhood were where Gene and his fellow touch-football players from his neighborhood would play out their high school football careers.

Except on those fabulous Friday afternoons! Lane Tech's football team played its games on Fridays and the 1950 season was shaping up to be a championship season for the Myrtle and Gold. Gene's adrenaline began pumping after lunch on Fridays and increased as the dismissal bell rang and a majority of its student body of nearly 5,000 students began their charge toward the stadium from all exits of the school. Maximum adrenaline rush was felt as the crowd of Laneites jamming the stands on the east side of the stadium stood to sing the rousing "Go Lane, Go!" Accompanied by Lane's ROTC military band, the Laneites sang their fight song with pride and zeal, then remained standing for the kickoff.

It was a kick to watch an outstanding defensive halfback like Dean Jyckowski, who played single safety as if he invented the position. It was through watching Jyckowski break up or intercept opponents' passes, or never missing a tackle but always nailing the ball-carrier solidly, that Gene Ryan could vicariously enjoy pass defense in high school football. When former gym classmate Wally Herzog ran a pass pattern downfield, then turned to look over his shoulder and haul in a long pass for big yardage, Gene, in his heart had caught the ball with him, and stride for stride was running with him. When a tough, single yard was needed for a first down, and team captain Mack Sonder led his offensive line's charge, Gene, in his mind, was down in the trenches with them, while cheering them on. This was to be an outstanding season for one student spectator, who had been too scrawny as a freshman, to try out for Frosh-Soph football.

The baseball season was not yet over and October's Fall classic offered baseball fans a World Series that was a battle between pin-striped uniforms, Yankee blue and Phillie red. The Phillies had snatched the pennant from the outstretched, grasping hands of the Dodgers in the 10th inning of the last game of the season on a home run by their resident slugger, Del Ennis. A short series, it was far from sweet for Eddie Sawyer's "Whiz Kids" who were swept clean in four games, ground-up by Casey Stengel's juggernaut, two-platoon, New York Yankees. The hapless Phillies were in good company however, since they were victim number two in the Yankees' string of five straight World Championships.

While Gene's fall afternoons were usually filled with the youthful excitement of some form of football, the more mundane activities of homework assignments demanded Gene's time during the evenings. Classes became more interesting each day, due to more interesting teachers and the development of friendships with his classmates. No longer were his Commercial Art contemporaries split into separate art classes and division rooms. Spending four periods or half the day, in Mr. Andrew Potts' very educational art class and division room with the same group of guys, allowed Gene to become part of a close-knit group. He was forging new friendships with the lucky guys who had spent the first two years in other art classes. He could also expand his friendships with Joe Garth, Pat Decker, and John Chavez, the classmates and friends who had shared his first two years of art classes.

A new friendship developed between Gene and Robert Gagnon, a good-looking, tall, dark-haired kid of French-Canadian descent, who as Gene was to learn, was very bright. In previous times they hadn't really hit it off but being assigned to the same lab bench in Physics enabled them to learn that they both were bright, had a mutual liking for Science, and an aptitude for Physics experiments. These qualities, coupled with the blessing that they were lucky enough that one of them could always come up with the right answer pushed them to the top of their Physics class. In knowing this subject so well, they had opened themselves up to repeated requests for help and tutoring from their fellow art classmates.

A gifted, albeit temperamental art instructor, Mr. Potts probably enjoyed many more years here on earth than he might have, had he been aware of some of the surreptitious shenanigans that went on in his class. He never knew how many art class hours had been used by Stan Janowicz, John Solice, and several others during the semester, to write up their Physics experiments. An attack of apoplexy might have accompanied such knowledge.

After learning from Gene and Robert, just where they went wrong in their previous day's experiments, these guys used part of each morning to redo their Physics homework, since it was due at the start of Physics class right after lunch. On countless mornings, neither Gene or Robert picked up a paint brush until after nine o'clock and they agreed that they had probably carried several of their friends through the rigors of elementary Physics. Fortunately for Gene and Robert, their classmates had few problems with English or U. S. History, else the additional tutoring time might have impacted Gene's and Robert's Commercial Art grades.

As a Junior, Gene found that his Gym class took on greater significance, since upperclass gym classes were held in Gym #1, the main gym, where Juniors and Seniors competed against each other. Here gym teams were organized along division room lines only, increasing intra-team camaraderie while promoting inter-team competition. What it meant to some of the Junior teams was that their heads could sometimes be handed to them by some of the Senior teams. This competition perhaps caused the "our team against all others" mentality among his team members that may have allowed Gene to really get to know his division room friends who opened up to him, taking him into their inner circle.

Gym #1 was also where Lane Tech upper-class students were introduced to two marvelous, loosely-organized, character-building activities known as, "Pushball" and Mass Basketball," two games having three basic rules each.

Pushball's equipment consisted of only a large, inflated, canvas ball, approximately four feet in diameter. Any number of foolhardy individuals could play but Rule #1 stipulated that half of the combatants, er, participants, should be on each side of the center line of the main basketball court. Rule #2 stated that a point was to be scored by the group on side A when the ball hit the floor on side B and vice-versa. Rule #3 stated that the group with the most points at the end of the game wins. End of rules.

While one cannot clearly recall in detail, the variety of physical fouls that those young men inflicted on each other along the line of contact between the two surging forces, these are recalled: pushing, elbowing, holding, and tripping. Amid frantic shouts like, "Keep the ball in the air!" body-blocks and stiff-arming were also employed by young men caught up in the heat of battle. As stated in Rule #2, a point was scored when the ball hit the floor. Zero points were awarded for bodies hitting the floor. It was a thoroughly enjoyable exercise and often the final whistle signaling the game's end was met with a volley of boos from the melee of disappointed, bloodthirsty, young savages.

Mass basketball, though short on rules, also seemed to be

short on equipment. There were eight to ten teams in the class, each assigned a backboard and hoop. It worked out so that each team had their own basket to shoot basketballs into and score points in the process. Alas, they were never given enough basketballs, usually two less than the number of teams. Rule #1 stated that a team could only score points in its own assigned basket. Rule #2 stated that the team with the most points at the end, wins. Rule #3 stated that if a team doesn't have a basketball, then that team must acquire one from a team that has one. End of rules. A mayhem-inducing activity, the game incorporated elements of track, wrestling, rugby, football, and of course, basketball, in a team's efforts to secure a basketball and keep it. A game of intense enthusiasm, it was exhilarating, even long after the whistle had blown to mercifully end the conflict, and the participants were down in the locker rooms, changing into street clothes.

Periodic track meets were held during gym classes, pitting team against team. The incessant running that Gene had forced himself to do for over a year, had conditioned his legs and lungs for endurance over the longer dashes. During one meet in late October, Gene finished second to Stan Janowicz against six other runners in a 100 yard dash and fourth of twenty runners in a 220 yard dash. Gene had loved running all out in the 100! He also liked to run with controlled effort during the longer races, running at various percentages of effort at different points of the race.

Heats of the 880 yard dash began and Gene and Pat Decker found that they had chosen the same 880 heat.

"What are we doing, running a half-mile dash? We never ran a dash that long. We must be nuts!" said Gene.

"There are eighteen other guys in this race! I just hope I can place in this thing!" responded Pat.

Lining up for the start, they wished each other luck, and the starting whistle blew. Once around the quarter-mile track, Gene was okay. At the 660 yard mark he was holding seventh place but fifth place was the last one that meant points to his team. Looking around for Pat, Gene saw his friend sixty yards ahead of him, leading the pack. Spurred on by that vision Gene made his move, summoning all of his remaining energy, and ten yards from the finish line, passed two guys dueling for fifth place! Pat, Gene, and a few others then collapsed to the ground in order to catch their breath but otherwise, they felt great, they had placed!

While Gene had grown and become proficient at sports, it was too late in his academic career to go out for any school team. His fate had been that in addition to starting high school a year younger than his peers, physically, he had also been a late-bloomer. Gene soon found that intramural sports offered a temporary way of playing on school teams.

Competing for Mr. Potts' division, Gene, Pat Decker, Robert Gagnon, and a few other friends who worked after school formed up a team and competed in the single elimination tournaments during the basketball and softball seasons. Although they didn't last long enough to win any trophies, his fellow team members enjoyed playing immensely, usually remaining in the tournament for three or four games until eliminated. These events brought the teammates closer together as friends, for they learned they could depend on each other while working as a team.

As the football season that began in September progressed, Lane continued to win all of its games, many by lop-sided scores, and the sports columns were giving space to the discussion of Lane's chances for the Public League championship.

Gene's brother, Bob, a Lake View grad, tried to pour cold water on Gene's enthusiasm by saying, "Lane has 5,000 male students, they should have the best teams in everything."

A tough argument for Gene who could only say, "Yeh, but only eleven players can be on the field at one time!"

Bob may have been resentful since he had attended Lane for his first semester of high school but then transferred to Lake View. Gene never learned the full story behind his brother's brief matriculation at Lane but he wasn't going to pry into his reasons. Bob was ready to put money on the outcome of the game being in Lake View's favor but Gene didn't want to jinx his team.

Came Friday afternoon and the game began with Lane kicking off to Lake View. The red-and-white-clad team's star halfback took the kickoff and ran it back for a touchdown, setting off an explosion of cheers from the stands on the west side of the field, that caused a feeling of dread in the pit of Gene's stomach. Those guys in red and white were serious about this game, thought Gene, who hoped he wouldn't have to go home and tell Bob that Lane had lost to this team. Although Lake View kept it close, Lane won by one slender touchdown. Hearing Gene's postgame report, Bob relished the news that his old school had scored on the opening kickoff, throwing a scare into his kid brother.

Sweeping their regular schedule, Lane was scheduled to play Chicago Vocational School in their quarter-final game at Lane on what turned out to be a rainy, dreary, fall afternoon; football weather. At the half, Lane was down by a touchdown after what seemed like a lethargic first half without any offense. Shortly after the third quarter began, two players got up from the bench and threw off their warm-up coats. Seeing their uniform numbers, Gene instantly realized why Lane was behind: Lane's starting halfbacks had been kept on the bench throughout the entire first half. With its first-string halfbacks ripping off yardage through and around the opponents line, Lane strongly controlled the field in the second half, and the final result was Lane 20, CVS 7.

The Lane gridders then encountered a formidable, semifinal opponent in Fenger High School's football team when they met at Soldier Field along Chicago's beautiful lake shore. Sunny skies augmented the cool, crisp air of a fall afternoon on that October Saturday when at the half, Lane was down, 12 to 6, despite playing their first string. Spectators wearing green and gold felt very uneasy as they stood for the second-half kickoff.

A few minutes later, when Lane's gridders seemed to have lost their spark, a cheer began. It began at one end zone, spurred by the common helplessness felt by 5,000 Lane students who couldn't be down on the field to help their team. It spread along the rows until all 5,000 were standing as one, shouting, "GO!" "GO!" "GO!" "GO!" "GO!" From early in the third quarter, the one-word cheer persisted throughout the entire second half until the final gun. Lane had won, 19 to 12.

Later on, Gene learned from Wally Herzog that the Lane players had heard their unyielding fans.

Wally admitted, "We players were flat until we heard that

steady, ongoing cheer and I felt chills down my spine. We were all inspired, not only by volume of the cheering but because it didn't stop. It just didn't stop!" Continuing, he said that, "We felt beaten until the cheering began and then we decided if the fans weren't quitting, then we better not either! We just dug in that much harder." Then Wally added, "We played that game but you guys in the stands won it for us!"

Aside from football games, there wasn't much other excitement in Gene's life. Always having to ask his mom for money to go to the show or buy anything put a crimp in his outside activities. He didn't want another paper route, which perturbed Kathleen at first but she came to understand that he felt he was getting too old for a paper route although there weren't many other jobs open to fifteen-year-olds.

Having free time on his hands after school, he occasionally walked the half-mile over to his aunt Maybelle and uncle Lew's place to see what his cousin Roy was up to. They'd spend a couple of hours playing in the vacant lot behind the outdoor billboard along Armitage near Oakley. Roy had the cutest little Beagle-mix dog that he had chosen to name "Rex," when more correctly she should have been named "Regina." Though he enjoyed his cousin's company, the games that they played were more suited to Roy's age, and he was nearly four years younger while Gene's interests ran to sports and games more suited to teenagers.

On one of his visits to Roy's, Lew came home while he was there and asked Gene, "Would you like to make some money on a painting job with me?"

Gene answered with an emphatic "Yes!"

"Okay," said Lew, "but be sure to bring a change of clothes so you won't have to wear your soiled clothes home."

"Paint job? Why do you need extra clothes for a paint job?" asked Lew's inquisitive nephew.

"You'll see when we get there!" replied his uncle.

The kid never saw the painting portion of the job. The job was to paint a 20 by 15 storeroom at a North Side seminary. Wooden chairs, tables, and all sorts of other furnishing castoffs had been relegated to this piled-high purgatory for furniture. Removing the clutter wasn't the problem as much as it was to clean up the surfaces. Dust that seemed to be a half-inch thick, covered every inch of wall and timber surface and needed to be removed before the room could be painted. Clouds of black, sooty dust which had lain there for years rose up to engulf them the moment they began cleaning the dust off timbers and moldings. In those days, protective masks weren't in vogue and a lot of coughing ensued. After about seven hours of removing the furniture and dust, the two sooty-faced workers left and drove back to Lew's where Gene was told by his aunt and uncle to shower and change because they didn't want him going home to Kathleen looking like he just came out of a coal-mine. He walked home realizing that he had just endured another of those character-building experiences: the dirtiest job he had ever undertaken in his young life.

Sometimes, early on Saturday evenings, after clearing it with Kathleen who would then make him two lunches, one for him and one for his grandpaw, Gene would walk five blocks down to the paperstand at Damen and Fullerton where Grandpaw Kelly worked. Staying with his forebear, Gene would run the papers to the people in cars pulling up at the curb to buy the Sunday paper until around midnight.

Grandpaw told him that he was a big help to him because early Saturday evening was the time when the Sunday paper news sections had to be "stuffed" with the advertising, feature, and magazine sections. Arriving early Saturday evening, Gene would spot the stacks of Sunday papers with the big "NORTHWEST" banner on each bundle, from half a block away, knowing that his evening was going to be busy.

Although he wouldn't think of taking any money from Grandpaw Kelly, he still felt that in some small way, he was earning his keep at home by helping out his mother's father. By midnight sales usually had fallen off and his grandpaw began closing the stand. Yawning and sleepy-eyed, Gene was more than ready to walk the half-mile home alongside his grandpaw who, with his artificial leg, always walked at a slower pace. In making conversation, Gene often told his grandpaw, "Hey Grandpaw, when I learn to drive and get a car, we'll ride home instead of walking!" Sometimes the old man's response was a weary, "I'd sure appreciate a ride home 'bout this time of night." Other times he might come back with a snappy, "Unless I lose my mind, I ain't so sure that I'm gonna let myself get into any rattle-trap with you, youngster!"

Strange as it may seem, in those days an old crippled man and a young teenaged boy were able to walk along Fullerton Avenue west of Damen at nearly one o'clock on a warm night and not feel that they were in any danger. Even lonely, dark streets seemed to be safer then, while courtesy was expected and shown to each other by neighbors in their neighborhood streets.

All too soon, those pleasant, warm, early fall evenings evolved into cool October nights. New fall television programs were in full swing the night of October 20, 1950, when a news bulletin announced the death of Al Jolson. The subject of two movies about his life and a man who had been an entertainer for fifty years had passed away in San Francisco. In his career Jolson had stopped the show many times, and in death he stopped the show once more when his passing caused the Broadway theatres to pause and dim their lights in his memory. Outside, in Times Square where 42nd Street and Broadway meet, traffic had come to a standstill out of respect for "Jolie."

Television and homework filled Gene's weekday evenings to the point of near-boredom and if it weren't for Lane's football games, the late fall weekends would have offered little to look forward to. Days became weeks and before Gene knew it, November had come and an icy wraith of wind whistled through the barren trees while snow often blanketed the ground.

On a frigid Saturday, with temperatures registering ten above zero, Lane Tech met Kelly in the Public League football championship final at Soldier Field. The lake front stadium, normally an enormous concrete box now felt like a concrete deep-freeze and Gene, loyally attending the game with Pat Decker, felt that his feet had become two blocks of ice.

At the end of the first-half, Pat threw in the towel, saying, "I quit! I'm going home and watch it on television. I gotta leave while I can still walk!" Then his friend asked, "Haven't you had enough, Ryan?"

Shivering and probably half-loony from the cold, Gene deferred, "No, I'm going to stay a little longer."

That was his second mistake. His first mistake had been showing up in the first place! Getting up to walk around for a while helped, and mercifully, the second half got under way soon after Gene returned to his seat. His seat? Due to the severity of the weather, he had his choice of thousands of empty seats! Within minutes he was sorry he hadn't left with Decker, thinking that Pat was probably sitting on a warm bus by then.

Finally, nearly frozen-through, Gene left a few minutes before the final gun, and looking back, saw the final score posted on the scoreboard, Lane 41, Kelly 21, as he slogged toward downtown Chicago where he could catch a warm bus back home.

When he arrived home, his mom asked, "Why did you stay so long in such weather?"

Gene answered, "I had to borrow the money from you for the ticket and I would've felt like I was wasting it, if I didn't stay until the game's end."

"Silly kid!" his mom answered, "You could have gotten frostbite out there. Money isn't that important!"

Amazingly enough, a short time later when Lane played against powerhouse Mount Carmel, the Catholic League champion, in the "Prep Bowl," the weather was entirely different. Inappropriately named, the game should have been called the "Fog Bowl," since a bank of pea-soup fog rolled in off Lake Michigan just to the east, obliterating the field of play. When the stadium's inadequate lights were turned on, the brightness only caused glaring of the lights off the fog and the crowd had to depend on the field announcer in order to know what was happening. Lane's faithful supporters would have rather not known what was transpiring down on that ghostly field of ghastly play.

Lane was rolled over by the Caravan. Downcast but not alone among the Lane Tech followers walking back across the bridge over the IC tracks, Gene contemplated what an inglorious end this fiasco had been, to a glorious 1950 season for Lane Tech.

Chapter 24

Duty Calls

Gene's family couldn't have known then, that the gray, chilly mist that permeated the morning air of Christmas Day, 1950, foreboded dire events yet to come. They only knew that it was Christmas, celebrating it as previous Yule holidays had been, yet unaware that it would be the last Yuletide for a long time, that all members of the family would be home to celebrate. The distant drums of war rumbling in far-off Korea would affect members of Gene's family in the coming year. The war had intensified when Chinese "volunteers" had entered the conflict on the side of North Korea back in late October, turning the tide of battle against the U. N. forces, and a quick end to the war now seemed unlikely. Home for the Christmas holidays was Pat, their aunt Etta's husband, who had been recalled to active duty by the Navy where he had served during World War II.

Shortly after Christmas came the wild celebration of a dawning new year, 1951, followed the next day by most male members of every Midwestern household watching the Rose Bowl game. Victorious again, the Big Nine had been represented by the University of Michigan, who won out over the Pacific Coast Conference school, the University of California, by a score of 14 to 6. Later in October of this year, the Western Conference's familiar nickname, the "Big Nine" would be changed to the "Big Ten" when the Michigan State Spartans would be admitted to conference play.

Deceptive, bright sunshine accompanied temperatures near zero on that frigid Thursday, the 18th of January, when Gene found the warm joy of arriving home lessened by the somber news that his brother Bob would be leaving home that Saturday. Despite having earlier served a two-year hitch in the Navy, Bob's Selective Service classification of 1C still left him draft eligible, and a draft notice seemed imminent. Preferring not to be drafted into the Army, Bob enlisted in the Air Corps earlier in the day and now had two days to clear up his affairs and report.

Saturday dawned gloomy and wet, due to a cold rain which pattered loudly on the porch's aluminum awning as they saw Bob off. He was driven to the induction center on Van Buren Street by Lew. Later, in the afternoon, Bob called to say he was being sent to Chanute Field outside Rantoul, Illinois, 120 miles from home. At least it was good news, he was going to be close to home.

Still, his absence in their home had left another void that couldn't be filled, with his presence missed immediately, by Kathleen, Dave, and Gene. Dave continued working at the downtown paper company office where he and Bob had worked for the past year. Dave was dating a pleasant, blonde, brown-eyed girl named Maryann Mathews, who lived about a mile away. They had met one night at the movie theatre where she worked after school and had been seeing each other exclusively for about six months and it seemed serious. Gene was glad for Dave, because Maryann had exerted a much-needed steadying influence on his heretofore aimless and disorganized brother.

Barely organized himself, Gene soon saw the end of his Junior year's first half, capping off a much-improved semester as February 2nd marked the end of a term of hard work. It had also been a time of gaining great new friends like Ron and Stan, while renewing his old friendship with Bill Milford. His grades had also improved to A's and B's.

Gradually, Gene got accustomed to his older brother's absence, for after all, Dave was still around to talk to, on those rare occasions when he was home. It was especially fun when Dave's live-wire buddy, Jack Gorr, came over to see Dave. Jack had just graduated in midyear from Lane Tech and hadn't a clue as to what he was going to do. To get a job or go to college? College was a viable option for him since he was a bright guy. But to get a job was going to be tough. Employers were leery of hiring young guys who were classified 1A and likely to be drafted soon.

294

Leastwise, Jack would no longer be strolling through the open hall between his Senior art class and Gene's Junior art class, yelling in his booming voice, "Hey, Ryan, go to work!"

One time he disrupted Gene's class as he walked through, shouting, "Hey Ryan, wake up!"

He hadn't seen short Mister Potts behind an easel, whereupon Potts shouted back, "Get outta here, Gorr!"

While it lasted though, it had been kind of nice to have an older friend like Jack nearby, to get straight advice from and kid around with.

In the late afternoon of Saturday, the 10th of February, Gene turned from watching the feathery snow falling past their bedroom window, and asked his brother, "Dave, what are you getting Mom for her birthday?"

Dave hesitated, stood up, pulled a cigarette from the pack on his dresser, flipped the top of his Zippo lighter and lit the end of his cigarette.

Taking a deep drag, he slowly blew the smoke toward the ceiling, then with furrowed brow he turned to his kid brother and said, "I dread Mom's birthday this year, because I'm going to really spoil it the day before, on Valentine's Day."

Accustomed to hearing Dave often speak in obtuse riddles when he wanted to spare someone's feelings, Gene said, "Okay, out with it! Tell me! What's wrong?"

Dave gave his younger brother a stern look, put his arm around his shoulder and replied, "Jack Gorr and me joined the Army today and we gotta report on Valentine's Day."

"Not you too!" Gene exclaimed "Why? Why do you have to go away too?"

His kid brother was near tears as he tried hard not to believe what he had been dreading since he saw that Korean War headline back in June of the year before. Gene thought, "That lousy war! That lousy war! Why did it have to be? Why did any wars have to be?" Gene had never forgotten about Earl, who was cut-down by enemy bullets and died at Salerno beach and now he feared for his own brother Dave.

Then Gene's thoughts turned to their mother and he worried how she would take the news.

"When are you going to tell Mom?" he asked.

"That's the hardest part! I gotta tell her and I don't know how or when."

"Maybe you should tell her now, so she'll be more accustomed to the idea before the 14th."

Dave nodded his head in agreement.

Kathleen took it very hard but even as she cried, she surprisingly admitted, "I have expected it ever since you turned seventeen and when the Korean War broke out I was sure it wouldn't be too long before my fearless second son would want to get into the fight. You've never been afraid of anything. And you always talked of being a Marine since you were a little boy. Why didn't you join the Marines?"

Dave told her, "Me and Jack did try to join the Marines together but Jack, unbelievably, was turned down, so we decided to join the Army instead."

"Well, at least you boys will be together and you'll be back home in fourteen weeks; that's not so awfully long," sighed Kathleen as she hugged Dave, who most resembled her, close to her.

The dreaded time had now come; the time to allow her beloved rowdy boy to spread his wings and fly.

On Valentine's Day, Gene came home from school to find his mother in tears, for his brother Dave had left earlier in the day with Jack. Both of them had been the subjects of several snapshots taken outside in the bright sunlight of a cold February day with Kathleen and Maybelle, who was about five months pregnant at the time with her second child. For a long time those pictures would be held and treasured by Kathleen, who loved all three of her sons but held closest in a loving mother's heart, the one farthest from home.

Not only were his brothers absent from home but so also was the extra money which they had given Kathleen, while living at home. Their money for board had been helpful, since Tom still persisted in stopping off on Friday evenings instead of coming home. Needless to say, a good percentage of his take-home pay was never taken home. Wanting to help out instead of collecting an allowance which his mother could now ill-afford, Gene found

296

out from Jerry Gales, a friend working part-time at the local drugstore that he was quitting school to join the Army.

"I'll recommend you to my boss, if you want the job," said Jerry.

"Sure, I'll give it a try," said Gene.

As soon as the words were out of his mouth fear gripped his throat as he thought of being in the public eye. Talking to strangers? Talking? To strangers? How would he be able to work with the customers who crowded into the well-located, busy drugstore or worse, the younger crowd who inundated the soda fountain during the hours after school and evenings?

Remembering the two-minute presentations that Mr. Neville forced his English class students to give and the advice that Mrs. Spies, his elderly paper-route customer and friend gave him about speaking up, he brightened. Gene thought, "This is it! Are you going to hide away all of your life or are you going to go out there and learn to handle yourself with people?" He decided to give the job a try. Kathleen was heartened to hear that he wanted to apply for the job and gave her permission.

On February 19th, he was employed by Mr. Feinstein, pharmacist and proprietor of the Western Pharmacy, located a block away from home at Western and Fullerton. To learn the ropes, Gene was told to work the first week with a honey blonde named Pam Carlson who was a thorough, helpful teacher, with whom he became friends. Some of the other kids, fellow regulars at the soda fountain, were mildly surprised to see Gene behind the fountain and chided him, saying that he had spent so much time there that he might as well work there and get paid for it.

Not realizing it then, Gene had taken a job that would play a very significant role in his social development as an individual during his sixteenth and seventeenth years. Learning to interact with people from all walks of life, all ages and types of personalities, fathoming the give and take with peers on the other side of the counter, and becoming well-known were all positive influences. So also was having to talk with these same people and express himself to them. Where up until that time he would have been considered an introvert, Gene would become more extroverted over the next year through interaction with the many people he would encounter during his working hours.

The number of friends he had would triple in the next year due to exposure to so many other guys and girls his own age, from farther off in the "Bucktown" area. Although he would gain many new friends he would still long for a "best friend" like Jack Gorr was to Dave. Throughout his young life, the role of best friend had been filled for the most part by his own brother Dave.

Gene's gradual progression toward extroversion often resulted in prolonged conversations with some of the younger customers which sometimes piqued Mr. Feinstein who reasonably and rightfully so, expected an hour's work for an hour's pay. Even if angered however, Mr. Feinstein would humorously point out the error of one's ways and he knew how to hold off on criticism in front of others. While Gene was unaware of it during the early months, Mr. Feinstein would affect his mental and spiritual growth during his year-and-a-half of employment there. In time to come, Gene would join the ranks of many other Feinstein alumni who had gained a friend, confidante and respected advisor for life, in Mr. Feinstein, a prince among men.

Assigned to work three afternoons and two evenings a week, Gene drew the Tuesday and Thursday night shift, working until 11:00 P.M. Sharing his evening shifts was a Tuley High School senior named Dan Witalski. Dan eased him into the evening routine, introducing Gene to the evening customers and cluing him in about life too. Curly-haired and gregarious, Dan was a good-looking, outgoing guy who had no enemies and whose mother was a widow. Having both grown up without a father around, Dan and Gene became good friends. Often, when things got busy, the two guys pitched in and worked very well together, weaving back and forth and around each other in perfect choreography as they covered different counters.

When their shift was over at 11 o'clock at night, Dan and Gene usually dashed across the street through the cold night over to Mardy's restaurant for a cup of hot coffee, a cinnamon roll, and time to carry on meaningful discussions. They were always treated warmly by the waitresses who quite often stopped by the drugstore and knew them to be hardworking kids. The late hour prevented the two soda-jerks from staying too long, before leaving for their respective homes. Gene often got home after his folks had gone to bed and a snack at the restaurant kept him from clattering around in the kitchen, waking them up.

While Dan wasn't from a rich family either and probably couldn't afford a new winter coat, he made do by wearing a poplin jacket under a rayon school jacket. Gene thought Dan was so cool that maybe Dan was way ahead in starting a new fashion trend, so out of hero worship or sincere imitation, Gene ceased wearing his winter coat and wore a poplin jacket under his school jacket too.

Because he was an upperclassman, had an after school job, and a last-period study hall, Gene was, with a note from his employer, able to apply for and receive an early-dismissal pass. This allowed him to leave school one period earlier in order to get to his part-time job. Early-dismissal came to be a blessing, since so few students left at that time in the afternoon, that one could even get a seat on the streetcar that left the corner of Addison and Western at exactly 1:55 P. M. A speedy Green Hornet, it was able to roll to a stop at Cornelia, the stop at Lane's main Western Avenue door, just a few seconds later.

That's right. The stop was directly in front of Lane's front door. The only hitch was that the school's door was set back about 600 feet from the street. Each day, as predictably as the annual return of San Juan Capistrano mission's swallows, the anointed few early dismissal guys would burst through the doors and race hell-for-leather for that early streetcar. They needed to get a few good scouts onto the Cornelia Avenue stop's safety island, just a few, to consume enough boarding time, so that the other slower guys could catch up to the streetcar before it pulled away.

Proving only to himself, that his self-imposed running regimen had worked, the former 90-second wonder was usually one of the leaders of the pack racing for transportation. Often Gene threw open the school's front door, saw the streetcar pulling away from Addison, and knew he had to race at top speed in order to arrive at the stop at the same time as the streetcar. One day he ran far ahead of one of Lane's state champion soccer players, who was recovering from an injury, delaying the streetcar a few seconds.

It was just long enough for the soccer jock, who shouted, "Good man!" as he limped breathlessly up the trolley's steps.

Since the streetcar was usually almost empty, it made very few stops between Cornelia and Fullerton and at the speed at which it traveled, their ETA at Fullerton was usually about 2:00. Jumping off the trolley, Gene dashed across the street dodging cars, in order to clock in at approximately 2:00 P. M. Hurrying to the back of the store to hang up his jacket and put on an apron, he was always glad that his mom had recommended that he begin using a deodorant. Probably not as glad as those who had to work closely with him for the next four hours.

All did not run smoothly however as one day his early-dismissal pass was suspended indefinitely. Don Stanky, one of his longtime classmates got both of them in trouble. Don was great, a really, good-looking guy, who had a white-toothed smile, dark-complexion, black hair, and a penchant for mischief. Each day after lunch, Gene cut through the art rooms, past the long sinks meant for washing out art materials, toward the row of lockers outside the door on the other side.

As he passed the sinks, he would sometimes find that all twelve faucets had been left running and since he hated waste, would turn them off. One day Gene happened to be right behind a chuckling Don as Don hurriedly turned on the faucets right in front of Gene. In the process of turning off the first couple of faucets, from behind them, Gene heard the voice of doom.

A gleefully-stressed voice shouted, "Aha! Now I've got you!" from behind them.

It was Potts! Mr. Potts had been furious for some time, wondering who the idiot was who had been leaving the water faucets running, and now believed he had TWO of the culprits. He marched Don and Gene down to the Discipline Office and told Herr Ruesselsheimer of the crime that these two wasteful vandals had consistently perpetrated. Mr. Ruthless offered his opinion that indefinite discipline seemed to be in order, to which Mr. Potts agreed.

Indefinite discipline!!? An unspecified number of periods to be served after school but at least five had to be served. The student served those discipline periods until the teacher or Old Ruthless let him off the hook. Even though the next day, Potts came to believe Don Stanky who assumed full blame for turning on the faucets, the full five periods still had to be served by Gene. Don, for his part was made to serve ten periods after school.

Within a month of Dave's departure, Bob came home on a weekend pass from Chanute Field. Gene was overjoyed to see him and surprised at the uniform which Bob wore. It wasn't olive drab like other Army dress uniforms, it was slate blue. And he already had a stripe which looked upside-down.

"Why are you wearing a blue uniform?" he asked his Airman Third-Class brother.

"There isn't any Army Air Corps anymore," Bob explained. Continuing, he said, "It's been replaced by the U. S. Air Force and our uniforms are blue."

"Snappy color; it even makes you look good!" cracked his kid brother.

It was out of necessity that Bob soon purchased an old Hudson Terraplane sedan, built around 1937 with which he was able to come home just about every other weekend, driving the nearly 120 miles back and forth to the base. His visits eased somewhat the pain Kathleen and Gene felt, missing Dave and his presence was a comfort to Kathleen on Tom's "lost weekends." Dave who wrote about once a week was surviving basic infantry training at Camp Breckinridge, outside Morganfield, Kentucky.

In April, Gene was reminded of the spectre of war in Korea, a war that could engulf his brothers, especially Dave who was destined to be an infantryman. In a startling change, General MacArthur was relieved of his command by President Truman and replaced by General James Van Fleet. It was a dirty war, fought in bitter cold during the winter of 1950-51 and it seemed that the end was nowhere in sight. Some GI's were coming home now, a few were kids like Jerry Walen, from the neighborhood. Jerry limped badly, having lost frostbitten toes, due to combat boots not designed for the extreme cold of the Korean winter.

Weeks passed and now that late spring was in the air it wouldn't be long before Dave would be coming home on leave.

Torrential rains were falling on that happy afternoon in early June, when the phone rang and Kathleen picked up the receiver. In a moment her eyes lit up and a warm, happy smile filled her face. It was Dave calling to say he was downtown at the train station and was trying to catch a cab to come home.

By suppertime Dave and Jack were banging on the door, and in a mock threat, yelling, "If you don't open the door, we'll bust it down!"

Daredevil, whirlwind brother Dave was home! That evening, Bob rolled in from Chanute Field on a weekend pass and to Kathleen's great joy, home was in its normal state of chaos once again!

June was in full bloom and a stifling humidity hung in the air on that sunny afternoon which found Gene serving a counter full of high-school kids, mostly female, when out of the corner of his eye he saw two guys in summer khaki uniforms walking into the drugstore. Omigod! His brothers were here and he had to wait on them. But that was the easy part. The hard part was answering the girls' sotto voce probes for information about his brothers' ages, eligibility, discharge dates, and other personal insights while he was attending to the customers at the counter. Even Mr. Feinstein engaged them in conversation, asking when Bob and Dave would know where their duty stations were going to be and when they would get out.

When Gene was finally able to talk to his brothers, he asked, "Where did you go this afternoon?"

Bob answered, "We visited Lane Tech with Jack Gorr, touring the school. We also toured your art room where we saw some of your work," then commenting for all to hear that "but we think you're a sick kid who needs psychiatric help."

Whereupon Gene asked, "What have you got against paintings of graveyards and mausoleums?"

"No, not those paintings; we were referring to the paintings of those gorgeous, naked girls!"

While no such paintings existed, Gene's brothers had put the spotlight on him and made the girls at the counter notice their kid brother, wondering if what Bob and Dave said, was true.

A family photo opportunity was suddenly called by Kathleen

late the next afternoon and while each of her posing progeny squinted into the low-hanging sun's glare, Kathleen clicked away with her old Brownie camera. Achieving respectable poses from her sons had been a trial for her, what with various hand signs and gestures being displayed by one brother above an unsuspecting brother's head.

Afterwards, Kathleen said, "Okay, let's everybody wash up for dinner."

Gene and Dave didn't move toward the house but lingered. Then Gene, not wanting this pleasurable time to end, began walking through the gangway toward the front of the house.

Catching up to him Dave asked, "Didn't you hear Mom? Get back here!"

His younger brother refused, snarling, "You'll have to catch me first!"

Instantly the two youths kicked into high gear, racing up Montana toward Western, with Dave only a step or two behind his heretofore always slower younger brother. Reaching the alley east of Star Cleaners, Gene turned abruptly into the alley, racing toward Fullerton. He heard his brother right behind him but only kicked his speed up that last final notch, coming out of the alley at Fullerton and turning up the sidewalk toward the intersection. Stopping for the traffic signal at Western, Gene was overtaken by Dave.

Walking across the street to the drugstore, they both flopped down on counter stools and breathlessly ordered up quick Cokes.

"That's the first time I couldn't catch you!" gasped Dave, as he lit up a cigarette.

"Out of breath and you're lightin' up a lung-warper? Maybe that's why you couldn't catch me!" chided Gene.

"Damn, when did you get so fast?" Dave asked.

To answer, Gene had to explain how he had been running for nearly three years. The race was still foremost in his mind, for it had revealed a change in one constant of their relationship: Dave had always been faster than he. No longer would Dave seem to be the fastest guy he knew. Gene was now just as fast as Dave; in Gene's mind, he had arrived.

Coming to an early end as all good times do, Dave's ten-day leave was up and he had to move on to his duty station, in Europe. While it was a common occurrence in those times, with so many young men going overseas, it was a unique time of sorrow for the family of one who was leaving. To loved ones remaining behind it meant that they wouldn't see him again for over two years.

At about 2:15 on that Friday afternoon, Gene arrived home for the going-away party already in progress for Dave and Jack, who would be traveling to Europe together. Everyone had gathered for the imminent goodbyes, which would be soon, since a taxicab had already been called. Bob had made it there earlier, having left Chanute Field earlier. Dave's girl, Maryann was there, as was Jack's girlfriend, Marsha Towers, one of the gorgeous Towers sisters from the old neighborhood on George Street.

Abruptly, like a light switched off, the hearty, warm merriment halted when someone said, "Your taxi's here!" A pall of sadness crept across the living room as the women began to cry and Gene, with so much he wanted to say, was unable to clear the lump from his throat, saying nothing to the brother he loved so much. Like Bob, all he could do was throw his arms around his beloved brother and hold back his own tears. As Dave and Jack made their way to the front door, the radio that had been on throughout the gathering now began to air Guy Mitchell's Columbia recording of "My Heart Cries For You," which touched the hearts of everyone present.

Not wanting to prolong the oppressive, sad agony of saying goodbye, Dave and Jack made their way slowly out the door, the women each trying to give them one last kiss, until they were finally across the threshold. They walked down the sidewalk to the curb, went to the back of the taxicab with the driver, threw their duffel bags in the trunk, and slid into the back seat of the cab. As the yellow car pulled away and drove east toward Oakley Avenue, their smiling faces could be seen mugging in the back window, while they waved until the cab turned right down at the corner of Oakley then went out of sight. Brother Dave was gone.

At sixteen, Gene hadn't known a heartache like this pain deep within his chest for a long time. Once he again he felt the hurt of watching a loved one go away for a long time with no certainty that he would see them again. Maintaining a cheerful front for his mother's sake, Gene could only wait until later that night, when the thought of all those months yet to be without Dave around would overwhelm him, and he wept for his brother.

As the days passed, it was soon the end of June and during the last week of the semester, Gene found that the interminable Physics final wasn't too difficult, while Mrs. Barrett's U. S. History test was also a long one but he felt that he did well. Proficiency tests in gym didn't seem as hard as they once had been and he had actually come to enjoy their physical challenge. Somehow the week's activities aided in taking his mind off his brother Dave's absence. Getting his grades, he found that he had received B's in everything except Gym where he got an A.

Gene had been passed into his senior year. A Senior! Looking back at his first three years, he remembered the pain of exclusion he had endured but he had also gained new friends and now felt accepted. There had been some pretty memorable occasions during those three years, such as the speaking engagement by Jack Dempsey, "The Manassa Mauler" who still looked like he could go a couple of rounds in the ring. Laneites had also been treated to a concert by a former alumnus, Frankie Laine, who belted out every song he had recorded, during two separate assemblies. Gene had also been a student at Lane during the season when their football team had won the Public League Championship, and Lane teams were perennial baseball and swimming champions. He had always felt the pride that all Lane students felt and tried to remember the good times over the bad.

At home, it had been a blessing for Kathleen, that Bob could still come home every other weekend from Chanute Field, for he was her primary source of strength. She looked forward to Bob coming home and enjoyed the warmth of his charm and wit. Bob was the most Irish of her sons, having the gift of blarney, the dark, handsome looks, and the ability to lift his mother's spirits with a joke or brogue-inflected comment. Since he had become an adult, not a Saint Patrick's Day evening had gone by without his donning of a bright, Kelly green tie and engaging in the traditional search of local dance-halls and pubs for the elusive, fabled Unicorn.

Bob, as a gesture of faith in his kid brother, promised to teach him to drive during his stay at Chanute. A gesture yes, but never a certainty as weeks became months that slipped into memory as Gene never even got behind the wheel of the old Hudson. It may have been a case of too many things to be done in so little time while he was home, that Bob never had the time. Or maybe he realized that the old car was the difference between him driving home on pass or having to hitchhike. If his kid brother drove it into a lamp post over a weekend, he'd have had no transportation back to the base.

After weekends with Bob, it was back to the everyday grind, except for mail, that fragile thread linking so many families and their far-off servicemen together, which had begun to arrive from Dave. He wrote that it was fortunate that he and Jack had each other's company and were too busy to be lonesome yet. Dave and Jack had been sitting at Camp Kilmer, New Jersey, waiting for a ship to take them to Europe. They had gone into New York City and made the grand tour of Manhattan and the other boroughs. Dave wrote that they would be shipping out on the 3rd of July and he asked that his family and of course, Maryann, keep writing, so that when he arrived at his permanent duty station, the mail would catch up to him.

A couple of weeks later, Dave wrote, saying that he was stationed with an Army medical company near Deggendorf, Germany, not too far from Munich. In his letter, he conveyed the fear that his being gone for thirty months might be too long for Maryann to wait, but he was hoping for the best. While he worried about it being tough on Maryann, he didn't let on about the despair he must have felt as an eighteen-year-old kid, away from home for so long, when his sweetheart was five-thousand miles away. Quite often folks back home would just have to "read between the lines" of letters they received from afar.

Chapter 25

The Social Whirl

Summer of 1951 might have slipped into history unremembered were it not for certain memorable lessons in young Gene's social life. Dan, his evening-shift sidekick had left his job at the drugstore, taking a summer vacation before going off to college. The place wasn't the same without Dan's ever-present relaxed air and sense of humor.

Dan's absence had also come at a bad time, since it seemed that of the four remaining high-school students working at the drugstore that summer, never more than two of them were in the city of Chicago at the same time. Overlapping vacations forced the working of double and split-shifts by Gene and whoever else wasn't away on vacation at that time.

The clear, clean glass window on the drugstore's front door was ablaze in sunlight one hot day as Gene worked one of the afternoon shifts when the red-haired dental assistant from the dentist's office across the street came in. Behind the fountain, Gene could see that she was purchasing cigarettes from Mr. Feinstein at the front register.

Turning to leave, she walked to the door but then stopped to extend her conversation with the Boss. Wearing a white uniform but no slip, the image of her shapely legs was fully defined by sunbeams bursting through the glass door behind her. As her conversation went on, Gene continued to watch. Hormones already active inside his sixteen-year-old body were stirred as if by an egg-beater by the demon of lust until he realized that he was being aroused, and might soon embarrass himself, if he couldn't get his mind on something else. Suddenly, he had an idea: Grab a drink of ice-water from the soda-fountain. Quickly filling a paper cup, he chugged down the chilly fluid and within seconds he noticed that the impending urgency he had felt was beginning to subside. Not a moment too soon, he thought. He learned a lesson about the effects of cold water and cold showers that afternoon. A lesson that he'd remember.

On another hot day Gene came off his shift as Pam, now the senior and only other member of the drugstore's student workers still in town, came on. Accompanying her were two tall, hard-looking guys who came in, sat down at the fountain counter and engaged Pam in conversation. He guessed that they were old school friends which was confirmed when she introduced Bill and Ed to Gene.

"If you're a friend of Pam's you're a friend of ours," one of them said, to Gene's relief.

A few minutes later, Gene said, "I'm glad to have met you but I've got to get going."

Pam inquired, "Where are you going, Gene?"

Gene replied, "I'm going over to Goethe school's playground and see if I can play softball."

Bill then said, "Wait a few minutes. We're going over there too!"

Gene thought it prudent not to decline their company. After they departed the drugstore, the three of them talked on the way over to the playground, discussing school, family, and brothers away. Gene learned that Bill and Ed each had an older brother serving in Korea.

Ed asked Gene, "What team do you play for?"

Gene replied, "I don't play as a regular. All of the teams have regular rosters but usually one of the teams is short a player. But some nights I sit it out."

Arriving at the school yard Gene was to find that Bill and Ed must have known everybody there. As they walked over to the bleachers, Bill stopped at one of the benches out of Gene's earshot, where he spoke to one of the team captains. Whatever Bill said, it helped! The team captain came over and asked him if he wanted to play, receiving an affirmative from Gene. Strangely enough, Gene never again had to stand around on the sidelines hoping to play. What he hadn't known that night was that Bill and Ed were two of the hardest guys around with tough reputations, but who didn't look for trouble, and seemed to have the respect of everyone at the schoolyard. It was another short but sweet lesson in life for Gene that taught him about making friends whenever the opportunity presented itself.

Those two lessons came to mind on that humid, August day, when an eighteen-year-old acquaintance named Alvina Stinson, strolled in with another girl. Wearing sheer, clingy blouses and straight linen skirts, they looked very cool, in a sense unrelated to temperature.

They slid effortlessly onto two chrome-trimmed stools at the soda-fountain and cooed, "Hello Gene."

Straightening up from washing out glasses, Gene was stupefied by the greenest eyes he had ever seen. Set in a lovely, light-complexioned face framed by shimmering coal-black hair, those eyes belonged to the stranger.

Alvina introduced the stranger, "Alice, this is my friend, Gene. Gene, this is my cousin, Alice Smith."

Alice smiled warmly and instantly won herself a lifelong admirer. Gene remembered to make friends with the lovely stranger and perhaps just as important, he casually drew himself a cup of ice-water which he kept close at hand.

After about twenty glorious minutes during which Gene enjoyed their company, the two young ladies finished their sodas and left. Gene who lamented having to remain at his post, watched Alice in her white sleeveless blouse and baby-blue straight skirt as she glided out the door, noticing as she departed that Alice's legs were as exceptional as her face. As he took a long sip of ice-water, he hoped fervently that this would not be the last time he would see that lovely girl.

Seeing Alvina later that week, Gene asked her all of the important questions regarding Alice's commitments versus availability and learned from Alvina that Alice was going with somebody but it didn't seem too serious. On a sunny day soon after, Gene sat in Tony the barber's chair, squinting into the late afternoon sun through the window along the sidewalk. At the point where Tony began shaving behind Gene's ear, the dark-haired illusion of loveliness named Alice Smith passed the window strolling toward the drugstore. Unbelievably, Gene jerked slightly forward at seeing her and only the barber's years of experience and dexterity prevented him from taking off a piece of Gene's ear. Seeing Gene through the window, Alice gave him a big, friendly smile and waved to him. Without any further ado, Tony, who had cut Gene's hair for the last couple of years, brushed off the young man, collected $3.50, and sent him out the door while he still had both of his ears.

Hurrying out of the barber shop and walking a few doors north, Gene encountered the stunning Alice inside the drugstore. He sat down with her and ordered up a cold Coke for himself, she having already ordered. Afterwards he proceeded to walk along with her to her home, which was only four blocks away. Arriving at her house, they sat down on her front porch and talked for a couple of hours, wherein he learned that she was indeed going with someone who had asked her not to date anyone else and she was still considering the idea. Alice thanked Gene for his interest however, and said that they could still talk to each other when they met. Walking back north on Western Avenue with shoulders hunched, Gene tried to tell himself that the walk back home only seemed to be twice as long.

Until then Gene had never had an actual date with a girl and began to wonder if he was even ready for a date. Just sixteen, he had never learned to dance and thought he'd better ask his mom what he should do about that. Kathleen impressed on him, how much it was appreciated by a girl or woman, if her date really knew how to dance but she couldn't teach him. She said he should ask his aunt Betty if she would teach him because she was an instructor at a well-known dance studio.

To his pleasant surprise, Betty, who had always been like a big sister to him since he was little, had the time and the inclination to teach one more nephew to dance. Seems that his brother Dave had already preceded him in going that route!

As a dancer, Gene might have made an excellent grape-stomper. He was terrible. He moved stiffly, as if a board were shoved down the back of his pants. Gene also seemed to possess someone else's uncoordinated, mismatched feet, and he couldn't have found rhythm in the dictionary! By September, he was able to sustain the pattern of steps for more than a minute or so but still hadn't mastered flexing his knees and loosening up.

It is unknown, even today, how much painful punishment poor Betty's toes had endured at the feet of her fledgling nephew.

She praised him for taking the initiative and wanting to learn because, as she put it, "A guy doesn't need to be good-looking, if he really knows how to dance; dancing can be of immense help to him socially."

Heeding her words of dubious inspiration, Gene practiced hard and slowly became a dancer. What did Betty mean when she said, "A guy doesn't need to be good-looking?"

By late September, Gene thought that he was ready. He had already practiced dancing with his mom and his aunt Etta, just so he wouldn't only be used to dancing with Betty who said he had to get accustomed to dancing with different partners.

It was September 28th, a pleasant clear evening of firsts which found a nervous Gene executing his first shave, trying hard to shave nearly non-existent whiskers from his face in preparation for his first Lane Social. Various public high schools hosted coed dances every other Friday night and tonight's social was the first dance of the season hosted by Lane Tech. His nerves were shaky because for the first time in his life, tonight he was going to have to walk up to a girl and ask her to dance. What if she said no? For that matter, what if she said yes and he, in his inexperience, danced all over her feet instead of the floor? What if he forgot the steps right in the middle of a number? Fortunately he stopped asking himself questions before he talked himself out of going!

All slicked-up, he hopped the Western Avenue streetcar a block further north, at Altgeld instead of Fullerton just so he wouldn't run into any smart aleck acquaintances of his who might be loitering around the drugstore. Arriving at Lane after a swift ride on the streetcar, he walked west along Addison Street. Hearing his leather heels make a lot of noise on the pavement he was afraid others might hear him coming. He continued on to the west end of the building, past the auditorium wing, past the administration wing, to the gym.

Wow! Gym #1 certainly looked different from the outside! At the top of the stairs, he paid his admission to two pretty young women in a booth. "I know they don't go here," he said, sotto voce. Approaching the door of Gym #1, two burly heavyweights from Lane's wrestling team were there to make sure that each person had a ticket before allowing them inside. Security here certainly seemed adequate!

Walking into Gym #1 from the outside was another first for Gene and he noticed how the gym's bright lights had been severely dimmed and what a nice effect it had created. Looking around the softly-lit gym, Gene couldn't help noticing how many girls had shown up and they all looked pretty! But first, he had to find someone he knew, someone to talk to and lean on if necessary. He ran into Ron Luzinski, a buddy of Robert Gagnon, a friend and classmate of Gene's. They talked for about ten minutes, when the band began playing "It's No Sin." Gene noticed a girl with a friendly smile and decided to ask her to dance.

Surprisingly, the young lady said yes. As they clung to each other for support on the dance floor, Gene learned her name was Lorene Deming, a cute girl of average height, with brown hair, warm brown eyes, and a very friendly personality.

As they danced she told Gene, "This is the first social that I've been to."

Gene quickly reassured her, "You aren't alone in that respect. I haven't been dancing before."

"I'm a sophomore at Carl Schurz High School but I had heard that Lane had the best socials and decided to see what one was like."

Great, thought Gene. She goes to Schurz, Lane Tech's arch rival. Even though she only knew a two-step while Gene knew the foxtrot, they somehow managed to dance together for the balance of the evening. During one number Gene looked up to see Bill Ferris, a guy from the neighborhood, who was a semester ahead of him, dancing like a pro. Bill saw him, smiled, and continued on.

312

When the band played their last number, Gene asked Lorene, "Can I see you home?"

"I came here with my girlfriend, the tall blonde who's coming this way. Gene, meet Barbara Witte."

Meeting Barbara, Gene offered to see them both home and they accepted. Not unheard of in those times, the three of them rode the bus to Irving and Kostner in the Portage Park area. There Gene and Lorene walked Barbara to her home and then the two of them walked slowly back to Lorene's home on Tripp.

They had talked all evening and they still had so many things to talk about until they got to her door where they said goodnight and Gene walked back up to Irving Park Road. Lorene was nice. Gene couldn't get over how nice she was and how well the evening had gone. Arriving home at 12:45 in the morning, he had so much to talk about but he thought his folks were already asleep. As he hung up his suitcoat, he heard his mother's voice asking how the evening had gone. Surprised that she was still up, he was glad to be able to tell someone close about his very pleasant, first evening out.

Mr. Feinstein made a slight mistake the next morning, when in a slow moment at the drugstore he casually asked how his young employee's evening had gone. Mercifully, a customer came in ten minutes later to have a prescription filled by a grateful pharmacist. Gee, thought Gene, Mr. Feinstein didn't usually hurry off like that, stepping quickly into the back of the store behind the prescription counter to fill a prescription. Maybe it's an emergency.

Back at school on Monday, Gene encountered Bill Ferris who told him, "I saw you at the social Friday night and noticed you're a new dancer. You need to get out and dance with different girls. You've got the steps down and the rhythm right, but you've got to flex those knees, man. You danced like you had plaster casts on your legs. Loosen up!"

Gene replied, "I didn't realize that I'd been dancing so stiffly but I really do appreciate the tip and will work on it."

It wasn't difficult for Gene to change, he just began to practice flexing his knees when dancing and his style did smooth out.

Between after-school work, homework and dancing practice,

Gene's free hours were gainfully occupied. His part-time job was a way of earning money for himself and to help out at home. The routine of hurrying home from school was eased somewhat by a change in starting time from 2:15 back to 3:00 P. M. Now he had time to stop by his house for a little while before he went to work.

October 3rd, 1951 was the day when he stopped at home to turn on the TV and catch the score of the third and final playoff game between the New York Giants and the Brooklyn Dodgers. In mid-August, the Giants had been down 13 1/2 games behind the Dodgers but had roared back to wind up in a tie with the Dodgers on the last day of the season. Each of the teams had won one of the playoff games and this third game was for the pennant! As the set warmed up, Gene heard the Giants were at bat, down 4 to 1, and there was one out in the bottom of the ninth inning. He had to go to work at 3 o'clock but he couldn't leave. Gene watched tensely, issuing his own running commentary triggered by the urgent need to leave for work and the pedantic pace of the baseball game.

Alvin Dark, the Giants' shortstop came up to bat. Interminable balls and strikes. "Hit it will you?" CRACK! Dark singles! "Hurry, you guys, I gotta get going!" Then outfielder Don Mueller steps up to the plate. More balls and strikes. "Come on, swing at it!" WHAM! Mueller keeps the inning alive by singling! "What? A conference on the mound? Why now? Let's get back to the game!" Giant left-fielder Whitey Lockman steps into the batter's box. Standing up, Gene prepares to push the off button when Lockman blasts a booming double down the alley, driving in Dark to score. Mueller comes up lame going into third base and now they're taking a time out to replace him with a pinch runner. More delays! By then Gene was really ready to dash out the door.

That's all for Dodger pitching great Don Newcombe as Lockman's double causes the Dodgers to bring in Ralph Branca as a relief pitcher. "Warm-up pitches? Come on guys! Let's see, more warm-up pitches, then Thomson will come up. He'll foul off a couple because Branca won't throw him anything good to swing at. If I leave now I'll get to work about the time Branca's ready to pitch. That's it! I'm outta here!"

Turning off the TV, Gene raced out the front door like a thoroughbred out of the gate, running the city block to work in an attempt to get there in time to hear what Bobby Thomson was going to do. Breathless, he arrived at the drugstore in time to hear only pandemonium over the store's table model radio.

"What happened?" he asked those gathered around the small white box.

"Bobby Thomson just hit a three-run homer! The Giants won!" They asked, "Didn't you see it?"

"No, I was on my way here," replied Gene to no one listening.

Thomson hadn't waited. On a 0-1 count, he drove a Branca fastball into the left-field seats of the Polo Grounds, for a three-run homer. It was the home run that would forever be remembered as "The shot heard 'round the world." And Gene had missed it!

That night, Gene went over to Lorene's home where he met her mom and dad. The two high-schoolers agreed to meet each other at Lane's main stadium gate after the Lane/Schurz football game on Friday, October 5th. Although Lane lost the game by a score of 9 to 6, it didn't bother Gene quite as much since he was looking forward to seeing Lorene after the game.

When he met her at the gate, he couldn't help feeling warm all over just seeing Lorene's vivacious, smiling face in the warm, amber glow of late afternoon sunshine in autumn. In return, she had also seemed glad to find him in the crush of the crowd. They talked for a while, then confirmed their plans made earlier in the week, that they would meet each other again, later that evening at the Schurz social.

Gene had no way of knowing beforehand, that Schurz students would be turning the dance into a victory celebration. That theme didn't play well with Gene because it had been close, hard-fought game which Lane lost 9 to 6. He may have been the only Laneite there but hadn't felt threatened, not while Lorene was along. He wasn't going to let the antics of other Schurz students put a damper on his evening with her.

Also unknown to Gene, was the fact that Lorene had a boyfriend at Schurz and when he showed up, Lorene grew increasingly indifferent toward Gene, until by ten o'clock, Gene decided to fade out of the dance and caught the bus home. It hadn't been hard to put together. Lorene probably wanted Gene around just to make her other interest jealous enough to be interested in her. Gene felt a great sense of disappointment in her and in himself for being such a patsy. As he lay in his bed, in the darkness of his room, he made up his mind that he would just put Lorene Deming out of his life, but he couldn't put her smiling face, aglow in the amber cast of the late afternoon sun, out of his mind.

The next Lane social was on October 11th, a Thursday, because there was no school on Friday since it was Columbus Day. Debating whether or not to go, Gene finally conceded and gave it another try. He enjoyed the music and the dancing, and since Lane wasn't coed, he looked forward to the opportunity to meet girls. A veteran now, he staked out a spot of his own from which to watch the crowd, of girls. Looking over at the band, he saw the saxophone player put down the sax and pick up his clarinet. Dun! Dun! Dun! Suddenly the wailing strains of "Clarinet Polka" filled the gym and Gene, who had just recently added the polka to his quickly growing list of dances that he had learned to do, looked around for a partner. Several girls had said no when he asked if they did the polka before he found her. A polka partner! Well, she was until they got out on the floor and she sheepishly admitted that she didn't really know how, so they went through the motions and faked it rather well.

Remaining on the floor for the slow dance that followed, he found out that her name was Mimi Sesona and she was a junior at Alvernia, an elite Catholic high school for girls on Chicago's Northwest side. When he asked if she had a part-time job after school too, she said that she worked after school at a restaurant as a part-time cashier. As fate would have it, she worked at Mardy's, the restaurant across the street from the drugstore where he worked. Since they worked on the same afternoons he had never seen her there when he was off.

Somehow, they danced together the entire evening and when the last dance was over, he offered to see her home. Declining his offer, she said it wasn't necessary but he insisted because he didn't want her to ride the bus alone late at night. Still he accompanied her to the Addison Street bus stop, although on the way, she repeated her protests that it wasn't necessary for him to escort her, citing that it was too far, it was too late, she liked riding alone, ad infinitum.

Persistent in his gallant though unsolicited and unappreciated endeavors to see her home safely, he sat with her on the bus and walked her home at the end of the line out past Harlem Avenue, nearly the city limits. Walking past large, mist-laden vacant lots, he told her that it was the first time he had been this close to being out of the city, and wondered if she thought he was a boob. Seeing her to the door of her home, she said goodnight in a huff and slammed the door behind her. She certainly had spirit!

The cool night air had a sobering effect on our young swain, who had begun to wonder why he had traveled so far, only to receive little or no appreciation in return. The long walk back to the bus stop and the even longer wait for a bus gave him cause to reflect on the relative merits of seeing this girl, even if she were to agree to see him! Arriving home from his trip to Addison Street and Plowed Ground at 1:30 in the morning, he found that even his mother fell asleep sometime, and somehow didn't mind not having to tell her about the abrupt end to his evening.

Sitting on his bed in the dark, he looked out his window at the many glittering stars set like tiny diamonds in a dark blue velvet background. Too late to wish on the first star, he thought about the evening and about the girl he had just met. Perhaps Mimi was just being careful and particular about who takes her home or wanted to know if he was easily discouraged. Somehow, her aloofness hadn't deterred him but had only piqued his interest. Through it all, he actually liked her, for her dark hair and blue eyes, but mostly for her smile. He was a sucker for an overbite.

The next day was Columbus Day, a day without school or work, so a curious and yet foolhardy Gene decided to wander over to Mardy's Restaurant and visit Mimi, unannounced and uninvited. Working at the cash register, she was in plain view of everyone there, including her boss. When she saw Gene, she asked why he had come there and he replied that he had just wanted to talk to her. Mimi then informed him that she was going steady with a guy from the neighborhood who was in the Army.

"Is that true?" asked Gene.

"Yes, it is," replied Mimi.

Thinking for a moment, Gene then responded with, "I won't bother you anymore. You hadn't told me. I've got two brothers in the service and I wouldn't want to horn in on a soldier's girl while he was away."

Then turning around, Gene walked out of the restaurant and slogged over to the drugstore where he thought he might find solace in a soft-drink among friends. Walking into the drugstore and saying hello to a stony-faced Pam, two things occurred simultaneously: he remembered that he had previously agreed to cover for Pam today since she had covered for him the night before and she scolded him furiously as soon as he walked into the store. His sincere apologies received superficial acceptance and shortly after, he went home. Soon night fell, bringing a merciful end to a double-zero day.

Moping around the next day, Gene felt as though he had no friends left but it wasn't true. During the eight months he'd been working at the drugstore, Gene had made many new friends from the many acquaintances who were steady customers. For some time, a slender guy in his early twenties had been coming into the drugstore with several teenaged guys from the local park and parish.

His full name was Louis Polesniak but everyone knew him simply, as "Louie." He was unable to join the guys in their athletic pursuits since his spastic body wouldn't allow him. But Louie's mind was a source of knowledge and information to them all. Over the months, Gene had also come to make friends with Louie who ofttimes seemed to possess a bit of ESP or at least a great amount of empathy. Louie could sense when someone was up or down. If they had a problem, he had good advice for them, for Louie was like everyone's big brother. Contrary to the customary behavior among young people toward someone with a disability, these guys didn't pick on Louie; they held him in high esteem and respected him because of his openness, honesty, and his high intelligence. Often, when a bunch of the guys were talking about going over to the bowling alley or to one of the theatres, Louie was usually invited to tag along with them.

On that next day, Gene worked his usual Saturday early shift and was pleasantly surprised when Louie happened to come in. Asking Gene, in Polish as he always did, how things were, he followed quickly with, "What's her name?" Gene ignored the latter statement until Louie said "You look like you've got woman problems, kiddo. Tell Uncle Louie about it." Then Gene mentioned forgetting all about covering for Pam, whom he really liked as a friend, and the other incident with Mimi.

Louie told him not to worry about Pam, because she wouldn't stay angry long. He then said, "I admire your sense of honor in not pursuing a girl who's going with a soldier. Honor is a virtue that too many guys lack nowadays. Continuing, Louie confided, "Don't be down, kiddo. Your girl will come along someday! How old are you? Sixteen? You've got lots of time."

Listening to Louie somehow made Gene feel a lot better. It wouldn't be the only time Louie would be able to solidly advise or teach Gene. The two of them already shared a liking for historical events, politics, geography, and different languages. Being a former seminary student, Louie had taught Gene several phrases in Latin. Generally, most of their discussions took place at the soda fountain of the drugstore. Other times, a friend of Louie's, tall, lanky Don Schubert would drop in and the three of them and a few other guys would go up to the Fireside Bowl and bowl several games.

It was good to have friends like Don and Louie around, to help ease the emptiness of those times when Gene really missed his brother Dave. Don was Dave's age and was wary of being drafted any day, since he was classified 1A. He was also the guy who got Gene interested in roller skating when he let Gene tag along with him to the Riverview Roller Rink where Gene got hooked on skating around the big circle to Russ Young's organ music.

One night, while he and Don were there, Gene bumped into his aunt Betty who, like Don, was an expert skater. After Gene introduced them to each other, Don asked Betty to skate and the two of them looked great! Gene envied them and thought that someday he might learn some of those great skate dances like the Foxtrot, Romp, Fourteen-step, and Collegiate. But for now and for the sake of his wrists and knees, his first skating priority was to learn to skate better and stop falling down so much!

While friends like Don and Louie were good to have, they weren't close friends. Envying brother Dave's close friendship with Jack Gorr, Gene lamented the persistent lack of a best friend in his life. The close friend that Gene had wanted and needed still hadn't come along.

From what Dave had written in his letters, Gene surmised that he hadn't yet overcome his homesickness. Dave was just eighteen and alone over there, since he and Jack had been split up by the Army on the day they arrived in Germany. An armored cavalry regiment in Regensburg acquired Jack's services while Dave was serving as a medic with an infantry outfit in Deggendorf and writing about how much he missed Maryann. Bob was alone down at Chanute Field, so all three Ryan boys were sort of in the same boat. Gene had no way of knowing but in weeks to come his search for a close, best friend would end.

For several weeks now, Gene had been training a new guy at the drugstore, a guy with a real attitude, toward Gene. About six-feet tall and weighing in around 200 pounds, the new kid, Joe Kolski just didn't seem to like Gene. In addition to taking instruction reluctantly, Joe was a bigot. During one busy time when two teenaged black kids, who worked at the huge cleaning plant just up Western, came in for service at the fountain, Joe ignored them, continuing to serve others in the crowd.

Gene reminded Joe of the two guys, "When are you going to take care of them, Joe?"

Joe snarled, "I'm not waiting on them."

Gene replied angrily, "Forget it, jerk! I'll wait on them!" and took care of the two long-waiting guys, saying to them, "If you ever have to wait too long again, you let me know."

Sadly, in a reflection of the times, one of the young men replied, "It's okay man. We're used to it!"

Then the two young men thanked him and left.

Their parting comment rang a bell in Gene's mind. He also knew, what it was like, having to get "used to it." Hadn't he gotten used to the slights and taunting, that came with being different?

Needless to say, Mr. Feinstein, even though busy himself, had observed Joe's slight of the two young men and later called him into the back of the store, perhaps for a re-orientation of his attitude toward minority customers. Since Dan Witalski, Gene's friend and former co-worker, had left for college, Joe was assigned to Dan's old shift, working with Gene on Tuesday and Thursday nights. After a few weeks of working together, Joe's attitude seemed to improve and the two of them actually became friends of sorts.

In early November, Gene noticed two solid-looking guys in blue windbreakers who always came in together and sat at the fountain, talking to Joe. It turns out that all three of them went to Weber High School, an all-boys Catholic high school at Lockwood and Palmer. After a couple of weeks, Gene had also made their acquaintance and became friends with Ted Marcinski and Walt Mikolzyk. He knew this for certain when they mentioned that Weber was having a dance on Thanksgiving Eve and suggested that Gene come along with them. Why not? Walt would be giving him a lift, driving his dad's car!

At the dance Walt and Ted introduced Gene to most of their classmates and friends. It was then that Gene was glad that Louie Polesniak had taught him some Polish pronunciations, since those guys had names that were pronounced much more easily in Polish than English. Afterwards, the three of them drove Ted's kid sister, Barbara, home then they drove down to where Ted's Dad worked and brought him home. Hungry by then, the three of them chowed down at Coleman's hamburger grill over on Western near Diversey where really great hamburgers were served. Gene had a great time, and on the way home, Walt and Ted suggested that they get together the next night which was Thanksgiving night and take in a movie. By the time the weekend was over, it was as though they were old friends. What a great feeling it was for Gene, having two good friends with whom to share good times.

Walt and Ted then clued Gene in to their phone code, used to determine if the other was willing to meet at the drugstore, the halfway point between their homes. One would call the other and hang up after one ring. If the receiving party was inclined to go out into the cold, they would ring back once, if not, they would ring back twice. It saved on the phone bill and prevented fruitless trips to the drugstore on frigid nights. Wanting to be a part of future gatherings, Gene suggested that if he called, he could ring twice, then the called party could respond to him with one or two rings. Ted could initiate a signal with one ring to Gene while Walt could start with two rings to Gene. Simple. As the days went by, Ted became the more frequent caller, meeting Gene about twice as often as Walt.

Over the months to come, Gene was to spend many evenings at Ted's house, kidding his sister, Barbara, and bantering with their mother, a second-generation Pole who took him under her wing and began teaching him Polish. She lamented her own son not learning Polish and kidded Gene that he knew more Polish than Ted. Visits weren't always smooth, like the time when Mrs. Marcinski mentioned the time when her brother had to change his name to an Irish name in earlier years in order to get work and she derided young Gene Ryan, the closest Irish guy.

Gene's response was, "While you may have reason to be resentful of some Irish, I didn't keep your brother from working. I didn't make him change his name. Your son is my best friend and I've asked you to teach me Polish! You oughta realize by now that I admire you Poles. So don't try to pin that old injustice on me!"

To Gene's surprise, Mrs. Marcinski laughed and said, "That's why I like you; you've got a mouth! You don't let anybody walk on you!"

It was in remembering his rebuttal that Gene realized he finally had a best friend.

The evening of December 7th found Gene still in search of a girlfriend at a Lane Social where he met a girl who really impressed him, named Dorothy Haneghen, from Schurz. After giving him her phone number, she and her girl friend were picked up by her father. Gene would have been better off had he just torn up the phone number and wrote the evening off as a total loss.

Yet how would he have learned to recognize when he was being jerked around unless he experienced it? His education in the wiles of young women was accelerated in the three weeks that followed, when Dorothy came down with the flu twice, breaking two dates, although the second time she recovered in time to have gone out when he called back to set up an alternate date. Her Dad's car wouldn't start, twice, keeping her from meeting Gene. Giving it one more try, Gene accepted Dorothy's invitation to accompany her to a Christmas party at the home of one of her friends. Upon picking her up at her home, he gave her a Christmas present of a makeup compact. Arriving at the party, it wasn't long before she began hanging all over a guy she knew from school. Having been that route before, with another Schurz girl who had a boyfriend stashed at school, Gene held out little hope that anything further would develop between he and Dorothy. He saw her home and called her the next day to tell her to get lost, but she opened by saying that she had decided to go steady with someone else. He wisely never contacted her afterwards.

Christmas Eve found Gene a little down while working at the drugstore during the day but his spirits lifted as he worked the front register and Mimi Sesona came in from cashiering at Mardy's across the street.

Gene asked her, "Are you getting off early for Christmas Eve?"

She replied, "I just got off and am on my way home."

"I'll be here until six. But it was so nice of you to stop in and wish me a Merry Christmas."

"I stopped in for a pack of gum, but Merry Christmas anyhow." She then kidded him saying, "I'll be home by the time you get off work."

"Should I call you then?" he joked.

"Sure. If you like the sound of a slammed phone receiver in your ear," she said, smiling as she left.

Not put off by her aloofness he enjoyed seeing her.

Late that night he wandered over to Mardy's and saw his brother Bob in the cocktail lounge. Bob was sitting at the bar with a frequent drugstore customer named Bud Graves and as Gene walked up to them, Bud spoke first.

After their exchange of greetings, Bud said, "Gene, I'd like you to meet Bob. Bob, this is Gene."

"We've already met."

"You have?"

"Yeh, he's my kid brother!"

"I'll be damned! And here I tried to introduce you two to each other. How come I never put two and two together? Gene told me about a brother in the Air Force and I was friends with an airman. Never thought it was the same guy."

After talking for a while Gene decided to go to church. Since his church didn't have an evening service, he walked over to St. John Berchman's on Logan Boulevard to attend Midnight Mass. Despite being confused by the liturgy and responses, he was moved by the congregation's solemnity and reverence and felt that he wanted to learn more about this religion.

The Martin-Ryans celebrated Christmas Day as always but despite Bob being home on leave, Dave's vacant chair next to Gene at the dining room table was so much more noticeable. Their first Christmas without Dave's mirth and zaniness was a somber one, but two more Yuletides might pass without his presence, although he wrote about coming home on furlough for the next Christmas. His girl, Maryann, had been invited to come over and share their Christmas dinner but she had declined. Perhaps without Dave there, it might have been too sad for her, so Gene's family tried to understand.

Two days later, on his birthday, his mom and brother Bob went with Gene over to the six-corner shopping center of Lincoln-Belmont-Ashland where they helped him pick out his first adult suit. With Bob along, it was a certainty that Gene wouldn't be spending his hard-earned money withdrawn from the bank on anything less than the best in taste. Bob was a fashion plate who always seemed to select sharp jackets and sweaters to give Gene for Christmas and his birthday. They settled on a dark blue, worsted wool suit with two pairs of pants. Gene hadn't brought enough money for extra pants.

Bob said, "You need the second pair of pants because they will help in longer wear of the entire suit."

"I understand, but I don't have the money with me."

"You don't need the money. I'll pay for the extra pair of pants as a birthday present."

Every kid should've had a big brother like Bob, who then drove them home.

A few days later at year's end, Gene tried to take stock of how his social life had been affected by his job at the drugstore and the dances at Lane and other schools. He was amazed at how much more extroverted he had become in dealing with the public and with friends at school. Gene also believed that he had learned a lot about the ways of the opposite sex, yet felt as if he had so much more to learn.

Finally, he experienced a revelation when he realized just how limited a man's knowledge of women really is, and probably always would be.

Chapter 26

Candles Burn Brighter, At Both Ends

December it seemed, had zoomed past, bringing 1951 to a rapid and welcome end. Gene had become so busy with friends and activities now, that he didn't feel the usual loneliness of Christmas spoiled by the rantings of a drunken stepfather who left him alone. His turn had already come and gone for him to stand up to Tom, just as his brothers had done. His stepfather now was aware that even though Kathleen's older sons were away, there was still one son around to defend his mom. "Don't you ever lay a hand on her!" was the warning that always stood and was still enforceable. Christmastime also made Gene miss Dave and he was glad that he had been setting time aside to write to his faraway brother. At least Dave would have gotten his Christmas letter and the lighter that he sent him.

Of late, the loneliness of being just nineteen and so far away in Germany where he would be for another two years at least, was beginning to come through in Dave's letters. Fearless Dave, who had never been afraid of anything, was now afraid. Fearful that his long absence might cause him to lose his sweetheart, Maryann, he was concerned about how lonely she might be. Often he asked Kathleen and Gene if they kept in touch with her, which they tried to do.

Rather than call her, thinking that to see her in person might have more impetus, Gene often walked six blocks up to the Congress Theatre where Maryann worked, to talk to her. In fact he went to the movies at the Congress just before Christmas to see if she would be coming over on Christmas Day but she had deferred. Never having had a sister, Gene really hoped that Maryann might someday be like a sister as his sister-in-law.

January opened up 1952 like a fast break down the court! Two of Gene's activities were playing basketball, once a week on a team that he started up in the Park District league and once or twice a week for a Methodist church over on Armitage Avenue in Old Town. With only seven players on the church team and usually having only five players show up by game time, Gene had suddenly become a starter.

At five-feet-ten, Gene preferred playing forward but because Will Slater, their regular center at six-two hadn't been showing up, Gene had been pressed into playing center. Being the Methodist Church League's shortest center, he was able to compete primarily because his young legs allowed him a vertical leap advantage over the other guys on the team in their mid-twenties. Often he had been able to hold his own in tip-offs and rebounds with centers averaging six-feet-two, but against this big guy, Wayne, of Avon who stood six-feet-four, Gene needed to plant a foot on one of Wayne's feet at tip-off time until the ref caught him!

Fortunately, they didn't play basketball on weekends, so on Saturday, January 5th, Ted, Walt, and Gene decided to go to a dance at Weber. The three of them piled into Walt's dad's car, and drove up Fullerton in style. While Ted and Walt both had dark hair and were good-looking guys, Ted at 175 pounds and about Gene's height while Walt was an athletic six-feet-two, weighing around 200 pounds.

It was good that the car was a four-door sedan, because after they all had a good time at the dance, two more of their Weber friends, strong, tall guys named Jim Konski and Bob Kazmier joined the trio. Earlier in the evening, Jim had introduced Gene to his younger, very pretty sister, Jan. Gene managed to file her name and face away in his mental file cabinet for future reference. As the quintet drove around looking for someplace to go, hunger overcame them. The ravenous five descended on a spaghetti joint down at Damen and Milwaukee near closing time and nearly cleaned out the place. The hour was getting late and since there were few places where under-aged guys could go after the restaurants closed, they decided to call it a night. It had been a really fun, fabulous time and Jim had been the life of the party. Gene wondered how a young man like Jim, who attended a good Catholic school could learn so many off-color and downright dirty, but humorous jokes.

Monday morning, back at school, the week slowly built up momentum for the big game. Well, not so big to anyone else, but significant to Gene and Joe Garth. Joe, who was Gene's bench-mate in Art class and good friend since freshman year, just happened to play basketball for the Wesleyan team and while they had looked forward to a really great game on January 11th, Wesleyan had to forfeit because Joe and his twin, Jerry, were the only two guys to show. A practice game was started after splitting up the eight players who showed; a game which turned out to be a blast!

Naturally, the next day in class, a boastful Joe bragged to Gene that, "It was fortunate for Armitage that my team didn't show up or we would have rolled over you guys like a Sherman tank."

Gene replied, "You know, I bet you and your brother are the only team members Wesleyan has!"

Because Gene played for a church team, he was required to attend a church function at least once a week. He overdid it. On Sunday mornings, if he didn't work at the drugstore, he went to church, then hung around with the other young men and women his age. His two primary friends at church were tall, lanky Will Slater, and big, friendly Otto Forst. Otto's main goal on Sundays was to put mileage on his big, new, '51 Mercury. They and others usually grabbed a burger and a malt after church, then whiled away the afternoon riding around or going to some point of interest. One time, eight of them piled into Otto's car and went to the Field Museum for a couple of hours until it was time to hurry back to the church for the fellowship meeting in late afternoon.

Gene, whose activities cup was already spilling over, decided to join the church choir as one of the tenors, which behooved him to attend choir practice.

"What's that? You practice on Wednesday nights? Oh sure, I can fit that in! Let's see, I work two nights, do homework three nights, play at least two basketball games a week, attend Friday night dances, bowl on Saturday nights, or attend parties, Sunday afternoon church meetings, and sometimes Sunday night roller skating. Sure, I can make choir practice."

Unfortunately for Gene, he was able to sing both the tenor and baritone parts, practicing with the tenors on Wednesday nights but having to sing without practice, with the baritones on some Sunday mornings when one or two baritones failed to show. Without burning his fingers, Gene had the candle burning at both ends but he had the energy to do so and still enjoyed all of it, the people, the gatherings, and most of all, the feeling of belonging.

On January 21st, he came home from working after school to find Kathleen in tears.

Immediately concerned, he asked, "Mom, what's wrong?"

His mom replied, "Bob called earlier this afternoon to tell me that he's being transferred to an air force base in Germany in February. But that's not all," she said, handing him a letter from Dave.

Reading it, Gene felt such a letdown, for his brother Dave had volunteered, along with about 400 other soldiers of the 18th Infantry Regiment, for combat duty in Korea. Dave just hadn't felt right, sitting out a hot war while other guys were doing the fighting.

Gene put the letter down and wrapped his arms around his anguished mother, blurting out, "This sure has been a lousy day for you! But they're going to be alright! Didn't they learn to survive anything that comes their way?"

Kathleen managed a weak smile and wiped away her tears, saying, "Yes, all of you boys have been through times that should have made you tough enough to survive anything."

Gene wished that he could say something to make himself feel better. In his letter, Dave had written that if he was accepted for duty in Korea, he would be getting combat pay, and that could help pay Gene's way through college. Gene admired his brother's courage but didn't want to take Dave's money, because he wanted to make his own way in life and not take from his brother who just might need it to get married on. Had Dave forgotten about needing money for that? Bummed out the rest of the day, Gene prayed for his brothers that night, that they would both come home safely and for his mother, Kathleen, whose loving heart had already endured enough travail over the years.

The 29th was a cold January night and brother Bob was home on leave. He had been fortunate in getting a two-week furlough at home before he went overseas. Bob was curious how well his kid brother played basketball, so he came with the family to watch. It would be Gene's most memorable basketball game that season but not due to any points he scored. Armitage was playing against the Ravenhorst team, the league-leading team of strong, athletic guys from the far North Side who beat them by sixty points the last time. A wide-open game, in which Armitage trailed by a bunch, it became a physical game but the referees were letting the game proceed, since there were no blatant fouls.

In going up for a rebound, Gene and a muscular opposing forward collided under the basket, resulting in the other guy falling to the floor. On his feet, Gene helped the guy up and looked to pick up the action but his view was blocked by Ravenhorst's captain who probably outweighed him by thirty pounds. Apparently this guy was miffed about his teammate winding up on his duff and began jawing with Gene.

Before he could think of a snappy response, Gene was shoved aside by Bob, who was more than willing to take up the matter with his brother's adversary. Players from both teams and the refs quickly intervened, to cool things down but Bob didn't really lighten up until after the game during the drive home.

Gene looked over to his brother at the wheel and offered, "Thanks for stepping in back there."

Bob acknowledged Gene's remark, "You don't have to thank me. You're my kid brother and nobody is going to get away with muscling either of my brothers while I'm around."

Hours later, lying in his bed, Gene remembered how quickly his older brother had come to his defense and realized that Bob really cared about him and now he was going away for a long time. He marveled in how Bob was a real scrapper who, as a five-foot-eight welterweight, would've given away about twenty pounds to his younger brother's antagonist from Ravenhorst. A throwback to the old-time boxers like Mike McTigue or Mickey Walker, Bob was able to take care of himself. Just before he fell asleep, Gene realized that he had been worrying about Bob for nothing for he was a guy who could handle serving overseas for three years!

The next night found Gene with time on his hands because Bob had gone out with some old friends from his days at the Home. Signaling his buddies Ted and Walt by phone, Gene met them shortly after at the drugstore. Gene's major concern was beginning to be that of getting a date for the Prom.

After talking for a while, Ted asked Gene, "Whatever happened to that Alvernia girl that you liked? What was her name, Mimi?"

As soon as the words were out of Ted's mouth, Gene realized that he hadn't yet called Mimi, the girl that he wanted so much to ask to the Senior Prom. But first he had to find out if she was still seeing that guy in the Army.

Gene responded to Ted by saying, "Sorry buddy, but I've got to make a fast phone call!"

He sprang off the counter stool on his way to the phone booth with Ted close behind. A best friend doesn't let important matters like this pass without paying close attention and the glass door of a phone booth wouldn't prevent him from hearing at least one side of Gene's conversation.

Gene quickly dialed Mimi's number which was forever imprinted in his memory and when she answered, they began a conversation that would go on for an hour. To his chagrin, she was still seeing the soldier, which kept him from asking her to the Prom. He would rather have gone with her than anyone else yet honor got in his way. But honor didn't keep him from telling her all about it while not asking her to go with him. Somehow, during the conversation, they discussed getting together at her house so he could teach her how to dance the polka! Gene would like that. After an hour of close air in the phone booth, Gene had worked up a sweat and the wave of fresh air striking his face felt refreshing as he exited the booth.

Ted asked, "What the hell did she say to you that kept you on the phone so long? Geez!"

You'll never know!" replied Gene coyly.

Beginning on a Friday, early February would be a roller-coaster ride of joy and sadness that began on a high note when Gene got his grades and learned that he had passed into 4A, the last semester of high school. That night, he celebrated by taking a bus over to the church for its fund-raising "Spaghetti Dinner Night" and by washing dishes afterwards with his friends Will, Otto, and a few of the girls from the choir. Finishing up, they all went out to eat again, as a group and had an enjoyable time.

Impressing him the most was a petite girl wearing glasses, with brown hair and blue eyes, named Phoebe Kent who sang alto in the choir. Gene made a mental note to call her the next week just to talk with her. He did so on Monday after school, asking her if she and any other choir members might be going to the church basketball game that night. Fans were always appreciated but he wished that she would be one of them. Playing his best game of the season as Armitage won 56 to 47, Gene was disappointed that no choir members showed up, not even just one.

By midweek, just two basketball games and three working days later, a Saturday night going-away party for Bob had been arranged at a local hall owned by a friend of the family. Not wanting to spend the evening dancing with his aunts like some kid, Gene got on the phone. He called Phoebe and asked her if she would like to attend a family party with him. To his surprise, she assented.

A fun-filled, festive weekend began on Friday of that week, when Gene attended a meeting of the youth group at the church and afterwards, Phoebe invited him to her house where he met her family. Over homemade pizza, Gene and her older brother hit it off pretty well. At evening's end, her brother and his girlfriend drove him home.

On Saturday, after finishing work at the drugstore, Gene got dressed and hopped a bus over to Phoebe's house where he called for her and they rode a bus back to the neighborhood hall for the party. What a great evening they had dancing all of the different dances together, struggling with some, yet still having fun. Everyone thought she was so nice, even Grandmaw Kelly, who usually gave her approval sparingly, sometimes reluctantly. At the end of the evening, they got a ride back to Phoebe's house from Bob and his date. When they got to her door, they stood and talked for a while. Since she seemed to like being with him, Gene asked Phoebe if she wanted to go to his Senior Prom with him. "I'll have to ask my parents and then let you know later." They then bid each good night and Gene caught a bus home.

On Sunday evening, Gene met Phoebe at the Youth Fellowship meeting which was followed by Phoebe inviting everyone back to her mother's house for coffee and cake. There, Phoebe's brother put on a dance record and asked Phoebe and Gene to show them their stuff. It was their good fortune that they had been able to practice the night before. Abruptly, their dancing was halted when Phoebe's mother came into the living room and put an end to it by saying that it wasn't right to dance on the Lord's day!

Wisely attempting to pour oil over troubled waters, Otto Forst segued into posing a religious question to the group, leading to an open discussion and a calming of the atmosphere. As usual, Otto and his big, blue Mercury conveyed everyone home afterwards. Otto was such a great guy and a good friend but for some reason, Gene just never got around to telling him so. Phoebe however, didn't have to wonder what Gene thought of her, for he made sure that he let her know how nice he thought she was.

If Gene's emotions reached their zenith over the weekend, they fell to nadir level on Monday, the 11th, when he came home from working at the drugstore to see Bob packing his last bag.

"I wish you didn't have to go to Germany," said a teary-eyed Gene.

"I wish I didn't have to go either" said Bob, "but it's my duty, and a man meets his responsibilities. I want you to always remember that! Oh, by the way, since they'll fit you, you might as well wear my shirts, suits, and other clothes, since I won't be able to wear civilian clothes in occupied Germany, and by the time I get back they'll be out of style."

Then, always dapper Bob looked at the loose knot in Gene's tie and shook his head. "I never did get around to teaching to you to tie a Windsor knot, did I? Tell you what, I'll teach you now but you've got to learn quickly, 'cause I only have five minutes!"

Twice the two brothers went through the steps of tying a Windsor knot, after which, with the tie still hanging around his neck, the sad, young man hugged his brother goodbye, and followed his mentor down the stairs. A solemn-faced, duty-bound man of twenty-three, Bob then kissed their mom goodbye, carried his bags out the door to his friend's car and suddenly was gone. Gone for the next three years. Bob's quick lessons stuck in his brother's mind. From that day on, Gene tied his tie for work with a Windsor knot. And of course he followed his oldest brother's advice and helped him out by wearing those shirts, pants, and suits that would have gone out of style in three years!

Three days later on Valentine's Day, with his spirits lifted by the thought of seeing Phoebe, Gene brought a heart box of candy with him to her house. After presenting the candy to Phoebe, Gene sat and talked with Phoebe and Mrs. Kent. After about a half-hour, he mentioned that he had to leave because it was his night to work at the drugstore. As she walked him to the doorway, Phoebe thanked him for the candy, then, in a near-whisper, asked him not to call her anymore. Asking her for a reason, Gene held back the emotion that began to build within him. "My mother doesn't want me to get serious with you. She says I'm too young to go out with just one boy." Then Phoebe finished with a familiar phrase, "I hope you understand that it's not just you."

As Gene made his way back to the bus stop, he told himself, "Happy Valentine's Day, sucker! Is there anyone else you want to care about? Have you had enough of this yet? Wise up!" He was really feeling sorry for himself but would eventually get over it.

There was always basketball, school, or work to throw himself into and that's how he was able to, for a time, block out disappointments like starting to care for somebody who didn't care back. Good thing it happened now, in the middle of the basketball season, when being involved in the intensity of competing against other teams left no room for other negative thoughts that might have occupied his mind. He felt slightly better when six-foot-two Will returned to the team to play center.

Will came over before their next game and said, "I heard that Phoebe isn't going to see you anymore. You didn't know it, but last summer I went out with her for a a couple of weeks before she told me she was too young to get serious about one boy. She's just a heartbreaker!"

"I don't know if she's that," was Gene's response, then he went on, "but at least I wasn't the only one she dumped. Thanks for telling me, Will."

One of the more exciting games occurred against Avon, on the icy night of February 19th, when an even colder Armitage team had fallen behind 21 to 8 at the quarter, falling back to what looked like an insurmountable twenty-six point deficit at the half. Firing up in the third quarter, Will hauled down rebounds like a man possessed! Armitage came back to edge past Avon in the final minute, 68 to 66, and then Gene sank an insurance basket to make the final score 70 to 66. Starting at forward, his favorite position, twelve of Gene's fourteen points had come in the second half. He, his teammates, and his mom and aunts, were exhilarated by a such a come-from-behind win. He felt so good that he shouted out in the locker room, "It was a great game, Will. Too bad Phoebe missed it!" Will laughed out loud.

Having kept a low profile until the middle of March, Gene thought maybe it was time to go to another Lane Social, and late in the evening he again met Patsy Campbell. Patsy was a comely long-haired blonde with very pretty, deep, blue eyes, and she was from the neighborhood, a few blocks away. They had met through a mutual friend, Betty Cashmann, at a sorority dance a few months earlier and gone out a couple of times in groups.

It was a timely meeting, since earlier in the evening he had been ditched by a girl named Karen from Steinmetz High School who, halfway through the evening, went to the powder room with her girlfriend. After waiting about fifteen minutes, Gene decided she wasn't coming back and began to dance with other girls. He hadn't seen that move before, where a girl who went to the powder room never came back. It was a diversionary tactic that he, unfortunately, would see again in his travels! Patsy laughed when he told her but somehow she made him feel much better about the whole thing. He asked if she would like to go out the next week and she told him yes. Patsy was a girl whom he had been very interested in since he met her and now he finally had her phone number.

Helping Gene keep his sense of humor were letters like the ones he received Bob and Dave around the third week in March. Bob's letter noted that he had arrived in Germany on March 11th and was stationed at small Fuerstenfeldbrueck Air Force Base, in southern Bavaria, near Munich or Muenchen as the Germans called it.

It had taken Bob a full month to the day since his departure from home to make it to Germany. Disappointed that he went from home to a replacement depot rather than going right overseas, his letter described how he rattled around for over two weeks at Camp Kilmer, New Jersey, where soldiers and airmen were temporarily billeted prior to shipment to Europe. Having no permanent assignment there, all personnel were fair game for whatever dirty details were available.

Bob's least favorite job at home had always been cleaning the bathroom and so, to temper the steel of this fine Airman 2nd Class, Fate allowed him to be assigned to daily latrine duty while he was at Kilmer. While there over two weekends, he caught a K. P. assignment for the entire first weekend at Kilmer. As the second weekend approached, he smartened up, laid low, and grabbed a pass into New York City the first chance he had.

Fate found him again, as he laid low on board the USS General Rose, his transport ship to Bremerhaven. As duty officers established work details, Bob was selected for, you guessed it, latrine detail all the way over. While Gene felt sorry for his brother, he had to laugh when he pictured his duty-bound, polished, dapper brother Bob, up to his elbows in toilet bowls!

Dave's letter, while having lesser content than Bob's, was interesting when one visualized the conditions under which it had been written. Dave wrote the letter while his outfit was out on maneuvers. After slogging through the rain down a muddy, boggy, country road near his bivouac area he found a dry place. Along that road, was a decrepit, old booth, probably used as a telephone booth or kiosk at one time.

The dark, murky skies darkened even more as dusk fell, making the light too dim to see by, inside the walls of the old booth. Planning ahead, Dave had brought a candle with him. In his letter he apologized that, "My handwriting might not be too legible since the rain is dripping off my helmet and I'm writing by the light of a candle out of a ration box. I stuck it to the helmet on my head with melted candle wax! It's what the Army would have called 'utilizing a field expedient.'"

Between letters, Gene passed some of his free time playing his and Bob's record collections, although Bob's tastes ran along a slightly higher plane, with selections like "Grieg's Piano Concerto" and "Tchaikovsky's Piano Concerto," which Gene had liked. When Bob was still home he had brought home a couple of expensive operatic record albums borrowed from a friend.

At first Gene deprecated what he heard, saying, "I don't understand the words."

Bob's response had been, "This is the greatest music in the world and some of it has been around nearly a hundred years! Music is universal. You don't have to understand the words to love the music, Jocko. Listen!"

As Gene listened, he heard the opening strains of a duet from the first act of "La Boheme" during which, as the accompanying synopsis described, Rudolfo sings of his simple life and simple needs to Mimi who joins him in song. The paired notes of the duet and the quality of voices singing them made him turn away where his brother couldn't see him for tears came to his eyes the first time he heard it and would again, each of the few times in his early life when he would hear it again. He either couldn't or had neglected to remember the name of the duet and years would pass before he learned that the duet was named, "O Soave Fanciulla."

His interest in certain operatic arias, spurred by his brother Bob began to grow within Gene, perhaps encouraged by the movie, "The Great Caruso" which starred Mario Lanza, their generation's greatest tenor voice. One of the opera bits shown in the movie was from "La Boheme." Instead of hearing a scratchy old recording, Gene wondered what it might be like, to be in the audience attending a performance of "La Boheme" at the Met and hear the beauty of that duet performed by God-given voices singing the roles of Rudolfo and Mimi. He had a soft spot for a real-life Mimi and ofttimes imagined himself as Rudolfo and her as Mimi but definitely without the tuberculosis!

This bent for opera and his growing interest in the Catholic church were behind his purchase of a few records by Lanza, including "Ave Maria" and "Vesti La Giubba" from the opera "I, Pagliacci." It wasn't difficult for him to envision Canto's painful, poignant dilemma of being a clown whose heart was broken yet who had to go on with the show.

Perhaps it was not wanting to continue running into Phoebe at church or maybe the long, long sermons at the Methodist church were losing their appeal to him, so Gene thought that perhaps he should back away from involvement in it for a while, until he was in a better position to make up his mind.

In April, wanting the advice of his brothers, Gene wrote them of this religious confusion and wanted their assurance that if he ever changed his religion that it wouldn't cause a rift between them. All he wanted to do at this point was find out more about different religions. Remarkably, at this time, Look magazine was running articles explaining the beliefs of various religions, a different religion in each issue, until they had covered most major religions, even Judaism. Poring over each issue, Gene studied their differences and become better informed, believing that if everyone learned more about other religions, perhaps the world would see less prejudice.

Receiving answers from Bob and Dave near the end of April, Gene was relieved to know that they were together in their statement that religion was a very important issue in one's life, not to be taken lightly. They also agreed in saying that it was Gene's life and his decision to make, but it would never cause them to change their feelings for him.

Bob added one more very important caveat; "Be sure you are making the decision for yourself and not with or for anyone else."

A few days later, Gene walked over to the St. Hedwig rectory, to learn if it were possible to learn about the Catholic church without taking catechism classes. Entering the foyer of the rectory in which he detected the strong, pleasant smell of good cooking punctuated with a trace of fine cigar smoke, Gene rang the bell at what resembled a cashier's cage.

A portly, kindly-looking man of fifty soon responded, asking, "What is the purpose of your visit?"

Asking the priest, "Do you have any literature with information about the Catholic church which I can read without having to take catechism classes?" Gene hoped he sounded interested but not too interested.

"Not sure yet, eh son? I've got just the thing for you."

Turning to open a cabinet door behind him, the priest removed a booklet from the shelf, turned and handed it to Gene.

"You read this over, then take the whole summer to think about what you have read. If in the Fall you are still interested come back and you and I will talk about it. If and when you come just ask for Father Ed."

Leaving the rectory, Gene began reading the explanatory booklet on the way home, continuing to read it when he had the chance. He decided to think about his choice of religion over the long Summer.

Chapter 27

Last Go Around

Spring had really settled in by April 25th, and the warm, balmy evening was a perfect Friday night for a dance. Lane's usual social had been pre-empted by the girls of Jones Commercial High School who had extended an invitation to the Lane Tech student body of 5,000 boys. Nowhere near that number had shown up as the contingent from Lane was a small representation; good news for the guys who showed.

What a sight for sore eyes she was! Gene couldn't believe that it was Marjorie Cribbens because she had gone on to Waller High School from Agassiz after graduation. Exuding an air of refinement as a hostess for Jones, greeting newcomers at the door, Marjorie was the girl Gene had a crush on during his years at Agassiz grammar school since the first grade.

After talking for a minute or so Gene asked her, "How about saving a dance when you get a break from greeting at the door?"

She replied "I certainly will."

"Oh boy," said Gene to himself, "I've found her again and maybe now we can go out like we never did at Agassiz."

Shortly after, Marjorie found him and asked if he had time for the dance she saved for him. Gleefully answering that it was, Gene escorted her to the dance floor where they danced well together.

"You've learned a lot since seventh grade. Did your mother teach you?"

Gene was glad that he could answer, "No, I learned from a dancing instructor."

"You learned well!" Marjorie quipped.

Not one to beat around the bush, Gene asked her, "Are you seeing anyone?"

"Yes, I'm engaged to a senior at Notre Dame University."

A college senior? At Notre Dame? At that moment, if Gene had been piloting a jet fighter, his plane would be shot full of Notre Dame bullet holes, engulfed in flames, and falling in a death spiral from which it wouldn't recover. Mercifully, the band broke for a well-deserved intermission, whereby Gene thanked Marjorie for the dance and she went back to greeting at the door and out of his life.

Resuming their music, the band opened with a nice mixer-type slow number. Spying a petite brunette, Gene approached her and asked her if she would like to dance. She said that she would and they danced together. She hadn't been dancing very long but Gene was willing to go along with teaching her when he could.

Gosh, he thought, looking into her crystal-clear blue eyes, she was really cute, when she broke his concentration, "I'm Patrice Hoffman."

Her name sounded as if it could be Jewish although it made no difference to him, since he had several Jewish friends at Agassiz and Lane. Besides, he liked her, so they continued to dance together the rest of the evening.

Before they knew it, the band was playing the last number and Gene asked if he could escort her home.

"I live pretty far," she said.

"Not at the end of the bus line I hope!" said Gene, remembering another long ride.

"Oh no, there's a streetcar route all the way. I live in the area around Roosevelt and Kostner."

Gene was hoping that Patrice didn't see him blanch as he remembered that except for a few deliveries he made out south for the drugstore, he was totally lost south of Division Street, and Roosevelt was three miles south of Division.

A light spring rain had fallen during the dance, lacing the streets and sidewalks with a light dampening. The air was warm and heavy as they walked to Western Avenue to catch the streetcar south. Rolling past his neighborhood, Gene pointed out his street, and realized to his regret that from her perspective, she probably noticed that four taverns stood in the same block. Nice impression, he thought. After transferring at Roosevelt, they rode a Roosevelt streetcar westward and along the route, Gene saw many Kosher delicatessen signs and indications that they were in a Jewish section of the city. It still didn't matter to Gene, especially since she was cute, bright, and seemed so nice.

Alighting from the streetcar several minutes later, they found themselves walking the quiet streets of her West Side neighborhood at nearly one o'clock in the morning, passing the corner of 14th Street and Kedvale twice. Seeing no one else on the street, and with the heavy, humid air muffling any traffic noise from up on Roosevelt, it seemed that only the two of them were sharing this night. Patrice was very friendly and bright, a girl who could maintain an interesting conversation. He liked her!

A few days later, on Monday, Gene called Patrice and was invited over to her house. Arriving about eight o'clock he met her mother, after which they walked around her neighborhood again and returned to her home where she mentioned that she would like to improve her dancing. Wanting to please her, Gene agreed to show her the steps to other dances. He liked dancing with Patrice because she seemed to fit perfectly in his arms. At ten o'clock, as he was leaving, they thanked each other for the nice evening and Gene walked up to Roosevelt. He then made the long trip back home, a trip that seemed to be so much longer without her along. He liked her a lot despite his own warnings to take things slowly this time.

Three days later Gene left his buddy Ted sitting at the drugstore soda fountain after he told Ted that he was going to ask Patrice to the Prom. Gene hurried over to the phone booth, dropped a nickel and called Patrice, anxious to hear her voice. He had decided after Monday night at her house, to ask her if she would like to go with him to his Senior Prom.

Patrice replied that for her part, she would love to go but she had to ask him a question before she asked her parents if she could go to his Prom.

Gene said, "Go ahead, ask me anything."

Patrice opened with, "I'm sure you know I'm Jewish, don't you?"

"Yes," replied Gene who continued, "I believed that you were but it doesn't make any difference to me."

Then Patrice asked the 64 dollar question, "I wasn't sure if you were but your answer implies that you're not Jewish, are you?"

"No, I'm not but I really like you," said Gene.

"I really like you too, Gene," replied Patrice softly, "but my parents would rather that I didn't go out with boys who aren't Jewish. Please understand, that while I think they are being old-fashioned, they're still my parents and I am only honoring their wishes when I say it would be better if I didn't see you anymore."

Fighting against a wave of disappointment, Gene took a moment, then replied "I do understand, Patrice."

"I'm glad that you do."

Gene knew that he had no way to resolve this religious and cultural impasse.

Composing his thoughts, he closed with, "Good luck to you Patrice, and please know that I will always remember you. Goodbye."

Gene hung the receiver up on the phone, held it there for a few moments and tried to ease the tightening lump in his throat. Bracing himself for his return to his best friend Ted at the soda-fountain who would be dying of curiosity, Gene opened the door of the phone booth.

"So, how did it go? Did you ask her? Damn, the look on your face tells me she's not going! What did you do wrong now?"

Gene slowly explained what had happened.

Ted offered, "Geez, that's tough! She really sounded like a great girl. But it's probably better this way, that religious differences split you up now, long before you started caring about her. Right?"

"Yeh, Ted. Right," muttered Gene, struggling for a subject to which to change the conversation. In a moment he had it, and exclaimed, "Hey, guess what, I stopped by St. Hedwig's rectory and looked into learning about the Catholic church."

"That's great buddy," beamed Ted, "but are you sure you want to convert?"

Gene sputtered, "Convert? When did I say I wanted to convert? I didn't say I wanted to convert! I just want to learn more about it! Geez, you'll have me wearing a cassock and saying Mass next."

The next afternoon, having been volunteered by his mom to paint the trim below the second floor windows at Grandmaw Kelly's, Gene found himself up on the extension ladder. Being just above the kitchen windows, he overheard her and his grandpaw talking in the kitchen. Grandmaw Kelly had just gotten back from the Milwaukee Avenue shopping area and was grousing about being shortchanged. An item which she believed to be on sale hadn't been and she ended up paying the regular price. Her ire aroused, Grandmaw Kelly had fumed all the way home where she launched into a tirade of choice derogatory terms for Jewish store-owners while Grandpaw Kelly criticized her for using ethnic slurs.

In his mind, Gene remembered Patrice's sweetness and thought at least she would be spared having to hear remarks like these one day from someone in his family, whom he loved despite their faults. He and Patrice had found each other in the wrong time and place. Perhaps in a different time they might have found a place together, or better yet, in a different world.

Knowing by then that the best way to get a girl off his mind was to date another girl, Gene called Patsy Campbell, the girl he had gone out with in late March. A junior at Tuley High School, Patsy was attractive in Gene's eyes. After talking for about an hour, he asked her to go to the movies and they agreed to go to a movie downtown the next night, Saturday night.

The next afternoon was Saturday, May 3rd. A warm and sunny day, it prompted Ted, Walt, and Gene to hop a bus down to the beach at North Avenue for a couple of hours, where they found that the water temperature was still more relative to winter than summer. Undaunted, Walt and Gene went out into the cold, frothy waves while Ted stayed on the warm sand and took their pictures.

"So this is what an ice cube feels like in a cold drink!" said Gene to Walt.

"I'm not staying out here for long," said Walt through chattering teeth.

A few minutes later, as his extremities began to numb, Gene caved, "Okay guys, I've had it, I coming in!" shouted Gene to Walt. He was shouting to Walt's back, since Walt had already begun trudging through the cold surf toward shore.

Back on shore, they warmed up rather quickly as they observed three girls sharing a blanket nearby. A dark-haired vision of loveliness in a dark brown one-piece bathing suit got up to splash herself in the surf and returned to the girls' blanket to towel off. Facing the trio of young men nearby, she held the towel so that it appeared that all she was wearing was the towel. The impression had not been lost on the three guys who decided that it was time to head back home before they got themselves in trouble.

Had it been too much sun too soon or the girl with the towel? For some reason, they got on the wrong bus, noticing it when the bus didn't take the usual turn up Diversey.

Walt asked the bus driver, a would-be Ralph Kramden, "Is this bus going to Logan Square?"

The driver quipped, "Not while I'm driving it!" Then he told them, "I'm taking this bus up to Sheridan Road in the Uptown neighborhood."

Not dressed for going to the Aragon Ballroom, the guys asked the driver to let them off to walk back to catch the Diversey bus.

The overweight driver, perspiring profusely in the afternoon heat, muttered something under his breath about harebrained teenagers who could get lost in their own backyards and abruptly braked the bus to an unscheduled stop.

"Here you are!"

The guys yelled, "Thanks!" as the door slammed shut in their faces and the bus drove off leaving them standing in a cloud of noxious fumes.

Catching the right bus, the trio arrived at Logan Boulevard and Western without further incident.

That evening, Gene walked over to Patsy Campbell's home

and the two of them strolled to the Milwaukee Avenue "El" where they caught the train for downtown. An already open window was alongside the empty seat which they sat in and they enjoyed the roar of the train reverberating off the concrete tunnel walls. Gene had always enjoyed the noise plus the pyrotechnic display of sparks as the train roared into the subway, crossing different tracks and switchings, throwing showers of sparks as electrical contact was broken over and over.

It was great to be able to hop an "El" train and not be concerned about safety. Unfortunately, they had been so preoccupied with the sounds, sights, and their conversation that they had missed their stop and got off four blocks farther down the line.

Arriving downtown, they walked up the steps out of the subway into a face full of Lake Michigan breeze wafting through the concrete and brick canyons of Chicago's Loop. Walking the several blocks from the subway station to Eitel's Palace Theatre, the sun had not yet set and it was a beautiful evening. They passed several downtown theaters which, though not The Palace, were all palaces back then and usually filled on Saturday night, because to go downtown on a date was special; downtown was special. "Singing In The Rain" was the first-run movie at the Palace, which Patsy and Gene thought was a terrific musical. When the show was over they walked a couple of blocks over to Anne's Restaurant where they had something to eat. After they finished their meal, they walked back to the subway where they caught a train to the Northwest Side.

Back in the neighborhood as Gene was walking Patsy to her house, he remembered that in order to walk Patsy to her door they had to walk through the gangway first. But he had a sudden uneasy feeling! There is no more menacing sight to a seventeen-year-old guy with a girl than a large group of other guys in their path. Must've been twenty guys sitting around the front of the darkened grocery store next door to her gangway! To Gene's relief, a couple of them just exchanged hellos with Patsy as she and Gene passed by.

As the two young people stood by her door, in the darkened gangway, Gene asked her if she would go to the Senior Prom with him on May 28th and to his surprise, the pretty-eyed girl said, "Yes. I will." They kissed goodnight and Gene glided out of her gangway, levitated by her answer. He was no longer concerned about the mob in front. As he passed the group alone, he recognized a couple of them in the dim light as guys who had come into the drugstore, and acknowledged them, "Hey Frank, how are you doing? Haven't seen you in a while, Caz." These weren't hard guys. If they had been, they would've stomped him the minute he came out alone. That way they wouldn't have gotten his blood all over Patsy!

The kid finally had a Prom date and she didn't live ten miles away! Since he got home so late that night, he had to wait until the next day to write to his brothers and tell them. On Monday, Gene met his buddy, Pat Decker at their locker and exclaimed, "Hey, it's all set! I got a Prom date! You and me are doubling up!" Only slightly impressed Pat replied, "It's about time, Romeo!"

Later in the week, Gene called Patsy to ask her out on Saturday.

She told him, "I'd better tell you that I can't go to the Prom with you after all. My parents won't let me spend the money on a formal gown. Oh, and I can't go out with you on Saturday, since I have to go to my grandma's birthday party with my parents."

Believing her, Gene was to catch her in a lie, when while walking past Mardy's Restaurant on Saturday evening with Ted and Walt, Gene saw Patsy through the plate-glass window in a cozy booth with some swarthy-looking guy who wasn't from the neighborhood. It wasn't her seeing someone else that infuriated Gene. It was having Patsy lie to him and bring the guy right into his neighborhood.

Lucky for Gene, or unlucky, depending on one's perspective, he met a tall girl with long blonde hair and hazel eyes, at the Lane social the night before, who was an Amundsen High School drum majorette. He asked her out a few times, going dancing, then downtown to movies and a play. Her name was Irene Stempel and what a bright girl she was. She was also seventeen going on twenty-five, naming all of those fabulous, expensive clubs and restaurants downtown that they should take in. Gene's early warning system began flashing inside his mind when he noticed that the stars in her eyes looked more like dollar signs.

On the 19th of May, nine days before the Prom, she agreed to go to the Prom with Gene when he asked her. Again, the desperate kid had a Prom date, and none too soon! Telling Pat Decker about having a Prom date again, his buddy of four years seemed unsure. Pat had been watching Gene's carousel ride of no date, a date, no date, a date, until he was dizzy.

Needless to say, Decker asked Gene, "Are you sure you're going to the Prom with this one?"

"I certainly am," chuckled Gene, "it's getting too late to switch now!"

Pat, of course, had no problem with an uncertain Prom date since his sister had agreed to go with him months before when he didn't have a date lined up. Gene had even thought of asking Pat's sister, when he hadn't even known her name or seen her, just from Pat's description but then Pat wouldn't have had a date and he was going to be driving!

"She sounds like a gold-digger to me!" said Ted after hearing Gene describe his dates with Irene.

"I know she is but I'm not going to marry her!" said Gene who went on, "After the Prom I probably won't see her anymore. Geez, what are you, my mother?"

The third week in May; shakedown tests in Gym and Civics. The 440 yard dash: a race that once took him 90 seconds as a freshie he ran in 62 seconds flat. The time for a passing grade was 70 seconds or less. The Civics test had posed little difficulty for him but his grade of only 85 would come back in a few days which he accepted with the intent of doing better on the final.

Gene's focus had been on two major events in a Senior's life: the Prom, a personal thing with him: wanting to be as good as anyone else and proving it by being there; Graduation: because he would be graduating from the school through which his own brother doubted he would make it. Gene was cognizant however, that after graduation, his four-year Commercial Art course would leave him unprepared to continue on to college work that wasn't art-related, and he wasn't a good enough artist to make a living at it. His job at the drugstore certainly wasn't the kind of career one followed to earn a living.

With the goal of a full-time job in mind, on May 22nd, he hitched a ride with Pat Decker to the electric appliance wholesaler where Pat worked and got a part-time job with the understanding that it would become full-time work upon graduation. Giving notice to Mr. Feinstein of his leaving wouldn't be easy but it was time to move on to the next phase of his life to begin soon.

"Of course you've got to get another job, Gene. I don't want you to be a clerk at my store for the rest of your life and you haven't gone to Pharmacy college. If you can get full-time work, take it and good luck to you." Then Mr. Feinstein asked, "Can you still work your two nights next week until we break someone else in?"

"Sure, Boss! I can do that. You've always been more than fair with me!" replied Gene to his employer, friend, and adviser.

Dan Witalski had started it when he worked there, calling Mr. Feinstein, "Boss" and the other guys who worked for him had picked it up until Mr. Feinstein asked them to address him as "Mr. Feinstein." After they left his employment, the male former employees addressed him afterwards as "Boss." It was their title of respect for him.

On Monday, the 26th, Gene began his job, picking electrical supplies from stock to fill orders and, being the new guy, sweeping the floors and burning the cardboard trash before leaving for the day. The job would do until he found a better one, maybe in printing where he could employ his Print Shop training from school.

Picking up his rented tux early on the 28th, Gene worked nearly four hours, then got ready for Prom Night which had finally arrived. Enduring the ordeal of the Brownie photo op: snapshots of him in his tux taken by Kathleen, the afternoon quickly became evening and suddenly Pat and his sister were pulling up. Instead of driving his dad's old, black '46 Oldsmobile as he had planned, Pat had rented a still-new, sharp, white '51 Ford hardtop. Gene hurried out to the car and sat up front with Pat and his sister as they all drove off to pick up Irene, who lived on the North Side. Her name was Terry. Whose name? Pat Decker's sister, that's who. A fresh-faced, blonde, blue-eyed Doris Day look-alike, wearing a rose-pink formal, she took Gene's breath away when he first sat down next to her. He almost wished that he had asked her brother to fix him up with her instead; Gene would have found some way to get to the country club.

After calling for Irene, who was elegantly adorned in a yellow gown, they doubled back to Gene's house so that Irene could meet his mom. Then it was off to Medinah Country Club which they didn't find until after 10 o'clock, for somehow they got lost on the way. While Gene wanted to dance and mix with the other couples, Irene suggested that they first have photos taken, which they did.

After a few dances the foursome left at 11:45 to enjoy dinner at Allgauer's Fireside Restaurant up north where everyone else from their division room had made reservations. It was a heady experience, all dressed up for the first time and eating out at a posh restaurant. It was about 2:30 when Pat dropped Irene and Gene off at her house and drove on. Talking for a while with Irene in her downstairs hallway, it was 3:15 in the morning when he caught a cab for home. Riding along with the balmy night air blowing through the open cab window, Gene pondered the merits of the Prom and felt that it probably hadn't been worth the worry, the hassle of getting a date, and the expense but at least he hadn't missed it. He also hadn't missed the chance to meet Terry Decker.

While other Prom-goers had a picnic the next day, most of Gene's friends hadn't planned such an activity. Sleeping until 10 in the morning, Gene returned his tux downtown where he ran into Robert Gagnon and John Solis who dropped him off at Pat Decker's. He and Pat then drove around in the rental car most of the day. Calling Irene later in the day, she invited him to come to watch the Amundsen majorettes march in their outfits in the Memorial Day parade on Friday.

Memorial Day came and while watching the parade and taking pictures of Irene in her majorette outfit, Gene couldn't help but notice that she had nice long legs! After saying that she would see him Saturday night, she went home. Taking in a movie at the downtown McVickers theatre downtown on Saturday night, Irene and Gene then walked to a restaurant where they dined on shrimp, a first for Gene who liked the shrimp. Gene was beginning to think of a viable, credible reason to give Irene for breaking up with her, for her tastes were just too expensive for his budget.

Gene could have been knocked over with a feather on June 3rd, as he called Irene, in an effort to gauge the possibility of ending their dating, when Irene surprised him by asking him to take her to her Prom three days later. And he thought he had asked her to his Prom on short notice! Strangely, yet erroneously feeling obliged, since she had accompanied him to his Prom, Gene agreed to take her.

Kathleen was, needless to say, mildly perturbed when Gene gave her the news.

She asked, "Have you come into a sudden windfall? Where are you getting all the money for these Proms? It seems that Irene certainly likes to go to expensive places. Is she just going out with you because of your money?"

"I'm earning a little more money on the new job and my income tax refund is due any day now!" replied Gene.

Then an argument ensued over the refund check.

"Tom and I think that you should turn the refund over to us since we couldn't claim you as a dependent on our return," said his mom.

After some discussion, they agreed on splitting Gene's refund check.

He piqued Kathleen's anger a bit more by saying that he wasn't going with Irene for much longer. Kathleen's emotional floodgates opened up and she let it all out.

"You're never home anymore. You're either working, out somewhere, over at your friends' homes, or out with some girl. Who are you going to go out with now? Why are you always going out with different girls? What you need is one nice girl, like the one in pink you brought by, who was going to the dance with her brother. What was her name, Sherry?"

"Terry, Mom, her name was Terry," Gene replied.

Then Gene responded to her tirade. He defended himself by

explaining to his mom, the philosophy which he and his friends followed, handed down to some degree through the mores of their parents.

He choked a bit when he said, "What I would like most in the world is to go out with just one girl who I could really care about, who could care about me in return, and maybe someday get married to. Ted and Walt want that in their lives too, but most of the girls won't go out with us. So I keep looking. I'm out a lot 'cause it's lonely here; I miss my brothers, too! I just don't stay at home much because it seems that Tom won't allow anyone else to be comfortable at home. He won't allow even my best friends to come over here, so I visit their homes. But when they stopped by for me the night the new concrete laundry tubs had been delivered, Tom thought they were good enough to help when he told me to ask them to help carry those heavy tubs into the basement."

"Tom works hard and likes to relax when he comes home, son."

"Mom, you're just defending his selfish domination of this house. Who wouldn't like to be able to relax in their home; I would," exclaimed Gene. "As for Pat's sister, Terry, I'd like to see her but she has to want to go out with me. I can't twist a girl's arm! I let her brother know that I was interested in her but I haven't heard anything yet."

Kathleen then told him, "I had mistakenly thought that Terry was your date when they all came in, until you introduced Irene as such. Terry seemed so sweet, it would be nice if you asked her out?" asked his mom.

"Maybe I can sometime, but not right now, okay? I've got to get past this Prom Friday night first."

A bittersweet letter arrived on June 5th, from an apologetic Dave, who hadn't written for a couple of weeks. He and Bob had finally gotten to see each other down at Fuerstenfeldbrueck back on May 7th and 8th and planned to get together at least once a month. It sounded great to Gene because at least each of them knew that they weren't really alone over there. More good news: Dave and Jack had both been turned down for combat duty in Korea.

But then, in response to Kathleen's question in her last letter about how often he heard from Maryann, Dave's answer read, "Mom, I've had one letter from Maryann since Christmas and that letter was to say goodbye. She wrote that she had found someone else that she wanted to marry him and I just wished her luck. I just didn't want to tell you, until now. I should also tell you that I won't be coming home on furlough for Christmas since she's no longer waiting and I might get out earlier then."

Feeling sad for his brother, Gene couldn't believe it. Dave had kept the sadness and pain to himself for five months, not getting it off his shoulders by telling his family, but just living with what he had feared most: the loss of Maryann. What a sad time Dave must have had. No wonder he had written in January about offering his potential Korean combat pay for Gene's education instead of his own future marriage. Dave's letter informed them that he wouldn't be home for Christmas which meant three Christmases away from home.

Getting back to his own trivial problems, Gene easily rented a tux but his lack of a driver's license forced Irene to arrange for someone at her Prom to give them a lift to Mangam's Chateau after her Prom. Came Friday night and after once more undergoing the ritual of the Brownie camera with Kathleen, Gene hailed a cab to take him downtown to the hotel where he was to meet Irene at her Prom. The evening was a fiasco. While they managed to have a so-so time at the Prom, upon their arrival at the Chateau, they found that no one in the party had made reservations so they ended up driving to Club Hollywood out on River Road where they saw the show and left around 2:30 in the morning. Dropped off at Irene's house, they talked briefly and Gene again caught a cab home.

"That's it! No more of this Prom stuff!" muttered a disappointed, weary Gene.

The cabbie asked, "Sorry sir, were you talking to me?"

Gene answered, "No, just thinking out loud!"

Dragging himself in the house at 4:30 A. M., he was up again at 7 o'clock to go to work from 8 until 1 o'clock in the afternoon.

"Geez, you must be dyin'," volunteered Ted, "how the hell did you get up this morning?"

"It wasn't easy," said Gene as they walked down to Armitage and Western to the Oak theatre to see a movie.

"So how was this Prom?"

"Not as good as Lane's, probably because the first Prom had better planning for it," replied Gene.

"So what's this you mentioned about your friend's sister? You gonna go out with her?" quizzed Ted.

"What is this, Twenty Questions? Yeh, I'd like to see her. Yeh, and maybe her brother can fix me up. Hey, maybe she won't even want to go out with me. I'm still going with Irene and you tell me where I'm going to get the money to date anybody else at the same time," lamented Gene.

"So stop going out with her! Geez, how hard is that to decide?" offered Gene's best-friend.

"You know, you're right! I guess I've just been putting it off. Who would I rather be going out with, Ted?"

"Your buddy's sister, I think."

"Right again, pal. Hey, thanks a lot!"

"Somebody's got to straighten you out," needled Ted, who smiled from ear to ear as they neared the theatre.

During midweek on the 10th, with his mental script prepared, Gene called Irene and after a few minutes of small talk he began working up to telling her that he wasn't going to see her anymore. He offered that they seemed to have differences of opinion regarding an enjoyable time. Gene further explained that it seemed that she couldn't have a good time unless they went to expensive places, when for his part, he could enjoy just walking and talking with a girl. His comments may have struck a nerve for she retorted that she hadn't insisted on going to some of the places that she had suggested such as Don Roth's Blackhawk Restaurant or the Ambassador East.

"That's just what I'm talking about. I don't think I can afford to go out with you," stated Gene.

Irene then blurted out, "Oh, I get it! You're trying to dump me. Well, let me tell you, you piker, NOBODY dumps Irene Stempel! GOODBYE!!!" and she slammed the phone receiver down.

With the sound of crashing receiver still vibrating in his ears, Gene joined his friends Ted and Walt outside the drugstore, where the three of them got into Walt's dad's boxy 1950 Dodge, and drove around for a while. Gene remained silent causing curiosity to hang so thickly in the atmosphere of the car that a machete would have been needed to slice through it.

Who else but Ted then opened with, "Didya tell Irene to get lost?"

"Nope," replied Gene.

Then Walt chimed in with, "I'll bet he chickened out and didn't even tell her."

"You're right. I didn't tell her."

"Let's stop and get the mouse some cheese, Walt, he was afraid to tell her!"

Then Gene interjected with, "You guys finished? Geez. I didn't tell her because I never got the chance. As soon as she detected that I was going to call it off with her, she dumped me. Imagine that, I finally had a chance to be the dumper instead of the dumpee, and she aced me out by saying goodbye first!"

Erupting into laughter, Walt and Ted laughed until their eyes teared, at which point, Gene joked, "What would I do without back-stabbing friends like you, to laugh at my misery? Hey Walt, can this tank get us as far as Coleman's?" Minutes later they were sitting in Coleman's, their favorite hamburger joint. The realization came upon Gene that the simple things in life, like good music, good friends, and good hamburgers, were what he liked the most.

Chapter 28

220 To Life

Turmoil! Tension! Suspense! Anticipation! All ingredients necessary to bring a class of graduating Seniors to a boil! In contrast, Mr. Jung, their Art and division room teacher had a remedy for his stressed-out seniors who called themselves the Junger boys. Twice during their last full week of school, while other teachers buried Seniors in final exams, Mr. Jung took them out on field trip art classes. One day they walked to the Western Avenue bridge over the Chicago River where they climbed down the river bank and sketched the factories. But on this day they had walked over to the Addison Street bridge near California to sketch the bridge from the river bank.

The very warm morning sun beat down on the would-be artists as Gene sat alongside Pat Decker.

"Say, Pat, did your sister Terry ever mention me after the Prom?" asked Gene hopefully.

Without looking up from his sketch pad, his friend answered, "Yeh, she asked me how could I put up with a jerk like you for four years."

"Come on! She didn't say that! Did she?" asked a worried Gene.

"No, she didn't. In fact she hasn't mentioned you at all," Pat confessed.

Not knowing if that was much better, Gene, the supplicant begged, "Do you think she would go out with me? I mean could you maybe find out for me?"

"Oh yeh, I guess I could. But what do I tell her about Irene? Terry knows you went to the Prom with Irene; she was there."

"Uh, we broke up. There was nothing there," replied Gene, unsure who had really broken up with whom.

"If I get the chance, I'll ask her. She's almost never home, what with so many guys taking her out. You know how it is with really popular girls!" teased Pat.

"Yeh, right. That's why she went to the Prom with you," retorted Gene.

Mysteriously, a softball appeared and eventually everyone was drawn into a game of catch, including Mr. Jung. The game halted abruptly when an errant throw propelled the ball into the river, too far from shore to reach. "I'll be right back," said Jim Silvestri who lived down the street, and went home for his canoe. A few minutes later he reappeared with his canoe and paddled out to retrieve the ball.

Class hours for other subjects were being preempted by final exams in English and Civics, while Seniors' gym classes were now being used to practice the graduation march. That endearing, petite, middle-aged Civics teacher, Miss Simkowski had been recruited to call the pedantic cadence for the slow-marching Senior class. Marching alongside her charges, she would have done any marine drill instructor proud, for her voice could be heard above the amplified "Pomp and Chivalry" march music, drifting over the heads of the slow-moving six-hundred. "And one! And two! And three! And four!" Over and over she repeated that cadence as the Seniors marched the roughly two-hundred and twenty yards from the south end of Lane's quarter-mile track to the north end of it, the area where they would one night soon be seated.

By the 19th of June all of the finals were over and grades were out on the 20th. School was out for the graduates but they still had to report for graduation ceremony practice on Monday through Wednesday mornings. A festive feeling filled the air as Friday afternoon came to an end but not before Pat Decker told Gene some good news.

"We're having a house party Saturday night and you are invited." Before Gene could ask, Pat assured him, "Yes, Terry'll be there and without a date. You coming?"

"Hey, I'll be there. I've waited quite a while for this chance," exclaimed Gene.

As parties go it was strictly family with Terry's family and girl friends occupying much of her time, but Gene also enjoyed chumming with Pat and Rich, his slightly younger brother. Gathered outside their small first-floor apartment, the guys were talking about cars, when the screen door squeaked open and there was Terry, coming out into the fresh air. Suddenly remembering that they had to go get some ice, the two brothers hustled to the car and drove off. Thrust together alone by fortunate circumstance, the two young people shyly began a tentative conversation.

Between numerous interruptions and questions by any and all of her three younger sisters who wanted to see what was going on, Terry agreed to go out with Gene the Saturday after graduation. They might go dancing but they'd have to touch base during the week.

Moments later the two grinning brothers returned with a bag of ice and Pat asked, "Did you miss us?"

"I didn't know you guys had left! But I'm glad you did, when you did. Thanks!" beamed Gene.

Saying that he had better leave early in order to get some sleep for their Senior picnic the next day, Gene said goodbye to Pat's parents, and family. Terry was busying herself in the kitchen helping to clean up.

Pat and Rich came by in the old Oldsmobile at 8 o'clock the next morning and Gene ran out of the house with his equipment bag.

"Are you moving out of the house?" asked his buddy Pat.

"No, I just want to make sure I've got all my stuff for the different sports we're gonna play today. Right?"

Sherwood Park on Cedar Lake could be heard long before it could be seen, due to its public address system being hooked up to the juke box in the pavilion which played pop music all day long. Percy Faith's recording of "Delicado" greeted them as they pulled into the parking lot where they met up with some of the other guys from Jung's division. The first scheduled activity of the day for those young men was having an early lunch! Setting up at some of the picnic tables, the guys bragged boisterously back and forth to each other above the blaring music.

Sides were already being chosen for a softball game and shortly after lunch Gene trotted out to center-field, flanked on his right by Pat and on his left by Rich. "At least we've got a solid outfield!" shouted Gene to the infielders who were already busy baiting the guys on the other side.

After three grueling hours in the heat, the sun had moved to the high side of noon, when the guys ended the game. After changing into swimming trunks, several of the young Seniors, including Gene, cooled off in the lake while the remaining celebrants hung around the dance pavilion. A few guys who hadn't brought dates were cutting on their friends who had, which led to a heated encounter between two old friends, Steve Barkis and Lee White, which was quickly broken up and settled.

A vigorously played touch-football game picked up in mid-afternoon and upon its completion, Gene had no soda left and it was a long way back to the concession area. Going over by Robert Gagnon and Steve Barkis who were savoring a beverage, Gene asked if they could give him a drink. Steve pulled out a half-full quart bottle of beer and handed it to a very thirsty Gene, who quizzically looked at the two of them and hoisted the cool brew to his lips and drank some of it down. He had hated beer since his uncle Chick's wedding eleven years before but on that hot day, it certainly relieved his thirst.

Three tired, overheated guys occupied the old Oldsmobile early that evening as they made their way back home. It had been a hot but beautiful day which everyone attending from Jung's division had really enjoyed. Being their last get-together as a group, it had been a fitting cap to their four years of camaraderie.

Graduating Seniors were only required to come to school for practice Monday morning through Wednesday morning, practicing in the auditorium on Tuesday, just in case it rained on Wednesday night. At their final practice Wednesday morning they were requested by the assistant principal to maintain decorum while marching back after commencement exercises.

"Hold your formations as long as you can, it will look better, gentlemen!"

He also reminded them that in spite of having four stadium

tickets each for members of their families, if it rained, only those two tickets each marked "good for auditorium" would be honored. Since Gene had invited seven people to his graduation, he still had to get three more tickets. Mentioning this to Abe Samuelson, who sat next to him for a year of Civics, Abe mentioned that he only needed one ticket and Gene could have his other three. The catch was that Abe's mom had all the tickets and she was working downtown.

"Want to go for a ride?" asked Abe.

"Sure, I've got time to kill," Gene replied.

Abe drove Gene all the way downtown where they got the tickets, stopped for lunch at Henrici's, and drove back out to Gene's home where Abe dropped Gene off and wished him luck.

"Thank's a lot Abe! And lots of luck in your endeavors to be a good lawyer someday."

"Thanks, we did have a great Civics class, didn't we?"

"Sure did, Abe," said Gene. "Maybe I'll bump into you tonight at graduation. So long."

Hot mid-afternoon breezes were blowing, when with tickets in hand, Gene walked into the house where he presented them to Kathleen, to distribute to his aunts and uncles. As she looked at the tickets in her hand, Gene's mom, who encouraged him through all the trials he had encountered in life, hugged him.

Then backing away slightly, tears welled in her eyes as she quietly said, "My son, many years ago, when I had to leave you at your Grandmaw's and your brothers at the Home, I came back to an empty room and prayed to God, asking him to let me see my sons grow to manhood. He is answering the third and last part of my prayer today. Tonight, when you receive your diploma, completing high school, you will be fulfilling that dream which I've carried inside me for all of these years. Now that you're finishing high school, my last son can now be on his own if he has to be. You'll soon be a man and I am so proud of you."

With that she opened the top buffet drawer and removed a gift-wrapped box and handed it to Gene.

"Congratulations son, you deserve this."

He opened the brightly-wrapped package to find a gold Bulova watch which brought a big smile to his face, for he had never had a good watch.

"Thanks, Mom," he said, glowing, "it's my first real watch."

"I know, son," she replied, then she added "now you won't be late for your own graduation."

Excitement was building as Gene, his folks, and his cousin Roy, rode the Western Avenue streetcar to school.

"Sure wish Bob and Dave could have been here for this like they were at your graduation from Agassiz," lamented Kathleen.

"I'm sure they're here in thought, anyway," replied Gene.

Wearing his brother Bob's nice, light gray suit Gene thought, "Yeh, I'll bet Bob's thinking about me. He's probably wondering which one of his suits I'm wearing to graduation."

As he rode along, the clicking of the streetcar's steel wheels along the rails set the cadence for the phrase, "I'm graduating! I'm graduating!" repeating itself over and over in his mind.

Alighting from the streetcar at Addison, they walked to the stadium side of the building, where Gene told his parents and Roy that he had to go to the building entrance farther down, to get his cap and gown but they should go into the stadium here and he would see all of them at this same spot after the ceremony.

Continuing on along the building, Gene couldn't believe his good luck as he encountered Pat, Terry, Rich, and Mr. and Mrs. Decker strolling north from the parking lot. Gene hoped that he wasn't smiling too much, looking like a goof to Terry. Stopping to say "Hi!" they stood and talked for a few moments. Gene whispered to Terry that he would like to pick her up at 7:30 Saturday night and they could go dancing at the Aragon, if it was alright with her. She smiled and said it was okay.

What a smile, thought Gene.

"What are we standing here for?" asked Pat who then shouted, "Let's go graduate!" and the two guys hurried off into the school building to get their caps and gowns.

Suddenly, his long reminiscence ended as Gene heard "Eugene Ryan," over the public address. Had his name been called? "Casimir Rybarczyk."

Casey Rybarczyk gave Gene a stiff nudge with his elbow and

said, "Hey, Ryan! Quit daydreaming! They're calling our names to come up and get our diplomas. You wanta wait another four years? Move it! Move it!"

Hurrying between the rows of chairs, Gene caught up with Tony Rutherford, whose name was called just before his and who had been ten feet up the aisle ahead of Gene and Casey.

After the balance of the nearly six-hundred names had been called, it was a matter of minutes until the graduating class was dismissed. The orchestra hit the downbeat and as one, the graduates stood, turned and began marching in a stately manner back toward the other end of the field. Suddenly in a roaring crescendo, like Tennyson's Light Brigade, this six hundred began their charge toward the other end of the field, toward the stairway leading out of the stadium, 220 yards away. Now free of high school, each of them wanted to be the first to reach the stairway, racing at top speed as caps flew off and gown hems sailed.

It was a 220 yard dash - into their adult lives.